MASTERING DATA SCIENCE

FROM FUNDAMENTALS TO CUTTING-EDGE TECHNIQUES

MASTERING DATA SCIENCE

FROM FUNDAMENTALS TO CUTTING-EDGE TECHNIQUES

Pooja Mittal
Ramesh Kait

The Readers Paradise
New Delhi - 110002

Mastering Data Science - From Fundamentals to Cutting-Edge Techniques
Pooja Mittal, Ramesh Kait

Ist Edition

ISBN - 978-93-5977-046-8

Published by
THE READERS PARADISE
103, 4787/23, Ansari Road, Daryaganj,
New Delhi - 110002
Phone - 9654444181
thereadersparadisesales@gmail.com
www.thereadersparadise.com

Pages - 290 | Paper - 80gsm | Size - 7.5x9.5

Typesetting by
Shri Sai Printographers, Mukherjee Nagar, Delhi

Cover Design by
Kamini Bijoria, Daryaganj, New Delhi - 110002

Printed in India
Trident Enterprises, Noida, Delhi

Preface

Data is everywhere. From healthcare systems that predict patient outcomes to recommendation engines that shape our daily choices, data science has become the backbone of innovation in the digital era. It is not just a technical discipline it's a way of thinking, analyzing, and solving problems using evidence drawn from data.

This book, ***Mastering Data Science: From Fundamentals to Cutting-Edge Techniques***, is designed to guide you through the evolving and multidisciplinary landscape of data science. Whether you're a student stepping into the field for the first time, a software engineer transitioning into analytics, or a data professional seeking to broaden your expertise, this book offers a structured and practical approach to mastering the skills required.

Chapter 1: Introduction to Data Science

This part lays the foundation of data science, exploring its definition, importance, and relationship with fields like AI and machine learning. It introduces the end-to-end data science workflow from problem formulation to model deployment and highlights essential tools and technologies such as Python, R, SQL, and cloud platforms. Designed to provide a big-picture understanding, this section equips readers with the context and capabilities needed to navigate the field effectively and prepares them to dive deeper into specialized areas in the chapters that follow.

Chapter 2: Data Acquisition and Preprocessing

Clean, high-quality data is the backbone of successful data science. This part focuses on sourcing data from APIs, public datasets, web scraping, and databases. It then covers essential preprocessing tasks like cleaning missing values, handling outliers, encoding, and feature engineering. The section concludes with visualization techniques for uncovering patterns and insights, using tools like Matplotlib, Seaborn, and Plotly. By mastering these steps, readers will develop the ability to prepare and explore data efficiently skills that are crucial for building accurate and meaningful models.

Chapter 3: Statistics and Probability for Data Science

Understanding statistics and probability is key to making informed, data-driven decisions. This part introduces foundational concepts like probability distributions, Bayes' Theorem, and statistical inference. Readers will learn how to describe and interpret data using measures like mean, variance, and p-values, and will gain confidence in hypothesis testing and confidence intervals. The section also explores linear algebra and optimization core building blocks behind most machine learning algorithms. Together, these topics provide the mathematical rigor needed to deeply understand and evaluate models.

Chapter 4: Machine Learning Fundamentals

This part introduces machine learning by covering both supervised and unsupervised learning techniques. Readers will explore regression and classification models, evaluation metrics, and clustering algorithms. It also addresses dimensionality reduction and anomaly detection essential for real-world applications. The section concludes with deep learning fundamentals, including neural networks, CNNs for image data, and RNNs and transformers for sequential data. Each topic is explained with practical use cases and implementations, preparing readers to develop, tune, and evaluate powerful models across varied domains.

Chapter 5: Advanced Topics in Data Science

Expanding into cutting-edge applications, this part covers advanced areas like natural language processing (NLP), time series analysis, and reinforcement learning. It walks through text processing, sentiment analysis, and the rise of large language models. Time series models such as ARIMA and LSTMs are introduced for forecasting. Reinforcement learning principles are explored through Q-learning and policy gradients, with real-world applications in robotics and game AI. These chapters deepen the reader's technical skill set and offer insight into how modern innovations are built.

Chapter 6: Big Data and Data Engineering

Scalability and automation are critical for modern data systems. This part covers big data technologies such as Hadoop, Spark, and NoSQL databases, essential for handling massive datasets. It introduces data pipelines, ETL processes, and workflow orchestration using tools like Apache Airflow. The section also explores the integration of machine learning with cloud platforms, serverless computing, and MLOps best practices. Readers will learn how to build efficient, scalable solutions that can move seamlessly from development to production in real-world environments.

Chapter 7: Real-World Applications and Ethics

Data science is not just about building models it's about creating value and doing so responsibly. This part examines how data science is used across industries for decision-making, fraud detection, and personalized recommendations. It then explores ethical challenges, including algorithmic bias, fairness, and data privacy regulations like GDPR and CCPA. The final chapter guides readers in building a career in data science, highlighting key skills, certifications, portfolio strategies, and job paths. Together, these chapters connect technical knowledge to impactful, ethical, and sustainable practice.

Each part is designed to be modular yet connected, blending conceptual clarity with hands-on practicality. Code snippets, real-world case studies, and industry tools are integrated throughout, ensuring you gain not only knowledge but also experience.

In a world that is increasingly driven by data, this book is your guide to becoming a capable, thoughtful, and forward-thinking data scientist.

Authors

Contents

Preface

Pages

1. Introduction to Data Science **1**

1. What is Data Science?
   - Definition and Scope
   - Importance in the Modern World
   - Comparison with Related Fields (AI, Machine Learning, Big Data)
2. Data Science Workflow
   - Problem Formulation
   - Data Collection and Preparation
   - Exploratory Data Analysis (EDA)
   - Model Building and Evaluation
   - Deployment and Maintenance
3. Tools and Technologies for Data Science
   - Programming Languages (Python, R, SQL)
   - Data Science Libraries (Pandas, NumPy, Scikit-learn, TensorFlow, PyTorch)
   - Cloud and Big Data Technologies (AWS, Google Cloud, Hadoop, Spark)

2. Data Acquisition and Preprocessing **35**

4. Data Collection and Sources
   - Structured vs. Unstructured Data
   - Public Datasets and APIs
   - Web Scraping and Databases
5. Data Cleaning and Preparation
   - Handling Missing Data
   - Removing Duplicates and Outliers
   - Data Transformation and Encoding
   - Feature Engineering
6. Data Visualization and Exploratory Analysis
   - Importance of Data Visualization
   - Tools: Matplotlib, Seaborn, Plotly
   - Univariate and Multivariate Analysis
   - Identifying Trends, Correlations, and Anomalies

3. Statistics and Probability for Data Science **79**

7. Fundamentals of Probability

- Basic Probability Theory
- Bayes' Theorem
- Probability Distributions (Normal, Binomial, Poisson)

8. Descriptive and Inferential Statistics
   - Measures of Central Tendency and Dispersion
   - Hypothesis Testing and p-values
   - Confidence Intervals and Significance Testing

9. Linear Algebra and Optimization Techniques
   - Matrices and Vectors in Data Science
   - Eigenvalues and Eigenvectors
   - Gradient Descent and Optimization

4. Machine Learning Fundamentals **109**

10. Supervised Learning
    - Regression (Linear, Logistic)
    - Classification (Decision Trees, Random Forest, SVM)
    - Model Evaluation Metrics (Accuracy, Precision, Recall, F1-score)

11. Unsupervised Learning
    - Clustering (K-Means, DBSCAN, Hierarchical)
    - Dimensionality Reduction (PCA, t-SNE)
    - Anomaly Detection

12. Deep Learning and Neural Networks
    - Introduction to Neural Networks
    - Convolutional Neural Networks (CNNs)
    - Recurrent Neural Networks (RNNs) and Transformers

5. Advanced Topics in Data Science **157**

13. Natural Language Processing (NLP)
    - Text Preprocessing (Tokenization, Stemming, Lemmatization)
    - Sentiment Analysis and Topic Modeling
    - Large Language Models and Chatbots

14. Time Series Analysis
    - Trends and Seasonality
    - ARIMA and Exponential Smoothing
    - LSTMs for Time Series Forecasting

15. Reinforcement Learning
    - Basics of Reinforcement Learning
    - Q-Learning and Policy Gradients
    - Applications in Robotics and Game AI

6. Big Data and Data Engineering **199**

16. Big Data Technologies
    - Hadoop and MapReduce
    - Apache Spark and Distributed Computing
    - NoSQL Databases

17. Data Pipelines and Automation
- ETL (Extract, Transform, Load)
- Workflow Automation with Apache Airflow
- DataOps and MLOps

18. Cloud Computing for Data Science
- Deploying Models on AWS, GCP, and Azure
- Serverless Data Science Applications
- Scaling and Cost Optimization

7. Real-World Applications and Ethics **239**

19. Data Science in Business and Industry
- Data-Driven Decision Making
- Fraud Detection and Risk Management
- Recommender Systems

20. Ethics and Bias in Data Science
- Fairness and Transparency in AI
- Bias in Machine Learning Models
- Data Privacy and Compliance (GDPR, CCPA)

21. Building a Career in Data Science
- Essential Skills and Certifications
- Creating a Data Science Portfolio
- Job Roles and Salary Expectations

Appendices **269**
- Glossary of Data Science Terms
- Recommended Books and Courses
- Hands-on Projects for Practice

Chapter 1

Introduction to Data Science

Data science is an interdisciplinary field that focuses on extracting insights, patterns, and valuable knowledge from both structured and unstructured data. Combining elements of statistics, mathematics, computer science, and domain expertise, data science plays a vital role in decision-making and strategic planning across industries. The data science process typically begins with understanding a real-world problem and then collecting relevant data from various sources such as databases, APIs, web scraping, sensors, or user-generated content. Once collected, the data undergoes cleaning and preprocessing to handle missing values, remove outliers, and standardize formats. Exploratory data analysis (EDA) follows, where statistical tools and visualizations are used to identify trends, correlations, and anomalies. This stage is critical for understanding the behavior of the data and forming hypotheses. The insights gained from EDA guide the selection of appropriate machine learning models, such as regression, classification, clustering, or neural networks. These models are then trained, tested, and fine-tuned using performance metrics like accuracy, precision, recall, or mean squared error.

In addition to technical processes, data science requires strong communication and storytelling skills to translate complex analytical results into actionable insights for non-technical stakeholders. Ethical considerations also play a key role, especially as algorithms influence areas like hiring, lending, healthcare, and law enforcement. Responsible data scientists must account for fairness, privacy, transparency, and bias when designing and deploying models. Tools commonly used in data science include programming languages like Python and R, data management systems like SQL, and platforms such as Jupyter Notebooks, Tableau, and cloud computing environments. Big data technologies such as Hadoop and Spark are essential when working with massive datasets that exceed the capacity of traditional tools. As digital transformation accelerates, the demand for data-driven decision-making continues to rise, making data science a cornerstone of innovation in business, healthcare, finance, education, and government. With the rapid evolution of artificial intelligence, automation, and the Internet of Things (IoT), data science is expected to expand even further, shaping the future of how organizations understand and interact with their data.

1. What is Data Science?

Data science is an interdisciplinary field that uses scientific methods, processes, algorithms, and systems to extract knowledge and insights from data. It involves combining principles and practices from various fields like mathematics, statistics, computer science, and domain expertise to analyze large amounts of data, both structured and unstructured. The goal is to uncover hidden patterns, generate predictions, and support decision-making.

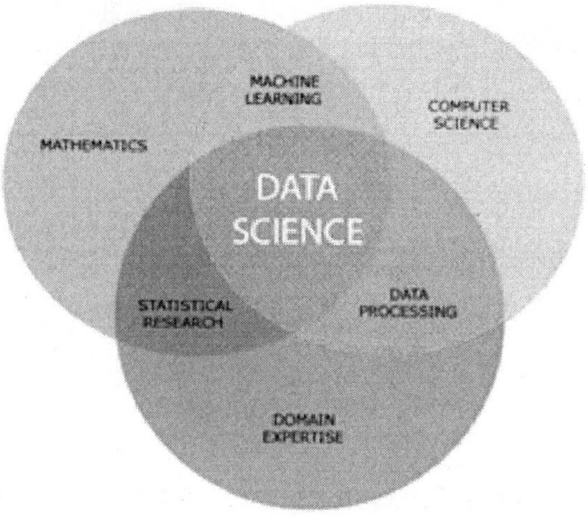

Fig.1.1

The different example of data science is as under:

1. **Mathematics:** Mathematics forms the theoretical backbone of data science. It provides the language and tools needed to describe and model real-world phenomena. In particular, linear algebra, calculus, probability, and statistics are heavily used. Linear algebra is essential for understanding data structures, especially in high-dimensional spaces, and for building models like neural networks. Calculus is used in optimization techniques, such as minimizing error functions in machine learning models. Probability helps data scientists model uncertainty, assess likelihoods, and handle random variables, while statistics allows for data summarization, inference, and hypothesis testing. These mathematical tools help data scientists develop, analyze, and interpret complex algorithms and data patterns. For example, logistic regression a common machine learning model relies on statistical concepts and functions derived through calculus. Mathematics ensures the precision and reliability of data science methods, helping professionals understand how and why a model works. Without strong mathematical grounding, it would be difficult to diagnose problems in models, interpret results accurately, or trust predictions made on new data. In short, mathematics provides the essential structure that underlies all analytical thinking in data science.

2. **Machine Learning:** Machine learning (ML) is a core part of data science that focuses on building systems that learn from data to make predictions or decisions. Unlike traditional programming, where rules are explicitly coded, ML models identify patterns in historical data and generalize them to new, unseen data. There are various types of machine learning: supervised learning (e.g., predicting sales), unsupervised learning (e.g., clustering customers by behavior), and reinforcement learning (e.g., teaching an agent to play a game). These models are used in tasks such as fraud detection, image recognition, recommendation systems, and natural language processing. In data science,

machine learning helps automate analysis, reduce manual intervention, and increase the scale of insight extraction. ML algorithms include decision trees, support vector machines, neural networks, and ensemble methods like random forests and boosting. The effectiveness of these models depends heavily on quality data, proper preprocessing, and appropriate performance evaluation. Machine learning is essential for uncovering hidden trends in data and turning raw information into actionable intelligence, making it one of the most powerful tools in a data scientist's toolkit.

3. **Computer Science:** Computer science supports data science through programming, software development, and computational problem-solving. It provides the practical tools and environments for building, testing, and deploying data models. Data scientists rely on programming languages like Python, R, and SQL for data manipulation, analysis, and automation. Knowledge of data structures (arrays, lists, hash tables) and algorithms (sorting, searching, optimization) is essential for writing efficient code and handling large datasets. Additionally, computer science introduces concepts like version control (Git), API usage, parallel computing, and cloud deployment, which are crucial in building scalable and maintainable data pipelines. Working with databases (e.g., MySQL, MongoDB) and big data technologies (e.g., Hadoop, Spark) also falls under this domain. Moreover, computer science plays a vital role in software engineering practices, such as modularity, testing, and debugging, which are critical for building reliable data applications. In essence, while mathematics and machine learning provide the "brain" of data science, computer science is the "hands" that execute and scale the ideas into real-world systems.

4. **Data Processing:** Data processing is a crucial step in the data science workflow that involves preparing raw data for analysis and modeling. It includes activities such as data cleaning, data transformation, feature engineering, and data integration. Raw data often contains errors, missing values, inconsistencies, or irrelevant information, which must be addressed before analysis. Cleaning ensures that the data is accurate and consistent. Transformation may involve normalizing values, encoding categorical variables, or converting time formats. Feature engineering creates new variables that help models perform better. In addition, data often comes from multiple sources APIs, databases, spreadsheets which need to be integrated into a unified dataset. Good data processing leads to higher-quality models and more trustworthy insights. It also helps reduce model bias and overfitting by ensuring the training data truly represents the real-world scenario. Tools like Python (with libraries like Pandas and NumPy), R, SQL, and ETL platforms (Extract, Transform, Load) are commonly used for these tasks. Efficient data processing ensures that downstream tasks—such as visualization, modeling, and deployment can proceed smoothly, making it a foundational pillar of any successful data science project.

5. **Domain Expertise:** Domain expertise refers to specialized knowledge in the specific field or industry where data science is applied, such as healthcare, finance, retail, manufacturing, or marketing. In data science, domain expertise is critical for understanding the context behind the data, formulating meaningful questions, interpreting results accurately, and making informed decisions. For instance, in healthcare, knowing clinical terminology and patient care practices can help a data scientist choose appropriate metrics and avoid misinterpretation of results. In finance, understanding risk, compliance, and market trends is essential for building effective predictive models. Domain experts help data scientists distinguish between useful patterns and irrelevant noise. They also play a key role in identifying ethical considerations, such as data sensitivity or regulatory constraints, that may affect data handling and model deployment. Without domain knowledge, even the most accurate models can lead to poor decisions if they misrepresent the problem or are applied incorrectly. Therefore, collaboration between data scientists and domain experts is essential to ensure that technical solutions align with real-world needs and add genuine value.
6. **Statistical Research:** Statistical research in data science involves the application of statistical methods to design studies, analyze data, and draw valid conclusions. It plays a critical role in evaluating the reliability of findings and ensuring that patterns in data are not just due to chance. Key concepts include sampling, descriptive statistics, inferential statistics, hypothesis testing, and confidence intervals. For example, a data scientist might use hypothesis testing to determine whether a new marketing strategy significantly increases sales or whether the observed difference is statistically insignificant. Regression analysis, ANOVA, and Bayesian inference are also widely used techniques. Statistical research supports model validation through techniques like cross-validation, bootstrapping, and significance testing, which help assess how well models generalize to new data. It also plays a role in identifying biases, understanding correlations vs. causations, and ensuring ethical data use. Without sound statistical reasoning, data science models can lead to misleading interpretations or flawed business strategies. Thus, statistical research brings rigor, credibility, and scientific grounding to the practice of data science.

Definition and Scope

Definition: Data Science is an interdisciplinary field that uses techniques from statistics, mathematics, computer science, and domain expertise to extract insights and knowledge from structured and unstructured data. It involves processes such as data collection, cleaning, analysis, modeling, and visualization to solve complex problems, make predictions, and support data-driven decision-making. By leveraging algorithms, machine learning, and statistical methods, data science turns raw data into actionable insights that can optimize operations, improve products, and forecast trends. It plays a crucial role across industries like healthcare, finance, marketing, and technology to drive innovation and efficiency.

Scope: The scope of data science is broad, dynamic, and continuously growing, as data becomes central to innovation, decision-making, and competitive advantage in nearly every industry. In today's digital world, massive amounts of data are generated daily from various sources social media, sensors, business transactions, mobile apps, and more. Data science plays a crucial role in extracting valuable information from this data to solve complex problems, automate processes, and optimize outcomes. Key areas include:

1. **Data Collection and Acquisition:** Gathering data from multiple sources such as databases, web servers, IoT devices, and user-generated content.
2. **Data Cleaning and Preprocessing:** Ensuring data quality by handling missing values, removing duplicates, and transforming data formats.
3. **Exploratory Data Analysis (EDA):** Understanding patterns, trends, and relationships in data using visualization and descriptive statistics.
4. **Machine Learning and Predictive Modeling:** Using algorithms to create models that predict outcomes, automate tasks, or classify information.
5. **Big Data and Cloud Computing:** Managing and analyzing massive datasets using tools like Hadoop, Spark, and cloud platforms (AWS, Azure, Google Cloud).
6. **Data Visualization and Communication:** Presenting findings through dashboards, reports, or storytelling to help stakeholders understand results.
7. **Domain-Specific Applications:** Tailoring data science to specific fields such as healthcare (predicting diseases), finance (fraud detection), retail (customer behavior analysis), and more.
8. **Ethics and Data Governance:** Ensuring responsible data use, privacy protection, and compliance with legal and ethical standards.

Importance in the Modern World: The importance of data science in the modern world are as follows:

1. **Data-Driven Decision Making**: Data science enables businesses and organizations to make informed decisions based on data insights rather than intuition, leading to better outcomes and strategies.
2. **Optimizing Operations:** Through predictive modeling and analytics, data science helps organizations streamline operations, reduce costs, and improve efficiency, enhancing overall performance.
3. **Personalization:** Data science allows businesses to create personalized experiences for customers, from personalized recommendations to tailored marketing campaigns, improving customer satisfaction and loyalty.
4. **Innovation and New Products:** By uncovering patterns in data, data science drives the development of new products, services, and solutions that meet evolving market needs and customer expectations.

5. **Automation and AI:** Data science is the foundation for automation and artificial intelligence, enabling machines to learn, adapt, and perform tasks that were previously handled by humans, increasing productivity.
6. **Predictive Analytics:** It helps organizations predict future trends and behaviors, such as market movements, customer actions, or even potential risks, allowing for proactive decision-making.
7. **Improved Healthcare:** In healthcare, data science supports early diagnosis, personalized treatment plans, and efficient management of medical resources, improving patient outcomes and reducing costs.
8. **Fraud Detection and Risk Management:** In finance and banking, data science is critical in detecting fraudulent activities and assessing risk, helping to prevent financial losses and improve security.
9. **Big Data Utilization:** Data science enables organizations to manage and extract value from vast amounts of structured and unstructured data, turning it into actionable insights for business and research.
10. **Enhanced Customer Insights:** It helps organizations better understand their customers by analyzing behavior, preferences, and feedback, leading to more targeted products, services, and strategies.
11. **Societal Benefits:** Data science contributes to societal development by addressing issues like climate change, urban planning, and public health through data-driven policies and innovations.
12. **Competitive Advantage:** Companies leveraging data science gain a competitive edge by making smarter, quicker decisions and responding more effectively to market changes and consumer demands.

Importance of Data Science: In a world flooded with user-data, data science is crucial for driving progress and innovation in every industry. Some key reasons data science is so important as:

1. **Helps Business in Decision-making:** By analyzing data, businesses can understand trends and make informed choices that reduce risks and maximize profits.
2. **Improves Efficiency:** Organizations can use data science to identify areas where they can save time and resources.
3. **Personalizes Experiences:** Data science helps create customized recommendations and offers that improve customer satisfaction.
4. **Predicts the Future:** Businesses can use data to forecast trends, demand, and other important factors.
5. **Drives Innovation:** New ideas and products often come from insights discovered through data science.

6. **Benefits Society:** Data science improves public services like healthcare, education, and transportation by helping allocate resources more effectively.

Comparison with Related Fields (AI, Machine Learning, Big Data)

Artificial Intelligence (AI): Artificial Intelligence (AI) refers to the simulation of human intelligence in machines that are programmed to think, reason, and make decisions. In data science, AI enables systems to analyze vast data sets, recognize patterns, and automate decision-making processes that previously required human intelligence.

Artificial Intelligence (AI) refers to the capability of machines to mimic human cognitive functions such as learning, reasoning, problem-solving, and decision-making. In data science, AI plays a critical role by leveraging large datasets to generate insights, automate analytical tasks, and drive decision-making. AI systems are built to simulate intelligence through a combination of algorithms, data inputs, and models, allowing machines to perform tasks that would normally require human intelligence. Key features include automation, adaptability, predictive modeling, natural language processing, and computer vision. These features empower AI to be deployed across sectors like healthcare, finance, marketing, and transportation. With AI, data science transcends basic statistical analysis and enters the realm of intelligent, autonomous decision-making. AI systems process and learn from massive data inputs, identify trends, detect anomalies, and offer recommendations making them indispensable in handling complex data science challenges.

Despite its transformative power, AI in data science also comes with notable challenges. One major disadvantage is its dependence on large volumes of high-quality data; without this, AI systems struggle to perform accurately. Furthermore, many AI models, especially deep learning models, operate as "black boxes" producing results without transparent reasoning, which raises trust and accountability issues. Developing and maintaining AI solutions can also be costly and resource-intensive. Ethical concerns such as data privacy, algorithmic bias, and decision accountability are also central issues in AI deployment. Nonetheless, when applied effectively, AI enhances the efficiency and intelligence of data-driven processes, making it a cornerstone of modern data science innovation.

Key Features

1. **Automation:** AI systems can automatically carry out complex data tasks.
2. **Adaptability:** They can adapt to new information and learn from experience.
3. **Natural Language Processing (NLP):** Enables understanding and interaction using human language.
4. **Computer Vision:** Interprets visual data such as images and videos.
5. **Predictive Analysis:** Uses past data to make informed predictions.

Advantages

1. **Efficiency:** AI dramatically speeds up data processing and insight generation.

2. **Scalability:** Capable of handling large volumes of unstructured data.
3. **Accuracy:** Minimizes human errors in data interpretation and analysis.
4. **Real-time Processing:** Supports immediate analysis and decision-making.
5. **Versatility:** Applicable across various industries, from healthcare to finance.

Disadvantages

1. **High Cost:** Developing and maintaining AI systems can be expensive.
2. **Complexity:** Requires expertise in AI theory, tools, and models.
3. **Black Box Problem:** Some AI models, especially deep learning, lack transparency.
4. **Data Dependence:** Requires large, high-quality datasets to perform effectively.
5. **Ethical Concerns:** Risk of biased decisions due to flawed data.

Machine Learning (ML): Machine Learning (ML) is a subset of AI focused on the development of algorithms that allow computers to learn from and make decisions based on data. In data science, ML is a critical tool used to create models that predict outcomes or classify data without being explicitly programmed for each task.

Machine Learning (ML) is a subset of AI that focuses on developing algorithms that allow systems to learn from data and improve over time without being explicitly programmed. It lies at the heart of modern data science, enabling computers to identify patterns, make predictions, and automate decisions based on historical data. ML techniques include supervised learning, unsupervised learning, and reinforcement learning. These methods allow models to be trained on input data and then generalize patterns to unseen cases. In data science, ML powers applications like fraud detection, recommendation engines, customer segmentation, and predictive analytics. Features such as scalability, adaptability, and automation make ML an essential tool for turning raw data into actionable insights.

However, ML also presents several limitations and challenges. A major concern is overfitting, where a model performs well on training data but poorly on new, unseen data. Additionally, ML models often require large datasets and careful preprocessing to achieve high accuracy. Interpretability is another issue many powerful ML models, such as ensemble methods or deep learning architectures, are not easily understood by humans, making it difficult to explain predictions. Moreover, biases present in training data can propagate through ML models, leading to unfair outcomes. Despite these challenges, ML remains a vital component of data science, offering the ability to analyze complex data structures and generate accurate, data-driven predictions at scale.

Key Features

1. **Learning from Data:** Models improve over time as more data is provided.
2. **Types of Learning:** Includes supervised, unsupervised, and reinforcement learning.

3. **Model Training and Testing:** Data is split into training and testing sets to validate performance.
4. **Pattern Recognition:** ML excels at finding patterns that are not obvious to humans.
5. **Feature Engineering:** Involves selecting the most relevant variables for model accuracy.

Advantages

1. **Automated Decision Making:** Helps make data-driven decisions quickly.
2. **Improved Accuracy:** Learns and improves continually, enhancing precision.
3. **Customization:** Models can be tailored to specific data science problems.
4. **Scalability:** Suitable for large and growing datasets.
5. **Wide Application:** Used in recommendation systems, fraud detection, image recognition, etc.

Disadvantages

1. **Requires Large Data Sets:** Poor performance on small or low-quality datasets.
2. **Overfitting:** Models may perform well on training data but fail on unseen data.
3. **Interpretability Issues:** Some algorithms are difficult to explain or interpret.
4. **Bias in Data:** Training on biased data can lead to unfair outcomes.
5. **Computationally Intensive:** Demands significant processing power for training.

Big Data: Big Data refers to large, complex datasets that cannot be effectively managed, processed, or analyzed using traditional data-processing tools. In data science, Big Data is both the input and the output fuelling data models and providing insights through analytics.

Big Data refers to extremely large and complex data sets that traditional data processing software cannot manage efficiently. Characterized by the 5 Vs Volume, Velocity, Variety, Veracity, and Value Big Data is generated from various sources including social media, IoT devices, web logs, and transaction records. In data science, Big Data provides the raw material from which insights and intelligence are extracted. Technologies like Hadoop, Spark, and NoSQL databases are employed to store, process, and analyze this data. Big Data enables organizations to uncover hidden patterns, predict trends, personalize experiences, and optimize operations. For data scientists, it forms the foundational layer on which advanced models and algorithms are built, particularly in AI and ML contexts.

Despite its vast potential, Big Data also introduces significant challenges. Managing such large volumes of data requires robust infrastructure, which can be costly and complex. Ensuring data quality and consistency is difficult, especially when dealing with unstructured or semi-structured data. Privacy and security are major concerns, as large datasets often contain sensitive personal or organizational information. Additionally, integrating diverse data sources into a cohesive and usable form requires advanced tools and expertise. Nevertheless, when handled effectively, Big Data unlocks immense opportunities for innovation and strategic advantage, playing a crucial role in driving data science forward.

Key Features

1. **Volume:** Refers to the massive amounts of data generated every second.
2. **Velocity:** Data is created and processed at unprecedented speeds.
3. **Variety:** Includes structured, semi-structured, and unstructured data.
4. **Veracity:** Ensures data quality and trustworthiness.
5. **Value:** Extracting meaningful insights is the ultimate goal.

Advantages

1. **Comprehensive Insights:** Analyzes more data for deeper, more accurate insights.
2. **Real-time Analysis:** Enables time-sensitive decision-making.
3. **Enhanced Customer Understanding:** Useful in personalization and behavioral analysis.
4. **Supports AI/ML:** Provides the necessary data scale for training advanced models.
5. **Competitive Advantage:** Organizations can better understand market trends and consumer behavior.

Disadvantages

1. **Data Storage:** Requires significant storage infrastructure and resources.
2. **Privacy Concerns:** Handling personal or sensitive information raises ethical and legal issues.
3. **Data Integration:** Combining data from diverse sources can be complex.
4. **Quality Issues:** Inaccurate or inconsistent data affects model performance.
5. **Cost of Infrastructure:** Investment in tools like Hadoop, Spark, and cloud services is required.

Comparison of Artificial Intelligence (AI), Machine Learning (ML), and Big Data based on various key attributes are listed in Table 1.1.

2. Data Science Workflow

The Data Science Workflow is a structured, repeatable process that data scientists follow to transform raw data into actionable insights. It ensures clarity, efficiency, and reproducibility in solving data-driven problems. While workflows may vary slightly

Table 1.1

S.No.	Feature / Aspect	Artificial Intelligence (AI)	Machine Learning (ML)	Big Data
1.	Definition	Simulation of human intelligence by machines	A subset of AI that learns from data automatically	Large, complex data sets that are difficult to process using traditional tools
2.	Goal	To create systems that mimic human decision-making and behavior	To enable systems to learn and improve from data	To extract meaningful insights and patterns from vast data
3.	Scope	Broad, includes ML, robotics, NLP, etc.	Narrower; a core part of AI	Independent domain used in conjunction with AI/ML
4.	Data Dependency	Not always data-driven (can include rule-based systems)	Highly data-dependent	Entirely data-centric
5.	Techniques Used	Rule-based systems, ML, neural networks, logic	Supervised, unsupervised, reinforcement learning	Data mining, ETL, distributed computing, analytics
6.	Output	Smart behavior, decision-making, automation	Models that predict or classify	Insights, trends, statistical summaries
7.	Real-world Examples	Chatbots, autonomous vehicles, virtual assistants	Fraud detection, recommendation systems	Market analysis, social media analytics, IoT data
8.	Tools & Frameworks	TensorFlow, Keras, OpenAI Gym, IBM Watson	Scikit-learn, TensorFlow, PyTorch, XGBoost	Hadoop, Spark, Hive, Kafka
9.	Relation to Each Other	Encompasses ML and often uses Big Data	A subset of AI; often relies on Big Data	Supports ML and AI by providing large-scale datasets
10.	Focus Area	Intelligent systems and behavior	Learning from data to make predictions	Volume, variety, velocity, veracity of data

based on the project or organization, most follow a core set of steps. A comprehensive breakdown of the typical data science workflow, with each stage playing a crucial role in the overall analytical pipeline is as:

1. Problem Definition / Problem Formulation: The very first and arguably most important step in the data science workflow is problem definition. Without a clear understanding of the problem, even the most advanced data modeling techniques may fail to deliver value.

In this phase, the data scientist works closely with stakeholders (business leaders, product managers, researchers, etc.) to translate a real-world challenge into a data science problem. For example, a retailer may want to reduce customer churn, a bank may want to detect fraudulent transactions, or a hospital may aim to predict patient readmission.

Problem formulation is the foundational step in any data science project. It involves translating a real-world issue into a structured, analytical problem that can be solved using data-driven methods. In data science, this often means defining whether the task is supervised (e.g., classification, regression), unsupervised (e.g., clustering, dimensionality reduction), or involves techniques like reinforcement learning. Collaborating with domain experts and stakeholders is essential to ensure alignment between business goals and analytical solutions. A poorly defined problem may lead to irrelevant models or misleading conclusions. For instance, a company seeking to improve customer retention might ask, "Why are customers leaving?" In data science terms, this becomes a binary classification problem: predict customer churn based on historical features. Key components of this step include identifying success metrics, understanding data availability, and outlining constraints like timelines or interpretability needs. Techniques such as hypothesis generation, feasibility studies, and requirement analysis are often employed. Clear problem formulation ensures that data collection, modeling, and interpretation are purpose-driven and measurable. Ultimately, this step bridges business intelligence and technical implementation, setting the stage for meaningful insights and impactful solutions. Key activities:

- Clarify the business objective
- Translate it into a data science problem (e.g., classification, regression, clustering)
- Define success metrics (e.g., accuracy, ROI, lift)
- Identify potential constraints (e.g., time, data availability, privacy issues)

2. Data Collection / Preparation: Once the problem is defined, the next step is collecting the data necessary to solve it. Data can come from various sources such as internal databases, APIs, third-party providers, or even through web scraping and IoT devices.

Data collection and preparation are critical steps that directly influence model performance and insight quality. Data may originate from databases, APIs, sensors, web scraping, surveys, or third-party sources. Once acquired, it typically requires significant preprocessing to ensure usability. Common challenges include missing values, inconsistent formatting, duplicates, and outliers. Preparation involves cleaning (e.g., imputation, removal), transforming (e.g., normalization, encoding), and integrating datasets to form a unified, analysable format. For example, categorical features may be one-hot encoded, while timestamps could be transformed into useful temporal features like "hour of day" or "day of week." This stage also includes feature engineering, where new variables are created to enhance model performance, and feature selection, to reduce dimensionality and noise. In data science, it's said that "80% of the work is data cleaning," reflecting how foundational this stage is. Data must also be split into training, validation, and testing subsets. Quality assurance through data profiling, summaries, and documentation is crucial. Tools like Pandas, NumPy, and SQL are commonly used. Without robust data preparation, even the most advanced models may yield unreliable or misleading outputs, emphasizing this stage's importance in the data science pipeline. Types of data include:

- **Structured Data:** Rows and columns (like SQL databases, Excel sheets)
- **Unstructured Data:** Text, images, audio, video
- **Semi-structured Data:** JSON, XML, log files

The quantity and quality of data collected at this stage significantly impact the downstream steps. Data scientists often work with data engineers or business analysts to ensure that relevant, accurate, and comprehensive data is collected. Key tasks:

- Identify data sources
- Query databases or use APIs
- Perform web scraping (if necessary)
- Store data securely and in a usable format

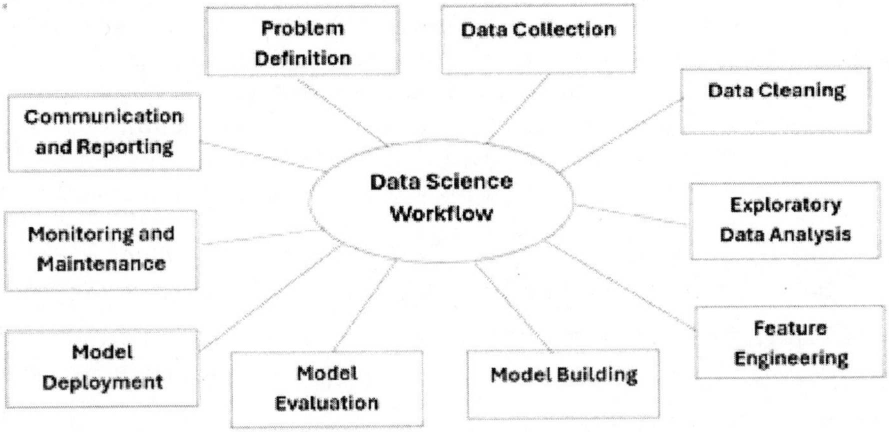

Fig. 1.2

3. Data Cleaning (Data Preprocessing): Data cleaning is often the most time-consuming step in the data science workflow but is critical to ensuring reliable outcomes. Raw data is rarely ready for analysis; it may have missing values, inconsistent formatting, duplicate records, or irrelevant fields. Data preprocessing involves:

- Handling missing values (e.g., imputation, deletion)
- Removing duplicates
- Correcting inconsistent entries
- Converting data types (e.g., string to date)
- Normalizing or scaling numeric values
- Encoding categorical variables

This step ensures that the data is accurate, consistent, and ready for analysis, which helps improve model performance and interpretability.

4. Exploratory Data Analysis (EDA): With clean data in hand, the data scientist moves to Exploratory Data Analysis (EDA). This is a critical phase where the data is explored in depth to understand its structure, distributions, trends, and relationships between variables.

Exploratory Data Analysis (EDA) is a core step in data science focused on understanding the structure, distribution, and relationships within the dataset. EDA helps uncover insights, detect anomalies, validate assumptions, and inform modeling choices. It typically involves both descriptive statistics (mean, median, standard deviation, correlation) and data visualization techniques (histograms, scatter plots, box plots, heatmaps). For example, data scientists might use EDA to discover that sales data is heavily right-skewed or that two variables are strongly correlated, influencing feature selection. EDA can also reveal data quality issues such as missing values, outliers, or inconsistent labeling, guiding decisions on cleaning strategies. In classification problems, visualizing class distributions can reveal imbalances that may necessitate resampling techniques. Data science tools like Python's Matplotlib, Seaborn, and Pandas Profiling or R's ggplot2 facilitate comprehensive EDA. Beyond numerical analysis, domain knowledge is crucial to interpret patterns meaningfully. EDA often sparks hypothesis generation and gives direction for feature engineering. Though sometimes overlooked, this phase can significantly improve model performance and interpretability. It's iterative in nature new findings during modeling may prompt additional exploration. Ultimately, EDA ensures the data is both trustworthy and informative before proceeding to model development. EDA serves two purposes:

- **Data understanding:** Identify patterns, outliers, or anomalies.
- **Feature insight:** Understand how each variable may contribute to the model.

Common tools and techniques used:

- Statistical summaries (mean, median, standard deviation)
- Correlation matrices
- Data visualization (histograms, scatter plots, box plots)
- Grouped analysis (e.g., churn rate by age group)

The insights gained from EDA help inform decisions on feature selection, modeling strategies, and business strategy alignment.

5. Feature Engineering: Feature engineering involves transforming raw data into features (input variables) that improve model performance. The goal is to create meaningful representations of the data that capture useful information for prediction or analysis. Tasks in this step include:

- Creating new features from existing data (e.g., age from date of birth)
- Encoding categorical variables (e.g., one-hot encoding, label encoding)
- Reducing dimensionality using methods like PCA (Principal Component Analysis)
- Binning or normalizing continuous variables
- Handling text or time series data with domain-specific techniques

Feature engineering often has a more significant impact on model accuracy than the choice of algorithm, and it relies heavily on domain knowledge and creativity.

6. Model Building: Once the features are ready, the next step is model building. In this phase, statistical or machine learning algorithms are used to train models on historical data so they can learn patterns and make predictions on new data.

Model building is a core phase in the data science lifecycle where algorithms are trained to recognize patterns or make predictions from data. After thorough data cleaning and feature engineering, data scientists choose appropriate models based on the nature of the problem classification, regression, clustering, or recommendation. For example, logistic regression, decision trees, or ensemble models like Random Forest and XGBoost are often used for classification, while linear regression or support vector regression are suited for numerical prediction.

In data science, model building begins with splitting the dataset into training, validation, and test sets. The training data is used to teach the model patterns using selected features, while validation sets are used to tune hyperparameters and prevent overfitting. Feature scaling, dimensionality reduction (like PCA), or transformations are commonly applied to optimize learning.

The model's complexity must match the problem too simple, and it underfits; too complex, and it overfits. Libraries such as Scikit-learn, TensorFlow, PyTorch, and Keras offer powerful tools for model development. Model building is iterative data scientists often test multiple models, compare performance, and refine features or algorithms. Successful model building in data science balances predictive power, efficiency, and interpretability, forming the foundation for reliable evaluation and deployment. Steps include:

- Splitting the dataset into training and testing (and sometimes validation) sets
- Choosing appropriate algorithms (e.g., linear regression, decision trees, SVMs, neural networks)
- Training the model on the training dataset
- Tuning hyperparameters using techniques like grid search or random search
- Using cross-validation to ensure the model generalizes well

Model building requires balancing complexity and performance while avoiding underfitting (too simple) or overfitting (too complex and memorizing the training data).

7. Model Evaluation: After training, the model's performance must be evaluated on unseen data (test set). This phase ensures the model is accurate, robust, and suitable for deployment.

Model evaluation in data science is the process of assessing how well a trained model performs on unseen or test data. It's a critical step to determine if the model generalizes beyond the training dataset and meets the defined objectives. The evaluation process begins after the model is trained, using a hold-out test set or through cross-validation techniques to assess stability across data subsets.

In data science, the choice of evaluation metrics depends on the problem type. For classification tasks, metrics include accuracy, precision, recall, F1-score, and the area under the ROC curve (AUC-ROC). For regression problems, Mean Absolute Error (MAE), Mean Squared Error (MSE), Root Mean Squared Error (RMSE), and R^2 (coefficient of determination) are commonly used. For clustering, metrics such as silhouette score and Davies–Bouldin index help gauge performance.

Beyond numerical scores, evaluation also includes error analysis and model explainability using tools like SHAP or LIME to understand why a model makes certain predictions especially important in sensitive fields like healthcare or finance. A good evaluation checks for overfitting, underfitting, data drift, and bias. Ultimately, evaluation ensures the model is not only statistically sound but also practically viable, ethical, and ready for deployment in real-world data science applications. Evaluation metrics depend on the type of problem:

- **Classification:** Accuracy, precision, recall, F1-score, ROC-AUC
- **Regression:** Mean Absolute Error (MAE), Mean Squared Error (MSE), R^2
- **Clustering:** Silhouette score, Davies–Bouldin index

Besides statistical performance, practical evaluation is also important: Does the model meet business objectives? Is it interpretable and fair? Are there biases?

8. Model Deployment: Once validated, the model is ready to be deployed in a real-world environment. This step involves integrating the model into existing systems where it can make predictions on new data.

Deployment in data science refers to the process of integrating a trained machine learning model into a live production environment where it can deliver value by making real-time or batch predictions. This step transforms a data science project from a research artifact into a functional component of a business system. Deployment strategies vary depending on the use case models may be embedded in applications via APIs, deployed as microservices using frameworks like Flask or FastAPI, or integrated into data pipelines using platforms like Airflow or cloud services (e.g., AWS SageMaker, Azure ML, or Google Cloud AI).

In a typical deployment process, the model is packaged with its preprocessing steps and dependencies using tools like Docker for containerization, ensuring consistency across environments. RESTful APIs, CI/CD pipelines, and monitoring systems are also established to facilitate continuous delivery and integration.

Key considerations in deployment include latency, scalability, security, and compliance, especially in sectors with strict regulations. Effective deployment ensures the model interacts seamlessly with incoming data and returns predictions efficiently to users or systems. Ultimately, deployment is about operationalizing data science turning analytical models into reliable, scalable tools that support decision-making and automate intelligent behavior within real-world systems. Deployment methods:

- **Batch deployment**: Running predictions periodically

- **Real-time deployment**: Using APIs for instant predictions
- **Embedded deployment**: Integrating models into software or hardware

Technologies used include Flask, FastAPI, Docker, AWS, Azure, or GCP. Deployment also involves setting up monitoring and feedback loops to track performance over time.

9. Monitoring and Maintenance: After deployment, models must be continuously monitored to ensure they perform as expected in the real world. Over time, the data or environment may change, leading to model drift or data drift.

Maintenance in data science involves monitoring and managing deployed models to ensure they continue to perform accurately and efficiently over time. Once in production, models face challenges like data drift (changes in input data patterns) and concept drift (changes in the relationship between features and target variables), which can degrade performance if not addressed. Therefore, regular performance checks are essential.

Maintenance includes logging predictions, collecting feedback, and periodically comparing real-world outcomes against model expectations. If accuracy declines, retraining may be necessary using more recent data. Tools like MLflow, Prometheus, Grafana, and custom dashboards help track performance metrics, latency, and system errors.

Version control for data, code, and models is also vital. MLOps practices machine learning operations bring DevOps principles to data science, ensuring reproducibility, traceability, and automation of model updates. Additionally, monitoring model fairness and bias over time is increasingly important, especially in regulated industries.

Maintenance also involves infrastructure management ensuring servers or cloud environments remain secure, cost-effective, and operational. Continuous improvement based on business feedback and new insights is encouraged to keep models aligned with evolving objectives.

In essence, model maintenance is critical for sustaining the value of data science solutions and ensuring long-term trust, reliability, and business impact in real-world applications. Ongoing activities include:

- Monitoring prediction accuracy
- Logging input/output data
- Updating the model with new data
- Detecting and addressing ethical or fairness concerns

A robust monitoring system ensures that the model remains reliable, relevant, and trustworthy over time.

10. Communication and Reporting: Finally, the results of the data science project need to be communicated effectively to stakeholders. This involves creating compelling visualizations, reports, and presentations that explain the insights and justify decisions based on the data. Good communication focuses on:

- **Clarity:** Use simple language and visuals
- **Context:** Align findings with business goals
- **Impact:** Highlight actionable insights and ROI
- **Transparency:** Explain the limitations and assumptions behind the model

Challenges in the Data Science Process

1. **Data Quality and Availability:** Data quality can affect the accuracy of the models developed and therefore, it is important to ensure that the data is accurate, complete, and consistent. Data availability can also be an issue, as the data required for analysis may not be readily available or accessible.
2. **Bias in Data and Algorithms:** Bias can exist in data due to sampling techniques, measurement errors, or imbalanced datasets, which can affect the accuracy of models. Algorithms can also perpetuate existing societal biases, leading to unfair or discriminatory outcomes.
3. **Model Overfitting and Underfitting:** Overfitting occurs when a model is too complex and fits the training data too well, but fails to generalize to new data. On the other hand, underfitting occurs when a model is too simple and is not able to capture the underlying relationships in the data.
4. **Model Interpretability:** Complex models can be difficult to interpret and understand, making it challenging to explain the model's decisions and decisions. This can be an issue when it comes to making business decisions or gaining stakeholder buy-in.
5. **Privacy and Ethical Considerations:** Data science often involves the collection and analysis of sensitive personal information, leading to privacy and ethical concerns. It is important to consider privacy implications and ensure that data is used in a responsible and ethical manner.

3. Tools and Technologies for Data Science

Tools and technologies for data science have rapidly evolved to support every stage of the data science lifecycle, enabling efficient data collection, analysis, modeling, and deployment. Programming languages like Python and R dominate the field due to their rich ecosystems of libraries such as Pandas, NumPy, Scikit-learn, TensorFlow, and ggplot2, which facilitate data manipulation, statistical analysis, machine learning, and visualization. For handling and visualizing data, tools like Tableau and Microsoft Power BI offer powerful, interactive dashboards that help translate complex data into actionable insights. Platforms like SAS provide comprehensive statistical analysis capabilities, especially favored in regulated industries. Open-source tools such as KNIME offer user-friendly, low-code environments for building data workflows, while BigML simplifies machine learning with cloud-based automation. For deep learning and AI applications, TensorFlow remains a leading framework with scalable solutions from research to production. Cloud-based data warehouses like Snowflake enable scalable, cost-efficient storage and processing of massive datasets with seamless integration into data science pipelines. Additionally, tools like Jupyter Notebooks and Google Colab foster collaboration and experimentation. Overall, the convergence of these diverse technologies empowers data scientists to tackle complex problems, streamline workflows, and deliver impactful, data-driven decisions across industries.

Programming Languages (Python, R, SQL)

Programming languages form the backbone of data science, enabling the extraction, manipulation, analysis, and visualization of data to uncover insights and build predictive models. Among the many programming languages available, Python, R, and SQL are the most widely used in the data science community due to their unique strengths and rich ecosystems tailored for different aspects of data workflows.

1. **Python:** Python is a versatile, high-level programming language widely used in data science due to its simplicity and powerful libraries. Its key features include an easy-to-read syntax, dynamic typing, and extensive community support. Python boasts numerous data science libraries such as Pandas for data manipulation, NumPy for numerical computations, Matplotlib and Seaborn for data visualization, and Scikit-learn for machine learning algorithms. For deep learning, frameworks like TensorFlow and PyTorch provide tools for building neural networks.

Python is used across the entire data science pipeline: data cleaning, exploration, statistical modeling, machine learning, and deployment. Its integration with Jupyter Notebooks makes interactive analysis and visualization intuitive and shareable. Python also supports big data processing through frameworks like Apache Spark (via PySpark). Additionally, its compatibility with web frameworks (Flask, Django) enables deploying models in production environments. Thanks to its readability and broad ecosystem, Python is the most popular language for both beginners and experienced data scientists.

Features:

- **Ease of Learning and Readability:** Python's simple syntax reduces the learning curve, making it accessible to beginners and efficient for rapid development.
- **Extensive Libraries:** Includes powerful libraries such as Pandas (data manipulation), NumPy (numerical computations), Matplotlib/Seaborn (visualization), Scikit-learn (machine learning), TensorFlow and PyTorch (deep learning).
- **Versatility:** Supports everything from data cleaning and analysis to building and deploying machine learning models.
- **Integration and Scalability:** Compatible with big data tools like Apache Spark (via PySpark) and production environments through frameworks like Flask and FastAPI.

- **Community Support:** Large and active community with vast resources, tutorials, and open-source contributions.

Usage in Data Science: Python is a go-to language for end-to-end data science workflows. It is widely used for cleaning and preprocessing data, exploratory data analysis, building predictive models, and deploying machine learning solutions. Its versatility allows seamless transitions from prototyping in Jupyter Notebooks to deploying scalable production applications. Python's integration with cloud platforms and data visualization tools makes it suitable for collaborative and enterprise environments.

2. R: R is a specialized programming language designed primarily for statistical analysis and data visualization. It offers powerful features like extensive statistical tests, hypothesis testing, and advanced data modeling. R's ecosystem includes thousands of packages, such as ggplot2 for creating elegant graphics, dplyr and tidyverse for data wrangling, and caret for machine learning. The language's syntax and data structures like data frames are optimized for statistical tasks.

R is widely used in academic research, bioinformatics, and industries where in-depth statistical analysis is critical. Tools like R Markdown enable reproducible reports combining code, output, and narrative text. Shiny allows users to build interactive web apps for data visualization and dashboards without extensive web development knowledge. While R is less commonly used for production deployment compared to Python, its strength in exploratory data analysis and statistical rigor makes it indispensable in many data science workflows.

Features:

- **Statistical computing focus:** R is designed for statistics and provides built-in functions for complex analyses, hypothesis testing, and modeling.
- **Rich package ecosystem:** Includes packages like ggplot2 (visualization), dplyr/tidyverse (data manipulation), and caret (machine learning).
- **Data visualization excellence:** Offers advanced, customizable visualizations for insightful data storytelling.
- **Reproducibility tools:** Supports reproducible research with R Markdown and interactive apps via Shiny.
- **Specialized domain support:** Widely used in bioinformatics, social sciences, and academia due to its statistical rigor.

Usage in Data Science: R excels in statistical analysis and exploratory data analysis, making it the preferred tool for statisticians and researchers. It is commonly used to analyze experimental data, create complex visualizations, and generate dynamic reports. R also supports machine learning tasks but is often combined with Python or SQL for deployment and data extraction. Its tools for interactive dashboards help communicate results effectively to stakeholders.

3. SQL: SQL (Structured Query Language) is the standard language for managing and querying relational databases. It features a declarative syntax that allows users to specify *what* data to retrieve without detailing *how* to get it, making it efficient for handling structured data. SQL commands enable filtering, joining, aggregating, and sorting data stored in tables, making it ideal for data extraction and preparation.

In data science, SQL is essential for accessing data stored in traditional databases like MySQL, PostgreSQL, and cloud warehouses such as Amazon Redshift and Snowflake. Data scientists use SQL to perform initial data cleaning and aggregation before feeding datasets into statistical or machine learning models. SQL also supports complex queries for trend analysis, reporting, and integration with programming languages like Python and R. Its universal adoption and efficiency in handling large datasets make it a foundational tool in any data scientist's toolkit.

Features:

- **Standardized query language:** SQL is the universal language for managing and querying relational databases.
- **Efficient data retrieval:** Enables filtering, joining, aggregating, and sorting large datasets quickly and reliably.
- **Compatibility:** Works with various database systems (MySQL, PostgreSQL, Oracle, SQL Server) and modern cloud warehouses (Snowflake, BigQuery).
- **Declarative syntax:** Allows users to specify desired results without defining detailed procedures.
- **Integration:** Easily integrates with data science tools and languages like Python and R for seamless data access.

Usage: SQL is fundamental in the data science workflow for extracting and preparing data from relational databases before analysis. Data scientists use SQL to clean, filter, and aggregate data efficiently at scale. It is essential for building data pipelines, conducting exploratory queries, and performing preliminary data transformations. SQL's ability to handle large structured datasets makes it critical in industries reliant on data warehousing and business intelligence.

Differences Between Python, R, SQL: Table 1.2 shows the differences between Python, R, SQL.

Data Science Libraries (Pandas, NumPy, Scikit-learn, TensorFlow, PyTorch)

Data science libraries are essential tools that simplify and accelerate the data science workflow. Libraries like Pandas and NumPy are used for data manipulation and numerical computations, making data cleaning and preparation efficient. Scikit-learn provides a wide range of machine learning algorithms for tasks like classification, regression, and clustering. For deep learning, TensorFlow and PyTorch offer powerful frameworks to build and train complex neural networks. These libraries integrate seamlessly with other tools and support scalable, real-world applications. Together,

Table 1.2

S.No.	Feature	Python	R	SQL
1.	Primary Purpose	General-purpose programming with strong data science support	Statistical analysis and data visualization	Data querying and manipulation from relational databases
2.	Strengths in Data Science	Machine learning, deep learning, automation, deployment	Statistical modeling, hypothesis testing, EDA	Data extraction, filtering, joining, aggregation
3.	Syntax Complexity	Easy to read and learn; highly readable and beginner-friendly	More statistical syntax; steeper learning curve for some	Simple and declarative, focused on querying
4.	Visualization Tools	Matplotlib, Seaborn, Plotly	ggplot2, Lattice, Shiny	Limited (basic tabular output, visualization done externally)
5.	Use in Production	Strong supports web frameworks (Flask, FastAPI)	Limited mostly used for research and reporting	Not used for modeling; supports production ETL pipelines
6.	Integration	Integrates well with other languages, APIs, and cloud platforms	Good integration with statistical tools and RStudio	Excellent with relational databases and cloud data warehouses

they form the backbone of data science by enabling data analysis, modeling, and deployment with speed, flexibility, and accuracy.

1. Pandas: Pandas is a powerful open-source Python library used extensively in data science for data manipulation, cleaning, and analysis. It provides two primary data structures Series and DataFrame which allow users to handle one-dimensional and two-dimensional labeled data respectively. Pandas simplifies tasks like reading data from various file formats (CSV, Excel, SQL, JSON), handling missing values, filtering, aggregating, and merging datasets. Its intuitive syntax makes operations such as group-by aggregations, pivot tables, and time-series analysis accessible even to beginners. In data science workflows, Pandas is often used in the initial stages for data cleaning and preparation, which are crucial before applying any machine learning or statistical techniques. It integrates seamlessly with other libraries like NumPy for numerical operations and Matplotlib/Seaborn for data visualization. Additionally, it supports efficient indexing and large dataset handling, enabling analysts and data scientists to preprocess data quickly. Whether it's preparing features for a model, conducting exploratory data analysis, or generating summary statistics, Pandas provides a reliable and efficient foundation. Its consistent API and widespread community support make it a standard tool in almost every data science project, contributing significantly to faster and more effective data-driven decision-making.

Features:

- Provides easy-to-use data structures: Series (1D) and DataFrame (2D).
- Handles missing data, merging, grouping, reshaping, and time-series.
- Supports reading/writing from various file formats (CSV, Excel, SQL, JSON).
- Integrates with NumPy and visualization libraries like Matplotlib.

Usage: Pandas is used for data cleaning, exploration, and transformation. It allows quick manipulation and analysis of structured data before feeding it into machine learning models. It's the go-to tool for handling tabular data during the preprocessing stage of any data science workflow.

2. NumPy: NumPy, short for Numerical Python, is a fundamental library for numerical computing in Python and serves as the foundation for many other data science libraries, including Pandas, Scikit-learn, and TensorFlow. Its core feature is the ndarray (N-dimensional array), a highly efficient structure for storing and manipulating numerical data. NumPy supports a wide array of mathematical operations such as linear algebra, statistical functions, random number generation, and Fourier transforms, all optimized for speed. In data science, NumPy is commonly used for handling large arrays and matrices of numeric data, which are essential in tasks like image processing, scientific computing, and machine learning model input preparation. It allows vectorized operations, reducing the need for explicit loops and enabling more readable and performant code. Data scientists rely on NumPy for tasks such as normalizing datasets, calculating performance metrics, implementing custom algorithms, or managing numerical simulations. Since many libraries in Python are built on top of NumPy, understanding its mechanics is crucial for advanced data science work. Its ability to interface with C and Fortran code also enables high-performance computing when needed. Overall, NumPy is indispensable in data science, especially for projects involving complex numerical computations and performance-critical operations.

Features:

- Provides fast, multidimensional arrays (ndarray).
- Supports mathematical operations like linear algebra, statistics, and Fourier transforms.
- Enables vectorized operations that boost performance.
- Serves as the foundation for other libraries like Pandas, TensorFlow, and Scikit-learn.

Usage: NumPy is used for numerical computation and efficient handling of large numeric datasets. It's essential for mathematical modeling, matrix manipulation, and scientific computing in machine learning and data analysis tasks.

3. Scikit-learn: Scikit-learn is one of the most widely used libraries in Python for classical machine learning in data science. Built on top of NumPy, SciPy, and Matplotlib, it offers simple and efficient tools for data mining and data analysis. Scikit-learn provides a consistent and user-friendly interface for implementing a variety of machine learning algorithms such as linear regression, logistic regression, decision trees, support vector machines (SVM), k-nearest neighbors (KNN), and ensemble methods like Random Forests and Gradient Boosting. It also includes utilities for preprocessing data (e.g., scaling, encoding, imputation), model evaluation (cross-validation, confusion matrix, accuracy, ROC/AUC), and feature selection. One of the key features of Scikit-learn is its pipeline system, which allows users to chain preprocessing and modeling steps into a single workflow, enhancing reproducibility and efficiency. In data science, Scikit-learn is used extensively for supervised and unsupervised learning tasks, including classification, regression, and clustering. Its simplicity makes it ideal for rapid prototyping, and it is commonly used in research, education, and production settings. Scikit-learn does not natively support deep learning or GPU acceleration but is highly efficient for moderate-sized datasets and classical algorithms. Overall, it is a cornerstone library for traditional machine learning workflows in data science.

Features:

- Offers a wide range of machine learning algorithms (classification, regression, clustering).
- Includes tools for preprocessing, model selection, and evaluation.
- Provides easy-to-use and consistent API.
- Supports pipeline creation for reproducible ML workflows.

Usage: Scikit-learn is ideal for implementing classical machine learning models quickly. It's widely used for building, testing, and validating models like decision trees, logistic regression, and SVMs, especially for structured/tabular data.

4. TensorFlow: TensorFlow is an open-source deep learning framework developed by Google, designed for building and training neural networks at scale. It supports a wide range of machine learning and deep learning tasks, including classification, regression, computer vision, natural language processing, and reinforcement learning. TensorFlow operates using computational graphs and offers both low-level and high-level APIs; the high-level API, Keras, simplifies the process of designing and training models. TensorFlow is highly scalable, supporting GPU and TPU acceleration for training large models efficiently. In data science, TensorFlow is used to create sophisticated deep learning models such as convolutional neural networks (CNNs) for image tasks, recurrent neural networks (RNNs) and transformers for sequence data, and autoencoders for anomaly detection or dimensionality reduction. It is also widely used in production environments due to tools like TensorFlow Serving for deploying models, TensorBoard for visualization, and TensorFlow Lite for mobile and embedded systems. TensorFlow integrates well with data pipelines (e.g., tf.data), supports distributed training, and is compatible with cloud platforms. While it has a steeper learning curve than Scikit-learn, its flexibility and performance make it ideal for enterprise-level and large-scale deep learning applications. In data science, TensorFlow is a top choice for building high-performance AI solutions.

Features:

- Supports large-scale machine learning and deep learning.
- Enables GPU/TPU acceleration for faster training.

- Includes Keras API for simplified model development.
- Offers tools for model deployment (TensorFlow Serving, TensorFlow Lite).

Usage: TensorFlow is used to build and train deep learning models for complex tasks like image recognition, NLP, and time-series forecasting. It's suitable for enterprise-grade applications and production environments requiring scalability.

5. PyTorch: PyTorch is a popular open-source deep learning framework developed by Facebook's AI Research lab (FAIR) and is widely used in both academia and industry. It is known for its dynamic computation graph, which allows more intuitive debugging and flexibility compared to static graphs used in TensorFlow. PyTorch's syntax is Pythonic and user-friendly, making it accessible to developers and researchers alike. It provides robust support for GPU acceleration, and its core library, torch, offers tensor computations similar to NumPy but with GPU support. In data science, PyTorch is frequently used for deep learning tasks such as image classification, object detection, speech recognition, and natural language processing using architectures like CNNs, RNNs, and transformers. Its ecosystem includes Torchvision (for image datasets and models), Torchtext (for NLP), and Lightning (for structured training). PyTorch is favored in research due to its flexibility and readability, but it also supports deployment via TorchScript and integration with tools like ONNX and Caffe2 for production use. As a result, it bridges the gap between research and real-world applications effectively. For data scientists working on deep learning models, particularly in research-heavy or experimental environments, PyTorch provides the ideal balance of performance, flexibility, and simplicity.

Features:

- Uses dynamic computation graphs (eager execution).
- Pythonic syntax with intuitive debugging.
- Offers GPU acceleration and robust support for neural networks.
- Includes ecosystem tools like Torchvision and Torchtext.

Usage: PyTorch is popular in research and experimentation for deep learning models. It's used for tasks such as computer vision and NLP, and it supports rapid prototyping with high flexibility. It's also increasingly used in production environments.

Differences Between Pandas, NumPy, Scikit-learn, TensorFlow, PyTorch: The differences between Pandas, NumPy, Scikit-learn, TensorFlow, PyTorch is listed in table 1.3.

Cloud and Big Data Technologies (AWS, Google Cloud, Hadoop, Spark)

Cloud and big data technologies are essential in data science for managing and analyzing large, complex datasets. Cloud platforms like AWS and Google Cloud provide scalable storage, computing power, and machine learning services, enabling data scientists to process data efficiently without on-premise infrastructure. Big data

Table 1.3

S.No.	Feature	Pandas	NumPy	Scikit-learn	TensorFlow	PyTorch
1.	Primary Use	Data manipulation and analysis	Numerical computing	Classical machine learning	Deep learning and large-scale ML	Deep learning and neural network research
2.	Core Data Structure	DataFrame, Series	ndarray (N-dimensional array)	Works with NumPy arrays, Pandas	Tensors (static computation graph)	Tensors (dynamic computation graph)
3.	Main Focus Area	Data preprocessing and EDA	Math, algebra, and scientific computing	ML algorithms (classification, regression, etc.)	Neural networks, production deployment	Neural networks, experimentation, research
4.	Ease of Use	High – very intuitive	Moderate – syntax less intuitive	High – simple and consistent API	Moderate – powerful but more complex	High – Pythonic and beginner-friendly
5.	GPU Acceleration Support	No	Limited (via third-party tools)	No	Yes – supports GPU and TPU	Yes – strong GPU support
6.	Common Use in Workflow	Cleaning, transforming, merging data	Matrix operations, numerical arrays	Building and evaluating ML models	Deep learning models, deployment	Deep learning research, NLP, CV tasks

tools such as Hadoop and Spark allow for distributed data storage and high-speed processing across clusters. These technologies support real-time analytics, predictive modeling, and AI applications. By combining cloud scalability with big data frameworks, organizations can accelerate insights, reduce costs, and drive data-driven decisions across various industries and use cases.

1. Amazon Web Services (AWS): Amazon Web Services (AWS) is the leading cloud computing platform that provides scalable, on-demand infrastructure and services for data storage, computing, analytics, and machine learning. In data science, AWS offers a wide range of tools that enable efficient data handling and model deployment at scale. Services like Amazon S3 are used for cost-effective data storage, while Amazon EC2 provides flexible virtual servers for running data pipelines or machine learning models. AWS Lambda enables serverless computing, which is helpful for lightweight tasks and event-driven processes. For data scientists, Amazon SageMaker is particularly valuable—it provides a managed environment for building, training, tuning, and deploying machine learning models with support for frameworks like TensorFlow, Scikit-learn, and PyTorch.

AWS also supports big data processing with services like Amazon EMR (Elastic MapReduce), which allows processing large datasets using Hadoop, Spark, and Presto. With its high scalability, security, and global infrastructure, AWS is ideal for enterprise-level data science solutions. Additionally, its pay-as-you-go pricing model allows organizations to manage costs effectively while scaling resources according to workload. The integration of AWS with data visualization tools, databases, and AI services makes it a comprehensive platform for full-cycle data science from raw data ingestion to real-time analytics and model deployment.

Features:

- **Scalable Cloud Infrastructure:** Auto-scaling EC2 instances for compute power.
- **Amazon S3 Storage:** Secure, scalable object storage for big datasets.
- **AWS SageMaker:** End-to-end machine learning model development and deployment.
- **Data Analytics Services:** Redshift (data warehouse), Glue (ETL), Athena (SQL querying).
- **Security and Compliance:** Identity & access management, encryption, and compliance tools.

Usage:

AWS is used for storing large datasets, training ML models at scale (with SageMaker), deploying AI services in production, and building scalable data pipelines in cloud environments.

2. Google Cloud Platform (GCP): Google Cloud Platform (GCP) is a suite of cloud computing services offered by Google, designed to support large-scale data processing, machine learning, and analytics. It provides robust infrastructure and pre-built services tailored for data science, including BigQuery, a powerful serverless data warehouse that allows fast SQL-based analysis of massive datasets. Cloud Storage serves as a reliable, scalable storage solution, while Compute Engine and Kubernetes Engine allow flexible deployment of data science applications and containerized environments. GCP is known for its tight integration with TensorFlow, Google's deep learning framework, making it an excellent choice for AI-heavy projects.

Data scientists also benefit from Vertex AI, a unified platform for developing, training, and deploying machine learning models. It includes tools for AutoML, feature engineering, model versioning, and experiment tracking. GCP's managed notebooks and support for Jupyter Notebooks enable collaborative and interactive development. Additionally, Dataflow and Dataproc support real-time and batch data processing using Apache Beam and Hadoop/Spark ecosystems, respectively. GCP offers advanced security, cost optimization tools, and deep integration with Google services, making it ideal for organizations already using Google's ecosystem. Its user-friendly interface and powerful APIs allow data scientists to innovate quickly and scale efficiently across projects of any size.

Features:

- **BigQuery:** Serverless, high-speed data warehouse for large-scale SQL analytics.
- **Vertex AI:** Integrated platform for ML model building, training, and deployment.
- **Cloud Storage:** Durable, secure, and scalable storage solution.

- **Compute Engine & Kubernetes:** VM and containerized deployment support.
- **Integrated AI APIs:** Pre-trained APIs for vision, language, and translation.

Usage: GCP is ideal for analyzing large datasets (via BigQuery), developing and deploying ML models (via Vertex AI), and running scalable compute jobs for AI/ML workloads.

3. Hadoop: Apache Hadoop is an open-source framework designed to store and process large volumes of data in a distributed computing environment. Its architecture is based on the Hadoop Distributed File System (HDFS), which splits data across multiple machines, and the MapReduce programming model, which processes data in parallel across clusters. Hadoop is fault-tolerant, meaning if one node fails, another can take its place without losing data. This makes it highly reliable for storing petabytes of data, particularly in data lakes and big data environments.

In data science, Hadoop is primarily used for large-scale batch processing tasks. It can handle unstructured, semi-structured, and structured data, making it useful for a variety of domains including finance, healthcare, and e-commerce. However, traditional Hadoop (MapReduce) can be slow due to its disk-based processing model. That's why many modern data science platforms integrate Hadoop with other technologies like Hive (SQL-like querying) and Pig (scripting), or replace MapReduce with faster engines like Apache Spark. Although Hadoop itself is not ideal for machine learning tasks, it is often used in the preprocessing phase collecting, cleaning, and organizing massive datasets before applying statistical or ML models. Hadoop remains a foundational technology in big data infrastructure, especially where data volume exceeds traditional system limits.

Features:

- **HDFS:** Distributed file system for storing huge datasets across clusters.
- **MapReduce:** Batch data processing model across distributed systems.
- **Fault Tolerance:** Automatically recovers from node failures.
- **Scalability:** Easily expands to thousands of nodes.
- **Ecosystem Integration:** Works with Hive, Pig, HBase, and more.

Usage: Hadoop is used to store and process large volumes of data for offline analytics, data lake management, and batch ETL tasks across various industries.

4. Apache Spark: Apache Spark is a fast, open-source big data processing engine designed for large-scale data analytics and machine learning. Unlike traditional Hadoop MapReduce, Spark performs in-memory computation, which significantly speeds up data processing tasks. It supports multiple programming languages, including Python (via PySpark), Scala, Java, and R, making it highly accessible to data scientists. Spark provides a unified platform for batch processing, real-time stream processing, SQL-based analytics, and machine learning (via MLlib), all within one ecosystem.

In data science, Spark is especially valuable for handling massive datasets that cannot fit into memory on a single machine. Its distributed computing model allows data scientists to scale operations across clusters, enabling fast processing of terabytes or even petabytes of data. With Spark SQL, users can perform SQL-like queries directly on structured data, while Spark Streaming supports real-time analytics from data sources like Kafka and Flume. GraphX enables graph processing for network analysis, and MLlib includes scalable machine learning algorithms such as regression, classification, clustering, and collaborative filtering. Spark integrates well with cloud platforms (AWS, GCP, Azure) and storage systems like HDFS, Amazon S3, and Google Cloud Storage. Overall, Spark is a powerful tool for data scientists working on complex, high-volume analytics and predictive modeling tasks.

Features:

- **In-Memory Processing:** Speeds up data processing significantly.
- **Support for Multiple Languages:** Python (PySpark), Scala, Java, and R.
- **Spark SQL:** Enables querying structured data with SQL.
- **Mllib:** Built-in machine learning library.
- **Streaming & Graph Processing:** Real-time data and network analysis support.

Usage: Spark is used for large-scale data analytics, real-time streaming, and distributed machine learning on massive datasets where performance and scalability are critical.

Differences Between AWS, Google Cloud, Hadoop, Spark: Table 1.4 shows the differences between features of AWS, Google Cloud, Hadoop, Spark.

Table 1.4

S.No.	Features	AWS	Google Cloud	Hadoop	Spark
1.	Core Service Focus	Broad cloud infrastructure & managed services	Cloud-native big data & AI/ML services	Distributed storage & batch processing framework	Fast in-memory data processing engine
2.	Data Storage	Amazon S3 (object storage), Redshift (data warehouse)	Cloud Storage, BigQuery (serverless warehouse)	HDFS (distributed file system)	Works on top of HDFS, S3, others
3.	Compute Model	Virtual machines (EC2), serverless (Lambda)	Compute Engine (VMs), Kubernetes Engine	MapReduce batch processing	In-memory processing with DAG execution
4.	Machine Learning Tools	SageMaker (managed ML platform)	Vertex AI (unified ML platform)	Limited (via ecosystem tools, e.g., Mahout)	MLlib (built-in scalable ML library)
5.	Real-time Processing	Kinesis (stream processing)	Dataflow (stream and batch processing)	Primarily batch-oriented	Native support for streaming via Spark Streaming
6.	Ease of Use / Integration	Extensive integrations, mature ecosystem	Strong integration with Google services	Requires setup and management of clusters	APIs in multiple languages, easy integration

SUMMARY OF INTRODUCTION TO DATA SCIENCE

Data Science is an interdisciplinary field that combines statistics, computer science, mathematics, and domain expertise to extract meaningful insights from structured and unstructured data. It involves a comprehensive workflow that includes problem formulation, data collection, data cleaning, exploratory data analysis (EDA), model building, evaluation, deployment, and ongoing maintenance. Data scientists use programming languages like Python, R, and SQL, and leverage libraries such as Pandas, NumPy, Scikit-learn, TensorFlow, and PyTorch. Cloud platforms (AWS, Google Cloud) and big data technologies (Hadoop, Spark) enable scalable storage and processing. Data Science plays a critical role in today's world, powering applications like recommendation systems, fraud detection, predictive analytics, and automation in industries including healthcare, finance, e-commerce, and manufacturing. It is closely related to machine learning and artificial intelligence but encompasses a broader scope, emphasizing data-driven decision-making and communication. Overall, Data Science is a vital tool for transforming raw data into actionable business and scientific value.

1. What is Data Science?

Data Science is a multidisciplinary field that uses techniques from statistics, computer science, and domain knowledge to extract insights and knowledge from data. It involves collecting, processing, analyzing, and interpreting large volumes of structured and unstructured data to solve complex problems and support decision-making. By applying methods such as machine learning, data mining, and predictive modeling, data scientists uncover patterns and trends that drive business strategies and innovations. Data Science is essential in various industries, including healthcare, finance, marketing, and technology, and plays a key role in enabling data-driven decisions in today's digital and information-rich world.

- **Definition and Scope:** Data Science is an interdisciplinary field that leverages statistical analysis, machine learning, data visualization, and domain knowledge to extract insights and knowledge from structured and unstructured data. At its core, it combines elements of computer science, mathematics, and business understanding to solve real-world problems using data.

  The scope of data science is vast. It includes data collection, processing, and analysis to make predictions, automate decisions, and uncover hidden patterns. Data science finds application in various sectors such as healthcare, finance, marketing, manufacturing, e-commerce, and more.

- **Importance in the Modern World:** In today's digital age, massive amounts of data are generated every second from online transactions and social media interactions to sensor data from IoT devices. Organizations that can harness this data effectively gain significant competitive advantages.

Data science enables evidence-based decision-making, personalization of services, fraud detection, recommendation systems, predictive maintenance, and much more. Businesses, governments, and scientific communities increasingly rely on data science to drive innovation and efficiency.

- **Comparison with Related Fields:** Artificial Intelligence (AI), Machine Learning (ML), and Big Data are interconnected technologies that drive modern data-driven applications. AI refers to the simulation of human intelligence in machines, enabling them to perform tasks such as reasoning, problem-solving, and learning. Machine Learning is a subset of AI that focuses on algorithms and statistical models that allow computers to learn patterns from data and improve over time without being explicitly programmed. Big Data refers to extremely large and complex datasets that cannot be processed efficiently using traditional tools. It is characterized by volume, velocity, and variety. Big Data provides the fuel for training ML models and powering AI systems. Together, Big Data supplies the information, ML creates predictive or analytical models, and AI applies intelligence to perform tasks like language translation, image recognition, or personalized recommendations. These technologies are widely used in industries such as healthcare, finance, e-commerce, and transportation.
  - **Artificial Intelligence (AI):** AI is a broader field aimed at creating systems that can perform tasks requiring human intelligence. Data science contributes to AI by providing data-driven models and algorithms, especially in areas like natural language processing and computer vision.
  - **Machine Learning (ML):** ML is a subfield of AI that involves algorithms that improve from experience. ML is a core part of data science, primarily during the model building phase. While data science uses ML as a tool, it also encompasses data preparation, interpretation, and communication of results.
  - **Big Data:** This refers to data sets so large and complex that traditional data processing tools can't handle them. Data science often involves working with big data using specialized tools and platforms. However, not all data science projects require big data.

2. Data Science Workflow

The data science workflow is a systematic approach that ensures data-driven problems are tackled effectively. It consists of the following key stages:

- **Problem Formulation:** The first and most crucial step is understanding and defining the problem. This involves communicating with stakeholders to identify business goals, constraints, and success criteria. Clear problem formulation sets the foundation for all subsequent steps.
- **Data Collection and Preparation:** Once the problem is defined, relevant data must be gathered. This can involve querying databases, using APIs, web

scraping, or collecting data from sensors. Data is often messy, so cleaning, filtering, and formatting (also called data wrangling or preprocessing) are essential to make it usable.

This stage may include handling missing values, removing duplicates, encoding categorical variables, and scaling features. High-quality data is essential for accurate and reliable analysis.

- **Exploratory Data Analysis (EDA):** EDA involves understanding the underlying structure and patterns in the data using statistics and visualization tools. Analysts use graphs, charts, and summary statistics to identify trends, detect anomalies, and form hypotheses.

  EDA helps in feature selection and engineering by highlighting which variables are most relevant. It also aids in choosing appropriate modeling techniques later in the workflow.

- **Model Building and Evaluation:** At this stage, predictive or descriptive models are built using machine learning or statistical algorithms. The dataset is typically split into training and testing sets. Models might include linear regression, decision trees, support vector machines, or deep neural networks, depending on the problem.

  Evaluation metrics such as accuracy, precision, recall, F1-score, RMSE (Root Mean Squared Error), or AUC (Area Under Curve) are used to assess model performance. Model tuning (hyperparameter optimization) and validation (cross-validation) are crucial steps in refining the model.

- **Deployment and Maintenance:** A model that performs well in testing must be deployed to a production environment. This means integrating it into applications, dashboards, or workflows where it can provide value to end users. Model deployment can be done using APIs, cloud services, or data pipelines. Maintenance involves monitoring model performance over time and updating it as new data becomes available or as business needs change. This ensures the model remains accurate and relevant.

3. Tools and Technologies for Data Science

Modern data science relies on a wide array of tools, programming languages, and platforms. These tools help in data manipulation, model development, visualization, and deployment.

- **Programming Languages:** Programming languages like Python, R, and SQL are essential tools in data science and analytics. Python is the most widely used language due to its simplicity, readability, and rich ecosystem of libraries such as Pandas, NumPy, Scikit-learn, TensorFlow, and Matplotlib. It is highly versatile, supporting data manipulation, machine learning, visualization, and deployment. R is preferred in statistical analysis and academic research, offering powerful packages like ggplot2, dplyr, and caret for data exploration and modeling. It is especially strong in statistical computing and data visualization. SQL (Structured Query Language) is fundamental for managing and querying relational databases. It allows data scientists to retrieve, filter, and aggregate data from large databases efficiently. While Python and R are used for advanced analysis and modeling, SQL is crucial for accessing and preparing data before analysis. Together, these languages form a strong foundation for building, analyzing, and interpreting data-driven solutions in various industries.

  - **Python:** The most widely used language in data science due to its simplicity and vast ecosystem of libraries. It supports everything from data cleaning and visualization to machine learning and deep learning.
  - **R:** Popular in academia and among statisticians. It excels in statistical modeling and data visualization with libraries like ggplot2 and caret.
  - **SQL (Structured Query Language):** Essential for querying relational databases. SQL helps retrieve and manipulate data stored in tables, making it a foundational tool for data collection and exploration.

- **Data Science Libraries:** Data science libraries such as Pandas, NumPy, Scikit-learn, TensorFlow, and PyTorch are fundamental tools in the data science and machine learning ecosystem. Pandas simplifies data manipulation and analysis with its DataFrame structure, ideal for handling structured data. NumPy provides efficient numerical operations on multi-dimensional arrays and serves as the foundation for many other libraries. Scikit-learn offers a comprehensive suite of machine learning algorithms for tasks like classification, regression, clustering, and model evaluation, making it ideal for traditional ML applications. For deep learning, TensorFlow and PyTorch are the most widely used frameworks. TensorFlow, developed by Google, supports scalable model training and deployment across various platforms. PyTorch, developed by Meta (Facebook), is praised for its intuitive design and flexibility, particularly in research and prototyping. Together, these libraries cover the full spectrum of data science from data preprocessing and statistical analysis to building, training, and deploying machine learning and deep learning models.

  - **Pandas:** Provides data structures (like DataFrames) and functions for manipulating structured data efficiently.
  - **NumPy:** Supports numerical computations and array operations. It forms the basis for many other scientific computing libraries.
  - **Scikit-learn:** A robust library for classical machine learning algorithms. It offers tools for regression, classification, clustering, dimensionality reduction, and model evaluation.
  - **TensorFlow:** Developed by Google, TensorFlow is widely used for building and training deep learning models. It supports deployment on mobile and cloud platforms.

  - **PyTorch:** Developed by Facebook, PyTorch is another popular deep learning library known for its flexibility and ease of use, especially in academic research and prototyping.

- **Cloud and Big Data Technologies:** Cloud and Big Data technologies refer to the tools and platforms that enable the storage, processing, and analysis of large-scale data over the internet. Cloud platforms like AWS, Google Cloud, and Microsoft Azure provide scalable infrastructure, data storage, and computing resources on demand. Big Data technologies such as Hadoop and Apache Spark are designed to handle massive datasets efficiently by distributing data and computation across clusters of machines. These tools support real-time processing, data lakes, and analytics at scale, allowing organizations to manage and analyze vast amounts of data quickly, cost-effectively, and without relying on physical infrastructure.
  - **AWS (Amazon Web Services):** Provides a suite of cloud computing services, including S3 for storage, EC2 for compute, and SageMaker for building, training, and deploying ML models.
  - **Google Cloud Platform (GCP):** Offers tools like BigQuery (for SQL-based analysis of massive datasets), Cloud ML Engine, and AutoML for machine learning.
  - **Hadoop:** A framework for distributed storage and processing of large datasets using a cluster of machines. Core components include HDFS (Hadoop Distributed File System) and MapReduce.
  - **Apache Spark:** A powerful big data processing engine that supports in-memory computation. It's faster than Hadoop for many tasks and integrates well with Python (via PySpark), making it popular among data scientists.

Chapter 2

Data Acquisition and Preprocessing

Data Acquisition is the foundational step in the data science workflow, involving the systematic collection of relevant data from various sources to address a specific problem or question. In today's digital landscape, data is generated continuously from diverse origins, including databases, web servers, sensors, social media platforms, APIs, and transactional systems. Effective data acquisition requires identifying the appropriate data sources that best represent the problem context, whether it is structured data like spreadsheets and relational databases or unstructured data such as images, text, and videos. This phase often involves extracting data using tools like SQL for databases, web scraping scripts for online content, or streaming services for real-time data. Additionally, organizations may combine internal data with external datasets, including open data or third-party data, to enrich their analyses. Acquiring high-quality data is critical because the insights, predictions, and decisions derived later heavily depend on the accuracy, completeness, and relevance of the initial data collected. Challenges during acquisition include dealing with disparate data formats, access restrictions, privacy concerns, and ensuring data integrity during transfer and storage. Selecting reliable data and adhering to ethical and legal guidelines are essential to maintain trust and compliance throughout the data lifecycle.

Once data is acquired, the next crucial step is Data Preprocessing, which transforms raw data into a clean, structured format suitable for analysis or modeling. Raw data is often incomplete, noisy, inconsistent, or contains errors, making preprocessing indispensable for ensuring data quality. This process involves several key tasks such as handling missing values by imputing or removing them, correcting errors, filtering outliers, and removing duplicate entries. Data normalization or scaling is applied to standardize features so they can be compared and modelled effectively, especially in algorithms sensitive to scale differences. Encoding categorical variables into numerical forms is also necessary because most machine learning algorithms require numerical input. Additionally, feature engineering during preprocessing creates new, meaningful variables derived from existing data to enhance model performance. Preprocessing may also include data reduction techniques like dimensionality reduction or sampling to make large datasets more manageable without significant loss of information. Automated tools and libraries like Pandas, Scikit-learn, and TensorFlow's data API support many of these preprocessing tasks, streamlining workflows and improving reproducibility. Effective preprocessing not only improves the accuracy and robustness of analytical models but also reduces computational complexity, leading to more efficient and interpretable results.

4. Data Collection and Sources

Data collection is a critical first step in any data science project, as the quality, relevance, and comprehensiveness of the collected data directly impact the insights and decisions that follow. It involves gathering raw data from various origins that best represent the problem being studied. Because data comes in many forms and from many places, understanding the diverse sources and methods of collection is essential for effective analysis. Data sources can broadly be classified into primary and secondary sources.

- **Primary Data:** Primary data is collected firsthand by the organization or researcher specifically for the project at hand. Examples include surveys, interviews, experiments, sensors, and direct observations. Collecting primary data allows for high control over data quality and relevance but can be time-consuming and expensive.
- **Secondary Data:** Secondary data refers to data that has been previously collected by other entities and made available for reuse. Examples include publicly available datasets, government databases, company records, web data, and data purchased from third-party providers. Secondary data is typically easier and cheaper to obtain but may lack customization or full control over quality and structure.

Common Data Collection Methods

1. **Databases and Data Warehouses:** Many organizations store structured data in relational databases like MySQL, Oracle, or PostgreSQL, or in large-scale data warehouses optimized for analytics. SQL queries extract relevant subsets for analysis.
2. **Web Scraping:** For unstructured or semi-structured data publicly available on websites, web scraping tools and libraries (e.g., BeautifulSoup, Scrapy) automate data extraction from web pages.
3. **APIs:** Application Programming Interfaces (APIs) provide programmatic access to data from web services, social media platforms (Twitter, Facebook), financial markets, weather services, and more. APIs offer real-time or batch data retrieval.
4. **Sensors and IoT Devices:** Internet of Things (IoT) devices and sensors collect real-time data in domains like manufacturing, agriculture, smart cities, and healthcare, providing continuous streams of data about environment, equipment, or human activity.

5. **Surveys and Questionnaires:** Primary data collection via surveys allows capturing specific information directly from people, providing qualitative and quantitative insights. Digital tools like Google Forms or SurveyMonkey simplify this process.
6. **Log Files and Event Data:** Web servers, applications, and network devices generate logs recording user activity, system events, or errors, which serve as valuable data sources for performance monitoring, security, and user behavior analysis.

Challenges in Data Collection: Data collection faces multiple challenges, including:

1. **Data Quality:** Ensuring accuracy, completeness, and consistency is vital. Poor-quality data can mislead analysis and lead to wrong conclusions.
2. **Data Privacy and Ethics:** Collecting sensitive data requires strict adherence to privacy laws (e.g., GDPR, HIPAA) and ethical standards to protect individuals' rights and prevent misuse.
3. **Data Integration:** Combining data from disparate sources often involves dealing with inconsistent formats, missing values, and varying granularity.
4. **Volume and Velocity:** The scale and speed at which data is generated (especially from IoT or social media) can overwhelm traditional systems, necessitating scalable and real-time data ingestion technologies.

Structured vs. Unstructured Data

Structured Data: Structured data refers to data that is organized and formatted in a predefined manner, typically using rows and columns. It is easily stored, processed, and retrieved using traditional database systems like relational databases (e.g., MySQL, Oracle, SQL Server). Each piece of structured data fits neatly into a table format, with defined data types and relationships. Examples include names, dates, credit card numbers, transaction details, and sensor readings. Because of its clear structure, structured data can be queried using SQL, making it efficient for analysis and reporting. It is commonly used in business systems like Customer Relationship Management (CRM), Enterprise Resource Planning (ERP), and financial records. Structured data is highly valuable for operational and decision-making tasks, but it has limitations in handling more complex or diverse data types. It is ideal when data is consistent, predictable, and regularly updated.

Unstructured Data: Unstructured data lacks a predefined format or organization, making it more complex to collect, store, and analyze. Unlike structured data, it cannot be stored in traditional row-column databases. Common sources include text documents, emails, social media posts, images, audio files, videos, and PDF files. This type of data is abundant, forming the majority of data generated daily, especially in domains like healthcare, marketing, and social media. Since unstructured data does not follow a clear schema, analyzing it requires advanced technologies such as Natural

Language Processing (NLP), computer vision, and machine learning. Tools like Hadoop, Apache Spark, TensorFlow, and PyTorch are often used to handle and process it. While more difficult to manage, unstructured data provides rich insights, especially when combined with structured data. For example, analyzing customer reviews (unstructured) alongside purchase records (structured) can reveal deeper patterns in consumer behavior. As data sources grow, managing and extracting value from unstructured data has become a major focus in modern data science and artificial intelligence applications.

Comparison Between Structured Data and Unstructured Data

Table 2.1

S.No.	Aspect	Structured Data	Unstructured Data
1.	Definition	Data organized in a predefined format (e.g., rows and columns)	Data without a fixed format or structure
2.	Storage Format	Stored in relational databases, spreadsheets	Stored in data lakes, NoSQL databases, cloud storage
3.	Examples	Customer information, transaction records, sensor data	Emails, social media posts, images, videos, PDFs
4.	Data Type	Typically text and numbers	Text, images, audio, video, documents
5.	Accessibility	Easy to search, query, and analyze using SQL	Requires advanced tools (e.g., NLP, computer vision) to analyze
6.	Schema	Fixed schema (predefined columns and data types)	No fixed schema, varies by source
7.	Processing Tools	SQL, Excel, RDBMS (MySQL, PostgreSQL)	Hadoop, Spark, TensorFlow, NLP and image processing libraries
8.	Ease of Analysis	Easier and faster to analyze	More complex and resource-intensive to analyze
9.	Use Cases	Financial reports, inventory management, CRM systems	Sentiment analysis, image recognition, video analytics
10.	Volume Handling	Handles moderate volumes well	Designed for high-volume, diverse data types

Public Datasets and APIs

Public datasets and APIs are valuable resources for data science, offering free or open access to structured or unstructured data for analysis, model training, and research. Public datasets are often provided by governments, academic institutions, and organizations like Kaggle, UCI Machine Learning Repository, and World Bank, covering topics such as health, economics, climate, and social trends. APIs (Application Programming Interfaces) allow programmatic access to dynamic data from platforms like Twitter, Google Maps, and OpenWeather, enabling real-time or automated data collection. These resources help data scientists prototype solutions, test algorithms, and gain insights without the need for original data collection.

Public Datasets: Public datasets are vital for data science, offering free access to structured information for analysis, model training, and research. They span various domains, including healthcare (e.g., MIMIC-III), finance (e.g., Yahoo Finance), environment (e.g., NOAA climate data), and social sciences (e.g., World Bank, Census data). Popular platforms like Kaggle, UCI Machine Learning Repository, and Google Dataset Search provide rich, curated datasets for machine learning and AI projects. These datasets help practitioners develop skills, validate models, and benchmark algorithms. Ethical use and awareness of data privacy are crucial when using public datasets, especially those containing sensitive or personally identifiable information. The different types of public datasets are as follows:

1. **Structured Datasets:** Structured datasets are highly organized and stored in tabular formats like CSV, Excel, or SQL databases. Each row typically represents an instance (e.g., a person or product), and each column represents a feature (e.g., age, price). These datasets are easy to manipulate using tools like pandas (Python), R, or SQL. Common examples include financial records, census data, and e-commerce transaction logs. In data science, structured data is commonly used for regression, classification, and clustering tasks. Since the data has a consistent schema, it's ideal for machine learning models that require numeric or categorical inputs. Datasets such as the UCI Machine Learning Repository or Kaggle competitions often provide structured data, allowing practitioners to test and compare algorithms. Preprocessing structured data typically involves handling missing values, encoding categorical variables, and normalizing numerical fields. The predictability and clarity of structured data make it one of the most accessible types for beginners and essential in business analytics.
2. **Unstructured Datasets:** Unstructured datasets do not follow a predefined format and include data such as text, images, audio, and video. Unlike structured datasets, these are more complex to process and often require advanced techniques in natural language processing (NLP), computer vision, or audio analysis. Examples include social media posts, emails, scanned documents, audio interviews, and video footage. Unstructured data makes up a large portion of the data generated globally, and its analysis provides deep insights into human behavior, sentiment, and trends. For data scientists, working with unstructured data involves preprocessing steps like text tokenization, image segmentation, or audio signal processing. Machine learning models such as convolutional neural networks (CNNs) and transformers are commonly used to analyze unstructured data. Tools like TensorFlow, PyTorch, and spaCy facilitate this work. Public sources of unstructured datasets include YouTube-8M for video, COCO for images, and the Enron email dataset for text. Despite the complexity, unstructured data offers rich opportunities for innovation in fields like AI, recommendation systems, and real-time analytics.

3. **Semi-Structured Datasets:** Semi-structured datasets fall between structured and unstructured data. They don't fit neatly into tables but contain organizational markers like tags or metadata that help identify elements. Examples include XML, JSON, and YAML files, as well as data from NoSQL databases, emails, or sensor logs. This type of data is common in web applications, APIs, and mobile systems. In data science, semi-structured data is valuable because it combines flexibility with enough organization to allow parsing and analysis. For instance, an e-commerce site might store order details in JSON format with varying fields depending on product type. Parsing tools like Python's json or xml.etree make it easier to convert semi-structured data into structured formats. Data scientists must often normalize this data for use in machine learning models. Public sources include Twitter APIs (which return JSON), GitHub repositories, and data.gov datasets with metadata. Working with semi-structured data develops critical skills in data wrangling, transformation, and schema inference essential for building scalable data pipelines and real-time analytics systems.
4. **Time Series Datasets:** Time series datasets consist of data points collected or recorded at regular time intervals, such as hourly, daily, or monthly. These datasets are crucial for tasks involving forecasting, anomaly detection, or trend analysis. Common examples include stock prices, weather records, IoT sensor data, and website traffic logs. The defining feature of time series data is temporal dependence current values are influenced by past ones. Data scientists analyze such datasets using techniques like ARIMA, exponential smoothing, or LSTM neural networks. Libraries like statsmodels, prophet, and tsfresh are popular for time series forecasting and feature extraction. Public sources of time series data include Yahoo Finance (stock data), NOAA (weather), and Kaggle (web traffic datasets). Proper handling of time series requires attention to stationarity, seasonality, and autocorrelation. Time series datasets often require resampling, smoothing, and differencing before model training. These datasets are central to fields like finance, operations, and energy management, where anticipating future trends can lead to significant strategic advantages.

Differences Between Structured, Unstructured, Semi-Structured, and Time Series Datasets

Application Programming Interfaces (APIs): Application Programming Interfaces play a crucial role in enabling seamless access to external data sources, integration of machine learning models, and automation of workflows. They act as intermediaries that allow different software systems to communicate by sending and receiving data, typically through web-based protocols like REST and data formats such as JSON. Data scientists commonly use APIs to retrieve real-time data from platforms like Twitter, Google Maps, or financial services for applications such as sentiment analysis, geospatial modeling, or stock forecasting. APIs also allow machine

Table 2.2

S.No.	Feature	Structured	Unstructured	Semi-Structured	Time Series
1.	Data Format	Tabular (rows & columns)	Free-form (text, images, audio)	Not tabular but organized (e.g., JSON, XML)	Tabular with a timestamp
2.	Organization	Highly organized schema	No predefined schema	Partial structure with tags or markers	Ordered by time intervals
3.	Examples	Titanic dataset, customer databases	Movie reviews, images, audio files	Twitter data (JSON), log files	Stock prices, weather data
4.	Data Processing Tools	SQL, Excel, pandas	NLP, image/audio processing, CNNs, RNNs	Parsers (e.g., JSON/XML readers) + structured tools	Time series libraries (e.g., Prophet, ARIMA)
5.	Common Use Cases	Classification, regression, business analytics	Sentiment analysis, image classification	Web scraping, API data, event logs	Forecasting, anomaly detection, trend analysis

learning models to be deployed and accessed remotely, making it possible to integrate predictive analytics into web apps or business systems. For example, a trained recommendation model can be hosted on a cloud server and queried via API to serve users personalized content in real time. Tools like Python's requests library make it easy to connect with APIs and process the data into usable formats for analysis. Overall, APIs enhance the efficiency, scalability, and interactivity of data science projects by enabling dynamic data exchange and system integration, which are essential for building modern, intelligent data-driven applications.

Accessing Data via APIs: A major use of APIs in data science is to fetch real-time or large-scale data from web services. Instead of manually downloading files, APIs allow automated access to updated datasets. For instance:

1. **Twitter API:** This provides access to tweets, hashtags, and user activity, commonly used in sentiment analysis and social media mining.
2. **Google Maps API:** This delivers geographic data, which can be integrated into geospatial analysis.
3. **Financial APIs:** Examples like Alpha Vantage, Yahoo Finance supply stock market and economic indicators for **financial forecasting.**
4. **Public Health APIs**: Like COVID-19 APIs enable real-time tracking of cases and vaccination data for **epidemiological modeling.**

This automated access is vital for keeping data pipelines current, especially when building dashboards or real-time analytics platforms.

Difference between Datasets and API: Table 2.3 shows the differences between datasets and API.

Table 2.3

S.No.	Feature	Datasets	APIs
1.	Definition	Collections of structured or unstructured data stored for analysis.	Interfaces that allow programs to request and exchange data or services.
2.	Data Access	Data is typically static or periodically updated and downloaded as files (CSV, JSON, etc.).	Provides real-time or on-demand access to data or functionality via network calls.
3.	Format	Often comes in files like CSV, Excel, JSON, or databases.	Data is usually returned in formats like JSON or XML via HTTP requests.
4.	Usage	Used for batch analysis, training models, exploratory data analysis.	Used to fetch live data, interact with services, or run remote processes dynamically.
5.	Interactivity	Data is passive and needs to be manually loaded and processed.	Enables dynamic, programmatic interaction and integration with external systems.
6.	Update Frequency	Fixed snapshots or updated periodically (daily, monthly).	Provides fresh, real-time or near real-time data on each request.
7.	Example	Titanic dataset (CSV file), ImageNet dataset (image files).	Twitter API for tweets, Google Maps API for geolocation data.
8.	Dependency	Self-contained; once downloaded, no external connection needed.	Requires internet connection and API authentication to access data/services.
9.	Flexibility	Limited to available data fields and size.	Can query, filter, or customize data responses dynamically.
10.	Complexity	Easier to use for offline analysis.	Requires understanding of API endpoints, authentication, and rate limits.

Web Scraping and Databases

In data science, gathering data is the first critical step toward meaningful analysis. Two fundamental methods for collecting and managing data are web scraping and the use of databases. Each serves distinct purposes, offers unique challenges, and is essential in the modern data ecosystem.

Web Scraping: Web scraping is an automated technique used to extract data from websites. Instead of manually copying and pasting information which is a slow and repetitive process it uses software tools to gather large amounts of data quickly. These tools can be custom-built or used across multiple sites. It also helps individuals and businesses to collect valuable data for research, marketing and analysis. Many websites restrict saving data so scraping offers a way to access information within legal limits. Web scraping is used across many fields to collect valuable data efficiently:

1. **Market and Competitor Analysis:** Businesses scrape product prices, customer reviews and competitor offerings from multiple websites. This helps them stay updated on market trends and adjust their strategies to remain competitive.
2. **Financial Data Collection:** Investors and analysts extract real-time stock prices, historical data and financial reports. This information supports better decision-making and timely responses to market changes.

3. **Social Media Monitoring:** Marketers collect data from social media platforms to track trending topics, customer sentiments and campaign effectiveness. This helps in shaping marketing strategies and improving customer engagement.
4. **SEO Tracking:** Companies use scraping tools to monitor how their websites rank on search engines for specific keywords over time. This helps optimize content and improve online visibility.
5. **Research and Machine Learning:** Researchers and data scientists collect large datasets from various websites to train machine learning models or conduct data-driven studies. Scraping automates this data collection helps in saving time and effort.

Web Scraping Works: Web Scraping methods follow three steps as mentioned below:

1. **Make an HTTP Request to The Website URLs** - In the first step, you need to provide a list of URLs to the Web Scrapers from which you want to extract the data and it will make HTTP requests to these URLs.
2. **Load and Parse the Websites Code** - Once the HTTP request is successfully executed to the URLs mentioned in the first step; Web Scrapers can load the HTML or XML code of the websites. Some Web Scrapers can also load CSS or JavaScript elements as well. Further, Web Scraper will parse the HTML code to identify and extract relevant data which is predefined by you.

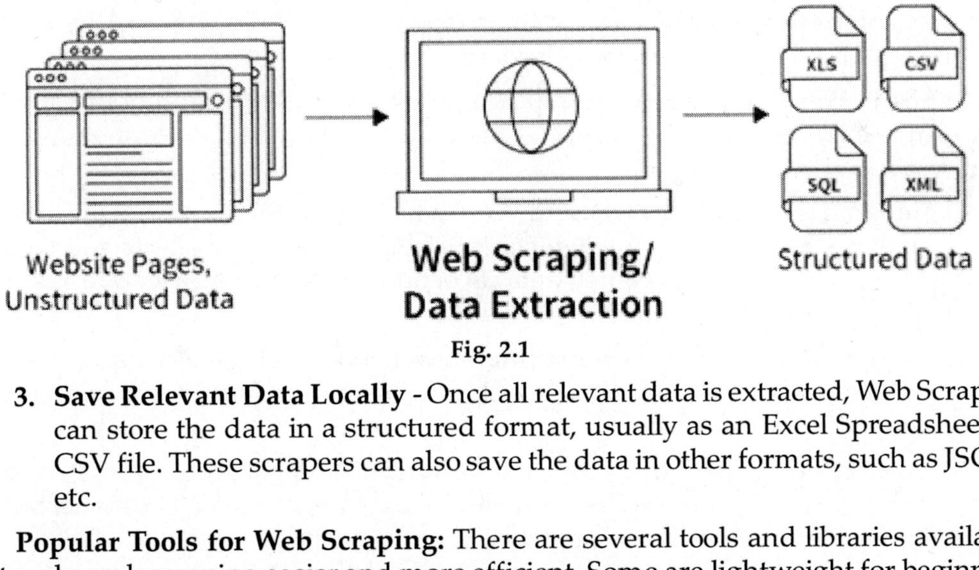

Fig. 2.1

3. **Save Relevant Data Locally** - Once all relevant data is extracted, Web Scrapers can store the data in a structured format, usually as an Excel Spreadsheet or CSV file. These scrapers can also save the data in other formats, such as JSON, etc.

Popular Tools for Web Scraping: There are several tools and libraries available that make web scraping easier and more efficient. Some are lightweight for beginners while others are built for large-scale data extraction:

1. **BeautifulSoup (Python):** BeautifulSoup is a beginner-friendly Python library used to parse HTML and XML documents. It allows us to navigate the page structure and extract specific elements using tags and classes.

2. **Requests (Python):** Requests is used with BeautifulSoup as it helps to send HTTP requests to websites and fetch the HTML content of web pages.
3. **Scrapy:** Scrapy is an advanced Python framework built for web scraping. It supports features like crawling, handling requests/responses, managing pipelines and storing scraped data efficiently.
4. **Selenium:** Selenium is a web automation tool that can control a browser like a real user. It's useful for scraping websites that use JavaScript to load content such as infinite scrolling or dropdown menus.
5. **Playwright:** Playwright is a newer alternative to Selenium, it supports modern web standards and provides better performance for scraping dynamic content with headless browser control.
6. **Commercial Platforms:** This includes:
   - **Bright Data (formerly Luminati)**: A premium proxy-based platform with strong scraping features.
   - **Import.io**: Allows scraping without coding which is ideal for non-programmers.
   - **Webhose.io**: Offers structured data feeds for news, blogs and online content.
   - **Dexi.io and Scrapinghub:** Provide cloud-based scraping services with built-in scheduling, storage and proxy support.

Each tool has its strengths and its choice depends on the complexity of the website, the volume of data and our technical background.

Future of Web Scraping: Web scraping is growing rapidly as the amount of online data grows exponentially. Its future is shaped by advances in technology, legal frameworks and business needs:

1. **Integration with Big Data and AI**: Combining web scraping with big data analytics and artificial intelligence will helps in deeper insights and smarter decision-making. Automated data collection will feed more accurate, real-time information into AI models.
2. **Improved Tools and Automation**: Newer tools will offer easier, faster and more reliable scraping solutions including better handling of dynamic content and anti-scraping measures.
3. **Greater Focus on Ethics and Compliance**: As legal frameworks develop, scraping will become more regulated helps in encouraging responsible and transparent data collection practices.
4. **More APIs and Structured Data**: Websites may provide more APIs or structured data feeds which helps in reducing the need for scraping and making data access easier and safer.

Mastering web scraping tools and techniques is important for anyone looking to see the full potential of online data in today's digital world.

Database: A database is an organized collection of data stored electronically. It allows users and applications to easily access, update, and manipulate information. This data contains text, numbers, images, videos and more. Databases are managed using specialized software known as a Database Management System (DBMS), which facilitates the storage, retrieval, and manipulation of data.

Databases are fundamental to modern computing, supporting various applications from online shopping platforms to social media networks. It is widely used in business, government, healthcare, and many other sectors to store and manage data, enabling informed decision-making and efficient operations. Reasons to use databases are as:

1. **Efficient Data Storage**: Databases can store large amounts of data and ensure it remains accessible and organized.
2. **Facilitate Transactions**: They enable smooth transactions in online banking, shopping, social media, and more by processing and retrieving data in real-time.
3. **Data Updates**: Databases allow for easy and quick updates to data, ensuring that the most current information is always available.
4. **Data Analysis**: Databases provide an excellent framework for analyzing trends and making data-driven decisions.

Types of Databases: Databases are the backbone of modern applications. They are designed to address specific data storage, retrieval and management needs. Databases can be classified based on their structure, use cases or storage methods. Let's explore the major types of databases:

1. **Relational Databases:** These databases organize data into tables with rows and columns, more like a spreadsheet. They use SQL to manage and query data. Accessing structured data is made most flexible and efficient by relational database technology. They ensure data is stored consistently and allow for complex queries, making them ideal for applications requiring structured data and relationships.
   - **Examples**: MySQL, PostgreSQL, Oracle, Microsoft SQL Server.
   - **Use Cases**: E-commerce platforms, banking systems, and HR management.
2. **NoSQL Databases**: These databases are designed to handle unstructured and semi-structured data. They do not use tables and SQL, instead store data in formats like documents, key-value pairs or graphs. They are highly scalable and flexible, making them ideal for real-time applications
   - **Examples**: MongoDB, Cassandra, DynamoDB.
   - **Use Cases**: Social media platforms, IoT applications and big data analytics.
3. **Distributed Databases:** These databases are made up of two or more files that are spread across multiple locations or servers. They work together to

provide a unified view of data. The database could be spread across many networks, housed in one physical place, or kept on several computers. They enhance performance and reliability by distributing data and workload across multiple servers.

- **Examples**: Google Spanner, Apache Cassandra.
- **Use Cases**: Global-scale applications, content delivery networks (CDNs).

4. **Cloud databases:** A collection of organized or unorganized data that is housed on a private, public or hybrid cloud computing platform is known as a cloud database. They can be relational or NoSQL databases. They offer scalability, flexibility, and cost-efficiency. Here users can pay for what they use without maintaining physical hardware.
   - **Examples**: Amazon RDS, Google BigQuery, Microsoft Azure SQL Database.
   - **Use Cases**: SaaS applications, startups, and dynamic workloads.
5. **Graph Databases**: These databases focus on the relationships between data objects. They use nodes (data entities) and edges (relationships) to model data. They efficiently handle complex relationships and are ideal for applications where connections between data points are crucial.
   - **Examples**: Neo4j, Amazon Neptune.
   - **Use Cases**: Social networks, recommendation engines, fraud detection.
6. **Object-Oriented Databases:** The type of database that uses the object-based data model approach for storing data in the database system is called Object-Oriented Databases. The data is represented and stored as objects which are similar to the objects used in the object-oriented programming language. They are suitable for applications that require complex data representations and interactions.
   - **Example**: ObjectDB.
   - **Use Case**: CAD systems and multimedia applications.
7. **Hierarchical Databases:** It is the type of database that stores data in the form of parent-children **relationship** nodes. Here, it organizes data in a tree-like structure. Data get stored in the form of records that are connected via links. Each child record in the tree will contain only one parent. They provide fast access to data with a known structure but can be inflexible when dealing with complex relationships.
   - **Examples**: IBM's Information Management System (IMS)
   - **Use Cases**: Legacy systems, Applications with a clear parent-child relationship
8. **Centralized Database:** It is the type of database that stores data at a centralized database system. It comforts the users to access the stored data from different

locations through several applications. These applications contain the authentication process to let users access data securely. An example of a Centralized database can be Central Library that carries a central database of each library in a college/university.

- **Examples:** Central library databases in universities
- **Use Cases:** Educational institutions, Organizations with centralized data management

Database Models: A database model is a framework that defines how data is structured, stored, and accessed in a database. It determines the relationships between data elements and how they can be queried or manipulated. Different common database models:

1. **Hierarchical Model:** The hierarchical model organizes data in a tree-like structure with parent-child relationships. Each parent node can have multiple child nodes, but each child node has only one parent. This model is ideal for applications with a fixed hierarchy, such as an organizational chart or file system.
    - **Example:** A furniture store database where "Bedroom" is a parent, and its children include "Bed," "Wardrobe," and "Nightstand."
    - **Limitation:** It is difficult to manage many-to-many relationships, and modifying the structure can be complex.
2. **Network Model:** The network model is an extension of the hierarchical model that supports many-to-many relationships between data entities. Data is organized in records, and each record can have multiple parent and child records, connected by links. This model uses a graph-like structure.
    - **Example:** In a university database, a "Course" can be linked to multiple "Students," and a "Student" can enroll in multiple "Courses."
    - **Advantage:** It allows for more complex relationships than the hierarchical model.
    - **Limitation:** It requires extensive programming for database operation
3. **Relational Model:** The relational model organizes data into tables (also called relations), where rows represent records and columns represent attributes. Relationships between tables are established using primary keys (unique identifiers) and foreign keys (references to primary keys in other tables).
    - **Example:** A customer database with a "Customers" table and an "Orders" table linked by a CustomerID.
    - **Advantages:** Simplicity and flexibility for data queries.
    - **Limitation:** It may struggle with very large datasets or unstructured data.
4. **Object-Oriented Model:** The object-oriented model integrates object-oriented

programming principles with database management. Data is represented as objects, which include attributes (properties) and methods (functions).

- **Example:** A "Car" object in a vehicle database could have attributes like Make, Model, and Year and methods like CalculateMileage().
- **Advantages:** Ideal for applications that involve multimedia, simulations, or complex data.
- **Limitation:** Less widely adopted compared to relational databases.

5. **Document Model:** The document model stores data in document-like formats such as JSON, XML, or BSON. Each document is self-contained and can include nested structures, making it suitable for semi-structured and unstructured data.
   - **Example:** A product catalog database where each product is represented as a JSON document with details like ProductID, Name, Category, and Price.

```
{
 "ProductID": "123",
 "Name": "Smartphone",
 "Category": "Electronics",
 "Price": 699.99
}
```

   - **Advantage**: Efficient for applications like content management systems and real-time analytics.
   - **Limitation:** Querying complex relationships can be less straightforward compared to relational models.

Future Trends in Databases

1. **AI-Driven Databases:** Artificial Intelligence is transforming databases by automating tasks like query optimization, performance tuning, and data management. AI-powered systems can predict workloads, identify inefficiencies, and self-heal, reducing the need for manual intervention and enhancing database efficiency.
2. **Blockchain Databases:** Blockchain-based databases ensure secure, decentralized, and immutable data storage. They are ideal for use cases requiring transparency, such as financial transactions, supply chain management, and digital identity systems, as they eliminate the need for centralized control.
3. **Edge Databases:** With the rise of IoT applications, edge databases are designed to process and store data closer to its source. This minimizes latency and bandwidth usage, making them essential for real-time applications like autonomous vehicles and smart devices.

4. **Multi-Model Databases:** These databases support multiple data types within the same system. which provides flexibility and simplies management for diverse data needs.
5. **Cloud-Native Databases:** These databases are Optimized for cloud, which offers automatic scalability, high resilience, and reduced operational complexity. It allows businesses to focus on growth.
6. **Serverless Databases:** They automatically scale and adjust resources based on demand of users. It offers cost efficiency and simplifies infrastructure management.
7. **Quantum Databases:** It uses quantum computing to process data much faster and handles complex calculations. It makes the performance for large datasets easier.

5. Data Cleaning and Preparation

Data cleaning and preparation is a crucial step in the data analysis process, ensuring that raw data is transformed into a structured and usable format. It involves identifying and correcting errors, handling missing values, removing duplicates, and standardizing formats to maintain consistency. This process may also include filtering out irrelevant data, converting data types, and normalizing values to improve data quality and integrity. Proper data preparation enables accurate analysis, better model performance, and reliable insights. It often requires domain knowledge to make informed decisions about which data to retain or modify. Automated tools and programming languages like Python and R are commonly used to streamline these tasks through libraries such as Pandas or dplyr. Ultimately, clean and well-prepared data forms the foundation for meaningful analytics, machine learning, and business intelligence, helping organizations make data-driven decisions with confidence.

Data Cleaning: Data cleaning in data science is the process of identifying and correcting or removing errors and inconsistencies from raw data to improve its quality and reliability. It is a vital step before any data analysis or modeling, as dirty data can lead to inaccurate insights and poor model performance. Common tasks in data cleaning include handling missing values, removing duplicates, correcting data entry errors, resolving inconsistencies, and ensuring proper formatting. This process often requires a combination of automated tools and manual inspection, along with domain knowledge to make informed decisions. In data science, tools like Python (using Pandas, NumPy) and R are widely used to perform data cleaning efficiently. Clean data is essential for building accurate predictive models, generating meaningful visualizations, and supporting data-driven decisions. Without proper cleaning, even the most advanced algorithms cannot yield reliable results, making this step foundational in the data science workflow.

The importance of data cleaning lies in the following factors:

1. **Improved Data Quality:** It is therefore very important to clean the data as

this reduces the chances of errors, inconsistencies and missing values, which ultimately makes the data to be more accurate and reliable in the analysis.

2. **Better Decision-making:** Consistent and clean data gives organization insight into comprehensive and actual information and minimizes the way such organizations make decisions on outdated and incomplete data.
3. **Increased Efficiency:** High quality data is efficient to analyze, model or report on it, whereas clean data often avoids a lot of foreseen time and effort that goes into handling poor data quality.
4. **Compliance and Regulatory Requirements:** There are standard policies the industries and various regulatory authorities set on data quality, and by data cleaning, one can be able to conform with these standards to avoid penalties and legal endangers.

The Data Cleaning Process: To find and fix flaws, inconsistencies, or inaccuracies in the data, the data cleaning process entails many procedures and techniques. The steps in the data-cleaning process are as follows:

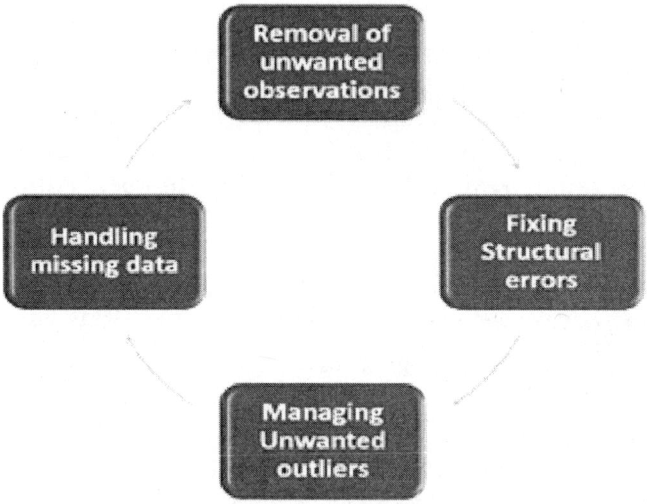

Fig. 2.2 Data Cleaning

1. **Removal of Unwanted Observations**: Identify and remove irrelevant or redundant (unwanted) observations from the dataset. This step involves analyzing data entries for duplicate records, irrelevant information or data points that do not contribute to analysis and prediction. Removing them from dataset helps reducing noise and improving the overall quality of dataset.
2. **Fixing Structure Errors:** Address structural issues in the dataset such as inconsistencies in data formats or variable types. Standardize formats ensure uniformity in data structure and hence data consistency.
3. **Managing Outliers:** Outliers are those points that deviate significantly from

dataset mean. Identifying and managing outliers significantly improve model accuracy as these extreme values influence analysis. Depending on the context decide whether to remove outliers or transform them to minimize their impact on analysis.

4. **Handling Missing Data:** To handle missing data effectively we need to impute missing values based on statistical methods, removing records with missing values or employing advanced imputation techniques. Handling missing data helps preventing biases and maintaining the integrity of data.

Common Data Issues: Before we explore the solutions, it's important to understand the problems. Some of the most common data issues that necessitate cleaning:

1. **Missing Data**: One of the most prevalent issues in datasets is missing values. This can occur due to data entry errors, system malfunctions, or simply because the information wasn't available at the time of collection. Missing data can significantly skew analyses and lead to incorrect conclusions if not handled properly.
2. **Duplicate Data**: Duplicate records can inflate dataset size and lead to biased analysis results. They often occur due to manual data entry errors, system glitches, or when merging data from multiple sources.
3. **Inconsistent Formatting**: Inconsistencies in data format can make analysis challenging. For example, dates might be recorded in different formats (MM/DD/YYYY vs. DD/MM/YYYY), or names might be entered with varying capitalization or order (Mohan Sohan vs. Mohan, Sohan).
4. **Typos and Spelling Errors**: Human error in data entry can lead to typos and misspellings. While seemingly minor, these errors can cause significant problems, especially when dealing with categorical data or when using the data for text analysis.
5. **Outliers**: Outliers are data points that significantly differ from other observations. While sometimes outliers represent genuine anomalies that require investigation, they can also be the result of measurement or data entry errors.
6. **Inconsistent Units**: When working with numerical data, inconsistent units can lead to severe misinterpretations. For instance, mixing metric and imperial measurements or using different currencies without proper conversion.
7. **Structural Errors**: These occur when there are issues with data labeling, categorization, or the overall structure of the dataset. For example, having inconsistent category names or mislabelled variables.
8. **Encoded or Garbled Data**: Sometimes data can become corrupted during transfer or storage, resulting in unreadable or nonsensical values. This is particularly common with special characters or when dealing with different character encodings.

9. **Inconsistent Naming Conventions**: Variables or categories might be named inconsistently across different parts of a dataset or across multiple datasets that need to be merged.
10. **Data Type Mismatches**: This occurs when data is stored in an inappropriate format. For example, storing numerical data as text, which can prevent mathematical operations.
11. **Truncated Data**: Sometimes data can be cut off or truncated due to system limitations or data transfer issues. This is particularly problematic with long text fields or large numerical values.
12. **Unnecessary Metadata**: Datasets might include extraneous information that isn't relevant to the analysis at hand, such as automatically-generated timestamps or system-specific identifiers.
13. **Inconsistent Aggregation**: When working with data that has been aggregated or summarized, there might be inconsistencies in how the aggregation was performed across different subsets of the data.

These common data issues is the first step in effective data cleaning. By being aware of what to look for, data scientists can develop targeted strategies to address these problems and ensure the integrity of their datasets.

Data Preparation: Data preparation is the process of making raw data ready for after processing and analysis. The key methods are to collect, clean, and label raw data in a format suitable for machine learning (ML) algorithms, followed by data exploration and visualization. The process of cleaning and combining raw data before using it for machine learning and business analysis is known as data preparation, or sometimes "pre-processing." But it may not be the most attractive of duties, careful data preparation is essential to the success of data analytics. Clear and important ideas from raw data require careful validation, cleaning, and an addition. Any business analysis or model created will only be as strong and validating as the very first information preparation. Data preparation acts as the foundation for successful machine learning projects as:

1. **Improves Data Quality:** Raw data often contains inconsistencies, missing values, errors, and irrelevant information. Data preparation techniques like cleaning, imputation, and normalization address these issues, resulting in a cleaner and more consistent dataset. This, in turn, prevents these issues from biasing or hindering the learning process of your models.
2. **Enhances Model Performance:** Machine learning algorithms rely heavily on the quality of the data they are trained on. By preparing your data effectively, you provide the algorithms with a clear and well-structured foundation for learning patterns and relationships. This leads to models that are better able to generalize and make accurate predictions on unseen data.
3. **Saves Time and Resources:** Investing time upfront in data preparation can significantly save time and resources down the line. By addressing data quality

issues early on, you avoid encountering problems later in the modeling process that might require re-work or troubleshooting. This translates to a more efficient and streamlined machine learning workflow.

4. **Facilitates Feature Engineering:** Data preparation often involves feature engineering, which is the process of creating new features from existing ones. These new features can be more informative and relevant to the task at hand, ultimately improving the model's ability to learn and make predictions.

Data Preparation Process: There are a few important steps in the data preparation process, and each one is essential to making sure the data is prepared for analysis or other processing. The following are the key stages related to data preparation:

Step 1: Describe Purpose and Requirements: Identifying the goals and requirements for the data analysis project is the first step in the data preparation process. Consider the followings:

- What is the goal of the data analysis project and how big is it?
- Which major inquiries or ideas are you planning to investigate or evaluate using the data?
- Who are the target audience and end-users for the data analysis findings? What positions and duties do they have?
- Which formats, types, and sources of data do you need to access and analyze?
- What requirements do you have for the data in terms of quality, accuracy, completeness, timeliness, and relevance?
- What are the limitations and ethical, legal, and regulatory issues that you must take into account?
- With answers to these questions, data analysis project's goals, parameters, and requirements simpler as well as highlighting any challenges, risks, or opportunities that can develop.

Step 2: Data Collection: Collecting information from a variety of sources, including files, databases, websites, and social media, to conduct a thorough analysis, providing the usage of reliable and high-quality data. Suitable resources and methods are used to obtain and analyze data from a variety of sources, including files, databases, APIs, and web scraping.

Step 3: Data Combining and Integrating Data: Data integration requires combining data from multiple sources or dimensions in order to create a full, logical dataset. Data integration solutions provide a wide range of operations, including combination, relationship, connection, difference, and join, as well as a variety of data schemas and types of architecture.

To properly combine and integrate data, it is essential to store and arrange information in a common standard format, such as CSV, JSON, or XML, for easy access and uniform comprehension. Organizing data management and storage using solutions such as cloud storage, data warehouses, or data lakes improves governance, maintains consistency, and speeds up access to data on a single platform. Audits, backups, recovery, verification, and encryption are all examples of strong security procedures that can be used to make sure reliable data management. Privacy protects data during transmission and storage, whereas authorization and authentication

Step 4: Data Profiling: Data profiling is a systematic method for assessing and analyzing a dataset, making sure its quality, structure, content, and improving accuracy within an organizational context. Data profiling identifies data consistency, differences, and null values by analyzing source data, looking for errors, inconsistencies, and errors, and understanding file structure, content, and relationships. It helps to evaluate elements including completeness, accuracy, consistency, validity, and timeliness.

Step 5: Data Exploring: Data exploration is getting familiar with data, identifying patterns, trends, outliers, and errors in order to better understand it and evaluate the possibilities for analysis. To evaluate data, identify data types, formats, and structures, and calculate descriptive statistics such as mean, median, mode, and variance for each numerical variable. Visualizations such as histograms, boxplots, and scatterplots can provide understanding of data distribution, while complex techniques such as classification can reveal hidden patterns and show exceptions.

Step 6: Data Transformations and Enrichment: Data enrichment is the process of improving a dataset by adding new features or columns, enhancing its accuracy and reliability, and verifying it against third-party sources.

- The technique involves combining various data sources like CRM, financial, and marketing to create a comprehensive dataset, incorporating third-party data like demographics for enhanced insights.
- The process involves categorizing data into groups like customers or products based on shared attributes, using standard variables like age and gender to describe these entities.
- Engineer new features or fields by utilizing existing data, such as calculating customer age based on their birthdate. Estimate missing values from available data, such as absent sales figures, by referencing historical trends.
- The task involves identifying entities like names and addresses within unstructured text data, thereby extracting actionable information from text without a fixed structure.
- The process involves assigning specific categories to unstructured text data, such as product descriptions or customer feedback, to facilitate analysis and gain valuable insights.
- Utilize various techniques like geocoding, sentiment analysis, entity recognition, and topic modeling to enrich your data with additional information or context.
- To enable analysis and generate important insights, unstructured text data is classified into different groups, such as product descriptions or consumer feedback.

Use cleaning procedures to remove or correct flaws or inconsistencies in your data, such as duplicates, outliers, missing numbers, typos, and formatting difficulties. Validation techniques like as checksums, rules, limitations, and tests are used to ensure that data is correct and complete.

Step 8: Data Validation: Data validation is crucial for ensuring data accuracy, completeness, and consistency, as it checks data against predefined rules and criteria that align with your requirements, standards, and regulations.

- Analyze the data to better understand its properties, such as data kinds, ranges, and distributions. Identify any potential issues, such as missing values, exceptions, or errors.
- Choose a representative sample of the dataset for validation. This technique is useful for larger datasets because it minimizes processing effort.
- Apply planned validation rules to the collected data. Rules may contain format checks, range validations, or cross-field validations.
- Identify records that do not fulfill the validation standards. Keep track of any flaws or discrepancies for future analysis.
- Correct identified mistakes by cleaning, converting, or entering data as needed. Maintaining an audit record of modifications made during this procedure is critical.
- Automate data validation activities as much as feasible to ensure consistent and ongoing data quality maintenance.

Differences Between Data Cleaning and Data Preparation: The differences between data cleaning and data preparation are listed in table 2.4.

Table 2.4

S.No.	Aspect	Data Cleaning	Data Preparation
1.	Definition	Process of correcting or removing inaccurate records	Broad process of transforming raw data into usable format
2.	Scope	Focused on fixing errors, missing values, duplicates	Includes cleaning, transforma tion, integration, and formatting
3.	Objective	Ensure accuracy and consistency of data	Make data suitable for analysis or modeling
4.	Activities Involved	Removing duplicates, handling nulls, correcting formats	Data cleaning + feature engineering, normalization, encoding
5.	Stage in Workflow	Initial step of data preparation	Happens before analysis or model training
6.	Tools Used	Excel, OpenRefine, Pandas (for missing values, duplicates)	Pandas, SQL, Scikit-learn, ETL tools (for full data prep)
7.	Outcome	Cleaned, error-free data	Structured, ready-to-use dataset
8.	Importance	Prevents inaccurate results due to bad data	Ensures data is not only clean but also analytically useful

Handling Missing Data: Handling missing data is a foundational preprocessing step, as incomplete datasets can lead to skewed analyses, inaccurate predictions, and misinformed decisions. Missing data can occur due to various reasons data corruption, non-response in surveys, system errors, or improper data collection. Before addressing the issue, it is essential to understand the nature of the missingness, categorized as MCAR (Missing Completely at Random), MAR (Missing at Random), or MNAR (Missing Not at Random), as each requires different treatment strategies. One common method is deletion, which includes listwise deletion (removing entire rows) or pairwise deletion (removing values only when required), but this is only viable if the missing data is minimal and random. Alternatively, imputation techniques are widely used, such as mean, median, or mode substitution for numerical or categorical features, forward-fill or backward-fill in time series, and more sophisticated methods like K-Nearest Neighbors (KNN), regression imputation, or multivariate imputation by chained equations (MICE). In modern machine learning, models like XGBoost and LightGBM are capable of handling missing values natively, though it's often still beneficial to preprocess the data. Creating a binary indicator column that flags missing values can sometimes improve model performance, especially when the pattern of missingness itself carries information. Visual tools like heatmaps and matrix plots (e.g., from Python's missingno library) help in understanding the structure and extent of missing data across features. The goal is not just to fill in gaps but to do so in a way that preserves the statistical properties of the dataset and avoids introducing bias. Careless handling can lead to overfitting or underfitting, depending on how predictive the missing values are. Therefore, a data scientist must carefully select the appropriate strategy based on the dataset's size, the proportion of missingness, domain context, and the modeling goals. Ultimately, addressing missing data with thoughtful preprocessing improves the robustness, accuracy, and fairness of machine learning models, making it a crucial skill in any data-driven project.

1. **Listwise Deletion:** Listwise deletion removes entire rows with any missing values. It's a straightforward approach but can significantly reduce the dataset size if missing data is widespread. It works best when data is missing completely at random (MCAR) and when the remaining data is sufficient for meaningful analysis.
2. **Pairwise Deletion:** Pairwise deletion uses all available data for each analysis by omitting only the missing values for the specific computation. This preserves more data than listwise deletion but can lead to inconsistencies across analyses. It's useful when performing correlations or regressions where data loss should be minimized.
3. **Mean/Median/Mode Imputation:** This method replaces missing values with the column's mean, median, or mode, depending on the data type. It is simple and fast but may distort data variability and relationships, especially if missingness is not random. Suitable for small amounts of missing data in low-impact features.

4. **Constant Value Imputation:** Missing values are replaced with a fixed constant such as 0, -1, or "Unknown." This is especially useful for categorical or flag-type variables and when missingness itself has meaning. However, it can introduce artificial clusters or bias if not used carefully with context.
5. **Forward Fill / Backward Fill:** Primarily used in time-series data, forward fill propagates the last known value, while backward fill uses the next known value. This assumes temporal continuity and is ideal when the variable doesn't change rapidly over time. It can, however, misrepresent actual changes in volatile data.
6. **K-Nearest Neighbors (KNN) Imputation:** KNN imputation finds the 'k' most similar rows to the one with missing data and imputes based on the average or mode of those neighbors. It's more accurate than simple methods when data has patterns, but it's computationally expensive and sensitive to outliers and scaling.

Removing Duplicates and Outliers

In the realm of data science, ensuring data quality through the removal of duplicates and outliers is a key aspect of preprocessing, directly impacting the reliability and interpretability of models. Duplicates typically arise during data collection, merging from multiple sources, or system errors, and if left unaddressed, they can cause certain observations to be overrepresented, leading to biased insights and models. These duplicates can be exact (identical records) or partial (same entities with slight variations), and tools like Python's Pandas library (drop_duplicates) or SQL queries are commonly used to detect and remove them. More complex scenarios may require fuzzy matching or deduplication based on custom business logic. On the other hand, outliers are data points that significantly deviate from the rest of the dataset, often indicating measurement errors, rare events, or genuine variability in the data. Their identification can be approached through statistical methods such as the Z-score (flagging values beyond 3 standard deviations), the interquartile range (IQR) rule, or visual tools like boxplots and scatter plots. In multivariate data, outliers may only be apparent when multiple features are considered together, requiring advanced methods like Mahalanobis distance, DBSCAN clustering, or model-based detectors such as Isolation Forest and One-Class SVM. Once identified, outliers can be removed, capped (using techniques like winsorization), or transformed (e.g., using log or square root functions) to reduce their influence on statistical metrics or machine learning models. The decision to remove or retain an outlier must be informed by domain knowledge what appears as an outlier statistically might be a critical signal in applications like fraud detection or anomaly monitoring. In regression and classification tasks, the presence of outliers can heavily skew model coefficients or lead to overfitting, particularly in sensitive algorithms like linear regression or SVM. Therefore, a data scientist must carefully assess the cause, context, and impact of duplicates and outliers to ensure that the data fed into models is clean, representative, and meaningful, ultimately supporting better generalization and more trustworthy conclusions.

1. **Improves Data Accuracy:** Duplicates can skew results and give false impressions in analysis.
2. **Reduces Data Size:** Eliminating redundant records helps in optimizing storage and processing time.
3. **Prevents Misleading Insights:** Repeated entries can distort averages, totals, and model predictions.
4. **Enhances Model Performance:** Machine learning algorithms can perform poorly on duplicated data due to overfitting or bias.
5. **Ensures Data Integrity:** Clean, unique data is more reliable for decision-making and reporting.
6. **Improves Statistical Accuracy:** Outliers can significantly impact mean, variance, and other statistical measures.
7. **Prevents Model Distortion:** Outliers can mislead regression lines and classification boundaries in ML models.
8. **Enhances Data Quality:** Removing anomalies ensures the dataset represents the general population better.
9. **Improves Visualization Clarity:** Outliers can stretch the scale and make visual interpretation harder.
10. **Detects Data Entry Errors:** Outliers often reveal input mistakes or sensor malfunctions that need correction.

Data Transformation and Encoding

Data transformation and encoding are fundamental processes in data science used to convert raw and often inconsistent data into structured numerical formats suitable for statistical analysis and machine learning models. Real-world datasets typically contain heterogeneous data types numerical, categorical, text, date-time, and more that require harmonization to facilitate model training. Transformation methods are used to scale, normalize, or restructure data to improve model convergence and performance. For instance, normalization (rescaling features to a 0-1 range) and standardization (centering around mean 0 and standard deviation 1) are often applied to numerical features to ensure uniform influence in distance-based models like KNN or gradient descent algorithms. Log transformations can help reduce skewness in right-tailed distributions, while discretization (binning) can simplify continuous features into ordinal categories. Date-time fields are often transformed into derived features such as day of week, hour of day, or time since an event, capturing temporal patterns. Equally important is encoding categorical variables, as most machine learning models require numeric input. Label encoding assigns unique integers to each category and is suitable for ordinal data, but for nominal (unordered) categories, one-hot encoding is preferred, creating binary indicator columns for each category to avoid introducing false ordinal relationships. However, one-hot encoding can cause a curse of dimensionality when applied to high-cardinality features. In such cases, binary encoding or target encoding where categories are replaced by a function of the target variable may be used, though the latter requires careful cross-validation to prevent data leakage. Embedding techniques are also increasingly popular, especially in deep learning, for representing high-dimensional categorical data in dense vector spaces. The choice of encoding and transformation strategy depends heavily on the model type (e.g., tree-based models are less sensitive to feature scaling), the feature cardinality, and the specific domain context. Without appropriate transformation and encoding, models may either fail to learn effectively or yield misleading outputs. Thus, mastering these preprocessing steps not only enhances model performance but also ensures data integrity, interpretability, and efficient use of computational resources, making it a cornerstone in the data science workflow.

Importance of Data Transformation and Encoding:

1. **Ensures Compatibility with Algorithms:** Many algorithms require numerical input; encoding transforms categorical data into a usable format.
2. **Improves Model Accuracy:** Normalizing or scaling data (e.g., MinMax, StandardScaler) improves convergence and performance.
3. **Handles Skewed Distributions:** Log transformation or Box-Cox can normalize highly skewed features, enhancing model results.
4. **Reduces Model Bias:** Proper encoding (e.g., one-hot, label encoding) prevents models from misinterpreting categorical values as ordinal.
5. **Facilitates Better Learning:** Transformed features help machine learning algorithms detect patterns more effectively.

Feature Engineering

Feature engineering is a pivotal component of the data science workflow that involves creating new, informative input features from raw data to improve the predictive power and interpretability of machine learning models. It is both a technical and creative process where domain expertise meets data manipulation to uncover hidden patterns, relationships, or signals within the data. Raw datasets often lack the complexity needed for accurate prediction, so feature engineering seeks to extract or construct new variables that capture underlying dynamics. Techniques vary widely and include mathematical transformations (e.g., squares, logs, ratios), aggregations (mean, count, sum by group), and interactions (products or differences between variables). For example, in financial data, constructing features like credit utilization ratio, income-to-loan ratio, or moving averages can significantly enhance model accuracy. Time-based features are especially valuable, where from a single timestamp, features like time since last event, hour of day, or day of week can be derived to model seasonality or user behavior. For categorical data, feature engineering may involve frequency encoding, target encoding, or combining categories into broader groups based on similarity. In the case of text data, feature extraction techniques like TF-IDF, sentiment scores, and n-grams help convert unstructured input into usable vectors. In image or sensor data, statistical summaries or embeddings often serve as engineered features. More advanced techniques include dimensionality reduction (PCA, t-SNE) to capture complex patterns in fewer features, or automated feature generation through deep learning or tools like FeatureTools and AutoFeat. Importantly, good features often improve model performance more than selecting a more complex algorithm, emphasizing the value of thoughtful design over brute-force modeling. Feature selection methods such as mutual information, recursive feature elimination (RFE), or regularization (Lasso) help retain only the most informative features and reduce overfitting. Ultimately, feature engineering is an iterative process: features are created, tested, evaluated, and refined based on feedback from model performance metrics. When done well, it reveals latent structure in the data, enhances model explainability, and drives more actionable insights, making it one of the most valuable and skill-intensive tasks in a data scientist's toolkit.

Importance of Feature Engineering:

1. **Enhances Predictive Power**: Creating meaningful features can significantly improve model accuracy and performance.
2. **Reduces Overfitting**: Smart feature selection or combination can simplify the model and reduce noise.
3. **Improves Model Interpretability**: Well-engineered features make it easier to explain the model's decisions.
4. **Encodes Domain Knowledge**: Integrating expert insights into features adds context and relevance to the data.
5. **Enables Use of Complex Relationships**: Polynomial features, interaction terms, or aggregations can capture nonlinear patterns.

6. Data Visualization and Exploratory Analysis

Data Visualization and Exploratory Data Analysis (EDA) play a critical role in understanding and interpreting complex datasets. Visualization transforms raw numbers into graphical representations like histograms, scatter plots, box plots, and heatmaps, allowing analysts to detect patterns, trends, and anomalies quickly. These visual tools make it easier to communicate findings, uncover relationships between variables, and assess data distribution. Effective visualization also aids in identifying missing values, outliers, and skewed distributions, which are essential for preparing the data for modeling.

Exploratory Data Analysis, on the other hand, is a foundational step in the data science process that involves summarizing the main characteristics of the data. Through techniques such as statistical summaries, correlation matrices, and graphical exploration, EDA helps in forming hypotheses, selecting relevant features, and shaping the direction of further analysis. It provides insights into the structure of the data and reveals underlying patterns that might not be obvious through raw data alone. Together, visualization and EDA enhance decision-making, reduce data complexity, and ensure that subsequent modeling is built on a well-understood dataset.

Data Visualization: Data visualization is the graphical representation of information and data through visual elements like charts, graphs, maps, and dashboards. In an age where organizations generate massive volumes of data daily, visualizing this data helps convert raw numbers into meaningful insights. Unlike rows of data in spreadsheets, visuals allow for quicker understanding, easier pattern recognition, and more effective communication. Common types of data visualizations include bar charts, line graphs, pie charts, scatter plots, heatmaps, and histograms, each serving a unique analytical purpose. For example, line graphs are ideal for identifying trends over time, while scatter plots are useful for visualizing relationships between variables. Visualization is not just about presenting data; it's about telling a story with that data highlighting key patterns, uncovering trends, and making complex information more accessible to both technical and non-technical audiences.

Beyond aesthetics, the true power of data visualization lies in its ability to drive smarter decision-making. Businesses use dashboards to monitor performance metrics in real time; healthcare professionals use visualizations to track disease outbreaks; and educators use charts to measure student progress. Effective data visualization helps identify outliers, spot errors, and make forecasts with confidence. Moreover, interactive visualization tools such as Tableau, Power BI, and Python libraries like Matplotlib and Seaborn enable dynamic exploration of data, allowing users to drill down into details and uncover deeper insights. However, poor visual design or misleading representations can lead to incorrect conclusions, making clarity, accuracy, and context essential in visual storytelling. Overall, data visualization plays a critical role in turning raw data into actionable knowledge, helping individuals and organizations make informed, data-driven decisions.

Benefits of Data Visualization: The benefits of data visualization include the following:

1. **Actionable Insights:** A broad spectrum of an organization's personnel can understand visuals presented in business intelligence dashboards. This lets users absorb information quickly, get better insights and figure out the next steps faster.
2. **Exploration of Complex Relationships:** Visualization platforms with advanced capabilities can display complex relationships among data points and metrics, allowing an organization to make faster data-based decisions.
3. **Compelling Storytelling:** Data dashboards that are visually compelling will maintain the audience's interest with information they can understand.
4. **Accessibility:** Visualization tools make data more accessible and understandable, so that laypersons or semi-technical users who aren't data scientists can interpret and analyze it.
5. **Interactivity:** Interactive dashboards have the functionality to allow users to click on various aspects of data displays to get more information. This is especially useful for those with less expertise on the subject area covered by the data. Static displays don't allow this.

Disadvantages of Data Visualization: While data visualization comes with many advantages, it can also pose several challenges, including the following:

1. **Complexity:** A highly complicated visualization could appear cluttered or make it difficult to glean a valuable insight. More complexity also means users need training on the tools being used or risk creating the wrong visual type for the data being used.
2. **Potential for misinterpretation:** Users might have good intentions when using a visualization platform, but they can draw incorrect conclusions from detailed visualizations.
3. **Data privacy and security:** Users must consider the security and privacy of the data being visualized. A platform might be susceptible to cyberattacks, thus compromising the security of data being used, or a data set could be used that isn't compliant with data privacy regulations.
4. **Bias:** Visualizations and the data they're based on should be scrutinized to ensure they aren't intentionally or unintentionally biased. Failing to do so could compromise the credibility of those analyses. For example, a data set that leaves out key demographics within a population could lead to a biased visualization of that data.

Importance of Data Visualization

1. **Simplifies Complex Data:** Visuals like charts and graphs make large and complex datasets easier to understand at a glance.
2. **Reveals Patterns and Trends:** Helps identify trends, correlations, and patterns that might be missed in raw data tables.
3. **Speeds Up Decision-Making:** Quick visual insights enable faster, more informed decisions across organizations.
4. **Detects Anomalies and Outliers:** Visualization makes it easier to spot data errors, outliers, or unusual behaviors.
5. **Improves Communication:** Translates data into a common language, making insights accessible to both technical and non-technical stakeholders.
6. **Supports Storytelling:** Engages audiences by presenting data in a compelling narrative form.
7. **Enhances Data Quality:** Visual exploration can reveal inconsistencies or missing data that need correction.
8. **Facilitates Interactive Exploration:** Tools enable users to drill down, filter, and analyze data dynamically.
9. **Encourages a Data-Driven Culture:** Visual data promotes transparency and reliance on evidence in business processes.
10. **Boosts Productivity:** Saves time compared to manually sifting through raw data or lengthy reports.

Tools: Matplotlib, Seaborn, Plotly

Matplotlib, Seaborn, and Plotly are prominent Python libraries used for data visualization.

Matplotlib: This is the foundational and most comprehensive plotting library in Python. It provides a vast array of tools for creating static, interactive, and animated visualizations, including line plots, scatter plots, bar charts, histograms, and more. Matplotlib offers extensive customization options, allowing fine-grained control over every element of a plot. While powerful, achieving complex or aesthetically pleasing plots can sometimes require more lines of code compared to higher-level libraries.

Matplotlib is a foundational and highly versatile data visualization library in Python, widely recognized as the go-to tool for creating static, animated, and interactive plots. It provides extensive control over every element of a figure, allowing users to customize axes, labels, ticks, colors, and more, making it suitable for creating publication-quality graphs. Its flexibility supports a broad spectrum of visualizations, including line plots, bar charts, histograms, scatter plots, and pie charts. Matplotlib integrates seamlessly with scientific computing libraries like NumPy and Pandas, enabling it to handle large datasets efficiently. It also serves as the underlying engine for many other higher-level visualization libraries, such as Seaborn, demonstrating its foundational role in the Python visualization ecosystem. While its powerful customization options are a strength, beginners may find Matplotlib's syntax and configuration verbose or complex. However, its extensive documentation and active community provide ample resources to learn from. Matplotlib is particularly valued in academia and industry where precise control and reproducibility of graphs are essential. Its ability to generate plots programmatically makes it a great choice for automating the creation of complex figures. Additionally, Matplotlib supports exporting visuals to multiple formats such as PNG, PDF, SVG, and more, making it versatile for use in reports, presentations, and web applications. Overall, Matplotlib's combination of flexibility, control, and robustness makes it an indispensable tool for data scientists, analysts, and researchers looking to create detailed and highly customized visualizations.

Features

1. Highly customizable plots with control over every element (axes, ticks, labels, colors).
2. Supports a wide range of plot types: line, bar, scatter, histogram, pie charts, error bars, etc.
3. Can create static, animated, and interactive visualizations.
4. Integrates well with scientific libraries like NumPy and Pandas.
5. Ability to export figures in multiple formats (PNG, PDF, SVG, EPS).
6. Supports subplotting and multiple figure management.

7. Extensive documentation and large community support.
8. Suitable for publication-quality figures.
9. Serves as the foundation for many other Python visualization libraries.

Seaborn: Built on top of Matplotlib, Seaborn is a high-level library specifically designed for creating attractive and informative statistical graphics. It simplifies the process of generating complex visualizations like heatmaps, violin plots, box plots, and pair plots, often with fewer lines of code and better default aesthetics than raw Matplotlib. Seaborn integrates seamlessly with Pandas DataFrames, making it ideal for exploratory data analysis.

Seaborn is a powerful Python data visualization library built on top of Matplotlib that focuses on making statistical graphics easier to create and aesthetically pleasing. It provides a high-level interface for drawing attractive and informative statistical graphics, allowing users to generate complex plots with minimal code. Seaborn simplifies the process of visualizing univariate and multivariate data by providing functions for common plot types like histograms, kernel density estimates, violin plots, box plots, scatter plots, heatmaps, and pair plots. One of its main strengths is built-in support for visualizing relationships and distributions, making it especially useful in exploratory data analysis (EDA). Seaborn also offers automatic color palettes and themes that improve the readability and visual appeal of charts without requiring users to spend time on design details. Additionally, Seaborn handles the integration of Pandas dataframes gracefully, allowing users to plot data directly from dataframe structures using column names. This tight integration streamlines the data exploration workflow. While Seaborn inherits Matplotlib's underlying capabilities, it abstracts much of the complexity, making it more user-friendly for those less experienced with Python's visualization intricacies. However, it still allows for customization by enabling users to modify Matplotlib objects as needed. Seaborn is widely adopted in data science and analytics communities for its balance of simplicity and functionality, making it an excellent choice when you need to quickly generate high-quality statistical visuals that are both insightful and visually compelling.

Features

- Built on top of Matplotlib with a higher-level API for easier plotting.
- Designed specifically for statistical data visualization.
- Offers beautiful default themes and color palettes for attractive charts.
- Simplifies visualizing univariate, bivariate, and multivariate distributions (e.g., box plots, violin plots, pair plots).
- Integrates smoothly with Pandas DataFrames, allowing plotting by column names.
- Provides tools for visualizing categorical data, time series, and regression fits.
- Supports heatmaps and correlation matrix visualization.

- Enables quick exploratory data analysis with minimal code.
- Allows customization by modifying underlying Matplotlib objects.

Plotly: Plotly is an open-source graphing library that specializes in creating interactive, web-based visualizations. Unlike Matplotlib and Seaborn which primarily generate static images, Plotly's charts allow for user interaction such as zooming, panning, hovering for details, and filtering. This interactivity makes Plotly particularly well-suited for web applications, dashboards, and interactive data exploration within environments like Jupyter notebooks. Plotly supports a wide range of chart types, including 3D plots and geographical maps.

Plotly is a dynamic, open-source graphing library for Python and other programming languages that excels in creating interactive and web-friendly data visualizations. Unlike static plotting libraries, Plotly generates charts that users can engage with through zooming, panning, hovering, and toggling features, which enrich the user experience and facilitate deeper data exploration. This interactivity is particularly beneficial for dashboards, reports, and web applications where user-driven data examination is important. Plotly supports a wide variety of chart types including line charts, bar charts, scatter plots, bubble charts, 3D plots, maps, and even complex visualizations like Sankey diagrams and contour plots. It also integrates smoothly with popular data science frameworks such as Pandas and supports exporting visualizations as standalone HTML files, which can be embedded in websites or shared without requiring specialized software. The library's declarative style of coding allows for concise and readable plotting commands while offering extensive customization options through configuration objects. Plotly is also compatible with Dash, a framework for building analytical web applications using Python, making it a preferred choice for interactive dashboards in professional environments. Although it may have a steeper learning curve compared to simpler libraries, Plotly's powerful features and ability to create responsive, aesthetically pleasing, and interactive visuals make it invaluable for users who require more engagement and flexibility in their data presentations. Overall, Plotly transforms static data insights into interactive experiences that drive better understanding and communication.

Features

1. Creates fully interactive and web-ready visualizations.
2. Supports zoom, pan, hover tooltips, and click events for user interaction.
3. Wide variety of plot types including 3D plots, maps, bubble charts, and advanced diagrams.
4. Exports charts as standalone HTML files for easy sharing and embedding.
5. Compatible with Pandas DataFrames and NumPy arrays.
6. Offers integration with Dash framework for building interactive web apps.
7. Declarative syntax that is concise yet flexible.

8. Suitable for dashboards, presentations, and live data monitoring.
9. Supports real-time data updates and dynamic visualizations.

Differences Between Matplotlib, Seaborn and Plotly: Table 2.7 shows the differences between Matplotlib, Seaborn and Plotly.

Table 2.7

S.No.	Features	Matplotlib	Seaborn	Plotly
1.	Type of Visualization	Primarily static and customizable plots	Statistical visualizations with better defaults	Interactive and web-based visualizations
2.	Ease of Use	Requires more code and customization	Higher-level API, easier for statistical plots	User-friendly for interactive plots, some learning curve
3.	Interactivity	Limited interactivity	Limited interactivity	Highly interactive (zoom, hover, click)
4.	Integration with DataFrames	Supports Pandas but more manual setup	Seamless integration with Pandas DataFrames	Good integration with Pandas and real-time data
5.	Plot Customization	Very high control over plot elements	Moderate customization, simpler defaults	Moderate customization with interactive features
6.	Typical Use Cases	Detailed, publication-quality static plots	Quick, attractive statistical plots and EDA	Interactive dashboards and web apps visualization

Exploratory Analysis: Exploratory Data Analysis (EDA) is a fundamental step in the data science process that involves examining and summarizing the main characteristics of a dataset. The primary goal of EDA is to understand the structure, patterns, and relationships within the data before applying any machine learning models or statistical tests. It helps data scientists uncover trends, detect anomalies, identify missing values, and spot outliers, ensuring data quality and integrity. EDA uses both statistical techniques and visual tools such as histograms, scatter plots, box plots, and correlation matrices to make the data more understandable. Summary statistics like mean, median, standard deviation, and skewness provide insights into the distribution and variability of the data. Visualization, on the other hand, helps in revealing patterns and relationships that are not obvious from raw numbers.

By performing EDA, data scientists can make informed decisions about feature selection, data cleaning, and transformation. It also assists in validating assumptions and identifying potential issues early in the analysis process. Ultimately, EDA sets the foundation for building accurate and robust predictive models by ensuring that the data used is well-understood and appropriately prepared.

Why Exploratory Data Analysis is Important: Exploratory Data Analysis (EDA) is important for several reasons in the context of data science and statistical modeling. Here are some of the key reasons:

1. It helps to understand the dataset by showing how many features it has, what type of data each feature contains and how the data is distributed.

2. It helps to identify hidden patterns and relationships between different data points which help us in and model building.
3. Allows to identify errors or unusual data points (outliers) that could affect our results.
4. The insights gained from EDA help us to identify most important features for building models and guide us on how to prepare them for better performance.
5. By understanding the data, it helps us in choosing best modeling techniques and adjusting them for better results.

Types of Exploratory Data Analysis: There are various types of EDA based on nature of records. Depending on the number of columns we are analyzing we can divide EDA into three types:

1. Univariate Analysis: Univariate analysis focuses on studying one variable to understand its characteristics. It helps to describe data and find patterns within a single feature. Various common methods like histograms are used to show data distribution, box plots to detect outliers and understand data spread and bar charts for categorical data. Summary statistics like mean, median, mode, variance and standard deviation helps in describing the central tendency and spread of the data.

Univariate analysis focuses on examining and understanding the distribution and characteristics of a single variable. It is the simplest form of data analysis and serves as the foundation for any data exploration process. The primary goal is to summarize and describe the variable's central tendency (mean, median, mode), dispersion (range, variance, standard deviation), and overall distribution shape. This analysis helps identify the data's general behavior, such as whether it is normally distributed, skewed, or contains outliers.

Visualization plays an important role in univariate analysis. Common charts include histograms, which show the frequency distribution of numerical data; box plots, which reveal the spread and potential outliers; and bar charts, which are often used for categorical data. These visual tools provide quick insights into the nature of the variable, helping analysts understand its variability and identify any unusual patterns.

Univariate analysis is crucial before any further analysis or modeling because it helps detect data quality issues like missing values or inconsistencies. It also aids in selecting appropriate statistical tests and machine learning algorithms. Overall, univariate analysis provides a clear snapshot of each variable's individual behavior, laying the groundwork for deeper, more complex analyses.

2. Bivariate Analysis: Bivariate Analysis focuses on identifying relationship between two variables to find connections, correlations and dependencies. It helps to understand how two variables interact with each other. Some key techniques include:

- Scatter plots which visualize the relationship between two continuous variables.

- Correlation coefficient measures how strongly two variables are related which commonly use Pearson's correlation for linear relationships.
- Cross-tabulation or contingency tables shows the frequency distribution of two categorical variables and help to understand their relationship.
- Line graphs are useful for comparing two variables over time in time series data to identify trends or patterns.
- Covariance measures how two variables change together but it is paired with the correlation coefficient for a clearer and more standardized understanding of the relationship.

3. Multivariate Analysis: Multivariate Analysis identify relationships between two or more variables in the dataset and aims to understand how variables interact with one another which is important for statistical modeling techniques. Multivariate analysis examines the relationships and interactions among two or more variables simultaneously. Unlike univariate analysis, which focuses on a single variable, multivariate techniques reveal how variables influence each other and uncover complex patterns within datasets. This type of analysis is essential when studying real-world phenomena where multiple factors interplay, such as predicting house prices based on size, location, and age, or understanding customer behavior influenced by demographics, purchasing habits, and preferences.

Common multivariate analysis methods include scatter plots for two variables, pair plots that visualize multiple pairwise relationships, correlation matrices to quantify linear associations, and heatmaps for visualizing complex data patterns. Advanced techniques like principal component analysis (PCA), factor analysis, cluster analysis, and multivariate regression help reduce dimensionality, group similar observations, and build predictive models.

Multivariate analysis helps identify dependencies, correlations, and potential causations, which are critical for hypothesis testing, feature selection, and building robust machine learning models. By analyzing multiple variables together, it provides a more comprehensive and realistic understanding of the data, supporting informed decision-making and deeper insights into the underlying structure of complex datasets.

It includes techniques like:

- Pair plots which shows the relationships between multiple variables at once and helps in understanding how they interact.
- Another technique is Principal Component Analysis (PCA) which reduces the complexity of large datasets by simplifying them while keeping the most important information.
- Spatial Analysis is used for geographical data by using maps and spatial plotting to understand the geographical distribution of variables.
- Time Series Analysis is used for datasets that involve time-based data and it involves understanding and modeling patterns and trends over time. Common

techniques include line plots, autocorrelation analysis, moving averages and ARIMA models.

Identifying Trends, Correlations, and Anomalies

Identifying trends, correlations, and anomalies is essential for understanding data patterns and making informed decisions. Trends show how data evolves over time, revealing upward, downward, or seasonal movements, often visualized with line charts or time-series plots. Correlations highlight relationships between variables, indicating whether they move together or inversely, commonly detected using scatter plots and heatmaps. Anomalies are unusual data points that differ significantly from the norm, signaling errors or rare events, and are spotted through box plots or statistical tests like Z-scores. Together, these analyses help uncover insights, improve data quality, and guide strategic actions.

Identifying Trends: Identifying trends in data involves recognizing patterns or movements that occur over time. Trends can be upward, downward, or seasonal cycles that repeat regularly. Detecting these helps in forecasting future values and making strategic decisions. Time-series plots, line charts, and moving averages are common tools used to visualize trends clearly. For example, a business might track monthly sales data to observe growth trends or seasonal dips.

Correlations: Correlations describe relationships between two or more variables, indicating how one variable changes in relation to another. Positive correlation means variables increase together, while negative correlation means one increases as the other decreases. Correlation matrices, scatter plots, and heatmaps are effective for identifying these relationships. Understanding correlations is essential for feature selection in predictive modeling and uncovering meaningful connections in data.

Anomalies: Anomalies (or outliers) are data points that deviate significantly from the expected pattern or distribution. They may signal errors, fraud, or rare but important events. Detecting anomalies is critical to maintain data quality and avoid misleading conclusions. Box plots, scatter plots, and statistical tests like Z-score or IQR methods help spot these irregularities. For instance, a sudden spike in website traffic might indicate a viral event or a bot attack.

Together, recognizing trends, correlations, and anomalies enables deeper data insight, improves model accuracy, and supports informed decision-making.

Steps for Performing Exploratory Data Analysis: It involves a series of steps to help us understand the data, uncover patterns, identify anomalies, test hypotheses and ensure the data is clean and ready for further analysis. It can be done using different tools like:

- In Python, Pandas is used to clean, filter and manipulate data. Matplotlib helps to create basic visualizations while Seaborn makes more attractive plots. For interactive visualizations Plotly is a good choice.
- In R, ggplot2 is used for creating complex plots, dplyr helps with data

manipulation and tidyr makes sure our data is organized and easy to work with.

Its step includes:

Step 1: Understanding the Problem and the Data: The first step in any data analysis project is to fully understand the problem we're solving and the data we have. This includes asking key questions like:

1. What is the business goal or research question?
2. What are the variables in the data and what do they represent?
3. What types of data (numerical, categorical, text, etc.) do you have?
4. Are there any known data quality issues or limitations?
5. Are there any domain-specific concerns or restrictions?

By understanding the problem and the data, we can plan our analysis more effectively, avoid incorrect assumptions and ensure accurate conclusions.

Step 2: Importing and Inspecting the Data: After understanding the problem and the data, next step is to import the data into our analysis environment such as Python, R or a spreadsheet tool. It's important to find data to gain a basic understanding of its structure, variable types and any potential issues. Here's what we can do:

1. Load the data into our environment carefully to avoid errors or truncations.
2. Check the size of the data like number of rows and columns to understand its complexity.
3. Check for missing values and see how they are distributed across variables since missing data can impact the quality of your analysis.
4. Identify data types for each variable like numerical, categorical, etc which will help in the next steps of data manipulation and analysis.
5. Look for errors or inconsistencies such as invalid values, mismatched units or outliers which could show major issues with the data.

By completing these tasks we'll be prepared to clean and analyze the data more effectively.

Step 3: Handling Missing Data: Missing data is common in many datasets and can affect the quality of our analysis. During EDA it's important to identify and handle missing data properly to avoid biased or misleading results. Here's how to handle it:

1. Understand the patterns and possible causes of missing data. Is it missing completely at random (MCAR), missing at random (MAR) or missing not at random (MNAR). Identifying this helps us to find best way to handle the missing data.
2. Decide whether to remove missing data or impute (fill in) the missing values. Removing data can lead to biased outcomes if the missing data isn't MCAR. Filling values helps to preserve data but should be done carefully.

3. Use appropriate imputation methods like mean or median imputation, regression imputation or machine learning techniques like KNN or decision trees based on the data's characteristics.
4. Consider the impact of missing data. Even after imputing, missing data can cause uncertainty and bias so understands the result with caution.

Properly handling of missing data improves the accuracy of our analysis and prevents misleading conclusions.

Step 4: Exploring Data Characteristics: After addressing missing data we find the characteristics of our data by checking the distribution, central tendency and variability of our variables and identifying outliers or anomalies. This helps in selecting appropriate analysis methods and finding major data issues. We should calculate summary statistics like mean, median, mode, standard deviation, skewness and kurtosis for numerical variables. These provide an overview of the data's distribution and helps us to identify any irregular patterns or issues.

Step 5: Performing Data Transformation: Data transformation is an important step in EDA as it prepares our data for accurate analysis and modeling. Depending on our data's characteristics and analysis needs, we may need to transform it to ensure it's in the right format. Common transformation techniques include:

1. Scaling or normalizing numerical variables like min-max scaling or standardization.
2. Encoding categorical variables for machine learning like one-hot encoding or label encoding.
3. Applying mathematical transformations like logarithmic square root to correct skewness or non-linearity.
4. Creating new variables from existing ones like calculating ratios or combining variables.
5. Aggregating or grouping data based on specific variables or conditions.

Step 6: Visualizing Relationship of Data: Visualization helps to find relationships between variables and identify patterns or trends that may not be seen from summary statistics alone.

1. For categorical variables, create frequency tables, bar plots and pie charts to understand the distribution of categories and identify imbalances or unusual patterns.
2. For numerical variables generate histograms, box plots, violin plots and density plots to visualize distribution, shape, spread and potential outliers.
3. To find relationships between variables use scatter plots, correlation matrices or statistical tests like Pearson's correlation coefficient or Spearman's rank correlation.

Step 7: Handling Outliers: Outliers are data points that differs from the rest of the data may cause by errors in measurement or data entry. Detecting and handling outliers is important because they can skew our analysis and affect model performance. We can identify outliers using methods like interquartile range (IQR), Z-scores or domain-specific rules. Once identified it can be removed or adjusted depending on the context. Properly managing outliers shows our analysis is accurate and reliable.

Step 8: Communicate Findings and Insights: The final step in EDA is to communicate our findings clearly. This involves summarizing the analysis, pointing out key discoveries and presenting our results in a clear way.

1. Clearly state the goals and scope of your analysis.
2. Provide context and background to help others understand your approach.
3. Use visualizations to support our findings and make them easier to understand.
4. Highlight key insights, patterns or anomalies discovered.
5. Mention any limitations or challenges faced during the analysis.
6. Suggest next steps or areas that need further investigation.

Effective communication is important to ensure that our EDA efforts make an impact and that stakeholders understand and act on our insights. By following these steps and using the right tools, EDA helps in increasing the quality of our data, leading to more informed decisions and successful outcomes in any data-driven project.

SUMMARY OF DATA ACQUISITION AND PREPROCESSING

Data Acquisition and Preprocessing are foundational steps in any data science project that ensure high-quality, reliable data for analysis and modeling. **Data acquisition** involves collecting data from diverse sources such as structured databases, unstructured files, public datasets, APIs, and web scraping. Structured data is highly organized, often stored in rows and columns, while unstructured data includes formats like text, images, and videos, requiring more processing effort. Once collected, **data preprocessing** prepares the raw data by cleaning and transforming it to improve its usability. This includes handling missing values through techniques like imputation or removal, eliminating duplicate entries that can bias results, and detecting and addressing outliers that might distort analysis. Additionally, preprocessing involves data transformation such as normalization or scaling, and encoding categorical variables into numerical formats suitable for algorithms. Feature engineering, a key part of preprocessing, creates new variables or modifies existing ones to enhance the dataset's predictive power. Together, acquisition and preprocessing ensure that the dataset is accurate, consistent, and in the correct format, forming a solid foundation for effective exploratory analysis, visualization, and machine learning. Efficient data acquisition and preprocessing save time and improve the quality of insights and model performance, making them critical for successful data-driven decision-making.

4. Data Collection and Sources

Data collection is a critical first step in any data-driven project, involving the acquisition of data from diverse sources to support analysis and decision-making. Structured data refers to well-organized information stored in tables with rows and columns, such as databases and spreadsheets, making it easy to search and analyze. On the other hand, unstructured data includes formats like text documents, images, audio, and videos, which require specialized techniques for processing and extraction. Common sources for data include public datasets made available by governments, organizations, or research institutions, providing free access to valuable information. APIs (Application Programming Interfaces) allow programmatic access to dynamic data from platforms like social media, finance, or weather services. When APIs are unavailable, web scraping techniques extract data directly from websites by parsing HTML content. Additionally, databases serve as structured repositories that store large volumes of data systematically, enabling efficient retrieval and management. Choosing the right data source depends on the project goals and data requirements.

- **Structured vs. Unstructured Data:** Structured data is highly organized and formatted in a way that is easily searchable and analysable by machines. It typically resides in relational databases or spreadsheets, arranged in rows and columns with defined data types and schemas. Examples include customer information, sales records, and sensor data. Its organized nature allows for straightforward querying using languages like SQL, making it ideal for traditional data analysis and reporting.

  In contrast, unstructured data lacks a predefined format or organization, making it more complex to process and analyze. This includes text files, emails, social media posts, images, audio, and videos. Unstructured data requires advanced techniques like natural language processing, computer vision, or audio analysis to extract meaningful insights. Despite the challenges, unstructured data contains rich information, especially in fields like sentiment analysis or multimedia content understanding. Both types of data are valuable; structured data offers ease of use, while unstructured data provides depth and context, often complementing each other in data projects.

- **Public Datasets and APIs:** Public datasets are collections of data made freely available by governments, organizations, or research institutions for public use. These datasets cover various domains such as health, finance, demographics, and environmental data. They serve as valuable resources for researchers, data scientists, and developers to analyze trends, build models, or benchmark algorithms without the need for costly data acquisition. Examples include datasets from the U.S. Census Bureau, Kaggle, and the World Bank.

  APIs (Application Programming Interfaces) provide a standardized way for software applications to communicate and access dynamic data. Many platforms, such as Twitter, Google Maps, or financial services, offer APIs that allow users to retrieve up-to-date data programmatically. APIs enable automated, real-time data collection and integration into applications or analyses. Unlike static public datasets, APIs often provide continuous streams of fresh data, making them ideal for projects requiring current or frequently updated information.

- **Web Scraping and Databases:** Web scraping is the automated process of extracting data from websites by parsing their HTML content. It is useful when data is not readily available through APIs or public datasets. Web scraping enables collecting diverse information such as product prices, reviews, or news articles directly from web pages. However, ethical and legal considerations must be observed, and website terms of service should be respected. Tools like BeautifulSoup and Scrapy are popular for building web scrapers.

  Databases, on the other hand, are structured storage systems designed to organize, store, and manage large volumes of data efficiently. They can be relational (SQL-based) or non-relational (NoSQL). Databases support complex queries, transactions, and data integrity, making them essential for business operations and analytics. Data collected via APIs or web scraping is often stored in databases for easier access, manipulation, and integration with analysis workflows. Combining web scraping and databases helps build comprehensive datasets from dispersed online sources.

5. Data Cleaning and Preparation

Data cleaning and preparation are essential steps to ensure the quality and usability of raw data before analysis or modeling. This process begins with handling missing data, where missing values are either filled using techniques like mean or median imputation, or removed if they are too numerous or irrelevant. Next, removing duplicates is important to avoid biased or skewed results caused by repeated records. Outliers, or extreme values that deviate significantly from the norm, are identified and addressed since they can distort statistical analyses and machine learning models. Data is then transformed and encoded to fit the requirements of analytical tools for example, normalizing numerical features or converting categorical variables into numeric formats using techniques like one-hot encoding. Finally, feature engineering creates or modifies variables to enhance the predictive power of the dataset by extracting meaningful information or combining existing features. Together, these steps create a clean, consistent, and well-structured dataset, forming a solid foundation for accurate analysis and modeling.

- **Handling Missing Data:** Handling missing data is a crucial step in data cleaning to ensure analysis accuracy. Missing values can occur due to errors in data collection, transmission, or storage. Ignoring missing data can lead to biased results or reduced statistical power. Common strategies include deletion, where rows or columns with missing values are removed if they are few or non-critical. Alternatively, imputation fills missing values using methods like mean, median, or mode substitution, or more advanced techniques like k-nearest neighbors (KNN) or regression imputation. Another approach is using algorithms that handle missing data internally. The choice depends on the nature and extent of missingness, whether data is missing completely at random, at random, or not at random. Proper handling of missing data preserves dataset integrity, prevents information loss, and improves model performance, making it a vital preprocessing step in any data science workflow.

- **Removing Duplicates and Outliers:** Removing duplicates and outliers is essential for maintaining data quality. Duplicates are identical or near-identical records that can bias analysis by over-representing certain data points. They often arise from data entry errors or merging datasets and should be identified and removed to ensure each observation is unique. Outliers are extreme values significantly different from the majority of data, which may result from measurement errors, data corruption, or genuine variability. Outliers can distort statistical analyses and model training by skewing means or inflating error estimates. Detection methods include visualization (box plots, scatter plots) and statistical techniques (Z-score, IQR). Once identified, outliers may be removed, transformed, or treated differently depending on their cause and impact. Cleaning duplicates and outliers ensures more reliable and robust analytical results.
- **Data Transformation and Encoding:** Data transformation and encoding prepare raw data for effective analysis and modeling by converting it into appropriate formats. Data transformation includes scaling numerical features through normalization or standardization to ensure consistent ranges, which improves the performance of many machine learning algorithms. It can also involve aggregation, discretization, or logarithmic transformations to reduce skewness and enhance interpretability. Encoding refers to converting categorical variables into numeric formats, as most algorithms require numerical input. Common encoding methods include one-hot encoding, which creates binary columns for each category, and label encoding, which assigns integer values to categories. More advanced techniques like target encoding consider the relationship between categories and target variables. Proper transformation and encoding help algorithms better understand and learn from the data, improving predictive accuracy and reducing computational complexity.
- **Feature Engineering:** Feature engineering involves creating, modifying, or selecting variables to improve the predictive power and performance of machine learning models. It transforms raw data into meaningful features that better capture underlying patterns and relationships. Techniques include creating interaction terms, extracting date/time components, aggregating data, or applying mathematical transformations. Domain knowledge often guides this process, enabling the creation of features that reflect real-world insights. Feature engineering also involves selecting relevant features through

techniques like correlation analysis or dimensionality reduction to remove redundant or noisy variables. Well-engineered features enhance model interpretability, reduce overfitting, and increase accuracy. Although time-consuming, feature engineering is often considered one of the most important steps in a data science pipeline because even powerful algorithms perform poorly without good features.

6. Data Visualization and Exploratory Analysis

Data Visualization and Exploratory Analysis are fundamental steps in understanding and interpreting data effectively. Data visualization transforms raw data into graphical representations such as charts, graphs, and plots, making complex information easier to comprehend and communicate. It helps uncover hidden patterns, trends, and outliers that might be missed in raw datasets. Tools like Matplotlib, Seaborn, and Plotly provide versatile options for creating static, statistical, and interactive visualizations, enhancing insight discovery. Exploratory Analysis complements visualization by systematically examining data characteristics through techniques like univariate analysis, which studies individual variables, and multivariate analysis, which explores relationships among multiple variables. Together, these approaches enable analysts to identify correlations, trends, and anomalies, guiding feature selection and model building. By revealing the underlying structure and quality of data, Data Visualization and Exploratory Analysis lay the groundwork for accurate modeling and informed decision-making in any data science project.

- **Importance of Data Visualization:** Data visualization is crucial because it transforms raw data into visual formats, making complex information easier to understand and interpret. It helps reveal patterns, trends, and outliers that might be missed in raw tables or spreadsheets. Effective visualization enhances communication between data analysts and stakeholders by providing clear insights. It also supports faster decision-making and problem-solving. Visualization tools allow interactive exploration, enabling users to dig deeper into the data. Overall, data visualization bridges the gap between data complexity and actionable knowledge, making it an essential step in any data analysis or data science workflow.
- **Tools: Matplotlib, Seaborn, Plotly:** Matplotlib is a versatile Python library for creating static, publication-quality plots with fine control over plot elements. Seaborn builds on Matplotlib, offering simpler syntax and attractive default styles, especially suited for statistical visualizations like heatmaps and categorical plots. Plotly provides interactive and dynamic visualizations that can be embedded in web apps, enabling user-driven data exploration. Together, these tools cover a wide range of visualization needs, from basic charts to complex, interactive dashboards, making them invaluable for data analysis and presentation.
- **Univariate and Multivariate Analysis:** Univariate analysis examines one variable at a time to understand its distribution, central tendency, and

variability using histograms, box plots, or frequency tables. It helps identify patterns like skewness or outliers. Multivariate analysis explores relationships between two or more variables simultaneously, using scatter plots, correlation matrices, or pair plots. This approach uncovers interactions, dependencies, and potential causal links within the data. Together, these analyses provide comprehensive insights: univariate for detailed single-variable understanding and multivariate for exploring complex variable interdependencies crucial for predictive modeling and hypothesis testing.

- **Identifying Trends, Correlations, and Anomalies:** Identifying trends involves detecting consistent patterns or movements in data over time, such as growth or seasonal cycles, often visualized with line charts. Correlations reveal relationships between variables, showing how changes in one variable relate to another, measured with correlation coefficients and visualized using scatter plots or heatmaps. Anomalies are unusual or rare data points that deviate from normal patterns and may indicate errors or significant events, detected using box plots or statistical tests like Z-scores. Recognizing these elements is key to understanding data behavior, improving model accuracy, and making informed decisions.

Chapter 3

Statistics and Probability for Data Science

Statistics and probability form the backbone of data science, providing essential tools for understanding, analyzing, and interpreting data. Probability offers a mathematical framework to model uncertainty, allowing data scientists to make predictions and assess risks. It includes key concepts such as random variables, probability distributions (like normal, binomial, and Poisson), and Bayes' theorem, which is foundational for machine learning and decision-making under uncertainty.

Statistics, on the other hand, focuses on collecting, summarizing, and drawing conclusions from data. Descriptive statistics mean, median, mode, variance, and standard deviation help summarize data patterns. Inferential statistics uses sample data to make generalizations about a population, applying techniques such as hypothesis testing, confidence intervals, and regression analysis.

In data science, these tools support tasks like data cleaning, exploratory data analysis, A/B testing, predictive modeling, and algorithm evaluation. For example, hypothesis testing can validate business strategies, while regression helps predict future trends. Understanding probability distributions enables better model selection and performance tuning.

Together, statistics and probability allow data scientists to make data-driven decisions, ensure analytical rigor, and build models that reflect real-world behaviors. Mastery of these concepts is critical for transforming raw data into actionable insights.

7. Fundamentals of Probability

Probability plays a critical role in data science by enabling the modeling of uncertainty and randomness in data-driven processes. It forms the theoretical foundation for many algorithms and techniques used in machine learning, predictive analytics, and statistical inference. In data science, probability distributions (such as normal, binomial, and Poisson) help describe how data is expected to behave. For instance, the normal distribution is commonly assumed in many models and is useful for understanding patterns and making predictions.

Bayesian probability is especially valuable for updating beliefs based on new evidence. It underpins Bayesian inference and models like Naïve Bayes classifiers, widely used in text classification and spam detection. Conditional probability and joint probability are essential for understanding relationships between variables. These concepts power algorithms such as Bayesian networks and are used in probabilistic reasoning.

In machine learning, probabilistic models help quantify uncertainty in predictions. For example, logistic regression estimates the probability of a binary outcome, and decision trees can output class probabilities.

Furthermore, probability is crucial in model evaluation concepts like precision, recall, ROC curves, and confusion matrices all involve probabilistic thinking.

Overall, probability provides the tools for making informed, data-driven decisions under uncertainty an essential skill in data science.

Fundamentals of Probability: Probability is the branch of mathematics that deals with quantifying uncertainty. It provides a framework for predicting the likelihood of future events based on known information or random experiments. Key Concepts:

1. **Experiment**: A process or action with uncertain outcomes (e.g., tossing a coin).
2. **Sample Space (S)**: The set of all possible outcomes (e.g., for a coin toss: {Heads, Tails}).
3. **Event**: A subset of the sample space (e.g., getting a Head).

Basic Rules:

1. **$0 \leq P(A) \leq 1$**: Probabilities range from 0 (impossible) to 1 (certain).
2. **Complement Rule**:

   $P(\text{not A}) = 1 - P(A)$
3. **Addition Rule** (for mutually exclusive events):

   $P(A \text{ or } B) - P(A) + P(B)$
4. **Multiplication Rule** (for independent events):

   $P(A \text{ and } B) - P(A) \text{ x } P(B)$

Classical Definition of Probability: As the name suggests the classical approach to defining probability is the oldest approach. It states that if there are ***n*** exhaustive, mutually exclusive and equally likely cases out of which ***m*** cases are favourable to the happening of event ***A***,

Then the probabilities of event A is defined as given by the following probability function:

Formula

$$P(A) = \frac{\text{Number of favourable cases}}{\text{Total number of equally likely cases}} = \frac{m}{n}$$

Thus, to calculate the probability we need information on number of favorable cases and total number of equally likely cases. This can he explained using following example:

Problem Statement: A coin is tossed. What is the probability of getting a head?

Solution:

Total number of equally likely outcomes ***(n)*** = 2 (i.e. head or tail)

Number of outcomes favorable to head ***(m)*** = 1

$$P(head) - \frac{1}{2}$$

Basic Probability Theory

Probability theory is a crucial foundation for data science, providing the mathematical framework to analyze uncertainty and randomness in data. It allows data scientists to quantify the likelihood of events, understand data variability, and make informed decisions. Key concepts include probability distributions, conditional probability, independence, and Bayes' theorem, all of which are essential for tasks like model building, risk assessment, and statistical inference.

Basic probability theory is the mathematical study of uncertainty and chance, providing a structured way to analyze random events and predict outcomes. At its core, it deals with experiments, outcomes, and events. An experiment is any process with uncertain results, such as rolling a die or flipping a coin. Each possible result is called an outcome, and the collection of all outcomes forms the sample space. An event is a subset of outcomes, and the probability of an event is a number between 0 and 1 that indicates the likelihood of that event occurring. If all outcomes are equally likely, the probability of an event is calculated as the ratio of favorable outcomes to total outcomes. Key rules in probability theory include the complement rule, which states that the probability of an event not occurring is one minus the probability that it does; the addition rule for mutually exclusive events; and the multiplication rule for independent events. Conditional probability, which measures the likelihood of one event occurring given that another has already occurred, plays a crucial role in complex problems. Bayes' Theorem builds on this, allowing for the revision of probabilities based on new evidence. Probability distributions such as uniform, binomial, and normal are used to model real-world phenomena. These concepts are widely applied in data science, statistics, machine learning, and decision-making processes, where understanding and quantifying uncertainty is essential. Overall, basic probability theory provides the foundational tools for analyzing randomness and making informed predictions in uncertain environments.

Bayes' Theorem

Bayes' theorem describes the probability of occurrence of an event related to any condition. It is also considered for the case of conditional probability. Bayes theorem is also known as the formula for the probability of "causes". For example: if we have to calculate the probability of taking a blue ball from the second bag out of three different bags of balls, where each bag contains three different colour balls viz. red, blue, black. In this case, the probability of occurrence of an event is calculated depending on other conditions is known as conditional probability.

Bayes Theorem Statement

Let $E_1, E_2, \ldots, E_n$ be a set of events associated with a sample space S, where all the events $E_1, E_2, \ldots, E_n$ have nonzero probability of occurrence and they form a partition of S. Let A be any event associated with S, then according to Bayes theorem,

$$P(E_i \mid A) = \frac{P(E_i)P(A \mid E_i)}{\sum_{k=1}^{n} P(E_k)P(A|E_k)}$$

Bayes Theorem Proof

According to the conditional probability formula,

$$P(E_i \mid A) = \frac{P(E_i \cap A)}{P(A)} \ldots (1)$$

Using the multiplication rule of probability,

$$P(E_i \cap A) = P(E_i)P(A \mid E_i) \ldots (2)$$

Using total probability theorem,

$$P(A) = \sum_{k=1}^{n} P(E_k)P(A|E_k) \ldots (3)$$

Putting the values from equations (2) and (3) in equation 1, we get

$$P(E_i \mid A) = \frac{P(E_i)P(A \mid E_i)}{\sum_{k=1}^{n} P(E_k)P(A|E_k)}$$

Note: The following terminologies are also used when the Bayes theorem is applied:

Hypotheses: The events $E_1, E_2, \ldots E_n$ is called the hypotheses

Priori Probability: The probability $P(E_i)$ is considered as the priori probability of hypothesis E_i

Posteriori Probability: The probability $P(E_i|A)$ is considered as the posteriori probability of hypothesis E_i

Bayes' theorem is also called the formula for the probability of "causes". Since the E_i's are a partition of the sample space S, one and only one of the events E_i occurs (i.e. one of the events E_i must occur and the only one can occur). Hence, the above formula gives us the probability of a particular E_i (i.e. a "Cause"), given that the event A has occurred.

Bayes Theorem Formula: If A and B are two events, then the **formula for the Bayes theorem** is given by:

$$P(A|B) = \frac{P(B|A)P(A)}{P(B)} \quad where \ P(B) \neq 0$$

Where $P(A|B)$ is the probability of condition when event A is occurring while event B has already occurred.

Bayes Theorem Derivation: Bayes Theorem can be derived for events and random variables separately using the definition of conditional probability and density.

From the definition of conditional probability, Bayes theorem can be derived for events as given below:

$P(A|B) = P(A \cap B)/ P(B)$, where $P(B) \neq 0$

$P(B|A) = P(B \cap A)/ P(A)$, where $P(A) \neq 0$

Here, the joint probability $P(A \cap B)$ of both events A and B being true such that,

$P(B \cap A) = P(A \cap B)$

$P(A \cap B) = P(A \mid B)\ P(B) = P(B \mid A)\ P(A)$

$P(A|B) = [P(B|A)\ P(A)]/ P(B)$, *where* $P(B) \neq 0$

Similarly, from the definition of conditional density, Bayes theorem can be derived for two continuous random variables namely X and Y as given below:

$$f_{X|Y=y}(x) = \frac{f_{X,Y}(x,y)}{f_Y(y)}$$

$$f_{Y|X=x}(y) = \frac{f_{X,Y}(x,y)}{f_X(x)}$$

Therefore,

$$f_{X|Y=y}(x) = \frac{f_{Y|X=x}(y) f_X(x)}{f_Y(y)}$$

Examples and Solutions: Some illustrations will improve the understanding of the concept.

Example 1: A bag I contains 4 white and 6 black balls while another Bag II contains 4 white and 3 black balls. One ball is drawn at random from one of the bags, and it is found to be black. Find the probability that it was drawn from Bag I.

Solution: Let E_1 be the event of choosing bag I, E_2 the event of choosing bag II, and A be the event of drawing a black ball.

Then,

$$P(E_1) = P(E_2) = \frac{1}{2}$$

Also, $P(A|E_1)$ = *P*(drawing a black ball from Bag I) = 6/10 = 3/5

$P(A|E_2)$ = *P*(drawing a black ball from Bag II) = 3/7

By using Bayes' theorem, the probability of drawing a black ball from bag I out of two bags,

$$P(E_1|A) = \frac{P(E_1)P(A|E_1)}{P(E_1)P(A|E_1)+P(E_2)P(A|E_2)}$$

$$= \frac{\frac{1}{2}\times\frac{3}{5}}{\frac{1}{2}\times\frac{3}{5}+\frac{1}{2}\times\frac{3}{7}}$$

$$= \frac{7}{12}$$

Example 2: A man is known to speak the truth 2 out of 3 times. He throws a die and reports that the number obtained is a four. Find the probability that the number obtained is actually a four.

Solution: Let *A* be the event that the man reports that number four is obtained.

Let E_1 be the event that four is obtained and E_2 be its complementary event.

Then, $P(E_1)$ = Probability that four occurs = 1/6.

$P(E_2)$ = Probability that four does not occur = 1- $P(E_1)$ = 1 – (1/6) = 5/6.

Also, $P(A|E_1)$ = Probability that man reports four and it is actually a four = 2/3

$P(A|E_2)$ = Probability that man reports four and it is not a four = 1/3.

By using Bayes' theorem, probability that number obtained is actually a four, $P(E_1|A)$

$$= \frac{P(E_1)P(A|E_1)}{P(E_1)P(A|E_1)+P(E_2)P(A|E_2)} = \frac{\frac{1}{6}\times\frac{2}{3}}{\frac{1}{6}\times\frac{2}{3}+\frac{5}{6}\times\frac{1}{3}}$$

$$= \frac{2}{7}$$

Bayes Theorem Applications: One of the many applications of Bayes' theorem is Bayesian inference, a particular approach to statistical inference. Bayesian inference has found application in various activities, including medicine, science, philosophy, engineering, sports, law, etc. For example, we can use Bayes' theorem to define the accuracy of medical test results by considering how likely any given person is to have a disease and the test's overall accuracy. Bayes' theorem relies on consolidating prior probability distributions to generate posterior probabilities. In Bayesian statistical inference, prior probability is the probability of an event before new data is collected.

Probability Distributions (Normal, Binomial, Poisson)

Probability distributions are mathematical functions that describe the likelihood of different outcomes in a random experiment. They can be discrete or continuous, depending on the nature of the outcomes. Here, we focus on three commonly used distributions are as follows:

1. **Normal Distribution:** The normal distribution is a continuous probability distribution often referred to as the Gaussian distribution. It is characterized by its bell-shaped curve, which is symmetrical around the mean. In a normal distribution, most of the data points cluster around the mean, with fewer values occurring as you move farther away from the center. The mean (μ) and standard deviation (σ) are key parameters that define the distribution. The probability density function (PDF) for a normal distribution is:

$$f(x) = \frac{1}{\sigma\sqrt{2\pi}} e^{-\frac{(x-\mu)^2}{2\sigma^2}}$$

This distribution is widely used in statistics, as many real-world phenomena (e.g., heights, test scores, measurement errors) approximate a normal distribution.

2. **Binomial Distribution:** The binomial distribution is a discrete probability distribution that models the number of successes in a fixed number of independent trials, each with two possible outcomes (success or failure). It is defined by two parameters the number of trials ***(n)*** and the probability of success in each trial ***(p)***. The probability of obtaining exactly ***k*** successes in ***n*** trials is given by:

$$P(X = k) = \binom{n}{k} p^k (1-p)^{n-k}$$

The binomial distribution is used when outcomes are binary (like flipping a coin) and is fundamental in hypothesis testing, quality control, and survey analysis.

3. **Poisson Distribution:** The Poisson distribution is a discrete probability distribution that models the number of events occurring in a fixed interval of time or space, given that these events happen with a known constant mean rate (λ) and independently of each other. The probability of observing ***k*** events in an interval is given by:

$$P(X = k) = \frac{\lambda^k e^{-\lambda}}{k!}$$

The Poisson distribution is often used to model rare events, such as the number of accidents in a day, the number of phone calls received by a call center, or the number of particles emitted by a radioactive substance.

Differences Between Normal, Binomial, Poisson: Table 3.1 shows the differences between Normal, Binomial, Poisson.

Table 3.1

S.No.	Feature	Normal Distribution	Binomial Distribution	Poisson Distribution
1.	Type of Distribution	Continuous	Discrete	Discrete
2.	Shape	Bell-shaped, symmetric	Discrete, can be skewed depending on pp	Skewed (can be left or right)
3.	Parameters	Mean (μ), Standard Deviation (σ)	Number of trials (n), Probability of success (p)	Rate of occurrence (λ)
4.	Use Case	Models natural phenomena like height, weight, and measurement errors	Models fixed number of trials (e.g., coin flips, success/failure)	Models the count of events occurring in a fixed interval (e.g., number of phone calls)
5.	Range of Values	Any real number (-8 , 8)	Discrete values from 0 to n	Non-negative integers (0, 1, 2, ...)
6.	Probability Mass/ Density Function (PMF/PDF)	PDF: $f(x) = \frac{1}{\sigma\sqrt{2\pi}} e^{\;\frac{(x\;\;\mu)^2}{2\sigma^2}}$	PMF: $P(X = k) = \binom{n}{k} p^k (1 - p)^{n\;\;k}$	PMF: $P(X = k) = \frac{\lambda^k e^{\;\;\lambda}}{k!}$

8. Descriptive and Inferential Statistics

Descriptive Statistics refers to the methods used to summarize and organize data in a meaningful way. It focuses on presenting data in a clear and concise manner, often through measures such as the mean, median, mode, standard deviation, and variance. These measures help in understanding the central tendency, spread, and distribution of the data. Additionally, graphs like histograms, bar charts, and pie charts, as well as tables, provide visual insights into data patterns, allowing for easier interpretation. Descriptive statistics are often the first step in data analysis, providing a snapshot of the data's key features without drawing conclusions beyond the data at hand.

Inferential Statistics, on the other hand, extends beyond merely describing the data. It involves making predictions, generalizations, or inferences about a larger population based on a sample of data. This branch of statistics relies heavily on probability theory and methods such as hypothesis testing, confidence intervals, and regression analysis. Through inferential statistics, researchers can estimate population parameters, test assumptions, and assess relationships between variables. It allows data scientists and statisticians to draw conclusions about a population from sample data and to quantify the uncertainty associated with these predictions, ultimately providing insights that guide decision-making and policy formulation.

Measures of Central Tendency and Dispersion

Measures of central tendency are statistical metrics used to summarize a dataset by identifying the central or typical value. The mean (average) is the sum of all data points divided by the number of observations, and it is highly sensitive to outliers. The median, the middle value when the data is ordered, is a more robust measure, especially when the data has extreme values. The mode is the value that appears most frequently and is useful in categorical data analysis. While measures of central tendency help to locate the "center" of the data, measures of dispersion show how spread out the data points are around the center. The range is the simplest measure of dispersion, defined as the difference between the maximum and minimum values in a dataset. The variance is the average of the squared deviations from the mean, providing a measure of data spread, while the standard deviation, the square root of the variance, offers a more intuitive understanding of variability, as it is expressed in the same units as the original data. Both central tendency and dispersion are essential in summarizing data, as they provide insights into the "typical" value and how much variation exists around that value.

Measures of Central Tendency:

1. **Mean:** The mean, also known as the average, is calculated by summing up all the values in a dataset and dividing the sum by the total number of values. It is sensitive to extreme values, making it susceptible to outliers.
2. **Median:** The median is the middle value in a dataset when the values are arranged in ascending or descending order. If there is an even number of values, the median is the average of the two middle values. Unlike the mean, the median is less affected by outliers.
3. **Mode:** The mode is the value that occurs most frequently in a dataset. It is particularly useful for categorical data but can also be applied to numerical data. A dataset may have one mode (unimodal), two modes (bimodal), or more than two modes (multimodal).

   Example: Let's consider a dataset of daily temperatures recorded over a week: 22°C, 23°C, 21°C, 25°C, 22°C, 24°C, and 20°C.

- **Mean:** (22 + 23 + 21 + 25 + 22 + 24 + 20) / 7 = 21.86°C
- **Median:** Arranging the temperatures in ascending order: 20°C, 21°C, 22°C, 22°C, 23°C, 24°C, 25°C. The median is 22°C.
- **Mode:** The mode is 22°C as it occurs most frequently in the dataset.

Measures of Dispersion:

1. **Range** In statistics, the range refers to the difference between the highest and lowest values in a dataset. It provides a simple measure of variability, indicating the spread of data points. The range is calculated by subtracting the lowest value from the highest value.

   For example, in a dataset {4, 6, 9, 3, 7}, the range is 9 - 3 = 6.
2. **Variance:** Variance is a statistical measure that quantifies the amount of variation or dispersion of a set of numbers from their mean value. Specifically,

variance is defined as the expected value of the squared deviation from the mean. It is calculated by:

- Finding the mean (average) of the data set.
- Subtracting the mean from each data point to get the deviations from the mean.
- Squaring each of the deviations.
- Calculating the average of the squared deviations. This is the variance.

3. **Standard Deviation:** Standard deviation is a measure of the amount of variation or dispersion of a set of values from the mean value. It is calculated as the square root of the variance, which is the average squared deviation from the mean.
4. **Interquartile Range (IQR):** Interquartile Range (IQR) is a measure of statistical dispersion that represents the middle 50% of a data set. It is calculated as the difference between the 75th percentile (Q3) and the 25th percentile (Q1) of the data i.e., IQR = Q3 – Q1.

Examples for Dispersion: Let's consider the same dataset of daily temperatures recorded over a week: 22°C, 23°C, 21°C, 25°C, 22°C, 24°C, and 20°C.

- **Range:** Maximum temperature - Minimum temperature = 25°C - 20°C = 5°C
- **Variance:** Variance = (Sum of squared differences from the mean) / (Number of data points)

  Mean = 21.86 °C

  Sum of squared differences from the mean = (22 - 21.86)2 + (23 - 21.86)2 + (21 - 21.86)2 + (25 - 21.86)2 + (22 - 21.86)2 + (24 - 21.86)2 + (20 - 21.86)2

  = (0.14)2 + (1.14)2 + (-0.86)2 + (3.14)2 + (0.14)2 + (2.14)2 + (-1.86)2

  = 0.0196 + 1.2996 + 0.7396 + 9.8596 + 0.0196 + 4.5796 + 3.4596

  = 19.0772

  Thus, Variance = 19.0772 / 7 ≈ 2.725 °C

- **Standard Deviation:** Take the square root of the variance to get the standard deviation.

  Thus, Standard Deviation √"2.725 ≈ 1.65 °C

- **Interquartile Range (IQR):** First Quartile (Q1) = 21°C Third Quartile (Q3) = 24°C

  Thus, IQR = Q3 – Q1 = 24°C - 21°C = 3°C

Importance of Measures of Central Tendency and Dispersion:

1. **Summarizing Data**: Central tendency provides a single value to represent the "center" of the data, making it easier to summarize large datasets for analysis.

2. **Understanding the Typical Value**: Measures like the mean and median help identify the typical or most common value in a dataset, aiding in quick interpretations.
3. **Identifying Skewness and Outliers**: The mean is sensitive to extreme values (outliers), while the median offers a better central value when data is skewed. This helps in identifying anomalies or unusual data points.
4. **Comparing Datasets**: Central tendency measures allow for the comparison of different datasets, helping analysts determine which dataset is higher, lower, or more consistent.
5. **Measuring Variability: Dispersion** (e.g., range, variance, standard deviation) indicates how spread out the data is, helping analysts assess the consistency and reliability of the data.
6. **Risk Assessment**: In fields like finance and risk management, understanding the spread of data through variance or standard deviation helps evaluate volatility and potential risks.
7. **Data Interpretation**: Dispersion measures help contextualize the central tendency, allowing for a fuller understanding of the data's characteristics, such as how clustered or dispersed the values are.
8. **Improved Decision-Making**: Together, central tendency and dispersion help businesses, researchers, and analysts make informed decisions, predictions, and conclusions by providing a clear picture of the data's typical behavior and variability.

Differences Between Central Tendency and Dispersion: The key differences between central tendency and dispersion are listed in the table 3.2.

Table 3.2

S.No.	Aspect	Central Tendency	Dispersion
1.	Definition	Indicates the typical or central value around which data tends to cluster	Indicates the spread or variability of data points in a dataset
2.	Purpose	Provides a single representative value summarizing the dataset	Describes how spread out the values are from each other and from the central value
3.	Examples	Mean, median, mode	Range, variance, standard deviation, interquartile range
4.	Calculation	Calculated using the values of the dataset	Calculated using deviations from the central value (usually the mean)
5.	Interpretation	Helps in understanding the center of the data distribution	Helps in understanding the spread of the data distribution
6.	Measure of Location	Indicates where the data is centered	Indicates how widely the data is spread out

Hypothesis Testing and p-values

Hypothesis testing is a statistical method used to assess whether there is enough evidence in a sample of data to support a specific hypothesis about a population. It begins with two competing hypotheses: the null hypothesis (H_0), which assumes no effect or no difference, and the alternative hypothesis (H_1), which suggests that there is an effect or a difference. To test these hypotheses, a test statistic is computed from the sample data, which is then compared against a critical value or used to calculate a p-value. The p-value represents the probability of observing the test results, or more extreme results, under the assumption that the null hypothesis is true. A smaller p-value (typically less than 0.05) suggests stronger evidence against the null hypothesis, leading to its rejection. Conversely, a p-value larger than the significance level (often 0.05) means the null hypothesis cannot be rejected. Hypothesis testing is a crucial tool in scientific research, allowing researchers to make data-driven decisions and determine whether their findings are statistically significant or due to chance. It is widely applied in fields such as medicine, economics, and social sciences.

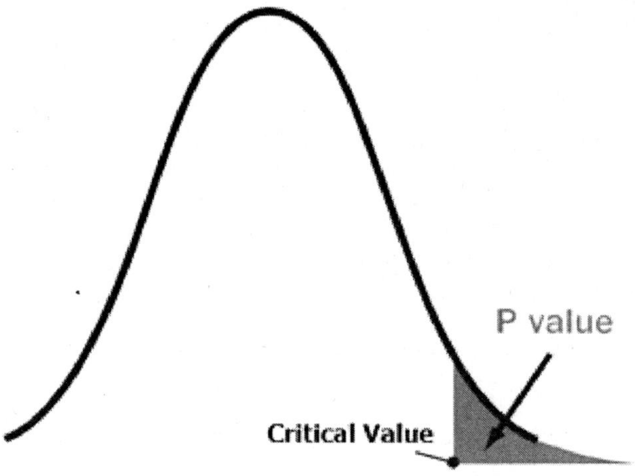

Fig. 3.1

Hypothesis testing compares two opposite ideas about a group of people or things and uses data from a small part of that group (a sample) to decide which idea is more likely true. We collect and study the sample data to check if the claim is correct.

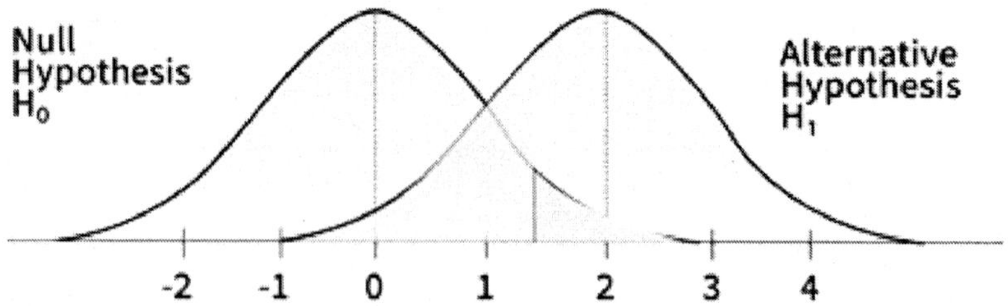

Fig. 3.2

For example, if a company says its website gets 50 visitors each day on average, we use hypothesis testing to look at past visitor data and see if this claim is true or if the actual number is different.

Defining Hypotheses

1. **Null Hypothesis (H_0):** The starting assumption. For example, "The average visits are 50."
2. **Alternative Hypothesis (H_1):** The opposite, saying there is a difference. For example, "The average visits are not 50."

Key Terms of Hypothesis Testing: To understand the Hypothesis testing firstly we need to understand the key terms which are given below:

1. **Significance Level (a):** How sure we want to be before saying the claim is false. Usually, we choose 0.05 (5%).
2. **p-value:** The chance of seeing the data if the null hypothesis is true. If this is less than a, we say the claim is probably false.
3. **Test Statistic:** A number that helps us decide if the data supports or rejects the claim.
4. **Critical Value:** The cutoff point to compare with the test statistic.
5. **Degrees of freedom:** A number that depends on the data size and helps find the critical value.

How does Hypothesis Testing work?

Working of Hypothesis testing involves various steps:

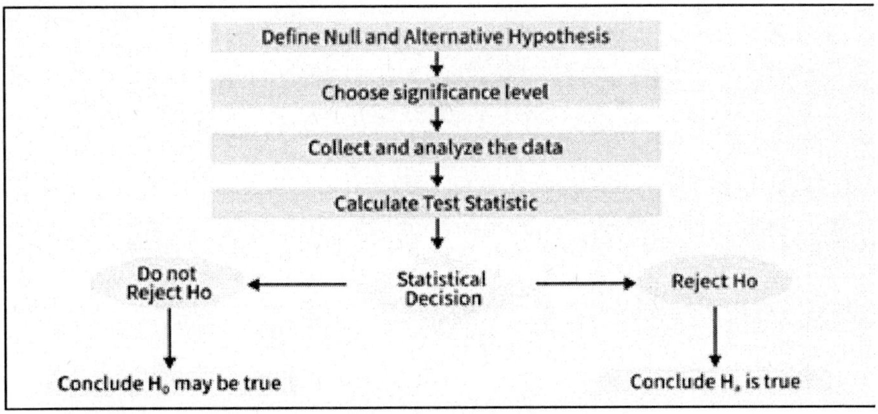

Fig. 3.3 Steps of Hypothesis Testing

Step 1: Define Hypotheses:

1. **Null hypothesis (H_0):** Assumes no effect or difference.
2. **Alternative hypothesis (H_1):** Assumes there is an effect or difference.

Example: Test if a new algorithm improves user engagement.

Step 2: Choose Significance Level: We select a significance level (usually 0.05). This is the maximum chance we accept of wrongly rejecting the null hypothesis (Type I error). It also sets the confidence needed to accept results.

Step 3: Collect and Analyze Data: Now we gather data this could come from user observations or an experiment. Once collected we analyze the data using appropriate statistical methods to calculate the test statistic.

Example: We collect data on user engagement before and after implementing the algorithm. We can also find the mean engagement scores for each group.

Step 4: Calculate Test Statistic: The test statistic measures how much the sample data deviates from what we did expect if the null hypothesis were true. Different tests use different statistics:

1. **Z-test:** Used when population variance is known and sample size is large.
2. **T-test:** Used when sample size is small or population variance unknown.
3. **Chi-square test:** Used for categorical data to compare observed vs. expected counts.

Step 5: Make a Decision: We compare the test statistic to a critical value from a statistical table or use the p-value:

1. **Using Critical Value:**
   - If test statistic > critical value → reject H0 .
   - If test statistic ≤ critical value → fail to reject H0 .
2. **Using P-value:**
   - If p-value ≤ a → reject H0 .
   - If p-value > a → fail to reject H0 .

Example: If p-value is 0.03 and a is 0.05, we reject the null hypothesis because 0.03 < 0.05.

Step 6: Interpret the Results: Based on the decision, we conclude whether there is enough evidence to support the alternative hypothesis or if we should keep the null hypothesis.

Real Life Examples of Hypothesis Testing: A pharmaceutical company tests a new drug to see if it lowers blood pressure in patients.

Data:

- **Before Treatment:** 120, 122, 118, 130, 125, 128, 115, 121, 123, 119
- **After Treatment:** 115, 120, 112, 128, 122, 125, 110, 117, 119, 114

Step 1: Define the Hypothesis

1. **Null Hypothesis (H0):** The new drug has no effect on blood pressure.
2. **Alternate Hypothesis (H1):** The new drug has an effect on blood pressure.

Step 2: Define the Significance Level: Usually 0.05, meaning less than 5% chance results are by random chance.

Step 3: Compute the test statistic: Using paired T-test analyze the data to obtain a test statistic and a p-value. The test statistic is calculated based on the differences between blood pressure measurements before and after treatment.

$t = m/(s/\sqrt{n})$

Where:

- **m** = mean of the difference i.e X after, X before
- **s** = standard deviation of the difference (d)
  $d_i = X_{\text{after},i} - X_{\text{before},i}$
- **n** = sample size

then m= -3.9, s= 1.37 and n= 10. we calculate the T-statistic = -9 based on the formula for paired t test

Step 4: Find the p-value: With degrees of freedom = 9, p-value $\approx$ 0.0000085 (very small).

Step 5: Result: Since the p-value (8.538051223166285e-06) is less than the significance level (0.05) the researchers reject the null hypothesis. There is statistically significant evidence that the average blood pressure before and after treatment with the new drug is different.

Importance of Hypothesis Testing and p-values:

1. **Supports Data-Driven Decisions:** Hypothesis testing helps organizations make objective, data-backed decisions instead of relying on assumptions or guesswork.
2. **Validates Research Findings:** It provides a structured method to confirm whether observed effects or patterns in data are statistically significant or due to random chance.
3. **Measures Evidence Against the Null Hypothesis:** The p-value quantifies the strength of evidence against the null hypothesis, helping to determine whether to accept or reject it.
4. **Establishes Statistical Significance:** By comparing the p-value to a predetermined significance level (e.g., 0.05), researchers can assess whether results are likely to be meaningful or due to variability.
5. **Controls Error Rates:** Hypothesis testing helps manage the risks of Type I errors (false positives) and Type II errors (false negatives), improving the reliability of conclusions.
6. **Used Across Various Fields:** It is widely applied in medicine, economics, psychology, business, and other fields to test claims, treatments, or interventions.

7. **Enables Comparisons:** Hypothesis testing allows comparison between groups (e.g., treatment vs. control), making it essential for experimental design and analysis.
8. **Foundation for Advanced Analytics:** It serves as a basis for more complex statistical methods and machine learning models, which often rely on statistical significance for model validation.

Confidence Intervals and Significance Testing

Confidence intervals are a range of values, derived from sample data, used to estimate an unknown population parameter. For example, a 95% confidence interval means that if the same population is sampled multiple times, 95% of the calculated intervals would contain the true population parameter. Confidence intervals provide a measure of uncertainty around a sample estimate, indicating the precision of the estimate. Wider intervals suggest greater uncertainty, while narrower intervals indicate more precise estimates. On the other hand, significance testing is a method to evaluate if the results of an experiment are statistically meaningful. The primary objective of significance testing is to determine whether an observed effect or difference is likely to have occurred by chance. This is often done by calculating a p-value and comparing it to a significance level (commonly 0.05). If the p-value is smaller than the chosen level, the result is considered statistically significant, implying that the observed effect is unlikely to be due to random variation. Together, confidence intervals and significance testing provide powerful tools for decision-making and help quantify the uncertainty associated with statistical estimates. While significance testing helps assess the presence of an effect, confidence intervals offer a broader view of the likely range of that effect in the population.

Confidence intervals and significance tests are both statistical methods used to analyze data, but they provide different types of information. Confidence intervals provide a range of plausible values for a population parameter, while significance tests assess the evidence against a null hypothesis. In simpler terms, confidence intervals tell you how sure you are about your estimate, and significance tests tell you if there's a real effect.

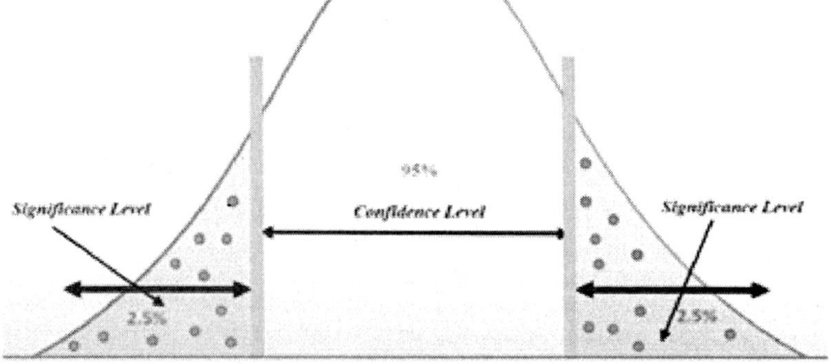

Fig. 3.4

Confidence Intervals: A confidence interval is a range of values that is likely to contain the true value of an unknown population parameter (like the population mean or proportion).

- **Interpretation:** A 95% confidence interval, for example, means that if we were to repeat the sampling process many times, 95% of the calculated intervals would contain the true population parameter.
- **Purpose:** Confidence intervals provide a measure of the precision of an estimate and give a range of plausible values for the parameter of interest.
- **Example:** A 95% confidence interval for the average height of adults in a city might be 5′6" to 5′10". This suggests that the true average height is likely within that range.

Significance Tests: Significance tests (also called hypothesis tests) assess the evidence against a specific null hypothesis (a statement about the population).

- **Process**: A test statistic is calculated, and its p-value is determined. The p-value is the probability of observing results as extreme as, or more extreme than, the observed results, assuming the null hypothesis is true.
- **Interpretation:** If the p-value is below a predetermined significance level (alpha, often 0.05), the null hypothesis is rejected. This suggests that the observed results are unlikely to have occurred by chance alone, and there is evidence against the null hypothesis.
- **Example:** A significance test might be used to determine if the average height of adults in a city is different from 5′8". The null hypothesis would be that the average height is 5′8". If the p-value is less than 0.05, the null hypothesis would be rejected, suggesting the average height is likely different from 5′8".

Relationship Between Confidence Intervals and Significance Tests:

- **Connection:** Confidence intervals and significance tests are related. A confidence interval can be used to perform a significance test. If the confidence interval for a parameter does not include the value specified by the null hypothesis, the null hypothesis can be rejected at the corresponding significance level.
- **Example:** If a 95% confidence interval for the mean difference between two groups does not include 0, it means the significance test would reject the null hypothesis of no difference at the 0.05 significance level.

Importance of Confidence Intervals and Significance Testing:

1. **Estimates Population Parameters:** Confidence intervals provide a range of values that likely contain the true population parameter, offering more information than a single point estimate.
2. **Measures Precision and Uncertainty:** Confidence intervals show the degree of uncertainty around an estimate narrow interval indicate more precise results, while wider intervals indicate more variability.

3. **Supports Reliable Decision-Making:** Both confidence intervals and significance testing help in making informed, statistically sound decisions in research, business, and policy.
4. **Assesses Statistical Significance:** Significance testing determines whether an observed effect is likely due to chance or represents a real difference, often using a p-value to guide conclusions.
5. **Interprets Effect Sizes More Clearly:** While significance testing tells if an effect exists, confidence intervals help understand the magnitude and direction of that effect.
6. **Improves Research Transparency:** Reporting confidence intervals alongside test results adds depth and clarity to findings, making research more transparent and credible.
7. **Guides Risk Assessment:** In areas like clinical trials or financial forecasting, confidence intervals help evaluate the risk and potential impact of decisions.
8. **Complements Hypothesis Testing:** Confidence intervals and significance tests work together if a confidence interval does not include the null value, the result is statistically significant.

9. Linear Algebra and Optimization Techniques

Linear Algebra and Optimization Techniques are fundamental components of data science, machine learning, and artificial intelligence. Linear algebra provides the mathematical foundation for handling and manipulating high-dimensional data. It deals with vectors, matrices, and linear transformations, which are essential for representing and computing data in models. For example, datasets are often structured as matrices, where rows represent observations and columns represent features. Operations like matrix multiplication, eigenvalue decomposition, and singular value decomposition (SVD) are key in dimensionality reduction, image processing, and recommendation systems. Concepts such as dot products, norms, and vector spaces help in understanding relationships between data points and are the backbone of algorithms like Principal Component Analysis (PCA), linear regression, and neural networks.

On the other hand, optimization techniques are used to find the best solution or minimize/maximize a function in a given context often a cost or loss function in machine learning. Optimization helps in tuning model parameters to improve performance. Techniques such as gradient descent, stochastic gradient descent (SGD), and constrained optimization are widely used for training models. Convex optimization is particularly important because many machine learning problems can be framed as convex, ensuring a global minimum is found. More advanced techniques like Newton's method and Lagrange multipliers are also used in specific scenarios. Together, linear algebra and optimization enable the design and training of efficient algorithms and models, making them indispensable tools for anyone working with data and building predictive or analytical systems. Their understanding is critical for interpreting model behavior and improving algorithmic performance.

Linear Algebra: Linear algebra is the branch of mathematics that deals with vectors, vector spaces, and linear transformations. Linear Algebra in data science offers essential tools for interacting with data in numerous approaches, understanding relationships between variables, performing dimensionality reduction, and solving systems of equations. Linear algebra techniques, including matrix operations and eigenvalue decomposition, are typically used for tasks like regression, clustering, and machine learning algorithms.

Importance of Linear Algebra: Linear algebra in data science is important because of its crucial role in numerous sector components.

1. It forms the backbone of machine learning algorithms, enabling operations like matrix multiplication, which are essential to model training and prediction.
2. Linear algebra techniques facilitate dimensionality reduction, enhancing the performance of data processing and interpretation.
3. Eigenvalues and eigenvectors help understand data records variability, influencing clustering and pattern recognition.
4. Solving systems of equations is crucial for optimization tasks and parameter estimation.
5. Furthermore, linear algebra supports image and signal processing strategies critical in data analysis.
6. Proficiency in linear algebra empowers data scientists to successfully represent, control, and extract insights from data, in the end driving the development of accurate models and informed decision-making.

Representation of Problems in Linear Algebra: In linear algebra, problems can frequently be represented and solved using matrices and vectors.

1. Many real-world situations can be translated into linear equations and converted right into a matrix structure.
2. Additionally, problems related to transformations, scaling, rotation, and projection, can be depicted using matrices.
3. Data units can be represented as matrices, in which every row corresponds to an observation and each column corresponds to a characteristic.
4. Eigenvalues and eigenvectors offer insights into dominant patterns and adjustments inside data, assisting in tasks like dimensionality reduction and understanding variability.
5. The usage of matrix operations can solve linear regression problems to discover optimal coefficients.
6. Classification problems can also be tackled using linear algebra strategies like

support vector machines, which involve mapping statistics into higher-dimensional spaces.

How is Linear Algebra used in Data Science?

Linear algebra in data science is considerably used for numerous tasks and strategies:

1. **Data Representation:** Data sets are often represented as matrices, wherein every row corresponds to an observation and every column represents a function. This matrix illustration permits efficient manipulation and data analysis.
2. **Matrix Operations:** Basic matrix operations like addition, multiplication, and transposition are used for numerous calculations, such as computing similarity measures, remodelling data, and solving equations.
3. **Dimensionality Reduction:** Singular Value Decomposition (SVD) and Principal Component Analysis (PCA) methods rely on principles from linear algebra to decrease the complexity of data while retaining critical information.
4. **Linear Regression:** Linear algebra is the base of linear regression, a widely used technique for modeling relationships between variables and depicting predictions.
5. **Machine Learning Algorithms:** Algorithms like support vector machines, linear discriminant evaluation, and logistic regression utilize linear algebra operations to build models and classify information.
6. **Image and Signal Processing:** Linear algebra strategies are vital in image processing responsibilities like filtering, compression, and edge detection. Fourier transforms, and convolutions contain linear algebra operations as well.
7. **Optimization:** Linear algebra is important for optimization algorithms utilized in machine learning, including gradient descent, based on calculating gradients.
8. **Eigenvalues and Eigenvectors:** These concepts assist in identifying dominant patterns and directions of variability in data, useful in clustering, feature extraction, and expert data characteristics.
9. **Data Visualization:** Dimensionality reduction techniques supplied through linear algebra, such as PCA, help visualize high-dimensional information in low-dimensional areas.
10. **Solving Equations:** Utilizing linear algebra techniques is a common approach to solving sets of linear equations, which emerge in scenarios involving optimization problems and the estimation of parameters.

Optimization Techniques: Optimization techniques are mathematical strategies used to find the most efficient solution to a problem, typically by maximizing or minimizing an objective function under certain constraints. In the context of data science and machine learning, optimization plays a central role, especially in training models, tuning parameters, and improving accuracy. The objective is often to minimize a cost or loss function, which measures the difference between predicted and actual outcomes, ensuring that the model learns to make better predictions over time.

One of the most widely used optimization techniques is Gradient Descent, a first-order iterative algorithm that adjusts model parameters in the direction of the negative gradient of the loss function. This process helps find a local minimum of the function. The size of each step is determined by the learning rate a critical hyperparameter. If the learning rate is too small, the convergence is slow; if too large, the model may overshoot the minimum or diverge. Variants of gradient descent include:

1. **Batch Gradient Descent:** Uses the entire dataset to compute gradients for each update.
2. **Stochastic Gradient Descent (SGD):** Uses one data point per update, adding noise that can help escape local minima.
3. **Mini-Batch Gradient Descent:** A hybrid approach that balances computational efficiency and convergence stability.

To further improve gradient descent, advanced optimization algorithms have been developed. Momentum helps accelerate updates by considering the past gradients, reducing oscillations. Nesterov Accelerated Gradient (NAG) improves on momentum by adjusting parameters based on an anticipated future position, leading to faster convergence.

Adaptive optimization algorithms adjust the learning rate during training. Adagrad increases the learning rate for infrequent parameters and decreases it for frequent ones. However, it may cause the learning rate to shrink too much over time. To address this, RMSprop maintains a moving average of squared gradients, normalizing them to maintain a more stable learning rate. Adam (Adaptive Moment Estimation) combines the benefits of both momentum and RMSprop, making it one of the most popular optimizers in deep learning tasks.

Besides gradient-based methods, second-order optimization techniques like Newton's Method use second derivatives (Hessian matrix) for faster convergence, especially in convex problems. However, they are computationally expensive and rarely used for large-scale problems due to the complexity of calculating the Hessian. In cases involving constraints (e.g., limited resources or specific conditions), constrained optimization methods like Lagrange multipliers and Karush-Kuhn-Tucker (KKT) conditions are applied. These are especially useful in economics, logistics, and operations research.

In combinatorial or non-differentiable problems, where gradient methods are ineffective, techniques like genetic algorithms, simulated annealing, and particle swarm optimization are used. These are known as heuristic or metaheuristic methods and are useful when the solution space is complex and traditional optimization is infeasible.

Optimization techniques are essential for efficiently solving real-world problems in data science, machine learning, and beyond. Choosing the right method depends on the nature of the problem, the complexity of the model, and the computational resources available. A deep understanding of these techniques enables data scientists to build better-performing and more robust systems.

Matrices and Vectors in Data Science

Matrices and vectors are core elements of linear algebra and play a vital role in data science. A vector is essentially a one-dimensional array that can represent a feature set, data point, or direction in space. For example, in a machine learning model, each data point (like a customer profile) can be represented as a vector of numerical features (e.g., age, income, location). A matrix is a two-dimensional array of numbers and is widely used to represent entire datasets, with rows as observations and columns as features. This structure allows for efficient storage and manipulation of data.

In data science, operations such as matrix multiplication, transpose, and dot products are used to implement and optimize algorithms. For instance, linear regression models use matrices to express the relationship between input variables and outputs, and predictions are computed using matrix-vector multiplication. Matrices are also essential in dimensionality reduction techniques like Principal Component Analysis (PCA), where the data is projected onto new axes. Vectors and matrices enable batch processing of data, leading to more efficient computation compared to looping over individual elements. Understanding how to work with them is crucial for building models, transforming data, and implementing scalable algorithms in real-world applications.

Importance of Matrices and Vectors:

1. **Efficient Data Representation**: Matrices and vectors provide a compact way to represent large datasets, where rows are observations and columns are features.
2. **Foundation of Machine Learning Models**: Many algorithms, such as linear regression, logistic regression, and neural networks, are built using matrix and vector operations.
3. **Enable Fast Computation**: Matrix operations allow for batch processing of data, making computations faster and more scalable using tools like NumPy and TensorFlow.
4. **Used in Dimensionality Reduction**: Techniques like PCA (Principal Component Analysis) rely on matrix algebra to reduce the number of features while preserving data variance.
5. **Facilitate Linear Transformations**: Matrices help perform transformations like rotation, scaling, and projection, which are important in data preprocessing and feature engineering.
6. **Core to Image and Text Processing**: In fields like computer vision and NLP,

images and word embeddings are represented as matrices and vectors, enabling effective analysis.

7. **Simplify Mathematical Notation and Derivations**: Using vectors and matrices makes complex statistical and machine learning models more interpretable and mathematically manageable.
8. **Power Optimization and Learning Algorithms**: Gradients, loss functions, and updates during model training are all calculated using vector and matrix operations.
9. **Support Parallel Computing**: Matrices can be processed in parallel on GPUs, making them ideal for handling big data and training deep learning models efficiently.
10. **Improve Model Performance and Accuracy**: Proper use of matrix algebra ensures precise computations, reducing errors and improving the performance of data-driven models.

Eigenvalues and Eigenvectors: Eigenvalues and eigenvectors are important concepts in linear algebra that help simplify matrix operations and are widely applied in data science, especially in areas like dimensionality reduction, feature extraction, and system stability analysis. Given a square matrix A, an eigenvector v is a non-zero vector that, when multiplied by A, results in a scalar multiple of itself $A \cdot v = \lambda \cdot v$, where λ is the eigenvalue. This property makes them powerful tools for analyzing linear transformations, allowing for the decomposition of complex systems into simpler components.

In data science, eigenvalues and eigenvectors are most notably used in Principal Component Analysis (PCA), where the goal is to reduce the number of features in a dataset while preserving as much variability as possible. The eigenvectors of the covariance matrix determine the principal components, and their corresponding eigenvalues indicate how much variance each component captures. This technique enables more efficient computation, improved model performance, and better visualization in high-dimensional datasets. Beyond PCA, eigenvalues are also used in spectral clustering, graph analysis, and assessing the stability of dynamic systems. Mastery of eigenvalues and eigenvectors allows data scientists to uncover hidden patterns, transform data more effectively, and build more interpretable models.

Importance of Eigenvalues and Eigenvectors:

1. **Dimensionality Reduction (PCA)**: Eigenvalues and eigenvectors are core to Principal Component Analysis (PCA), helping reduce the number of features while preserving maximum variance in the data.
2. **Feature Extraction**: They help identify the most informative directions (eigenvectors) in high-dimensional data, improving model performance and interpretability.
3. **Data Compression**: By projecting data onto the principal components

(eigenvectors), we can compress large datasets into lower-dimensional representations without significant information loss.

4. **Understanding Data Structure**: Eigenvectors reveal the structure and direction of data spread, while eigenvalues indicate the strength (variance) in each direction.
5. **Stability Analysis in Systems**: In dynamic systems and neural networks, eigenvalues are used to analyze stability and convergence behavior.
6. **Spectral Clustering**: Eigenvectors of graph Laplacians are used in spectral clustering to identify clusters in data based on graph structure.
7. **Graph and Network Analysis**: In social network analysis, eigenvector centrality measures a node's influence based on its connections and the importance of those connections.
8. **Solving Differential Equations**: Many machine learning models involve differential equations that are simplified using eigenvalue decomposition.
9. **Matrix Diagonalization**: Eigen decomposition allows complex matrices to be diagonalized, simplifying matrix operations and improving computational efficiency.
10. **Image and Signal Processing**: Eigenfaces (from eigenvectors) are used in face recognition, and similar methods apply in other pattern recognition tasks.

Gradient Descent and Optimization: Gradient descent is a widely used optimization algorithm in data science and machine learning for minimizing a cost or loss function. It works by computing the gradient (or derivative) of the loss function with respect to the model's parameters and iteratively updating these parameters in the direction that reduces the loss. In essence, gradient descent helps models "learn" by improving predictions through small, calculated adjustments. The learning rate, a hyperparameter, controls how large each step is; too high can overshoot the minimum, too low can slow convergence.

There are different variants of gradient descent, such as batch gradient descent, stochastic gradient descent (SGD), and mini-batch gradient descent, each with trade-offs in terms of speed and accuracy. Optimization techniques like momentum, RMSProp, and Adam build on gradient descent by adapting learning rates or smoothing gradients to enhance performance. These are essential when training neural networks and deep learning models, where loss surfaces are often complex and non-convex. Beyond machine learning, optimization is also used in operations research, logistics, and financial modeling. Understanding gradient descent and other optimization techniques is crucial for building efficient, accurate, and scalable models that perform well on real-world data.

Importance of Gradient Descent and Optimization:

1. **Core of Model Training**: Gradient descent is the backbone of training most machine learning and deep learning models by minimizing the loss function.

2. **Parameter Tuning**: Optimization techniques adjust model parameters iteratively to improve accuracy and reduce prediction errors.
3. **Works with Complex Models**: Gradient descent enables optimization of complex, high-dimensional, and non-linear models like neural networks.
4. **Efficient Learning from Data**: Optimization algorithms help models learn patterns from data efficiently, improving generalization and performance.
5. **Supports Large-Scale Computation**: Variants like stochastic and mini-batch gradient descent are well-suited for large datasets and big data environments.
6. **Enhances Convergence Speed**: Advanced optimizers like Adam, RMSprop, and Momentum accelerate convergence and avoid local minima.
7. **Minimizes Loss or Cost Functions**: The primary goal of gradient descent is to find the minimum value of loss functions, ensuring better model predictions.
8. **Improves Model Generalization**: Proper optimization reduces overfitting and underfitting, leading to models that perform well on unseen data.
9. **Applicable Across Domains**: Optimization is used not just in ML, but also in operations research, economics, logistics, and engineering problems.
10. **Supports Real-Time Learning**: Online learning algorithms use gradient-based optimization to update models in real time as new data arrives.

SUMMARY OF STATISTICS AND PROBABILITY FOR DATA SCIENCE

Data science relies heavily on statistics and probability to extract insights from data, build predictive models, and make data-driven decisions. These mathematical tools help data scientists understand patterns, measure uncertainty, and design intelligent algorithms. This summary outlines key concepts across probability theory, descriptive and inferential statistics, and the linear algebra and optimization techniques that power modern machine learning and analytics. Statistics and Probability for Data Science form the foundation for analyzing data, modeling uncertainty, and making informed decisions. Probability theory helps quantify the likelihood of events and supports techniques like Bayes' theorem and probability distributions (normal, binomial, Poisson). Descriptive statistics summarize data using measures of central tendency and dispersion, while inferential statistics enable hypothesis testing, p-values, confidence intervals, and significance testing to draw conclusions from samples. Linear algebra concepts such as matrices, vectors, eigenvalues, and eigenvectors facilitate data representation and dimensionality reduction. Optimization techniques like gradient descent are essential for training machine learning models efficiently and accurately.

7. Fundamentals of Probability

Fundamentals of Probability involve understanding how to measure the likelihood of events occurring in uncertain situations. It begins with basic concepts like sample space, events, and probability rules, including addition and multiplication rules for combined events. Conditional probability and independence help describe relationships between events. Bayes' Theorem allows updating probabilities based on new evidence. Probability distributions such as normal, binomial, and Poisson describe how probabilities are spread over outcomes, supporting data modeling and decision-making. These core principles form the basis for statistical inference, machine learning, and risk assessment in data science.

- **Basic Probability Theory:** Probability theory is the foundation of statistical reasoning and machine learning. It deals with quantifying uncertainty and predicting the likelihood of events. An event is any outcome or group of outcomes from a random process, and the probability of an event ranges from 0 (impossible) to 1 (certain). Key concepts include sample space, events, and conditional probability. The addition rule and multiplication rule help compute the probabilities of combined events. These basic rules form the basis for more complex modeling in areas like classification, recommendation systems, and anomaly detection.
- **Bayes' Theorem:** Bayes' Theorem is a fundamental concept in conditional probability that describes how to update the probability of a hypothesis based on new evidence. It is expressed as:

$$P(A|B) = \frac{P(B|A) \cdot P(A)}{P(B)}$$

  This formula allows us to reverse conditional probabilities and is widely used in Bayesian inference, spam filtering, diagnostics, and machine learning models like Naïve Bayes classifiers. Bayes' Theorem helps data scientists incorporate prior knowledge into predictions and decision-making processes, making it crucial for probabilistic modeling.
- **Probability Distributions (Normal, Binomial, Poisson):** Probability distributions describe how the values of a random variable are spread. In data science, three key distributions are:
  - **Normal Distribution**: A continuous, symmetric bell-shaped curve centered around the mean. It is commonly used due to the Central Limit Theorem, which states that the means of large samples follow a normal distribution.
  - **Binomial Distribution**: A discrete distribution representing the number of successes in a fixed number of independent trials with the same probability of success (e.g., flipping coins or customer conversions).
  - **Poisson Distribution**: A discrete distribution used to model the number of events occurring in a fixed interval of time or space, especially when the events happen independently (e.g., number of customer arrivals).

8. Descriptive and Inferential Statistics

Descriptive statistics summarize and organize data using measures like mean, median, mode (central tendency), and variance or standard deviation (dispersion), providing a clear overview of dataset characteristics. Inferential statistics use sample data to make predictions or decisions about a larger population through hypothesis testing, p-values, and confidence intervals. Hypothesis testing evaluates assumptions, while p-values measure result significance. Confidence intervals estimate parameter ranges with specified certainty. Together, these methods enable data scientists to understand data patterns, assess uncertainty, and draw meaningful conclusions, making them essential for data analysis and informed decision-making in various fields.

- **Measures of Central Tendency and Dispersion:** Descriptive statistics summarize and describe the main features of a dataset. Measures of central tendency mean, median, and mode help identify the "average" or typical value in a dataset. The mean is sensitive to outliers, while the median is more robust in skewed distributions. The mode is helpful for categorical data and identifying common values.

  Dispersion measures range, variance, and standard deviation describe how data is spread around the center. A high standard deviation means the data is more spread out, while a low standard deviation indicates tight clustering around the mean. These measures help understand data variability, detect outliers, and evaluate model accuracy.

- **Hypothesis Testing and p-values:** Hypothesis testing is a method to determine whether a statement about a population parameter is supported by sample data. It involves a null hypothesis *(H_0)* typically stating no effect and an alternative hypothesis *(H_1)* indicating the presence of an effect or difference.

  The result of the test is evaluated using a p-value, which indicates the probability of observing the sample results (or more extreme) under the assumption that the null hypothesis is true. A p-value less than 0.05 (common threshold) suggests that the observed results are statistically significant, leading to the rejection of H_0. This method is widely used in *A/B* testing, clinical trials, and model evaluation.

- **Confidence Intervals and Significance Testing:** Confidence intervals (CIs) provide a range of values within which the true population parameter is likely to fall, based on sample data. A 95% confidence interval means that if we repeated the sampling process multiple times, 95% of those intervals would contain the true value. CIs offer more information than p-values by indicating the precision and uncertainty of estimates.

  Significance testing, closely tied to hypothesis testing, assesses whether the results are likely to be meaningful or just due to random variation. Together, confidence intervals and significance testing allow analysts to make robust, statistically sound decisions and assess model reliability.

9. Linear Algebra and Optimization Technique

Linear algebra provides essential tools for data science through vectors and matrices, enabling efficient data representation and manipulation. Concepts like eigenvalues and eigenvectors help reveal underlying data structures and support dimensionality reduction techniques such as PCA. Optimization techniques, especially gradient descent, are crucial for training machine learning models by minimizing loss functions and improving accuracy. Advanced optimizers like Adam and RMSprop enhance learning speed and stability. Together, linear algebra and optimization form the mathematical backbone of modern data science, facilitating scalable computations, model training, and effective analysis of complex datasets.

- **Matrices and Vectors in Data Science:** Vectors and matrices are fundamental in organizing and computing data. A vector is a one-dimensional array representing features or data points, while a matrix is a two-dimensional array representing datasets (rows as samples, columns as features). These structures are used to represent data in linear models, neural networks, and data transformations.

  Operations like matrix multiplication, transpose, and dot products enable batch computation, which is much faster and more efficient than element-wise operations. Vectors and matrices also enable linear transformations key for data normalization, projection, and rotation. Tools like NumPy, Pandas, and TensorFlow are built around these mathematical structures.

- **Eigenvalues and Eigenvectors:** Eigenvalues and eigenvectors simplify matrix operations and provide insight into the underlying structure of data. In Principal Component Analysis (PCA), eigenvectors represent the principal components new feature directions while eigenvalues indicate the importance (variance) captured by each component. This makes PCA an effective tool for dimensionality reduction and noise elimination.

  Eigenvalues and eigenvectors are also used in spectral clustering, graph analysis, and to analyze system stability in dynamic models. Understanding them is crucial for advanced data modeling, especially when working with large or high-dimensional datasets.

- **Gradient Descent and Optimization:** Gradient descent is the most widely used optimization algorithm in data science. It minimizes a loss function by iteratively adjusting parameters in the opposite direction of the gradient (slope). This helps models learn patterns in data and improve prediction accuracy. Variants include:

  - **Stochastic Gradient Descent (SGD):** This updates weights based on a single data point per iteration.
  - **Mini-batch Gradient Descent:** This combines efficiency and stability by using subsets of data.
  - **Momentum, RMSprop, and Adam:** These are advanced optimizers that adapt learning rates and accelerate convergence.

Beyond gradient descent, constrained optimization (e.g., using Lagrange multipliers) is used in economics, resource allocation, and mathematical programming. In non-differentiable or complex solution spaces, heuristic methods like genetic algorithms and simulated annealing are used. Optimization is the key to training scalable and high-performing machine learning models.

Statistics and probability provide the mathematical language and tools that power data science. From understanding and summarizing data to building predictive models and optimizing performance, each concept plays a vital role. Probability theory helps quantify uncertainty, statistical techniques enable evidence-based decisions, and linear algebra and optimization support the computational frameworks behind modern AI systems. Mastery of these topics equips data scientists to tackle real-world problems with confidence, precision, and efficiency.

Chapter 4

Machine Learning Fundamentals

Machine learning plays a crucial role in data science, serving as one of its core components and enabling data-driven decision-making across various fields. In data science, the goal is to extract meaningful insights and knowledge from large and complex datasets, and machine learning provides the tools and techniques to automate this process. By using algorithms that can learn from data patterns, machine learning helps data scientists build predictive and classification models that can identify trends, forecast future events, and support business strategies. Supervised learning is often used for regression and classification tasks, such as predicting customer behavior or diagnosing diseases, while unsupervised learning is used for tasks like customer segmentation and anomaly detection. Reinforcement learning, although less common, is used in dynamic environments such as recommendation systems and robotics. The machine learning workflow in data science typically involves data preprocessing, model training, evaluation, and deployment, making it a systematic and iterative process that improves over time with more data.

In practical applications, machine learning empowers data scientists to tackle real-world problems with greater accuracy and efficiency. For example, in e-commerce, ML models can analyze customer purchase histories to recommend products, while in healthcare, they can identify patterns in patient records to predict potential illnesses. In the financial sector, machine learning is widely used for credit scoring, fraud detection, and market analysis. ML also plays a key role in natural language processing and image recognition, enabling innovations like chatbots, virtual assistants, and facial recognition systems. One of the major advantages of machine learning in data science is its scalability; it can process vast amounts of data far beyond human capability. However, it also requires careful consideration of model accuracy, bias, and interpretability. Data scientists must ensure that the models are not only accurate but also fair and explainable. As data science continues to grow, machine learning remains a driving force, transforming raw data into actionable intelligence and pushing the boundaries of what is possible through data analysis.

Need for Machine Learning: Machine learning is important because it allows computers to learn from data and improve their performance on specific tasks without being explicitly programmed. This ability to learn from data and adapt to new situations makes machine learning particularly useful for tasks that involve large amounts of data, complex decision-making, and dynamic environments. Some specific areas where machine learning is being used:

1. **Predictive Modeling:** Machine learning can be used to build predictive models that can help businesses make better decisions. For example, machine learning can be used to predict which customers are most likely to buy a particular product, or which patients are most likely to develop a certain disease.
2. **Natural Language Processing (NLP):** Machine learning is used to build systems that can understand and interpret human language. This is important for applications such as voice recognition, chatbots, and language translation.
3. **Computer Vision:** Machine learning is used to build systems that can recognize and interpret images and videos. This is important for applications such as self-driving cars, surveillance systems, and medical imaging.
4. **Fraud Detection:** Machine learning can be used to detect fraudulent behavior in financial transactions, online advertising, and other areas.
5. **Recommendation Systems:** Machine learning can be used to build recommendation systems that suggest products, services, or content to users based on their past behavior and preferences.

Overall, machine learning has become an essential tool for many businesses and industries, as it enables them to make better use of data, improve their decision-making processes, and deliver more personalized experiences to their customers.

Machine Learning Lifecycle: The machine learning lifecycle includes:

1. **Defining the Problem:** Clearly identify the real-world problem to be solved.
2. **Data Collection:** Gather necessary data from various sources.
3. **Data Cleaning and Preprocessing:** Resolve data quality issues and prepare the data for analysis.
4. **Exploratory Data Analysis (EDA):** Analyze data to identify patterns, outliers, and trends.
5. **Feature Engineering and Selection:** Enhance data features and select relevant ones to improve model performance.
6. **Model Selection:** Choose suitable models based on the problem type and data characteristics.
7. **Model Training:** Train the model using a split of training and validation datasets.
8. **Model Evaluation and Tuning:** Assess and optimize the model using relevant metrics.
9. **Model Deployment:** Implement the model in a production environment for real-time predictions.

10. **Model Monitoring and Maintenance:** Regularly check and update the model to maintain accuracy.

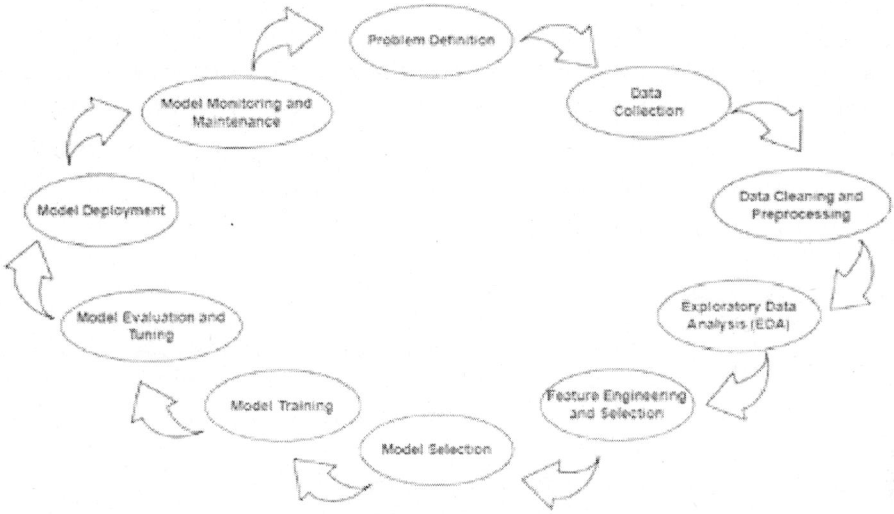

Fig. 4.1 Machine Learning Life Cycle

How machine learning algorithms work?

A machine learning algorithm works by learning patterns and relationships from data to make predictions or decisions without being explicitly programmed for each task. A simplified overview of how a typical machine learning algorithm works:

1. **Data Collection:** First, relevant data is collected or curated. This data could include examples, features, or attributes that are important for the task at hand, such as images, text, numerical data, etc.
2. **Data Preprocessing:** Before feeding the data into the algorithm, it often needs to be pre-processed. This step may involve cleaning the data (handling missing values, outliers), transforming the data (normalization, scaling), and splitting it into training and test sets.
3. **Choosing a Model:** Depending on the task (e.g., classification, regression, clustering), a suitable machine learning model is chosen. Examples include decision trees, neural networks, support vector machines, and more advanced models like deep learning architectures.
4. **Training the Model:** The selected model is trained using the training data. During training, the algorithm learns patterns and relationships in the data. This involves adjusting model parameters iteratively to minimize the difference between predicted outputs and actual outputs (labels or targets) in the training data.
5. **Evaluating the Model:** Once trained, the model is evaluated using the test

data to assess its performance. Metrics such as accuracy, precision, recall, or mean squared error are used to evaluate how well the model generalizes to new, unseen data.

6. **Fine-tuning:** Models may be fine-tuned by adjusting hyperparameters (parameters that are not directly learned during training, like learning rate or number of hidden layers in a neural network) to improve performance.
7. **Prediction or Inference:** Finally, the trained model is used to make predictions or decisions on new data. This process involves applying the learned patterns to new inputs to generate outputs, such as class labels in classification tasks or numerical values in regression tasks.

10. Supervised Learning

Supervised Learning is a type of machine learning where the model is trained on a labeled dataset—that is, a dataset that includes both the input data and the correct output. The goal of supervised learning is to learn a mapping from inputs to outputs, so the model can predict the correct output for new, unseen inputs. This approach is called "supervised" because the learning process is guided by the known answers (labels) in the training data.

Supervised learning is commonly used for two main types of tasks: classification and regression. In classification, the output variable is a category, such as identifying whether an email is spam or not. In regression, the output is a continuous value, such as predicting house prices or stock market trends. Popular algorithms used in supervised learning include Linear Regression, Logistic Regression, Decision Trees, Support Vector Machines (SVM), and Neural Networks. The success of supervised learning depends heavily on the quality and quantity of the labeled data, as well as careful tuning of the model to avoid problems like overfitting or underfitting.

How Supervised Machine Learning Works?

Where supervised learning algorithm consists of input features and corresponding output labels. The process works through:

1. **Training Data:** The model is provided with a training dataset that includes input data (features) and corresponding output data (labels or target variables).
2. **Learning Process:** The algorithm processes the training data, learning the relationships between the input features and the output labels. This is achieved by adjusting the model's parameters to minimize the difference between its predictions and the actual labels.

After training, the model is evaluated using a test dataset to measure its accuracy and performance. Then the model's performance is optimized by adjusting parameters and using techniques like cross-validation to balance bias and variance. This ensures the model generalizes well to new, unseen data.

In summary, supervised machine learning involves training a model on labeled data to learn patterns and relationships, which it then uses to make accurate predictions on new data.

Let's learn how a supervised machine learning model is trained on a dataset to learn a mapping function between input and output, and then with learned function is used to make predictions on new data:

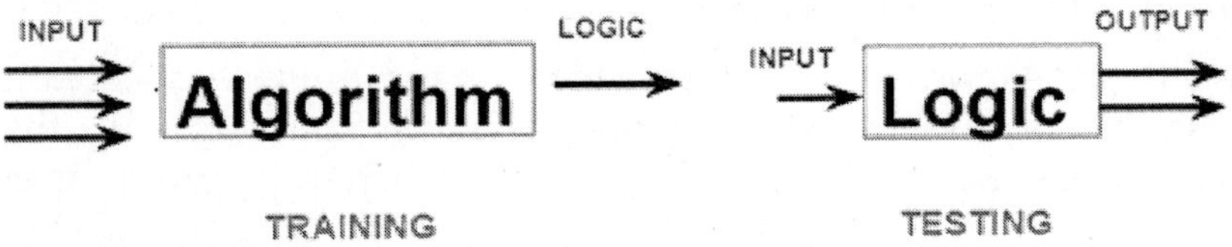

Fig. 4.2

In the image above,

1. **Training** phase involves feeding the algorithm labeled data, where each data point is paired with its correct output. The algorithm learns to identify patterns and relationships between the input and output data.
2. **Testing** phase involves feeding the algorithm new, unseen data and evaluating its ability to predict the correct output based on the learned patterns.

Supervised Machine Learning Algorithms: Supervised learning can be further divided into several different types, each with its own unique characteristics and applications. Here are some of the most common types of supervised learning algorithms:

1. **Linear Regression:** Linear regression is a type of supervised learning regression algorithm that is used to predict a continuous output value. It is one of the simplest and most widely used algorithms in supervised learning.
2. **Logistic Regression :** Logistic regression is a type of supervised learning classification algorithm that is used to predict a binary output variable.
3. **Decision Trees :** Decision tree is a tree-like structure that is used to model decisions and their possible consequences. Each internal node in the tree represents a decision, while each leaf node represents a possible outcome.
4. **Random Forests :** Random forests again are made up of multiple decision trees that work together to make predictions. Each tree in the forest is trained on a different subset of the input features and data. The final prediction is made by aggregating the predictions of all the trees in the forest.
5. **Support Vector Machine (SVM) :** The SVM algorithm creates a hyperplane to segregate n-dimensional space into classes and identify the correct category of new data points. The extreme cases that help create the hyperplane are called support vectors, hence the name Support Vector Machine.
6. **K-Nearest Neighbors (KNN) :** KNN works by finding k training examples closest to a given input and then predicts the class or value based on the

majority class or average value of these neighbors. The performance of KNN can be influenced by the choice of k and the distance metric used to measure proximity.

7. **Gradient Boosting :** Gradient Boosting combines weak learners, like decision trees, to create a strong model. It iteratively builds new models that correct errors made by previous ones.
8. **Naive Bayes Algorithm:** The Naive Bayes algorithm is a supervised machine learning algorithm based on applying Bayes' Theorem with the "naive" assumption that features are independent of each other given the class label.

The differences between supervised machine learning algorithms are in table 4.1.

Table 4.1

Algorithm	Regression, Classification	Purpose	Method	Use Cases
Linear Regression	Regression	Predict continuous output values	Linear equation minimizing sum of squares of residuals	Predicting continuous values
Logistic Regression	Classification	Predict binary output variable	Logistic function transforming linear relationship	Binary classification tasks
Decision Trees	Both	Model decisions and outcomes	Tree-like structure with decisions and outcomes	Classification and Regression tasks
Random Forests	Both	Improve classification and regression accuracy	Combining multiple decision trees	Reducing overfitting, improving prediction accuracy
SVM	Both	Create hyperplane for classification or predict continuous values	Maximizing margin between classes or predicting continuous values	Classification and Regression tasks
KNN	Both	Predict class or value based on k closest neighbors	Finding k closest neighbors and predicting based on majority or average	Classification and Regression tasks, sensitive to noisy data
Gradient Boosting	Both	Combine weak learners to create strong model	Iteratively correcting errors with new models	Classification and Regression tasks to improve prediction accuracy
Naive Bayes		Predict class based on feature independence assumption	Bayes' theorem with feature independence assumption	Text classification, spam filtering, sentiment analysis, medical

These types of supervised learning in machine learning vary based on the problem you're trying to solve and the dataset you're working with. In classification problems, the task is to assign inputs to predefined classes, while regression problems involve predicting numerical outcomes.

Regression (Linear, Logistic)

Regression is a fundamental concept in supervised machine learning, used to model relationships between input variables (features) and a target variable (output). It helps predict a continuous or categorical outcome based on past data. Regression is a supervised learning technique used to predict outcomes based on input features. Linear regression is used when the output variable is continuous, such as predicting a house price, temperature, or sales amount. It assumes a linear relationship between the input variables (features) and the target output. The algorithm fits a straight line through the data that best minimizes the error between the predicted values and the actual outcomes, using a method called least squares.

Linear regression is simple to interpret and quick to train, making it a strong baseline model for many real-world problems. However, it struggles with complex, non-linear relationships and can be influenced by outliers.

Logistic regression, despite its name, is used for classification tasks, typically binary classification such as spam vs. not spam or disease vs. no disease. It uses the logistic (sigmoid) function to map predicted values between 0 and 1, representing the probability that a given input belongs to a particular class. If the probability is above a certain threshold (commonly 0.5), it is classified into one category; otherwise, it falls into the other. Logistic regression is efficient and works well when the data is linearly separable. However, it cannot capture complex patterns in data, making it less effective for tasks requiring non-linear decision boundaries.

Linear Regression: Linear Regression is used when the target variable is continuous, meaning it can take any real value within a range (e.g., predicting house prices, temperature, or sales). The goal of linear regression is to find the best-fitting straight line (also known as the regression line) that describes the relationship between the independent variables (X) and the dependent variable (Y). The mathematical form of linear regression is:

$$Y = \beta_0 + \beta_1 X_1 + \beta_2 X_2 + \cdots + \beta_n X_n + \varepsilon$$

Where:

- Y is the predicted output
- $X_1, X_2, \ldots, X_n$ are the input features
- β_0 is the intercept
- $\beta_1, \beta_2, \ldots, \beta_n$ are the coefficients (slopes)
- ε is the error term

Why Linear Regression is Important? Reason why linear regression is important:

1. **Simplicity and Interpretability:** It's easy to understand and interpret, making it a starting point for learning about machine learning.
2. **Predictive Ability**: Helps predict future outcomes based on past data, making it useful in various fields like finance, healthcare and marketing.

3. **Basis for Other Models:** Many advanced algorithms, like logistic regression or neural networks, build on the concepts of linear regression.
4. **Efficiency:** It's computationally efficient and works well for problems with a linear relationship.
5. **Widely Used:** It's one of the most widely used techniques in both statistics and machine learning for regression tasks.
6. **Analysis:** It provides insights into relationships between variables (e.g., how much one variable influence another).

Best Fit Line in Linear Regression: In linear regression, the best-fit line is the straight line that most accurately represents the relationship between the independent variable (input) and the dependent variable (output). It is the line that minimizes the difference between the actual data points and the predicted values from the model.

1. **Goal of the Best-Fit Line:** The goal of linear regression is to find a straight line that minimizes the error (the difference) between the observed data points and the predicted values. This line helps us predict the dependent variable for new, unseen data.

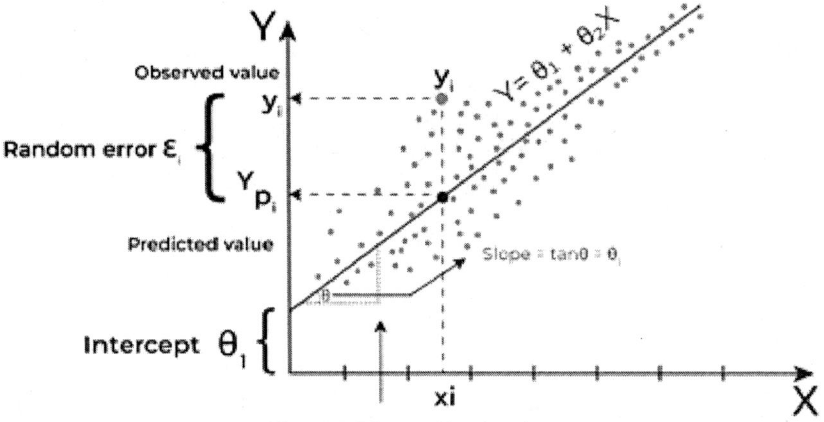

Fig. 4.3 Linear Regression

Here, *Y* is called a dependent or target variable and *X* is called an independent variable also known as the predictor of *Y*. There are many types of functions or modules that can be used for regression. A linear function is the simplest type of function. Here, **X** may be a single feature or multiple features representing the problem.

2. **Equation of the Best-Fit Line:** For simple linear regression (with one independent variable), the best-fit line is represented by the equation

   $y = mx + b$

   Where:

   - y is the predicted value (dependent variable)
   - x is the input (independent variable)

- *m* is the slope of the line (how much y changes when *x* changes)
- *b* is the intercept (the value of y when $x = 0$)

The best-fit line will be the one that optimizes the values of *m* (slope) and *b* (intercept) so that the predicted y values are as close as possible to the actual data points.

3. **Minimizing the Error: The Least Squares Method:** To find the best-fit line, we use a method called Least Squares. The idea behind this method is to minimize the sum of squared differences between the actual values (data points) and the predicted values from the line. These differences are called residuals.

   The formula for residuals is:

   $Residual = y_i - \hat{y}_i$

   Where:

   - y_i is the actual observed value
   - $\hat{y}_i$ is the predicted value from the line for that x_i

   The least squares method minimizes the sum of the squared residuals:

   $Sum of squared errors(SSE) = \Sigma(y_i - \hat{y}_i)^2$

   This method ensures that the line best represents the data where the sum of the squared differences between the predicted values and actual values is as small as possible.

4. **Interpretation of the Best-Fit Line**
   - **Slope (m):** The slope of the best-fit line indicates how much the dependent variable (y) changes with each unit change in the independent variable (x). For example, if the slope is 5, it means that for every 1-unit increase in x, the value of y increases by 5 units.
   - **Intercept (b):** The intercept represents the predicted value of y when x = 0. It's the point where the line crosses the y-axis.

Assumptions of the Linear Regression

1. **Linearity**: The relationship between inputs (X) and the output (Y) is a straight line.

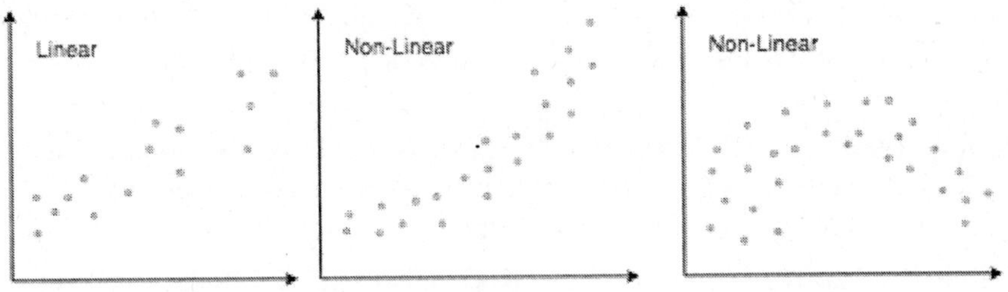

Fig. 4.4

2. **Independence of Errors**: The errors in predictions should not affect each other.
3. **Constant Variance (Homoscedasticity):** The errors should have equal spread across all values of the input. If the spread changes (like fans out or shrinks), it's called heteroscedasticity and it's a problem for the model.

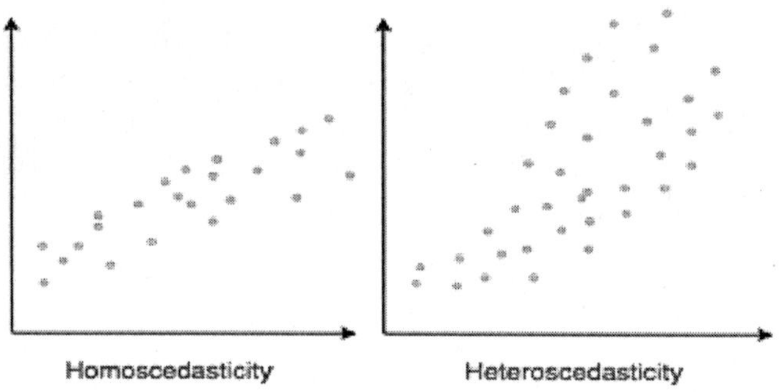

Fig. 4.5

4. **Normality of Errors**: The errors should follow a normal (bell-shaped) distribution.
5. **No Multicollinearity (for multiple regression)**: Input variables shouldn't be too closely related to each other.
6. **No Autocorrelation**: Errors shouldn't show repeating patterns, especially in time-based data.
7. **Additivity**: The total effect on Y is just the sum of effects from each X, no mixing or interaction between them.'

Logistic Regression: Logistic Regression is a supervised machine learning algorithm used for classification problems. Unlike linear regression which predicts continuous values it predicts the probability that an input belongs to a specific class. It is used for binary classification where the output can be one of two possible categories such as Yes/No, True/False or 0/1. It uses sigmoid function to convert inputs into a probability value between 0 and 1. In this article, we will see the basics of logistic regression and its core concepts. The assumptions behind logistic regression is important to ensure the model is applied correctly, main assumptions are:

1. **Independent Observations**: Each data point is assumed to be independent of the others means there should be no correlation or dependence between the input samples.
2. **Binary Dependent Variables**: It takes the assumption that the dependent variable must be binary, means it can take only two values. For more than two categories SoftMax functions are used.
3. **Linearity Relationship Between Independent Variables and Log Odds**: The model assumes a linear relationship between the independent variables and

the log odds of the dependent variable which means the predictors affect the log odds in a linear way.

4. **No Outliers:** The dataset should not contain extreme outliers as they can distort the estimation of the logistic regression coefficients.

5. **Large Sample Size:** It requires a sufficiently large sample size to produce reliable and stable results.

How does Logistic Regression work?

Logistic regression model transforms the linear regression function continuous value output into categorical value output using a sigmoid function which maps any real-valued set of independent variables input into a value between 0 and 1. This function is known as the logistic function.

Suppose we have input features represented as a matrix:

$$X = \begin{bmatrix} x_{11} & \cdots & x_{1m} \\ x_{21} & \cdots & x_{2m} \\ \vdots & \ddots & \vdots \\ x_{n1} & \cdots & x_{nm} \end{bmatrix}$$

and the dependent variable is *Y* having only binary value i.e., 0 or 1.

$$Y = \begin{cases} 0 & \text{if } Class\ 1 \\ 1 & \text{if } Class\ 2 \end{cases}$$

then, apply the multi-linear function to the input variables **X**.

$$z = \left(\sum_{i=1}^{n} w_i x_i\right) + b$$

Here ***xi*** is the ith*ith* observation of **X**, ***wi* = *[w1, w2, w3,ï", wm]*** is the weights or Coefficient and ***b*** is the bias term also known as intercept. Simply this can be represented as the dot product of weight and bias.

$$z = w \cdot X + b$$

At this stage, ***z*** is a continuous value from the linear regression. Logistic regression then applies the sigmoid function to ***z*** to convert it into a probability between 0 and 1 which can be used to predict the class.

Now we use the sigmoid function where the input will be *z* and we find the probability between 0 and 1. i.e. predicted *y*.

$$\sigma(z) = \frac{1}{1+e^{-z}}$$

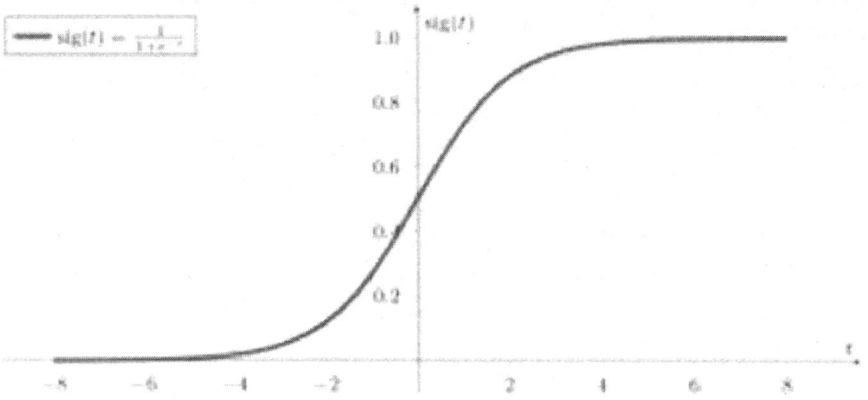

Fig. 4.6

As shown above in fig.4.6 the sigmoid function converts the continuous variable data into the probability i.e between 0 and 1.

- $\sigma(z)$ tends towards 1 as $z \to \infty$
- $\sigma(z)$ tends towards 0 as $z \to -\infty$
- $\sigma(z)$ is always bounded between 0 and 1

where the probability of being a class can be measured as:

$$P(y=1) = \sigma(z)$$
$$P(y=0) = 1 - \sigma(z)$$

Terminologies involved in Logistic Regression: Some common terms involved in logistic regression:

1. **Independent Variables:** These are the input features or predictor variables used to make predictions about the dependent variable.
2. **Dependent Variable**: This is the target variable that we aim to predict. In logistic regression, the dependent variable is categorical.
3. **Logistic Function**: This function transforms the independent variables into a probability between 0 and 1 which represents the likelihood that the dependent variable is either 0 or 1.
4. **Odds**: This is the ratio of the probability of an event happening to the probability of it not happening. It differs from probability because probability is the ratio of occurrences to total possibilities.
5. **Log-Odds (Logit)**: The natural logarithm of the odds. In logistic regression, the log-odds are modeled as a linear combination of the independent variables and the intercept.

6. **Coefficient**: These are the parameters estimated by the logistic regression model which shows how strongly the independent variables affect the dependent variable.
7. **Intercept**: The constant term in the logistic regression model which represents the log-odds when all independent variables are equal to zero.
8. **Maximum Likelihood Estimation (MLE)**: This method is used to estimate the coefficients of the logistic regression model by maximizing the likelihood of observing the given data.

Types of Logistic Regression: Logistic regression can be classified into three main types based on the nature of the dependent variable:

1. **Binomial Logistic Regression**: This type is used when the dependent variable has only two possible categories. Examples include Yes/No, Pass/Fail or 0/1. It is the most common form of logistic regression and is used for binary classification problems.
2. **Multinomial Logistic Regression**: This is used when the dependent variable has three or more possible categories that are not ordered. For example, classifying animals into categories like "cat," "dog" or "sheep." It extends the binary logistic regression to handle multiple classes.
3. **Ordinal Logistic Regression**: This type applies when the dependent variable has three or more categories with a natural order or ranking. Examples include ratings like "low," "medium" and "high." It takes the order of the categories into account when modeling.

Differences Between **Linear Regression and Logistic Regression:** Table 4.3 shows the differences between Linear Regression and Logistic Regression.

Table 4.3

S.No.	Aspect	Linear Regression	Logistic Regression
1.	Output Type	Continuous numeric values	Probabilities (ranging from 0 to 1)
2.	Target Variable	Continuous (e.g., price, temperature)	Categorical (e.g., yes/no, spam/not spam)
3.	Algorithm Purpose	Used for prediction of quantities (regression)	Used for classification (binary or multi-class)
4.	Function Used	Linear function	Sigmoid (logistic) function
5.	Evaluation Metrics	Mean Squared Error (MSE), R^2 score	Accuracy, Precision, Recall, F1-score, AUC
6.	Output Interpretation	Direct value prediction	Predicted probability converted to class label

Classification (Decision Trees, Random Forest, SVM)

Classification refers to predicting a category or class label from a set of input features. Decision trees are one of the most intuitive classification models. They split the data into branches based on conditions on the features, continuing until they reach a decision or class label. This model is easy to interpret and visualize, making it suitable for small datasets and scenarios where model explainability is essential. However, decision trees can easily overfit the data, especially if they grow too deep and start modeling noise rather than actual patterns.

To address overfitting, Random Forest is used. It is an ensemble method that builds multiple decision trees and combines their outputs using majority voting (for classification) or averaging (for regression). By training each tree on a random subset of the data and features, random forests increase accuracy and robustness while reducing variance. Another powerful classification algorithm is the Support Vector Machine (SVM), which aims to find the best hyperplane that separates different classes in the data. It works well in high-dimensional spaces and with non-linear data by using kernel functions. However, SVMs can be computationally intensive and difficult to interpret.

Decision Trees: A Decision Tree is a supervised machine learning algorithm used for both classification and regression tasks. It models decisions in a tree-like structure, where internal nodes represent features, branches represent decision rules, and leaf nodes represent outcomes or class labels. The tree splits the data based on the most significant feature at each node, typically using criteria like Gini impurity or information gain. One major advantage of decision trees is their interpretability they mimic human decision-making and can be visualized easily. They can handle both numerical and categorical data and do not require feature scaling. However, decision trees are prone to overfitting, especially when the tree becomes too deep or complex. Pruning techniques can help reduce overfitting by trimming unnecessary branches. Although they are relatively fast and easy to use, decision trees can be unstable small changes in data can lead to very different trees. Despite these limitations, decision trees are a popular choice for quick, interpretable models and are often used as building blocks in more advanced ensemble techniques like Random Forest and Gradient Boosting.

A Decision Tree helps us make decisions by showing different options and how they are related. It has a tree-like structure that starts with one main question called the root node which represents the entire dataset. From there, the tree branches out into different possibilities based on features in the data.

1. **Root Node:** Starting point representing the whole dataset.
2. **Branches:** Lines connecting nodes showing the flow from one decision to another.
3. **Internal Nodes:** Points where decisions are made based on data features.
4. **Leaf Nodes:** End points of the tree where the final decision or prediction is made.

How Decision Trees Work?

1. **Start with the Root Node:** It begins with a main question at the root node which is derived from the dataset's features.

2. **Ask Yes/No Questions:** From the root, the tree asks a series of yes/no questions to split the data into subsets based on specific attributes.
3. **Branching Based on Answers:** Each question leads to different branches:
   - If the answer is yes, the tree follows one path.
   - If the answer is no, the tree follows another path.
4. **Continue Splitting:** This branching continues through further decisions helps in reducing the data down step-by-step.
5. **Reach the Leaf Node:** The process ends when there are no more useful questions to ask leading to the leaf node where the final decision or prediction is made.

Example: A simple example to understand how it works. Imagine we need to decide whether to drink coffee based on the time of day and how tired we feel. The tree first checks the time:

1. In the morning: It asks "Tired?"
   - If yes, the tree suggests drinking coffee.
   - If no, it says no coffee is needed.
2. In the afternoon: It asks again "Tired?"
   - If yes, it suggests drinking coffee.
   - If no, no coffee is needed.

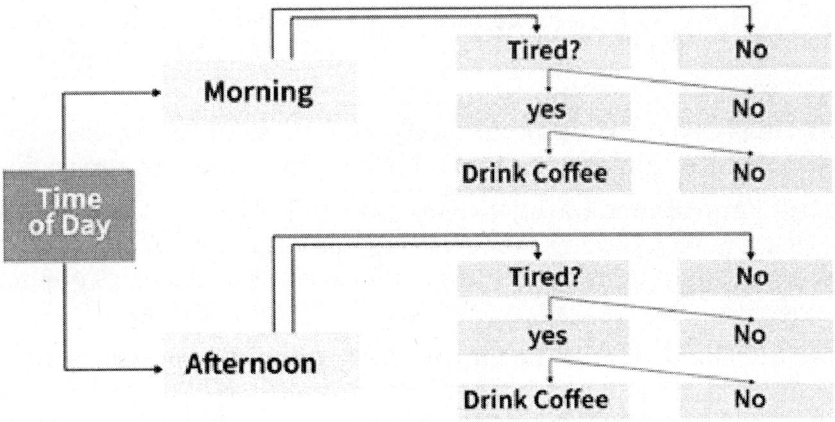

Fig. 4.7

Advantages of Decision Trees

1. **Easy to Understand:** Decision Trees are visual which makes it easy to follow the decision-making process.
2. **Versatility:** Can be used for both classification and regression problems.

3. **No Need for Feature Scaling:** Unlike many machine learning models, it don't require us to scale or normalize our data.
4. **Handles Non-linear Relationships:** It captures complex, non-linear relationships between features and outcomes effectively.
5. **Interpretability:** The tree structure is easy to interpret helps in allowing users to understand the reasoning behind each decision.
6. **Handles Missing Data:** It can handle missing values by using strategies like assigning the most common value or ignoring missing data during splits.

Disadvantages of Decision Trees

1. **Overfitting:** They can overfit the training data if they are too deep which means they memorize the data instead of learning general patterns. This leads to poor performance on unseen data.
2. **Instability:** It can be unstable which means that small changes in the data may lead to significant differences in the tree structure and predictions.
3. **Bias towards Features with Many Categories:** It can become biased toward features with many distinct values which focuses too much on them and potentially missing other important features which can reduce prediction accuracy.
4. **Difficulty in Capturing Complex Interactions:** Decision Trees may struggle to capture complex interactions between features which helps in making them less effective for certain types of data.
5. **Computationally Expensive for Large Datasets:** For large datasets, building and pruning a Decision Tree can be computationally intensive, especially as the tree depth increases.

Applications of Decision Trees: Decision Trees are used across various fields due to their simplicity, interpretability and versatility, some key applications:

1. **Loan Approval in Banking:** Banks use Decision Trees to assess whether a loan application should be approved. The decision is based on factors like credit score, income, employment status and loan history. This helps predict approval or rejection helps in enabling quick and reliable decisions.
2. **Medical Diagnosis:** In healthcare they assist in diagnosing diseases. For example, they can predict whether a patient has diabetes based on clinical data like glucose levels, BMI and blood pressure. This helps classify patients into diabetic or non-diabetic categories, supporting early diagnosis and treatment.
3. **Predicting Exam Results in Education:** Educational institutions use to predict whether a student will pass or fail based on factors like attendance, study time and past grades. This helps teachers identify at-risk students and offer targeted support.

4. **Customer Churn Prediction:** Companies use Decision Trees to predict whether a customer will leave or stay based on behavior patterns, purchase history, and interactions. This allows businesses to take proactive steps to retain customers.
5. **Fraud Detection:** In finance, Decision Trees are used to detect fraudulent activities, such as credit card fraud. By analyzing past transaction data and patterns, Decision Trees can identify suspicious activities and flag them for further investigation.

Random Forest: Random Forest is a machine learning algorithm that uses many decision trees to make better predictions. Each tree looks at different random parts of the data and their results are combined by voting for classification or averaging for regression. This helps in improving accuracy and reducing errors. Assumptions of Random Forest

1. **Each tree makes its own decisions**: Every tree in the forest makes its own predictions without relying on others.
2. **Random parts of the data are used**: Each tree is built using random samples and features to reduce mistakes.
3. **Enough data is needed**: Sufficient data ensures the trees are different and learn unique patterns and variety.
4. **Different predictions improve accuracy**: Combining the predictions from different trees leads to a more accurate final result.

Working of Random Forest Algorithm:

1. **Create Many Decision Trees:** The algorithm makes many decision trees each using a random part of the data. So, every tree is a bit different.
2. **Pick Random Features:** When building each tree, it doesn't look at all the features (columns) at once. It picks a few at random to decide how to split the data. This helps the trees stay different from each other.
3. **Each Tree Makes a Prediction:** Every tree gives its own answer or prediction based on what it learned from its part of the data.
4. **Combine the Predictions:**
   - For **classification** we choose a category as the final answer is the one that most trees agree on i.e., majority voting.
   - For **regression** we predict a number as the final answer is the average of all the trees predictions.
5. **Why It Works Well:** Using random data and features for each tree helps avoid overfitting and makes the overall prediction more accurate and trustworthy.

Key Features of Random Forest

1. **Handles Missing Data:** It can work even if some data is missing so you don't always need to fill in the gaps yourself.

2. **Shows Feature Importance:** It tells you which features (columns) are most useful for making predictions which helps you understand your data better.
3. **Works Well with Big and Complex Data:** It can handle large datasets with many features without slowing down or losing accuracy.
4. **Used for Different Tasks:** You can use it for both classification like predicting types or labels and **regression** like predicting numbers or amounts.

Advantages of Random Forest

1. Random Forest provides very accurate predictions even with large datasets.
2. Random Forest can handle missing data well without compromising with accuracy.
3. It doesn't require normalization or standardization on dataset.
4. When we combine multiple decision trees it reduces the risk of overfitting of the model.

Limitations of Random Forest

1. It can be computationally expensive especially with a large number of trees.
2. It's harder to interpret the model compared to simpler models like decision trees.

Support Vector Machines (SVM)

Support Vector Machine (SVM) is a supervised machine learning algorithm used for classification and regression tasks. It tries to find the best boundary known as hyperplane that separates different classes in the data. It is useful when you want to do binary classification like spam vs. not spam or cat vs. dog.

The main goal of SVM is to maximize the margin between the two classes. The larger the margin the better the model performs on new and unseen data.

Key Concepts of Support Vector Machine

1. **Hyperplane:** A decision boundary separating different classes in feature space and is represented by the equation $wx + b = 0$ in linear classification.
2. **Support Vectors:** The closest data points to the hyperplane, crucial for determining the hyperplane and margin in SVM.
3. **Margin:** The distance between the hyperplane and the support vectors. SVM aims to maximize this margin for better classification performance.
4. **Kernel:** A function that maps data to a higher-dimensional space enabling SVM to handle non-linearly separable data.
5. **Hard Margin:** A maximum-margin hyperplane that perfectly separates the data without misclassifications.
6. **Soft Margin:** Allows some misclassifications by introducing slack variables, balancing margin maximization and misclassification penalties when data is not perfectly separable.

7. **C:** A regularization term balancing margin maximization and misclassification penalties. A higher C value forces stricter penalty for misclassifications.
8. **Hinge Loss:** A loss function penalizing misclassified points or margin violations and is combined with regularization in SVM.
9. **Dual Problem:** Involves solving for Lagrange multipliers associated with support vectors, facilitating the kernel trick and efficient computation.

How does Support Vector Machine Algorithm Work? The key idea behind the SVM algorithm is to find the hyperplane that best separates two classes by maximizing the margin between them. This margin is the distance from the hyperplane to the nearest data points (support vectors) on each side.

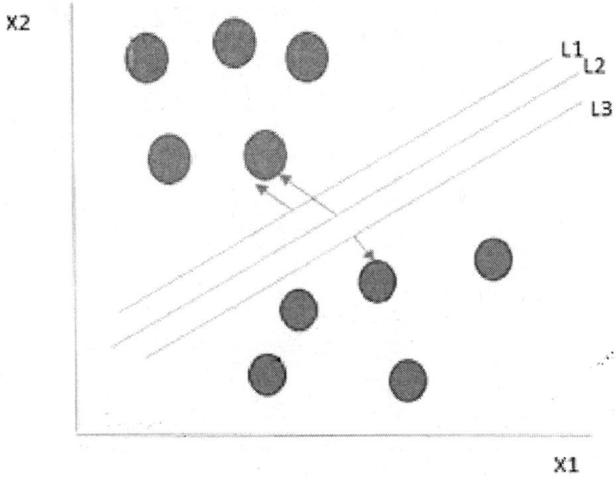

Fig. 4.8

The best hyperplane also known as the "hard margin" is the one that maximizes the distance between the hyperplane and the nearest data points from both classes. This ensures a clear separation between the classes. So, from the above figure, we choose L2 as hard margin. Let's consider a scenario like shown below:

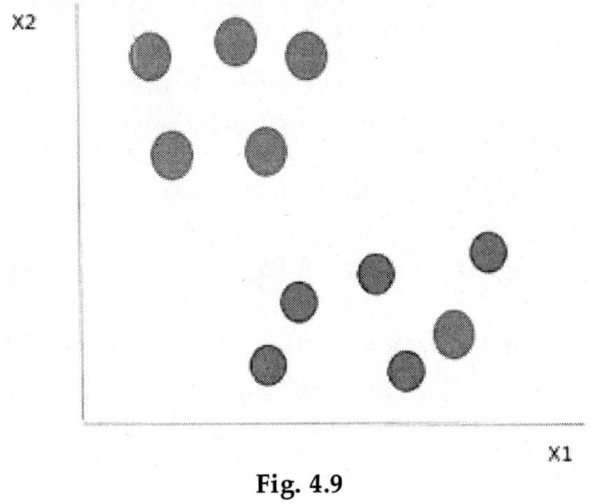

Fig. 4.9

Here, we have one blue ball in the boundary of the red ball.

Differences Between Decision Trees, Random Forest, and Support Vector Machines (SVM): Table 4.6 shows the differences between Decision Trees, Random Forest, and Support Vector Machines (SVM).

Table 4.6

S.No.	Aspect	Decision Trees	Support Vector Machines (SVM)	Support Vector Machines (SVM)
1.	Algorithm Type	Supervised (classification & regression)	Ensemble (Bagging of decision trees)	Supervised (mostly classification, also regression)
2.	Model Structure	Tree-like structure with nodes and leaves	Multiple decision trees combined	Hyperplane-based classifier
3.	Interpretability	Highly interpretable and visual	Less interpretable due to multiple trees	Low interpretability
4.	Overfitting Risk	High, especially with deep trees	Low (trees are averaged to reduce overfitting)	Low to moderate (depends on parameters)
5.	Performance on Large Data	Fast on small data, slower on large data	Slower due to many trees, but scales better	Computationally expensive on large datasets
6.	Handling non-linearity	Limited (no kernel-based transformation)	Better than single tree due to ensemble voting	Excellent (with kernel trick)
7.	Accuracy	Moderate	High (more robust and stable)	High (especially in high-dimensional data)
8.	Sensitivity to Noise	High	Lower (due to averaging over multiple trees)	Can be sensitive without proper tuning

Model Evaluation Metrics (Accuracy, Precision, Recall, F1-score)

Evaluating a machine learning model goes beyond just accuracy, especially in classification problems where class imbalance is an issue. Accuracy is the ratio of correctly predicted instances to the total instances. While it gives a quick measure of performance, it can be misleading in imbalanced datasets. For example, if 95 out of 100 samples belong to one class, predicting all as that class gives 95% accuracy but fails to detect the minority class entirely.

Precision, Recall, and F1-score are more informative in such cases. Precision is the proportion of true positives out of all predicted positives it measures how many selected items are relevant. Recall (or sensitivity) is the proportion of true positives out of all actual positives it shows how many relevant items were selected. The F1-score is the harmonic mean of precision and recall, providing a balance between the two, especially useful when the cost of false positives and false negatives is high. These metrics give a more complete picture of a model's performance, especially in real-world applications like medical diagnosis or fraud detection.

Accuracy: Accuracy is a fundamental model evaluation metric that represents the proportion of correct predictions made by a model out of the total number of predictions. It's calculated by dividing the number of correct predictions by the total number of predictions. While simple to understand and calculate, accuracy can be misleading when dealing with imbalanced datasets where one class has significantly more instances than others.

$$\text{Accuracy} = \frac{\text{Number of Correct Predictions}}{\text{Total Number of Predictions}}$$

In other words, it tells you how often the classifier is right. For instance, if a model makes 100 predictions and 90 are correct, the accuracy is 90%.

Accuracy is simple to understand and effective when the classes are balanced, meaning there are roughly equal numbers of examples from each class. However, it becomes misleading in the case of imbalanced datasets. For example, in a dataset where 95% of the samples belong to one class, a model that always predicts that class will achieve 95% accuracy even if it fails to identify any instances of the minority class.

Because of this limitation, accuracy is often used along with other metrics like precision, recall, and F1-score, especially in critical domains like healthcare or fraud detection, where false positives or false negatives can have serious consequences. While accuracy gives a quick general idea of model performance, it should not be the sole metric used for evaluation, particularly when the dataset is skewed or when one class is much more important than the others.

Precision: Precision measures how many of the positive predictions made by the model are actually correct. It's useful when the cost of false positives is high such as in medical diagnoses where predicting a disease when it's not present can have serious consequences.

$$\text{Precision} = \frac{\text{TP}}{\text{TP} + \text{FP}}$$

Where:

- TP = True Positives
- FP = False Positives

For example, in a spam detection system, if the model predicts 100 emails as spam but only 80 are actually spam, the precision is 80%. High precision indicates that the model is making very few false positive errors. Precision is particularly important in situations where false positives are costly. In medical testing, for instance, predicting a disease when a patient does not actually have it could lead to unnecessary treatments and anxiety. Similarly, in email filtering, classifying important messages as spam can cause users to miss critical information.

However, precision does not account for false negatives, which is where recall comes in. Therefore, it is often evaluated in combination with recall and the F1-score to get a more comprehensive understanding of a model's performance. A high precision score alone doesn't mean the model is great it simply means when the model predicts a positive, it's likely correct. If a model is too conservative and predicts very few positives, it might have high precision but very low recall.

Recall: Recall, also known as sensitivity or the true positive rate, is a model evaluation metric that measures a model's ability to correctly identify all relevant instances (positive cases). It's the proportion of actual positives that are correctly classified as positive by the model. A high recall score indicates that the model is good at detecting positive cases, minimizing false negatives.

$$\text{Recall} = \frac{\text{TP}}{\text{TP} + \text{FN}}$$

For example, in cancer detection, if 100 patients have cancer and the model identifies 85 of them correctly, the recall is 85%. High recall means the model captures most of the actual positives.

Recall is especially important in situations where missing a positive instance is critical. In healthcare, failing to detect a disease (false negative) can delay treatment. In fraud detection, not identifying fraudulent activity could result in significant financial loss. Hence, in such contexts, high recall is prioritized, even if it comes at the expense of lower precision.

However, a model can achieve high recall simply by classifying most instances as positive, which may result in many false positives. This is why precision and recall are usually considered together. A good model needs to balance both, which is where the F1-score becomes helpful. Overall, recall is a vital metric when the cost of false negatives is high, and it provides a deeper view into model performance than accuracy alone.

F1-Score: The F1-score is the harmonic mean of precision and recall, offering a single metric that balances both. It is especially useful when you need to strike a balance between false positives and false negatives, and when dealing with imbalanced datasets.

$$\text{F1 Score} = 2 \times \frac{\text{Precision} \times \text{Recall}}{\text{Precision} + \text{Recall}}$$

Unlike the arithmetic mean, the harmonic mean gives more weight to lower values. This means the F1-score will be high only when both precision and recall are high. If either metric is low, the F1-score drops significantly, making it a good measure of a model's overall classification effectiveness.

The F1-score is particularly important in situations where neither false positives nor false negatives can be ignored. For instance, in spam detection or credit card fraud detection, you want to catch most positive cases (high recall) without wrongly labeling too many normal cases (high precision). The F1-score helps assess this trade-off in a single number.

One limitation is that it gives equal weight to precision and recall. In some applications, you might care more about one than the other. In such cases, a weighted version like the F β -score can be used, where β allows you to favor recall or precision. Nonetheless, the F1-score is a widely used and reliable metric for classification model evaluation, especially in complex or imbalanced datasets.

Differences Between Accuracy, Precision, Recall and F1-score: The difference between Accuracy, Precision, Recall and F1-score is listed in table 4.5.

Table 4.5

Metric	Definition	Focus	Best For	Limitation
Accuracy	Ratio of all correct predictions to total predictions	Overall correctness	Balanced datasets with equal class importance	Misleading with imbalanced data
Precision	Ratio of true positives to total predicted positives	Correctness of positive predictions	When false positives are costly (e.g., spam filter)	Ignores false negatives
Recall	Ratio of true positives to total actual positives	Coverage of actual positives	When false negatives are costly (e.g., disease detection)	Ignores false positives
F1-score	Harmonic mean of precision and recall	Balance between precision & recall	Imbalanced data or when both errors are important	Hard to interpret, assumes equal importance of precision and recall

11. Unsupervised Learning

Unsupervised learning is a type of machine learning where the algorithm is given data without explicit labels or outputs. Unlike supervised learning, where the model is trained on input-output pairs, unsupervised learning works with unlabeled data and aims to discover hidden patterns, groupings, or structures within it. The goal is to make sense of the data by identifying similarities or relationships without any prior knowledge of the outcomes. Common tasks in unsupervised learning include clustering, dimensionality reduction, and association rule mining.

A popular example of unsupervised learning is clustering, where data points are grouped into clusters based on similarity such as customer segmentation in marketing. Another example is dimensionality reduction, used to simplify high-dimensional data while retaining its essential features; techniques like PCA (Principal Component Analysis) help visualize complex data or speed up model performance. Unsupervised learning is widely used in fields such as biology (e.g., gene grouping), cybersecurity (e.g., anomaly detection), and natural language processing (e.g., topic modeling). While powerful, its main challenge lies in evaluating results, as there is no ground truth to compare against. Despite this, unsupervised learning remains essential for exploring and understanding unstructured or unlabeled data.

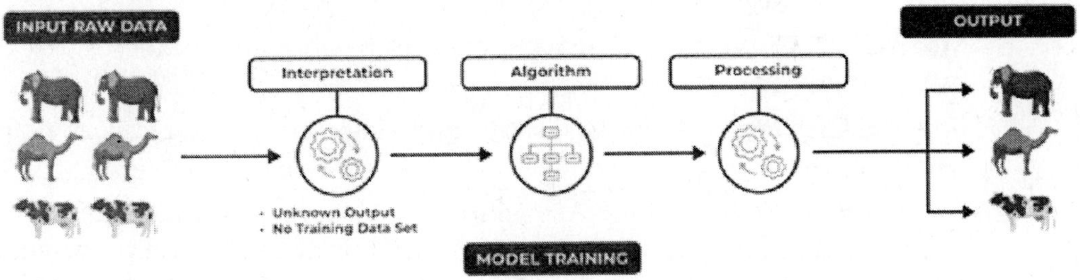

Fig. 4.10

The image shows set of animals: elephants, camels, and cows that represents raw data that the unsupervised learning algorithm will process.

1. **Interpretation:** The "Interpretation" stage signifies that the algorithm doesn't have predefined labels or categories for the data. It needs to figure out how to group or organize the data based on inherent patterns.
2. **Algorithm:** Algorithm represents the core of unsupervised learning process using techniques like clustering, dimensionality reduction, or anomaly detection to identify patterns and structures in the data.
3. **Processing:** Processing stage shows the algorithm working on the data.

The output shows the results of the unsupervised learning process. In this case, the algorithm might have grouped the animals into clusters based on their species (elephants, camels, cows).

Unsupervised Learning Algorithms: There are mainly 3 types of Algorithms which are used for Unsupervised dataset.

1. **Clustering Algorithms:** Clustering in unsupervised machine learning is the process of grouping unlabeled data into clusters based on their similarities. The goal of clustering is to identify patterns and relationships in the data without any prior knowledge of the data's meaning.

   Broadly this technique is applied to group data based on different patterns, such as similarities or differences, our machine model finds. These algorithms are used to process raw, unclassified data objects into groups. For example, in the above figure, we have not given output parameter values, so this technique will be used to group clients based on the input parameters provided by our data.

   Some common clustering algorithms:

   K-means Clustering: Groups data into K clusters based on how close the points are to each other.

   - **Hierarchical Clustering:** Creates clusters by building a tree step-by-step, either merging or splitting groups.
   - **Density-Based Clustering (DBSCAN):** Finds clusters in dense areas and treats scattered points as noise.
   - **Mean-Shift Clustering:** Discovers clusters by moving points toward the most crowded areas.
   - **Spectral Clustering:** Groups data by analyzing connections between points using graphs.
2. **Association Rule Learning:** Association rule learning is also known as association rule mining is a common technique used to discover associations in unsupervised machine learning. This technique is a rule-based ML technique that finds out some very useful relations between parameters of a large data

set. This technique is basically used for market basket analysis that helps to better understand the relationship between different products.

For example, shopping stores use algorithms based on this technique to find out the relationship between the sale of one product w.r.t to another's sales based on customer behavior. Like if a customer buys milk, then he may also buy bread, eggs, or butter. Once trained well, such models can be used to increase their sales by planning different offers.

Some common Association Rule Learning algorithms:

- **Apriori Algorithm:** Finds patterns by exploring frequent item combinations step-by-step.
- **FP-Growth Algorithm:** An Efficient Alternative to Apriori. It quickly identifies frequent patterns without generating candidate sets.
- **Eclat Algorithm:** Uses intersections of itemsets to efficiently find frequent patterns.
- **Efficient Tree-based Algorithms:** Scales to handle large datasets by organizing data in tree structures.

3. **Dimensionality Reduction:** Dimensionality reduction is the process of reducing the number of features in a dataset while preserving as much information as possible. This technique is useful for improving the performance of machine learning algorithms and for data visualization.

   Imagine a dataset of 100 features about students (height, weight, grades, etc.). To focus on key traits, you reduce it to just 2 features: height and grades, making it easier to visualize or analyze the data.

   Some popular Dimensionality Reduction algorithms:

   - **Principal Component Analysis (PCA):** Reduces dimensions by transforming data into uncorrelated principal components.
   - **Linear Discriminant Analysis (LDA):** Reduces dimensions while maximizing class separability for classification tasks.
   - **Non-negative Matrix Factorization (NMF):** Breaks data into non-negative parts to simplify representation.
   - **Locally Linear Embedding (LLE):** Reduces dimensions while preserving the relationships between nearby points.
   - **Isomap:** Captures global data structure by preserving distances along a manifold.

Challenges of Unsupervised Learning: Here are the key challenges of unsupervised learning:

1. **Noisy Data**: Outliers and noise can distort patterns and reduce the effectiveness of algorithms.

2. **Assumption Dependence**: Algorithms often rely on assumptions (e.g., cluster shapes), which may not match the actual data structure.
3. **Overfitting Risk**: Overfitting can occur when models capture noise instead of meaningful patterns in the data.
4. **Limited Guidance**: The absence of labels restricts the ability to guide the algorithm toward specific outcomes.
5. **Cluster Interpretability**: Results, such as clusters, may lack clear meaning or alignment with real-world categories.
6. **Sensitivity to Parameters**: Many algorithms require careful tuning of hyperparameters, such as the number of clusters in k-means.
7. **Lack of Ground Truth**: Unsupervised learning lacks labeled data, making it difficult to evaluate the accuracy of results.

Applications of Unsupervised Learning: Unsupervised learning has diverse applications across industries and domains. Key applications include:

1. **Customer Segmentation:** Algorithms cluster customers based on purchasing behavior or demographics, enabling targeted marketing strategies.
2. **Anomaly Detection:** Identifies unusual patterns in data, aiding fraud detection, cybersecurity, and equipment failure prevention.
3. **Recommendation Systems**: Suggests products, movies, or music by analyzing user behavior and preferences.
4. **Image and Text Clustering:** Groups similar images or documents for tasks like organization, classification, or content recommendation.
5. **Social Network Analysis:** Detects communities or trends in user interactions on social media platforms.
6. **Astronomy and Climate Science:** Classifies galaxies or groups weather patterns to support scientific research

Clustering (K-Means, DBSCAN, Hierarchical)

Distance or density-based methods, such as Local Outlier Factor (LOF), score each point based on the local density around it. Points in low-density areas relative to their neighbors are likely anomalies. Anomaly detection poses several challenges. Anomalies are rare and often not well-defined, making model training and evaluation difficult. Also, the definition of "anomalous" may vary by context. Model performance can be measured using precision, recall, and F1-score, especially important in imbalanced settings where anomalies are few. Visualization techniques like t-SNE or PCA can help visually assess anomaly separability.

K-Means: K-Means clustering is a popular unsupervised machine learning algorithm used to partition a dataset into K distinct, non-overlapping clusters based on feature similarity. The algorithm works by initializing K cluster centroids, assigning each data point to the nearest centroid using a distance metric (typically Euclidean), and then updating each centroid to be the mean of the points assigned to it. This process iterates until the centroids stabilize or a maximum number of iterations is reached. K-Means is valued for its simplicity, speed, and scalability, especially with large datasets. It is best suited for data with clearly separable, roughly spherical clusters of similar size. Common applications include customer segmentation, image compression, pattern recognition, and anomaly detection, where data points far from cluster centres may be considered outliers. Despite its strengths, K-Means has limitations it requires the number of clusters (K) to be defined in advance, is sensitive to outliers, and may converge to local minima depending on the initial centroid placement. Techniques like K-Means++ help mitigate initialization issues, and methods like the elbow method assist in selecting an optimal K. While K-Means assumes clusters are convex and isotropic, it remains a foundational algorithm for exploratory data analysis and clustering tasks, offering intuitive results that are easy to interpret and apply in real-world scenarios.

How K-Means Works:

1. **Initialization**: Select K initial centroids, either randomly or using strategies like K-Means++.
2. **Assignment**: Assign each data point to the nearest centroid based on a distance metric (typically Euclidean distance).
3. **Update**: Recalculate the centroids as the mean of all points assigned to that cluster.
4. **Repeat**: Continue the assignment and update steps until centroids stabilize or a set number of iterations is reached.

K-Means is computationally efficient, with a time complexity of O(n * k * i * d), where *n* is the number of data points, *k* is the number of clusters, *i* is the number of iterations, and *d* is the dimensionality. It's particularly effective for large datasets with clear, spherical-shaped clusters.

Importance and Applications: The importance and applications of K-Means are as:

1. **Scalability**: One of K-Means' greatest strengths is its scalability to large datasets. It can be used on millions of data points with relatively low computational cost, making it ideal for big data environments.
2. **Simplicity and Interpretability**: The output of K-Means a set of clusters with centroids is easy to interpret. This makes it a popular first step in exploratory data analysis, customer segmentation, and pattern recognition.
3. **Market Segmentation**: In business and marketing, K-Means is frequently used to identify customer groups with similar behaviors or demographics, enabling personalized marketing strategies.
4. **Image Compression and Segmentation**: In computer vision, K-Means can

reduce the number of color in an image (compression) or separate objects in an image (segmentation) by clustering pixel values.

5. **Anomaly Detection**: Points far from their assigned cluster centres can be considered anomalies, useful in detecting fraud or unusual behavior in data.
6. **Recommendation Systems**: K-Means can group users or items into clusters, allowing systems to make group-based recommendations.

Limitations: The limitations of K-Means are as:

1. **Predefined K**: The need to choose the number of clusters beforehand can be challenging without domain knowledge.
2. **Sensitivity to Outliers**: Outliers can heavily skew centroids, leading to suboptimal clusters.
3. **Assumes Spherical Clusters**: It performs poorly when clusters have irregular shapes or are of varying densities.

Despite these limitations, enhancements such as K-Means++ initialization, elbow method for choosing K, and combination with other techniques (e.g., PCA for dimensionality reduction) have improved its robustness.

DBSCAN: DBSCAN (Density-Based Spatial Clustering of Applications with Noise) is an unsupervised clustering algorithm that groups data points based on density, making it highly effective for discovering clusters of arbitrary shapes and identifying outliers. It requires two parameters: epsilon (å), which defines the neighbourhood radius, and minPts, the minimum number of points required to form a dense region. Points are classified as core points (dense areas), border points (near core points but not dense enough), or noise (isolated points). DBSCAN starts from a core point and recursively expands clusters by exploring its å-neighbourhood. Unlike K-Means, it does not require specifying the number of clusters in advance and is robust to noise and outliers. This makes it ideal for applications like geospatial analysis, fraud detection, and biological data clustering. However, DBSCAN can struggle in datasets with varying densities and is sensitive to the choice of å and minPts. Despite this, its ability to discover complex structures without assumptions of cluster shape or size makes it a powerful and flexible clustering method, especially in real-world data where traditional methods like K-Means may fail.

How DBSCAN Works: DBSCAN classifies data points into three types:

1. **Core Points**: Have at least minPts points (including themselves) within a distance ε (epsilon).
2. **Border Points**: Are within ε of a core point but have fewer than minPts neighbors themselves.
3. **Noise Points**: Are neither core nor border points.

The algorithm starts from a random point and explores its neighbourhood:

1. If it's a core point, a new cluster is formed.

2. Border points are added to the cluster, but don't expand it.
3. The process continues recursively until all points are processed.

Importance and Applications: The importance and applications of DBSCAN are as:

1. **No Need to Specify K**: Unlike K-Means, DBSCAN doesn't require the number of clusters in advance, making it ideal for exploratory analysis when the number of natural clusters is unknown.
2. **Handles Arbitrary Shapes**: DBSCAN excels at discovering clusters of any shape, unlike K-Means which assumes spherical clusters. This is especially useful in geographic or biological data where natural groupings aren't convex.
3. **Robust to Noise**: One of DBSCAN's key strengths is its ability to label outliers explicitly. This is critical in fields like fraud detection, network security, and fault diagnosis.
4. **Geospatial Applications**: DBSCAN is heavily used in mapping and location-based services to find dense areas (e.g., groups of users, vehicles, or crime hotspots).
5. **Astronomical and Scientific Data**: Because of its density-based nature, DBSCAN is used in scientific research to identify celestial objects or experimental anomalies that deviate from normal density patterns.
6. **Social Network Analysis**: Clusters of densely connected individuals can be identified, aiding in understanding community structures and information flow.

Limitations: The limitations of DBSCAN are as:

1. **Parameter Sensitivity**: The results depend heavily on the choice of ε and minPts. Incorrect values can lead to missed clusters or misclassified noise.
2. **Performance Degrades with High Dimensions**: In high-dimensional data, distance metrics become less meaningful (curse of dimensionality), and DBSCAN's accuracy can drop.

Hierarchical: Hierarchical refers to a system or structure in which elements are ranked or organized according to levels of importance, authority, or status. It is commonly used in organizational, social, and biological contexts. In a hierarchical organization, authority flows from the top down, with each level subordinate to the one above. For example, in a corporate setting, the CEO sits at the top of the hierarchy, followed by executives, managers, and employees at the base. Hierarchies help maintain order and clarify roles and responsibilities. They provide a clear chain of command and streamline decision-making processes. However, they can also create barriers to communication and innovation, especially when lower levels feel disconnected or disempowered.

Hierarchical structures are not limited to organizations. In computer science, file systems are often hierarchical, with folders containing subfolders and files. Similarly, in biology, taxonomy is hierarchical, classifying life from broad categories (kingdoms) down to specific species. While efficient in many cases, hierarchical systems can become rigid and slow to adapt. Modern trends in management and technology often favor flatter, more collaborative structures that promote agility and open communication, challenging traditional hierarchies and encouraging more distributed forms of leadership and responsibility.

Importance and Applications: The importance applications of hierarchical systems are as:

1. **Clear Structure:** Provides an organized framework with defined levels of authority and responsibility.
2. **Efficient Decision-Making:** Decisions flow from top levels, reducing confusion and streamlining processes.
3. **Accountability:** Clear reporting lines make it easier to assign responsibility and evaluate performance.
4. **Scalability:** Easy to manage large organizations or systems by dividing them into smaller, manageable units.
5. **Control and Supervision:** Enables consistent oversight and enforcement of rules, policies, and objectives.
6. **Organizations and Businesses:** Corporate structures from CEO to entry-level staff.
7. **Government and Military:** Clear chains of command and authority.
8. **Education Systems:** From national ministries down to local schools and classrooms.

Limitations: The limitations of hierarchical systems are as:

1. **Inflexibility:** Can be slow to adapt to change or innovation.
2. **Communication Barriers:** Information may get distorted as it moves up or down levels.
3. **Bureaucracy:** May result in excessive procedures and red tape.
4. **Employee Disempowerment:** Lower levels may feel undervalued or less motivated.
5. **Overcentralisation:** Decisions from the top may not reflect ground realities.

Differences Between K-Means, DBSCAN, Hierarchical: The differences between K-Means, DBSCAN, Hierarchical is listed in table 4.7.

Table 4.7

S.No.	Feature / Criteria	K-Means	DBSCAN	Hierarchical Clustering
1.	Number of Clusters	Must be specified in advance	Not required; determined by density	Not required; can be cut at different levels
2.	Shape of Clusters	Works best with spherical clusters	Can find clusters of arbitrary shapes	Can find clusters of arbitrary shapes
3.	Noise Handling	Does not handle noise well	Can identify and exclude noise (outliers)	Does not handle noise explicitly
4.	Scalability	Very scalable to large datasets	Less scalable to very large datasets	Least scalable due to high time complexity
5.	Deterministic Output	No (depends on initial centroids)	Yes (deterministic)	Yes (deterministic)
6.	Use Case Suitability	Suitable for compact, well-separated clusters	Good for data with noise and varying densities	Good for nested or hierarchical relationships

Dimensionality Reduction (PCA, t-SNE)

Dimensionality reduction is a data preprocessing technique used in machine learning to reduce the number of input features or variables in a dataset while preserving its essential patterns and structure. High-dimensional data can be challenging to visualize, analyze, or model effectively due to noise, redundancy, and increased computational complexity a challenge known as the "curse of dimensionality." Dimensionality reduction simplifies such datasets by transforming them into a lower-dimensional space, making them easier to interpret and process. Two popular methods are Principal Component Analysis (PCA) and t-distributed Stochastic Neighbour Embedding (t-SNE). PCA is a linear method that transforms data into new variables called principal components, which capture the maximum variance in the dataset using fewer dimensions. It is widely used for noise reduction and speeding up algorithms. In contrast, t-SNE is a non-linear technique that focuses on preserving the local relationships between data points, making it particularly effective for visualizing complex patterns in high-dimensional data such as images or word embeddings. While PCA is computationally efficient and interpretable, t-SNE offers better visual clustering but is slower and harder to generalize. Overall, dimensionality reduction is essential for improving model performance, interpretability, and data visualization in modern machine learning workflows.

PCA: PCA, or Principal Component Analysis, is a dimensionality reduction technique used to simplify complex datasets by transforming them into a smaller set of uncorrelated variables called principal components. These components capture the most significant variations in the original data, allowing for easier analysis and visualization. Applications:

1. **Data analysis:** PCA helps in identifying patterns and relationships within data.
2. **Data visualization:** It can be used to reduce the number of dimensions for easier visualization of high-dimensional data.

3. **Machine learning:** PCA can be used to preprocess data before feeding it to machine learning models, improving their performance and efficiency.
4. **Feature extraction:** PCA can identify the most important features in a dataset, which can be used in other machine learning tasks.
5. **Noise reduction:** By focusing on the principal components that capture the most variance, PCA can help filter out noise and irrelevant information in the data

How it works:

1. **Data transformation:** PCA transforms the original data into a new coordinate system where the axes (principal components) are orthogonal (uncorrelated).
2. **Eigenvectors and eigenvalues:** The principal components are derived from the eigenvectors of the covariance matrix of the data. The corresponding eigenvalues indicate the amount of variance explained by each component.
3. **Selection of components:** The principal components are ranked by their corresponding eigenvalues, with the first component explaining the most variance, the second explaining the next most, and so on.
4. **Dimensionality reduction:** By selecting only the top few principal components (those that explain most of the variance), you can reduce the dimensionality of the data.

t-SNE: t-SNE, or t-distributed Stochastic Neighbor Embedding, is a machine learning algorithm used for visualizing high-dimensional data by reducing its dimensions to two or three dimensions while preserving the relationships between data points. It's particularly useful for understanding the structure and patterns within complex datasets by creating interpretable visualizations.

How it works:

1. **Calculates probabilities:** t-SNE first calculates probabilities that represent the similarity between data points in the high-dimensional space.
2. **Creates a low-dimensional map:** It then tries to create a low-dimensional map where the similarities between points are also represented by probabilities.
3. **Minimizes the difference:** The algorithm iteratively adjusts the positions of points in the low-dimensional map to minimize the difference between the high-dimensional and low-dimensional probabilities.

Advantages:

1. **Excellent for visualization:** t-SNE produces clear and informative visualizations that can reveal complex relationships in high-dimensional data.
2. **Preserves local structure:** It's particularly good at maintaining the relationships between nearby data points.
3. **Non-linear dimensionality reduction:** It can capture more complex patterns than linear methods.

Disadvantages:

1. **Computational cost:** t-SNE can be computationally expensive, especially for very large datasets.
2. **Non-deterministic output:** The output can vary slightly with each run, unless a fixed random seed is used.
3. **Difficult to interpret:** The algorithm can make adjustments that are not always easy to interpret, so it's important to understand how it works to avoid misinterpretations.

12. Deep Learning and Neural Networks

Deep learning is a subset of machine learning that uses algorithms inspired by the structure and function of the human brain, called artificial neural networks. These networks consist of layers of interconnected nodes (neurons), where each layer processes input data and passes its output to the next layer. Deep learning models are particularly effective at recognizing patterns in large and complex datasets, such as images, audio, and text, making them a foundational technology for advancements in areas like computer vision, natural language processing, and speech recognition.

Neural networks operate by learning weights and biases through training, where data is fed into the system and predictions are compared to actual outcomes using a loss function. The system adjusts itself using optimization algorithms like stochastic gradient descent to minimize errors. Deeper networks, with many hidden layers, can model complex relationships but require substantial computational power and large datasets. Breakthroughs in GPU technology, availability of big data, and innovations like convolutional and recurrent neural networks have propelled deep learning to the forefront of artificial intelligence research and application.

Introduction to Neural Networks

Neural networks are machine learning models that mimic the complex functions of the human brain. These models consist of interconnected nodes or neurons that process data, learn patterns and enable tasks such as pattern recognition and decision-making. Neural networks are a fundamental concept in artificial intelligence (AI) and machine learning, modelled loosely after the human brain. They are designed to recognize patterns and relationships in data through a system of interconnected nodes, called neurons, organized into layers. Each neuron receives inputs, processes them using mathematical functions, and passes the result to the next layer. Neural networks are particularly effective for tasks such as image recognition, speech processing, and language translation. Layers in neural network architecture are as:

1. **Input Layer:** This is where the network receives its input data. Each input neuron in the layer corresponds to a feature in the input data.
2. **Hidden Layers:** These layers perform most of the computational heavy lifting. A neural network can have one or multiple hidden layers. Each layer consists

of units (neurons) that transform the inputs into something that the output layer can use.

3. **Output Layer:** The final layer produces the output of the model. The format of these outputs varies depending on the specific task like classification, regression.

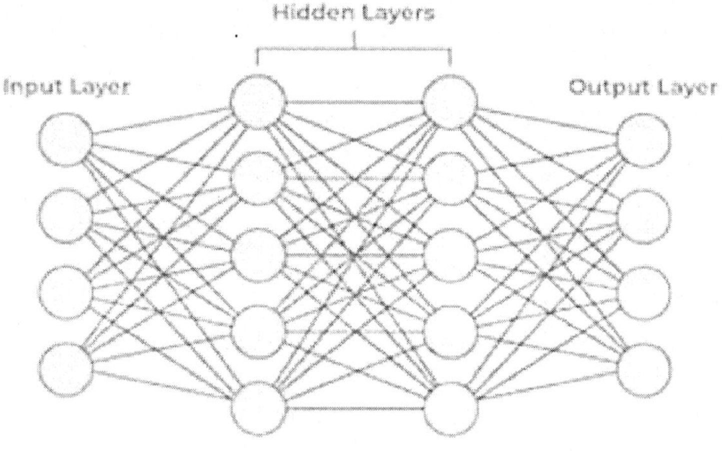

Fig. 4.11

Working of Neural Networks

1. **Forward Propagation:** When data is input into the network, it passes through the network in the forward direction, from the input layer through the hidden layers to the output layer. This process is known as forward propagation. Here's what happens during this phase:

   - **Linear Transformation:** Each neuron in a layer receives inputs which are multiplied by the weights associated with the connections. These products are summed together and a bias is added to the sum. This can be represented mathematically as:

     $Z = w_1 x_1 + w_2 x_2 + \ldots + w_n x_n + b$

     Where,

     w represents the weights

     x represents the inputs

     b is the bias

   - **Activation:** The result of the linear transformation (denoted as z) is then passed through an activation function. The activation function is crucial because it introduces non-linearity into the system, enabling the network to learn more complex patterns. Popular activation functions include ReLU, sigmoid and tanh.

2. **Backpropagation:** After forward propagation, the network evaluates its performance using a loss function which measures the difference between the actual output and the predicted output. The goal of training is to minimize this loss. This is where backpropagation comes into play:
   - **Loss Calculation:** The network calculates the loss which provides a measure of error in the predictions. The loss function could vary; common choices are mean squared error for regression tasks or cross-entropy loss for classification.
   - **Gradient Calculation:** The network computes the gradients of the loss function with respect to each weight and bias in the network. This involves applying the chain rule of calculus to find out how much each part of the output error can be attributed to each weight and bias.
   - **Weight Update:** Once the gradients are calculated, the weights and biases are updated using an optimization algorithm like stochastic gradient descent (SGD). The weights are adjusted in the opposite direction of the gradient to minimize the loss. The size of the step taken in each update is determined by the learning rate.
3. **Iteration:** This process of forward propagation, loss calculation, backpropagation and weight update are repeated for many iterations over the dataset. Over time, this iterative process reduces the loss and the network's predictions become more accurate.

Through these steps, neural networks can adapt their parameters to better approximate the relationships in the data, thereby improving their performance on tasks such as classification, regression or any other predictive modeling.

Neural Networks in Deep Learning: Neural networks are capable of learning and identifying patterns directly from data without pre-defined rules. These networks are built from several key components:

1. **Neurons**: The basic units that receive inputs, each neuron is governed by a threshold and an activation function.
2. **Connections**: Links between neurons that carry information, regulated by weights and biases.
3. **Weights and Biases**: These parameters determine the strength and influence of connections.
4. **Propagation Functions**: Mechanisms that help process and transfer data across layers of neurons.
5. **Learning Rule**: The method that adjusts weights and biases over time to improve accuracy.

Learning of a Neural Network

1. **Learning with Supervised Learning:** In supervised learning, a neural network

learns from labeled input-output pairs provided by a teacher. The network generates outputs based on inputs and by comparing these outputs to the known desired outputs, an error signal is created. The network iteratively adjusts its parameters to minimize errors until it reaches an acceptable performance level.

2. **Learning with Unsupervised Learning:** Unsupervised learning involves data without labeled output variables. The primary goal is to understand the underlying structure of the input data (X). Unlike supervised learning, there is no instructor to guide the process. Instead, the focus is on modeling data patterns and relationships, with techniques like clustering and association commonly used.

3. **Learning with Reinforcement Learning:** Reinforcement learning enables a neural network to learn through interaction with its environment. The network receives feedback in the form of rewards or penalties, guiding it to find an optimal policy or strategy that maximizes cumulative rewards over time. This approach is widely used in applications like gaming and decision-making.

Types of Neural Networks: There are *seven* types of neural networks that can be used.

1. **Feedforward Networks:** A feedforward neural network is a simple artificial neural network architecture in which data moves from input to output in a single direction.

2. **Single-layer Perceptron (SLP):** A single-layer perceptron consists of only one layer of neurons. It takes inputs, applies weights, sums them up and uses an activation function to produce an output.

3. **Multi-layer Perceptron (MLP):** MLP is a type of feedforward neural network with three or more layers, including an input layer, one or more hidden layers and an output layer. It uses nonlinear activation functions.

4. **Convolutional Neural Network (CNN):** A Convolutional Neural Network (CNN) is a specialized artificial neural network designed for image processing. It employs convolutional layers to automatically learn hierarchical features from input images, enabling effective image recognition and classification.

5. **Recurrent Neural Network (RNN):** An artificial neural network type intended for sequential data processing is called a Recurrent Neural Network (RNN). It is appropriate for applications where contextual dependencies are critical such as time series prediction and natural language processing, since it makes use of feedback loops which enable information to survive within the network.

6. **Long Short-Term Memory (LSTM):** LSTM is a type of RNN that is designed to overcome the vanishing gradient problem in training RNNs. It uses memory cells and gates to selectively read, write and erase information.

Advantages of Neural Networks: Neural networks are widely used in many different applications because of their many benefits:

1. **Adaptability:** Neural networks are useful for activities where the link between inputs and outputs is complex or not well defined because they can adapt to new situations and learn from data.
2. **Pattern Recognition:** Their proficiency in pattern recognition renders them efficacious in tasks like as audio and image identification, natural language processing and other intricate data patterns.
3. **Parallel Processing:** Because neural networks are capable of parallel processing by nature, they can process numerous jobs at once which speeds up and improves the efficiency of computations.
4. **Non-Linearity:** Neural networks are able to model and comprehend complicated relationships in data by virtue of the non-linear activation functions found in neurons which overcome the drawbacks of linear models.

Disadvantages of Neural Networks: Neural networks while powerful, are not without drawbacks and difficulties:

1. **Computational Intensity:** Large neural network training can be a laborious and computationally demanding process that demands a lot of computing power.
2. **Black box Nature:** As "black box" models, neural networks pose a problem in important applications since it is difficult to understand how they make decisions.
3. **Overfitting:** Overfitting is a phenomenon in which neural networks commit training material to memory rather than identifying patterns in the data. Although regularization approaches help to alleviate this, the problem still exists.
4. **Need for Large datasets:** For efficient training, neural networks frequently need sizable, labeled datasets; otherwise, their performance may suffer from incomplete or skewed data.

Applications of Neural Networks: Neural networks have numerous applications across various fields:

1. **Image and Video Recognition**: CNNs are extensively used in applications such as facial recognition, autonomous driving and medical image analysis.
2. **Natural Language Processing (NLP)**: RNNs and transformers power language translation, chatbots and sentiment analysis.
3. **Finance**: Predicting stock prices, fraud detection and risk management.
4. **Healthcare**: Neural networks assist in diagnosing diseases, analyzing medical images and personalizing treatment plans.

5. **Gaming and Autonomous Systems**: Neural networks enable real-time decision-making, enhancing user experience in video games and enabling autonomous systems like self-driving cars.

A basic neural network consists of three types of layers: an input layer, one or more hidden layers, and an output layer. The network learns by adjusting the weights of connections between neurons during training, using algorithms such as backpropagation and optimization techniques like gradient descent. As the model is trained on data, it becomes better at making predictions or classifications. Neural networks are the building blocks of deep learning and have enabled many recent breakthroughs in AI.

Convolutional Neural Networks (CNNs)

Convolutional Neural Network (CNN) is an advanced version of artificial neural networks (ANNs), primarily designed to extract features from grid-like matrix datasets. This is particularly useful for visual datasets such as images or videos, where data patterns play a crucial role. CNNs are widely used in computer vision applications due to their effectiveness in processing visual data. Convolutional Neural Networks (CNNs) are a specialized type of neural network designed primarily for processing and analyzing visual data. Unlike traditional neural networks, CNNs automatically and adaptively learn spatial hierarchies of features from input images using layers like convolutional layers, pooling layers, and fully connected layers. The convolutional layers apply filters (kernels) that scan across the image to detect features such as edges, textures, or more complex patterns, preserving the spatial relationship between pixels. Pooling layers reduce the dimensionality of the data, helping to make the network more computationally efficient and less prone to overfitting. After several convolution and pooling layers, the data is flattened and passed through fully connected layers to perform tasks like classification or detection. CNNs are widely used in applications such as facial recognition, medical image analysis, self-driving cars, and more. Their ability to learn and extract meaningful features from images with minimal pre-processing has made them a cornerstone of modern computer vision.

CNNs consists of multiple layers like the input layer, Convolutional layer, max pooling layer, dense layer and output layer as shown in fig.4.12.

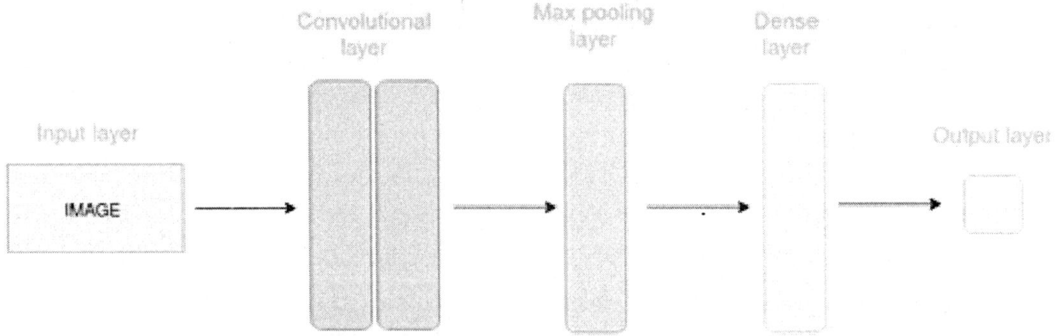

Fig. 4.12

How Convolutional Layers Works?

Convolution Neural Networks are neural networks that share their parameters. Imagine you have an image. It can be represented as a cuboid having its length, width (dimension of the image), and height (i.e the channel as images generally has red, green, and blue channels).

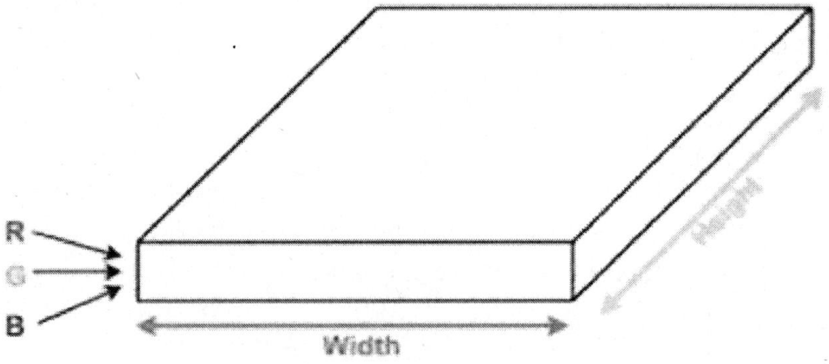

Fig. 4.13

Now imagine taking a small patch of this image and running a small neural network, called a filter or kernel on it, with say, K outputs and representing them vertically.

Now slide that neural network across the whole image, as a result, we will get another image with different widths, heights, and depths. Instead of just ***R, G,*** and ***B*** channels now we have more channels but lesser width and height. This operation is called Convolution. If the patch size is the same as that of the image it will be a regular neural network. Because of this small patch, we have fewer weights.

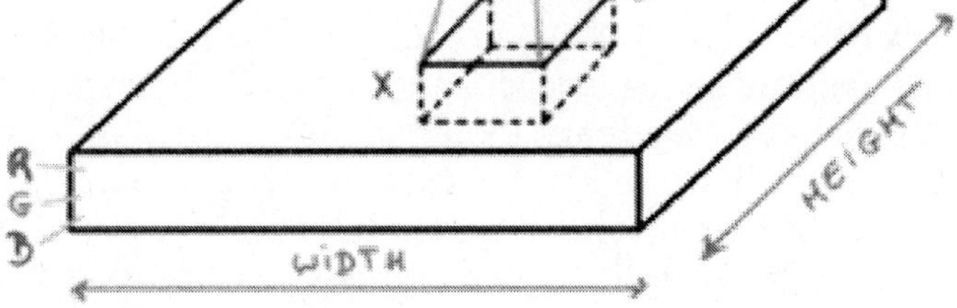

Fig. 4.14 Image source: Deep Learning Udacity

Mathematical Overview of Convolution: Now let's talk about a bit of mathematics that is involved in the whole convolution process.

1. Convolution layers consist of a set of learnable filters (or kernels) having small widths and heights and the same depth as that of input volume (3 if the input layer is image input).
2. For example, if we have to run convolution on an image with dimensions 34x34x3. The possible size of filters can be axax3, where 'a' can be anything like 3, 5, or 7 but smaller as compared to the image dimension.
3. During the forward pass, we slide each filter across the whole input volume step by step where each step is called stride (which can have a value of 2, 3, or even 4 for high-dimensional images) and compute the dot product between the kernel weights and patch from input volume.
4. As we slide our filters, we'll get a 2-D output for each filter and we'll stack them together as a result, we'll get output volume having a depth equal to the number of filters. The network will learn all the filters.

Importance of CNNs: There are several reasons why CNNs are important in the modern world, as highlighted below:

1. CNNs are distinguished from classic machine learning algorithms such as **SVMs** and **decision trees** by their ability to autonomously extract features at a large scale, bypassing the need for manual feature engineering and thereby enhancing efficiency.
2. The convolutional layers grant CNNs their translation-invariant characteristics, empowering them to identify and extract patterns and features from data irrespective of variations in position, orientation, scale, or translation.
3. A variety of pre-trained CNN architectures, including VGG-16, ResNet50, Inceptionv3, and EfficientNet, have demonstrated top-tier performance. These models can be adapted to new tasks with relatively little data through a process known as fine-tuning.
4. Beyond image classification tasks, CNNs are versatile and can be applied to a range of other domains, such as natural language processing, time series analysis, and speech recognition.

Recurrent Neural Networks (RNNs) and Transformers

Recurrent Neural Networks (RNNs) are a class of neural networks designed for sequential data, such as time series, speech, and natural language. Unlike traditional neural networks, RNNs have a feedback loop that allows them to maintain a memory of previous inputs, making them well-suited for tasks where context and order matter. However, RNNs often struggle with long-term dependencies due to issues like vanishing gradients, which led to the development of improved variants like Long Short-Term Memory (LSTM) and Gated Recurrent Unit (GRU) networks.

Transformers are a newer and more powerful architecture that has largely replaced RNNs in many applications, especially in natural language processing. Introduced in the paper *"Attention Is All You Need"*, transformers use a mechanism called self-attention to process entire sequences at once, allowing the model to weigh the importance of each word in the context of all others. This parallel processing capability makes transformers much faster and more effective at capturing long-range dependencies. Transformers are the foundation of state-of-the-art models like BERT, GPT, and T5, and have revolutionized tasks such as translation, summarization, and question answering.

Recurrent Neural Networks (RNNs): Recurrent Neural Networks (RNNs) are a class of artificial neural networks designed to handle sequential or time-series data. Unlike traditional feedforward neural networks that treat each input independently, RNNs incorporate a form of memory by using loops within the network. This allows them to maintain a "hidden state" that captures information about previous inputs, enabling them to make context-aware decisions over time.

The basic RNN architecture consists of repeating modules of neural networks, where the output from one time step is fed as input into the next. At each step, the RNN takes the current input and the previous hidden state to produce the new hidden state and output. This sequential nature makes RNNs suitable for tasks like language modeling, speech recognition, music generation, and time-series forecasting. However, vanilla RNNs suffer from the vanishing and exploding gradient problem. When sequences become long, it's difficult for the network to retain useful information from earlier steps, making it hard to learn long-range dependencies. To address this, more advanced variants were introduced:

1. **Long Short-Term Memory (LSTM)**: LSTMs use a more complex architecture with gates (input, forget, and output gates) and a memory cell that allows the network to retain or forget information over long periods. This greatly improves the model's ability to handle long sequences.
2. **Gated Recurrent Units (GRU)**: GRUs simplify LSTMs by combining the input and forget gates into a single update gate. They are computationally lighter while still managing long-term dependencies effectively.

RNNs are widely used in natural language processing tasks such as sentiment analysis, machine translation, and text generation. For example, in language modeling, an RNN can predict the next word in a sentence by considering the context of previous words. In speech recognition, it processes audio frames sequentially to produce the corresponding text. Despite their advantages, RNNs are inherently sequential in computation, meaning they process one time step at a time. This limits their ability to be parallelized during training, making them slower and less scalable compared to more modern architectures like Transformers. Additionally, even with LSTMs and GRUs, capturing extremely long-range dependencies remains a challenge.

Today, RNNs are still useful in real-time applications and low-power devices where model size and latency matter. Their step-wise nature makes them suitable for streaming data or online learning, where decisions are made one step at a time. In summary, Recurrent Neural Networks marked a major advancement in the ability of machines to understand and process sequential information. While they have been surpassed by newer models like Transformers in many areas, RNNs and their variants remain relevant in scenarios where lightweight, real-time processing of sequential data is essential.

Importance:

1. **Sequential Data Modeling:** RNNs are specifically designed to handle sequential or time-dependent data, such as text, audio, or time-series.
2. **Memory of Previous Inputs:** They maintain a hidden state that remembers information from previous timesteps, enabling context-aware predictions.
3. **Effective for Small Datasets:** RNNs (especially GRUs) can perform well even with smaller datasets compared to transformers.
4. **Used in Real-Time Systems:** Their step-by-step nature makes RNNs suitable for online and streaming data applications.
5. **Low Computational Footprint:** GRUs and lightweight LSTMs are ideal for mobile and embedded systems with limited computing resources.
6. **Speech and Audio Applications:** Widely used in speech recognition, text-to-speech systems, and music generation.
7. **Time-Series Forecasting:** Effective in modeling and predicting sensor data, stock trends, and weather sequences.
8. **Good for Short Sequences:** Performs efficiently when sequences are not too long and real-time response is important.
9. **Bi-directional Variants:** Bi-RNNs can access both past and future context in sequence classification tasks.

Transformers: Transformers are a groundbreaking neural network architecture introduced in the 2017 paper *"Attention Is All You Need"*. Unlike RNNs, which process input sequences step-by-step, Transformers use a mechanism called self-attention that allows them to process all tokens (words, symbols, etc.) in parallel. This architectural shift has dramatically improved both the performance and scalability of machine learning models for language and other sequential tasks. The key innovation of Transformers is the self-attention mechanism, which lets the model weigh the importance of each token in the input relative to others. For instance, in a sentence like *"The cat sat on the mat"*, the model can directly relate "cat" and "sat" even if they're not adjacent. This ability to capture relationships regardless of position allows Transformers to model long-range dependencies far better than RNNs or LSTMs. Each Transformer model is built from blocks consisting of:

1. **Multi-head self-attention layers**: Capturing multiple types of relationships.

2. **Feedforward neural networks**: Applied independently to each position.
3. **Residual connections and layer normalization**: Helping stabilize and speed up training.

To preserve the order of the sequence since self-attention doesn't inherently understand time or position Transformers use positional encodings added to the input embeddings. These can be learned or predefined (e.g., sine/cosine functions). Transformers are composed of encoder and decoder stacks:

1. The encoder reads and understands the input sequence.
2. The decoder generates an output sequence, step by step, attending to the encoder output and past generated tokens.

In natural language processing, Transformers have led to major innovations:

1. **BERT (Bidirectional Encoder Representations from Transformers):** Pretrained on large corpora and fine-tuned for tasks like question answering and sentiment analysis.
2. **GPT (Generative Pre-trained Transformer):** Focused on text generation, enabling chatbots, content creation, and more.
3. **T5, RoBERTa, XLNet:** Variants designed to push performance further in various language tasks.

Transformers are not limited to text. Vision Transformers (ViT) apply the same principles to images, treating patches of images like tokens. Multimodal models such as CLIP and DALL·E combine text and images, showing the versatility of the architecture. V Transformers are now the foundation of large language models (LLMs) like GPT-4, which power conversational AI, translation tools, summarization engines, and more. They scale well with data and model size, making them ideal for training "foundation models" that can be adapted to many tasks.

However, Transformers are resource-intensive. The self-attention mechanism scales quadratically with input length, making it costly for very long sequences. Research continues to develop efficient Transformer variants like Longformer, Reformer, and Performer to address this. Transformers have revolutionized deep learning by enabling more effective, scalable, and parallel processing of sequential data. They are the backbone of modern AI across text, vision, audio, and beyond.

Importance of Transformers

1. **Parallel Processing:** Unlike RNNs, transformers process entire sequences in parallel, significantly speeding up training and inference.
2. **Long-Range Dependency Modeling:** Self-attention allows the model to consider all positions in the input, making it excellent at handling long-range context.
3. **State-of-the-Art in NLP:** Transformers are the backbone of most modern NLP systems (e.g., GPT, BERT, T5, etc.).

4. **Scalable to Large Models:** They scale well to billions of parameters, enabling powerful "foundation models" used across tasks.
5. **Multimodal Capability:** Transformers are used in models that understand text, images, audio, and even video simultaneously (e.g., CLIP, GPT-4V).
6. **Transfer Learning:** Pretrained transformer models can be fine-tuned for a wide variety of downstream tasks with high accuracy.
7. **Improved Accuracy:** Outperform RNNs on most benchmarks in text classification, translation, summarization, and more.
8. **Flexible Architecture:** Adapted across domains (NLP, computer vision, bioinformatics, etc.) with minimal modification.
9. **Support for Attention Mechanism:** Attention provides explainability and focuses on important input parts, enhancing interpretability.
10. **Foundation of Generative AI:** Core to models like ChatGPT, DALL·E, Codex, etc., powering modern generative AI.

SUMMARY OF MACHINE LEARNING FUNDAMENTALS

Machine learning is a field of artificial intelligence that enables systems to learn patterns from data and make predictions or decisions without explicit programming. It is broadly classified into supervised learning, unsupervised learning, and deep learning.

In supervised learning, models are trained on labeled data. Key tasks include regression (e.g., linear and logistic regression for predicting continuous or binary outcomes) and classification (e.g., decision trees, random forests, and SVM for categorizing data). Models are evaluated using metrics like accuracy, precision, recall, and F1-score.

Unsupervised learning deals with unlabeled data, aiming to uncover hidden patterns. Common techniques include clustering (K-Means, DBSCAN, Hierarchical), dimensionality reduction (PCA, t-SNE), and anomaly detection for identifying outliers.

Deep learning is a subset of machine learning that uses neural networks to model complex patterns, especially in high-dimensional data. Artificial Neural Networks learn through layers of interconnected nodes. Convolutional Neural Networks (CNNs) are used for image data, while Recurrent Neural Networks (RNNs) handle sequences like text or time-series. Transformers, a newer architecture, outperform RNNs in tasks like natural language processing using self-attention mechanisms.

10. Supervised Learning

Supervised learning involves training a model on a labeled dataset, where the input data is paired with the correct output. The goal is for the model to learn the relationship between inputs and outputs so it can make accurate predictions on new, unseen data.

- **Regression:** Regression is a type of supervised machine learning used to predict continuous numerical values based on input features. It models the relationship between dependent and independent variables. Linear regression assumes a straight-line relationship, predicting output using a weighted sum of input features. Logistic regression, despite its name, is used for binary classification by predicting probabilities using a sigmoid function. Regression is commonly used in applications like forecasting sales, predicting prices, or estimating risk. Model performance is typically evaluated using metrics like Mean Squared Error (MSE) or R^2 score, which assess the accuracy of the model's predictions against actual values.
  - **Linear Regression**: It models the relationship between one or more independent variables and a continuous dependent variable using a straight line. The objective is to minimize the error between predicted and actual values using loss functions like Mean Squared Error (MSE).
  - **Logistic Regression**: Despite its name, it is used for binary classification problems. It predicts the probability that a given input belongs to a certain class using a sigmoid function and outputs values between 0 and 1.
- **Classification (Decision Trees, Random Forest, SVM):** Classification is a supervised learning task that assigns data points to predefined categories. Decision Trees split data based on feature values, creating a tree-like model of decisions that is easy to interpret. Random Forest is an ensemble of multiple decision trees, combining their outputs to improve accuracy and reduce overfitting. Support Vector Machines (SVM) find the optimal hyperplane that separates classes with the maximum margin, effective in high-dimensional spaces and with non-linear data using kernels. These algorithms are widely used for tasks like spam detection, image recognition, and medical diagnosis, evaluated by metrics such as accuracy and F1-score.
  - **Decision Trees**: These models split the data based on feature values, forming a tree-like structure where each internal node represents a decision rule and each leaf node represents an outcome. They are intuitive and easy to visualize.
  - **Random Forest**: An ensemble of decision trees, where each tree is trained on a random subset of the data. The final prediction is usually made by averaging (for regression) or majority vote (for classification). It helps reduce overfitting and improves accuracy.
  - **Support Vector Machine (SVM)**: SVMs aim to find the optimal hyperplane that separates data points of different classes with the maximum margin. They are effective in high-dimensional spaces and can use kernels to handle non-linear data.
- **Model Evaluation Metrics:** Model evaluation metrics measure how well a machine learning model performs, especially in classification tasks. Accuracy

calculates the proportion of correct predictions out of all predictions, useful for balanced datasets. Precision measures how many predicted positives are actually correct, focusing on reducing false positives. **Recall** (or sensitivity) measures how many actual positives were correctly identified, important for minimizing false negatives. The F1-score is the harmonic mean of precision and recall, providing a balanced measure when classes are imbalanced. These metrics help select, tune, and compare models to ensure reliable and effective predictions in real-world applications.

- **Accuracy:** The ratio of correct predictions to the total number of predictions. Useful when classes are balanced.
- **Precision:** The ratio of true positives to the total predicted positives. High precision means fewer false positives.
- **Recall (Sensitivity):** The ratio of true positives to the total actual positives. High recall means fewer false negatives.
- **F1-score:** The harmonic means of precision and recall. It provides a balanced metric when there is class imbalance.

11. Unsupervised Learning

Unsupervised learning deals with unlabeled data. The goal is to discover hidden patterns or structures within the data without predefined outputs. Unsupervised learning involves training models on unlabeled data to discover hidden patterns or structures without predefined outputs. Common techniques include clustering, which groups similar data points using methods like K-Means, DBSCAN, and Hierarchical clustering. Another key method is dimensionality reduction, such as PCA and t-SNE, which simplify high-dimensional data for easier analysis and visualization. Anomaly detection identifies rare or unusual data points, useful in fraud detection or fault diagnosis. Unsupervised learning is valuable in exploratory data analysis, customer segmentation, and recommendation systems, where understanding intrinsic data relationships is essential.

- **Clustering:** Clustering is an unsupervised learning technique that groups similar data points into clusters based on their features. It helps identify natural patterns or structures in data. Common algorithms include K-Means, DBSCAN, and Hierarchical Clustering, widely used in customer segmentation, image analysis, and market research. Clustering is the process of grouping similar data points together. Key algorithms include:
  - **K-Means Clustering:** A centroid-based algorithm that partitions data into *k* clusters. Each data point is assigned to the nearest cluster centroid, which is recalculated iteratively to minimize intra-cluster variance.
  - **DBSCAN (Density-Based Spatial Clustering of Applications with Noise):** It groups together closely packed data points based on density, allowing for the identification of clusters of arbitrary shapes and noise points (outliers).

  - **Hierarchical Clustering:** Builds a hierarchy of clusters either from the bottom-up (agglomerative) or top-down (divisive). Dendrograms are often used to visualize the cluster hierarchy.

- **Dimensionality Reduction:** Dimensionality reduction techniques simplify high-dimensional data while preserving important structures. They help in visualization and speed up learning. Dimensionality reduction simplifies high-dimensional data by reducing the number of input features while preserving essential information. It improves visualization, reduces noise, and speeds up model training. Techniques like Principal Component Analysis (PCA) and t-SNE help uncover hidden structures and patterns in complex datasets, aiding analysis and interpretation.
  - **PCA (Principal Component Analysis):** A linear technique that transforms data into a new coordinate system such that the greatest variance lies along the first axis (principal component), the second greatest along the second axis, and so on. It reduces redundancy and improves model performance.
  - **t-SNE (t-distributed Stochastic Neighbour Embedding):** A non-linear technique often used for visualizing high-dimensional data in 2D or 3D. It preserves local relationships and is effective for understanding data clusters.

- **Anomaly Detection:** Anomaly detection identifies rare events or data points that differ significantly from the majority. It is used in fraud detection, fault detection, and network security. Techniques include statistical methods, clustering-based outlier detection, and autoencoders. Anomaly detection identifies rare or unusual data points that deviate significantly from the norm. It is crucial in applications like fraud detection, network security, and equipment failure prediction. Techniques include statistical methods, clustering-based approaches, and machine learning models like autoencoders to detect outliers in unlabeled data.

12. Deep Learning and Neural Networks

Deep learning is a specialized branch of machine learning that uses artificial neural networks to model complex patterns in data. It is particularly effective for tasks involving large-scale data and high-dimensional inputs like images, audio, and text.

- **Introduction to Neural Networks:** Neural networks are inspired by the structure of the human brain. A basic neural network consists of an input layer, one or more hidden layers, and an output layer. Each layer contains neurons connected by weighted edges. During training, these weights are adjusted using backpropagation and optimization algorithms like stochastic gradient descent to minimize prediction error. Neural networks are capable of learning complex nonlinear relationships in data. As the number of layers increases, the model becomes "deeper," which allows for hierarchical learning of features. However, deep networks also require large datasets and high computational power to train effectively.

- **Convolutional Neural Networks (CNNs)** CNNs are a type of deep neural network primarily used for image data. They are designed to automatically and adaptively learn spatial hierarchies of features through convolutional layers. Key components of CNNs:
  - **Convolutional Layers**: Apply filters to the input to extract features like edges, textures, or patterns.
  - **Pooling Layers**: Down sample the data to reduce dimensionality and computation.
  - **Fully Connected Layers**: Connect all neurons to perform classification based on learned features.

  CNNs are widely used in computer vision tasks such as object detection, facial recognition, and medical image analysis due to their high accuracy and minimal preprocessing requirements.
- **Recurrent Neural Networks (RNNs) and Transformers:** RNNs are designed for sequential data like text, audio, and time series. Unlike feedforward networks, RNNs maintain a memory of previous inputs by passing information through hidden states across time steps. This allows them to capture temporal dependencies in data. Challenges with RNNs include the vanishing gradient problem, which makes it hard to learn long-term dependencies. Variants like LSTM (Long Short-Term Memory) and GRU (Gated Recurrent Unit) solve this by introducing memory cells and gating mechanisms to control the flow of information.

  Transformers are a more recent innovation that has largely replaced RNNs in many applications. They use a self-attention mechanism to weigh the importance of each word or token in a sequence, regardless of its position. This allows transformers to model long-range dependencies more effectively and in parallel, leading to faster training. Transformers are the foundation of state-of-the-art language models like BERT, GPT, and T5, which excel in tasks like machine translation, text summarization, question answering, and content generation.

Chapter 5

Advanced Topics in Data Science

Advanced topics in data science encompass sophisticated techniques that empower machines to process, learn from, and make intelligent decisions based on complex data. One key area is Natural Language Processing (NLP), which enables machines to understand and generate human language. Core tasks in NLP include text preprocessing techniques such as tokenization, stemming, and lemmatization, along with advanced applications like sentiment analysis, topic modeling, and the development of large language models and chatbots. Another essential domain is Time Series Analysis, which focuses on data collected over time to identify trends and seasonal patterns. Common methods include ARIMA and exponential smoothing, while modern deep learning approaches like Long Short-Term Memory (LSTM) networks are increasingly used for accurate forecasting. Lastly, Reinforcement Learning (RL) is a powerful area of machine learning where agents learn optimal actions through interactions with their environment. Key RL concepts include Q-learning, which involves learning the value of actions, and policy gradients, which optimize decision-making policies directly. Together, these advanced topics form the backbone of intelligent systems, enabling data scientists to solve real-world problems in areas ranging from language understanding to predictive analytics and autonomous decision-making.

13. Natural Language Processing (NLP)

Natural Language Processing (NLP) is a vital subfield of data science and artificial intelligence that focuses on enabling machines to understand, interpret, and generate human language. It bridges the gap between human communication and computer understanding, making it essential for applications such as chatbots, translation services, sentiment analysis, and search engines. The foundation of NLP involves text preprocessing techniques like tokenization, stemming, and lemmatization, which prepare raw text for further analysis by breaking it into manageable units and reducing words to their root forms. More advanced NLP tasks include sentiment analysis, which identifies emotions or opinions within text, and topic modeling, which uncovers hidden themes across large document collections. The rise of large language models such as GPT has significantly advanced the capabilities of NLP, enabling more accurate and context-aware language generation, conversation, and comprehension. These models underpin modern chatbots and virtual assistants, making interactions more natural and human-like. NLP continues to evolve rapidly, integrating deep learning techniques to improve performance across languages, domains, and tasks. Its growing importance is evident in industries ranging from healthcare and finance to customer service, where understanding and generating human language at scale is becoming increasingly critical for automation and insight extraction.

NLP Techniques: NLP encompasses a wide array of techniques that aimed at enabling computers to process and understand human language. These tasks can be categorized into several broad areas, each addressing different aspects of language processing. Here are some of the key NLP techniques:

1. **Text Processing and Preprocessing**
   - **Tokenization:** Dividing text into smaller units, such as words or sentences.
   - **Stemming and Lemmatization:** Reducing words to their base or root forms.
   - Stopword Removal: Removing common words (like "and", "the", "is") that may not carry significant meaning.
   - **Text Normalization:** Standardizing text, including case normalization, removing punctuation and correcting spelling errors.
2. **Syntax and Parsing**
   - **Part-of-Speech (POS) Tagging:** Assigning parts of speech to each word in a sentence (e.g., noun, verb, adjective).
   - **Dependency Parsing:** Analyzing the grammatical structure of a sentence to identify relationships between words.
   - **Constituency Parsing:** Breaking down a sentence into its constituent parts or phrases (e.g., noun phrases, verb phrases).
3. **Semantic Analysis**
   - **Named Entity Recognition (NER):** Identifying and classifying entities in text, such as names of people organizations, locations, dates, etc.
   - **Word Sense Disambiguation (WSD):** Determining which meaning of a word is used in a given context.
   - **Coreference Resolution:** Identifying when different words refer to the same entity in a text (e.g., "he" refers to "John").
4. **Information Extraction**
   - **Entity Extraction:** Identifying specific entities and their relationships within the text.
   - **Relation Extraction:** Identifying and categorizing the relationships between entities in a text.

5. **Text Classification in NLP**
   - **Sentiment Analysis:** Determining the sentiment or emotional tone expressed in a text (e.g., positive, negative, neutral).
   - **Topic Modeling:** Identifying topics or themes within a large collection of documents.
   - **Spam Detection:** Classifying text as spam or not spam.
6. **Language Generation**
   - **Machine Translation:** Translating text from one language to another.
   - **Text Summarization:** Producing a concise summary of a larger text.
   - **Text Generation:** Automatically generating coherent and contextually relevant text.
7. **Speech Processing**
   - **Speech Recognition:** Converting spoken language into text.
   - **Text-to-Speech (TTS) Synthesis:** Converting written text into spoken language.
8. **Question Answering**
   - **Retrieval-Based QA:** Finding and returning the most relevant text passage in response to a query.
   - **Generative QA:** Generating an answer based on the information available in a text corpus.
9. **Dialogue Systems**
   - **Chatbots and Virtual Assistants:** Enabling systems to engage in conversations with users, providing responses and performing tasks based on user input.
10. **Sentiment and Emotion Analysis in NLP**
    - **Emotion Detection:** Identifying and categorizing emotions expressed in text.
    - **Opinion Mining:** Analyzing opinions or reviews to understand public sentiment toward products, services or topics.

How Natural Language Processing (NLP) Works?

Working in natural language processing (NLP) typically involves using computational techniques to analyze and understand human language. This can include tasks such as language understanding, language generation and language interaction.

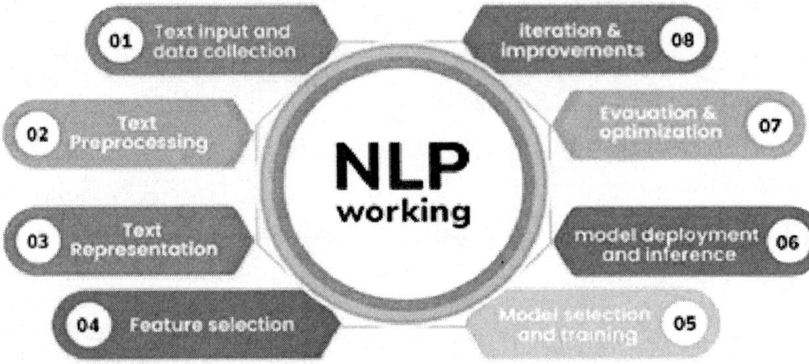

Fig. 5.1

1. **Text Input and Data Collection:** Text input and data collection are foundational steps in Natural Language Processing (NLP), forming the basis upon which all further analysis and model training are built. Text input refers to the acquisition of raw textual data from various sources such as websites, social media, emails, surveys, customer reviews, or internal documents. The nature and quality of this input significantly impact the effectiveness of NLP applications. Data collection involves systematically gathering this text in a structured or unstructured format, depending on the use case. Structured collection might include pulling data from databases or APIs, while unstructured methods involve web scraping, user submissions, or importing files. During this stage, it is important to ensure data diversity, relevance, and volume to train robust and unbiased models. Additionally, ethical considerations such as data privacy, user consent, and source credibility must be addressed. Once collected, the text data typically undergoes cleaning and preprocessing to remove noise, inconsistencies, or irrelevant content. High-quality input and thoughtful data collection strategies enable more accurate NLP outcomes in tasks like sentiment analysis, machine translation, and text classification, making this step a critical foundation for any successful NLP pipeline.
   - **Data Collection:** Gathering text data from various sources such as websites, books, social media or proprietary databases.
   - **Data Storage:** Storing the collected text data in a structured format, such as a database or a collection of documents.
2. **Text Preprocessing:** Text preprocessing is a crucial step in Natural Language Processing (NLP) that involves transforming raw text data into a clean and structured format suitable for analysis and model training. Since raw text often contains noise such as punctuation, special characters, inconsistent casing, and irrelevant words, preprocessing ensures that the data is normalized and meaningful. Key techniques in text preprocessing include tokenization, which splits text into individual words or sentences; lowercasing, which standardizes

all words to the same case; removal of stopwords like "and", "the", or "is" that carry little semantic value; and punctuation and number removal, which eliminates unnecessary symbols. Additionally, stemming and lemmatization are used to reduce words to their root or base forms stemming trims words to their stem (e.g., "running" becomes "run"), while lemmatization uses linguistic rules to derive the word's proper base form. These processes help reduce vocabulary size and improve the performance of NLP models. Other tasks, such as spelling correction and handling contractions (e.g., "don't" to "do not"), may also be included depending on the application. Effective text preprocessing not only cleans the data but also enhances model accuracy and efficiency by focusing on the most relevant linguistic features. Preprocessing is crucial to clean and prepare the raw text data for analysis. Common preprocessing steps include:

- **Tokenization:** Splitting text into smaller units like words or sentences.
- **Lowercasing:** Converting all text to lowercase to ensure uniformity.
- **Stopword Removal:** Removing common words that do not contribute significant meaning, such as "and," "the," "is."
- **Punctuation Removal:** Removing punctuation marks.
- **Stemming and Lemmatization:** Reducing words to their base or root forms. Stemming cuts off suffixes, while lemmatization considers the context and converts words to their meaningful base form.
- **Text Normalization:** Standardizing text format, including correcting spelling errors, expanding contractions and handling special characters.

3. **Text Representation:** Text representation is the process of converting textual data into a numerical format that machine learning models can understand and process. Since computers cannot interpret raw text directly, text must be transformed into structured numerical vectors while preserving its meaning and context. Traditional methods include Bag of Words (BoW), which represents text based on word frequency without considering word order, and Term Frequency-Inverse Document Frequency (TF-IDF), which weighs words based on their importance in a document relative to a collection of documents. While simple and effective for basic tasks, these methods often miss contextual nuances. More advanced techniques use word embeddings, such as Word2Vec, GloVe, and FastText, which map words into dense vector spaces where semantically similar words are located closer together. These embeddings capture relationships and meanings more effectively than sparse vectors. The most recent advancements in text representation involve contextual embeddings from large pre-trained language models like BERT or GPT, which generate dynamic word vectors based on context, allowing models to understand polysemy and syntax more accurately. Choosing the right representation method is crucial for achieving high performance in NLP tasks

such as classification, sentiment analysis, and machine translation, as it directly affects how well the model understands and processes language.

- **Bag of Words (BoW):** Representing text as a collection of words, ignoring grammar and word order but keeping track of word frequency.
- **Term Frequency-Inverse Document Frequency (TF-IDF):** A statistic that reflects the importance of a word in a document relative to a collection of documents.
- **Word Embeddings:** Using dense vector representations of words where semantically similar words are closer together in the vector space (e.g., Word2Vec, GloVe).

4. **Feature Extraction:** Extracting meaningful features from the text data that can be used for various NLP tasks. Feature extraction in Natural Language Processing (NLP) involves identifying and transforming relevant information from text into numerical features that can be used by machine learning models. It bridges the gap between raw text data and model input by highlighting the most informative aspects of the text. Common feature extraction techniques include frequency-based methods like Bag of Words (BoW) and Term Frequency-Inverse Document Frequency (TF-IDF), which capture how often words appear in a document or how important they are across a corpus. These methods create structured vectors but often ignore grammar and word order. To address this, n-grams (sequences of *n* words) are used to include some context. More advanced methods involve word embeddings like Word2Vec, GloVe, and FastText, which represent words as dense vectors based on semantic similarity, enabling better understanding of word relationships. Contextual embeddings from models like BERT or GPT take this further by generating dynamic vectors based on a word's context in a sentence. Additional features can include part-of-speech tags, named entities, sentiment scores, and syntactic dependencies, depending on the application. Effective feature extraction is essential for improving the accuracy and performance of NLP models, as it determines how well the model can learn patterns and make predictions from text data.

   - **N-grams:** Capturing sequences of N words to preserve some context and word order.
   - **Syntactic Features**: Using parts of speech tags, syntactic dependencies and parse trees.
   - **Semantic Features**: Leveraging word embeddings and other representations to capture word meaning and context.

5. **Model Selection and Training:** Selecting and training a machine learning or deep learning model to perform specific NLP tasks. Model selection and training are critical stages in the Natural Language Processing (NLP) pipeline, where appropriate algorithms are chosen and trained to perform specific tasks

such as classification, translation, sentiment analysis, or question answering. Model selection involves evaluating different machine learning or deep learning models based on the problem type, data size, complexity, and desired performance. For simpler tasks, traditional models like Naive Bayes, Logistic Regression, or Support Vector Machines (SVM) are often sufficient. For more complex problems requiring deeper understanding of language, neural networks, particularly Recurrent Neural Networks (RNNs), Long Short-Term Memory (LSTM) networks, or Transformer-based architectures like BERT and GPT, are preferred due to their ability to capture context and sequential patterns in text. Once the model is selected, the training process begins, where the model learns from labeled data by adjusting internal parameters to minimize prediction errors. This involves feeding the model training data, defining a loss function, and using optimization techniques like gradient descent. Proper validation during training helps prevent overfitting and ensures generalization to new data. Additionally, hyperparameter tuning is performed to find the optimal settings for the model. Effective model selection and training directly impact the performance, accuracy, and scalability of NLP applications.

- **Supervised Learning:** Using labeled data to train models like Support Vector Machines (SVM), Random Forests or deep learning models like Convolutional Neural Networks (CNNs) and Recurrent Neural Networks (RNNs).
- **Unsupervised Learning:** Applying techniques like clustering or topic modeling (e.g., Latent Dirichlet Allocation) on unlabeled data.
- **Pre-trained Models:** Utilizing pre-trained language models such as BERT, GPT or transformer-based models that have been trained on large corpora.

6. **Model Deployment and Inference:** Deploying the trained model and using it to make predictions or extract insights from new text data. Model deployment and inference are the final stages of the NLP pipeline, where a trained model is integrated into a real-world system to make predictions on new, unseen data. Model deployment involves taking the trained model and making it accessible through a production environment, such as a web application, API, or mobile app. This process requires considerations for scalability, latency, security, and resource efficiency. Popular deployment platforms include cloud services like AWS, Azure, Google Cloud, and tools like Docker and Kubernetes for containerization and orchestration. Once deployed, the model is ready for inference, which is the process of using the model to analyze incoming text and generate outputs such as classifying a review as positive or negative, generating a chatbot response, or extracting named entities. Inference must be fast and reliable, especially in real-time applications like virtual assistants or fraud detection. To maintain performance,

techniques like model quantization, caching, and batch processing may be used. Additionally, monitoring the model's predictions in production is crucial to detect issues like data drift or declining accuracy over time. Successful deployment and efficient inference ensure that NLP models deliver value in practical applications, transforming raw text into actionable insights and intelligent responses.

- **Text Classification:** Categorizing text into predefined classes (e.g., spam detection, sentiment analysis).
- **Named Entity Recognition (NER):** Identifying and classifying entities in the text.
- **Machine Translation:** Translating text from one language to another.
- **Question Answering:** Providing answers to questions based on the context provided by text data.

7. **Evaluation and Optimization:** Evaluating the performance of the NLP algorithm using metrics such as accuracy, precision, recall, F1-score and others. Evaluation and optimization are essential steps in the NLP pipeline to assess a model's performance and improve its accuracy, efficiency, and generalization. Evaluation involves using metrics appropriate to the specific NLP task. For classification tasks, common metrics include accuracy, precision, recall, and F1-score, which measure how well the model predicts correct labels. For tasks like machine translation or text generation, metrics such as BLEU, ROUGE, and METEOR evaluate the quality and relevance of the generated output. Confusion matrices and error analysis are also used to understand specific failure cases and model biases. Once performance is measured, optimization focuses on enhancing the model through techniques like hyperparameter tuning, feature engineering, or regularization to reduce overfitting. For deep learning models, optimization may involve adjusting learning rates, batch sizes, or using advanced techniques like dropout and early stopping. Cross-validation is often used to ensure the model performs well on different data subsets. Additionally, fine-tuning pre-trained models on task-specific data can significantly boost performance. Continuous evaluation and optimization help maintain high performance, especially when models are deployed in dynamic environments, ensuring they remain accurate, efficient, and aligned with real-world requirements.

   - **Hyperparameter Tuning:** Adjusting model parameters to improve performance.
   - **Error Analysis**: Analyzing errors to understand model weaknesses and improve robustness.

Applications of Natural Language Processing (NLP)

1. **Spam Filters:** One of the most irritating things about email is spam. Gmail

uses natural language processing (NLP) to discern which emails are legitimate and which are spam. These spam filters look at the text in all the emails you receive and try to figure out what it means to see if it's spam or not.

2. **Algorithmic Trading:** Algorithmic trading is used for predicting stock market conditions. Using NLP, this technology examines news headlines about companies and stocks and attempts to comprehend their meaning in order to determine if you should buy, sell or hold certain stocks.
3. **Questions Answering:** NLP can be seen in action by using Google Search or Siri Services. A major use of NLP is to make search engines understand the meaning of what we are asking and generate natural language in return to give us the answers.
4. **Summarizing Information:** On the internet, there is a lot of information and a lot of it comes in the form of long documents or articles. NLP is used to decipher the meaning of the data and then provides shorter summaries of the data so that humans can comprehend it more quickly.

Future Scope: NLP is shaping the future of technology in several ways:

1. **Chatbots and Virtual Assistants:** NLP enables chatbots to quickly understand and respond to user queries, providing 24/7 assistance across text or voice interactions.
2. **Invisible User Interfaces (UI):** With NLP, devices like Amazon Echo allow for seamless communication through voice or text, making technology more accessible without traditional interfaces.
3. **Smarter Search:** NLP is improving search by allowing users to ask questions in natural language, as seen with Google Drive's recent update, making it easier to find documents.
4. **Multilingual NLP:** Expanding NLP to support more languages, including regional and minority languages, broadens accessibility.

Text Preprocessing (Tokenization, Stemming, Lemmatization)

Text preprocessing is a foundational step in Natural Language Processing (NLP) that prepares raw text data for further analysis and modeling. Raw text often contains inconsistencies, noise, and variations that must be standardized to make the data suitable for computational processing. One of the first steps in preprocessing is tokenization, which involves splitting a large block of text into smaller units such as words, phrases, or sentences, called tokens. These tokens form the basic building blocks for any text analysis task. There are different types of tokenization word-level, sentence-level, or subword-level each useful in different contexts. For instance, subword tokenization is often used in transformer-based models like BERT to handle rare words more effectively. This step is crucial because it allows algorithms to understand the structure and components of text data.

Another critical part of preprocessing is stemming and lemmatization, both of which aim to reduce words to their root form to minimize vocabulary size and improve model generalization. Stemming is a rule-based process that chops off word endings (e.g., "running" becomes "run") without necessarily ensuring that the root word is valid in English. It's fast and simple but can be imprecise. On the other hand, lemmatization uses linguistic analysis to convert a word to its dictionary form, or lemma (e.g., "was" becomes "be," "better" becomes "good"), taking into account the word's part of speech. Though slower than stemming, lemmatization is more accurate and meaningful. Together, tokenization, stemming, and lemmatization help transform raw, unstructured text into a normalized format that is easier to analyze, improving the performance of machine learning and deep learning models used in NLP.

Tokenization: Tokenization is the process of breaking down a piece of text into smaller units called tokens. These tokens can be words, characters, subwords, or even phrases, depending on the type of tokenization used. It's a fundamental step in Natural Language Processing (NLP) used for tasks like text analysis, machine translation, and chatbot development. Types of Tokenization:

1. **Word Tokenization:** This is the most common type, where text is split into individual words. For example, the sentence "The quick brown fox" would be tokenized into ["The", "quick", "brown", "fox"].

   Example:

   Input: "Natural Language Processing is exciting!"

   Output: ["Natural", "Language", "Processing", "is", "exciting", "!"]

   Use Case: Common in tasks like sentiment analysis, text classification, and information retrieval.

2. **Sentence Tokenization:** This type focuses on splitting a text into individual sentences. For example, a paragraph might be split into multiple sentences.

   Example:

   Input: "NLP is fun. It helps computers understand language."

   Output: ["NLP is fun.", "It helps computers understand language."]

   Use Case: Useful for summarization, translation, and document-level processing.

3. **Subword Tokenization:** This method breaks down words into smaller units, often morphemes or sub-word units. For example, "unhappiness" might be tokenized into ["un", "happi", "ness"]. This is useful for handling rare words or languages with complex morphology.

   Example (using BERT-style WordPiece):

   Input: "unbelievable"

   Output: ["un", "##believ", "##able"]

Use Case: Used in transformer-based models like BERT, GPT, RoBERTa to improve generalization and vocabulary efficiency.

4. **Character Tokenization:** In this approach, each character in the text becomes a token. This is useful for languages without clear word boundaries (like Chinese or Japanese) or for tasks like spelling correction. For example, "hello" would be tokenized into ["h", "e", "l", "l", "o"].

   Example:

   Input: "NLP"

   Output: ["N", "L", "P"]

   Use Case: Helpful in language modeling, spelling correction, and when working with very short texts or noisy data.

5. **Phrase Tokenization:** This involves identifying and tokenizing multi-word phrases that carry a specific meaning, like "New York" or "artificial intelligence".

   Example (splitting on non-alphanumeric characters):

   Input: "Email: example@mail.com"

   Output: ["Email", "example", "mail", "com"]

   Use Case: Custom applications needing domain-specific rules, like extracting usernames, hashtags, or technical data.

Stemming: Stemming is a text normalization technique in Natural Language Processing (NLP) that reduces words to their root or base form, called a stem. This is done by removing affixes (prefixes and suffixes) from words. The stem might not be a valid word in the language. Common types of stemming algorithms include Porter, Snowball, Lancaster and Lovins. Types of Stemming Algorithms:

1. **Porter Stemmer:** A popular algorithm that uses a series of rules to remove suffixes in five steps, aiming to reduce words to their root form. For example, "eating" becomes "eat" and "happily" becomes "happi".
2. **Snowball Stemmer:** An improvement over the Porter stemmer, known for its ability to handle a wider range of words and often considered more accurate. It uses a set of rules to remove suffixes, and some consider it a better choice than Porter stemming.
3. **Lancaster Stemmer:** Another stemming algorithm that employs a more aggressive approach, potentially leading to more over-stemming (reducing words to forms that are not valid words).
4. **Lovins Stemmer:** This algorithm removes the longest suffix from a word and checks if the resulting stem is valid. It's known for its speed and ability to handle some irregular plurals, but can be less accurate.

Lemmatization: Lemmatization is a text normalization technique in Natural Language Processing (NLP) that reduces words to their base or dictionary form, known as the lemma. Unlike stemming, which simply chops off word endings, lemmatization considers the context and part of speech of a word to determine its lemma. This results in more accurate and meaningful base forms. Types of Lemmatization:

1. **Rule-Based Lemmatization:** This approach uses predefined rules and patterns to determine the lemma of a word. For instance, it might have rules to remove suffixes like "-ed" or "-ing" from regular verbs.

   Example: The word "better" would be lemmatized to "good" using a rule that handles comparative adjectives.

2. **Dictionary-Based Lemmatization:** This method relies on a dictionary or lookup table that maps words to their lemmas. When a word is encountered, the algorithm searches the dictionary to find its lemma.

   Example: A dictionary might map "better" to "good" and "running" to "run".

3. **Machine Learning-Based Lemmatization:** This approach uses machine learning models, like neural networks, trained on large text datasets to learn the relationships between words and their lemmas. These models can handle more complex linguistic patterns and exceptions.

   Example: A trained model might recognize that "better" in the context of an adjective should be lemmatized to "good".

Differences Between Tokenization, Stemming, Lemmatization: Table 5.1 shows the differences between Tokenization, Stemming, Lemmatization.

Table 5.1

S.No.	Feature	Tokenization	Stemming	Lemmatization
1.	Purpose	Splits text into smaller units (tokens)	Reduces words to their root form by removing suffixes	Reduces words to their base (dictionary) form
2.	Output	Tokens (words, sentences, or subwords)	Stems (may not be valid words)	Lemmas (valid dictionary words)
3.	Context Awareness	No	No	Yes
4.	Example Input	"running, runners ran"	"running" → "run", "runners" → "runner", "ran" → "ran"	"running", "ran" → "run", "was" → "be"
5.	Algorithms/Tools	Word/Sentence tokenizers, Regex-based tokenizers	Porter, Snowball, Lancaster Stemmers	WordNet, spaCy Lemmatizer
6.	Speed	Fast	Very fast	Slower (requires POS tagging and linguistic analysis)
7.	Accuracy	High (splits correctly)	Moderate (may over/under-stem)	High (produces linguistically correct base forms)
8.	Use Case	Text parsing, initial NLP preprocessing	Quick normalization, IR systems	High-accuracy NLP tasks like machine translation, NER

Sentiment Analysis and Topic Modeling

Sentiment analysis is an NLP technique used to determine the emotional tone behind a body of text. It is widely used in industries like marketing, customer service, and social media monitoring to gauge public opinion, customer satisfaction, or product reviews. The goal is to classify text as positive, negative, or neutral, and sometimes assign a sentiment score or probability. Traditional approaches to sentiment analysis involve machine learning models like Naive Bayes, Logistic Regression, or Support Vector Machines, trained on labeled data with sentiment tags. More advanced methods use deep learning models such as LSTMs or transformer-based architectures like BERT, which can better understand the context and nuances in human language. Sentiment analysis can be performed at the document, sentence, or aspect level each offering increasing granularity for insights.

Topic modeling, by contrast, is an unsupervised learning technique that automatically identifies the underlying themes or topics within a collection of texts. It is particularly useful for exploring large volumes of unstructured data without predefined labels. One of the most popular algorithms for topic modeling is Latent Dirichlet Allocation (LDA), which assumes that each document is a mixture of topics and each topic is a mixture of words. The output of topic modeling helps in organizing, summarizing, and discovering patterns in textual data. For example, it can be used to identify what subjects are most commonly discussed in customer feedback or news articles. Both sentiment analysis and topic modeling are valuable tools for extracting meaningful insights from text data. While sentiment analysis focuses on how people feel, topic modeling focuses on *what* they are talking about together, they offer a comprehensive understanding of textual content.

Sentiment Analysis: Sentiment analysis, also known as opinion mining, is the process of identifying and categorizing the emotional tone conveyed in a piece of text. It classifies text into sentiment categories such as positive, negative, or neutral, and sometimes even into more granular emotional states like anger, joy, sadness, or surprise. This technique is widely used in industries like marketing, politics, and customer service to monitor brand reputation, analyze product reviews, or assess public opinion. For example, a review like "The product quality is excellent" would be classified as positive, whereas "The service was terrible" would be classified as negative. Sentiment analysis can be performed at various levels document-level (entire text), sentence-level, or aspect-level (specific features or topics mentioned in the text).

The techniques used for sentiment analysis range from simple lexicon-based approaches, which use predefined dictionaries of positive and negative words, to more advanced machine learning and deep learning models. Traditional classifiers like Naive Bayes, Logistic Regression, and Support Vector Machines are used with labeled training data. Recently, transformer-based models such as BERT and RoBERTa have shown state-of-the-art performance in sentiment analysis due to their ability to understand context and word relationships. Despite its usefulness, sentiment analysis faces challenges such as sarcasm detection, ambiguity, and context sensitivity, which require careful model training and domain-specific customization.

Importance of Sentiment Analysis in NLP

1. **Measures Public Opinion**: Helps organizations understand how people feel about products, services, events, or policies.
2. **Improves Customer Experience**: Identifies positive and negative feedback from customer reviews, enabling faster resolution and service improvement.
3. **Enhances Brand Monitoring**: Tracks brand reputation in real-time across social media and other platforms.
4. **Supports Decision-Making**: Converts subjective opinions into measurable data to guide business and marketing strategies.
5. **Enables Real-Time Analysis**: Useful for monitoring live sentiment during product launches, political events, or crises.
6. **Personalizes User Interaction**: Powers chatbots and recommendation engines to respond empathetically based on user sentiment.
7. **Detects Emotion in Text**: Applicable in mental health analysis, content moderation, and social media behavior tracking.

Topic Modeling: Topic modeling is an unsupervised NLP technique that automatically discovers the abstract "topics" that occur in a collection of documents. Unlike sentiment analysis, which aims to classify emotions, topic modeling identifies what people are talking about by clustering related words and phrases into themes. This is especially useful when dealing with large amounts of unstructured text data, such as survey responses, research papers, or social media comments, where manual categorization is impractical. For example, in a dataset of restaurant reviews, topic modeling might reveal common topics such as "food quality," "service speed," or "ambience."

The most commonly used algorithm for topic modeling is Latent Dirichlet Allocation (LDA). LDA assumes each document is a mixture of topics and each topic is a mixture of words. The algorithm assigns probabilities to words and documents, enabling the identification of dominant themes. Other techniques include Non-Negative Matrix Factorization (NMF) and Latent Semantic Analysis (LSA). These methods work well when the data is well-pre-processed and structured. Topic modeling is valuable in exploratory data analysis, content recommendation, and document classification, but it also has limitations. For instance, the quality of topics can be hard to evaluate quantitatively, and the results are sensitive to the number of topics specified in advance.

Importance of Topic Modeling in NLP

1. **Extracts Key Themes Automatically**: Identifies hidden patterns and topics from large volumes of text without manual labeling.

2. **Organizes Unstructured Text**: Helps group and categorize documents, articles, or feedback based on topic similarity.
3. **Improves Content Summarization**: Useful in summarizing large documents or survey results into coherent themes.
4. **Aids in Trend Detection**: Reveals emerging issues or topics in real-time from news, research, or social media data.
5. **Enhances Search and Recommendation Systems**: Helps deliver relevant content by identifying user interests through topic analysis.
6. **Supports Exploratory Data Analysis**: Useful when there's no prior knowledge of the content, as it highlights what people are talking about.
7. **Increases Analytical Efficiency**: Saves time and resources in analyzing large textual datasets, such as reviews, legal documents, or academic papers.

Large Language Models and Chatbots

Large Language Models (LLMs), such as GPT (Generative Pre-trained Transformer), BERT (Bidirectional Encoder Representations from Transformers), and T5, represent a significant advancement in NLP. These models are trained on vast corpora of text data and can understand, generate, and manipulate human language with remarkable accuracy. Unlike traditional NLP systems that required hand-crafted rules and domain-specific training, LLMs are pre-trained on general-purpose tasks and can be fine-tuned for specific applications. Their strength lies in their ability to capture deep contextual relationships between words and sentences using transformer architectures. For example, BERT reads text bidirectionally, allowing it to understand both the left and right context of a word, which improves performance in tasks like question answering, named entity recognition, and summarization. GPT models, in particular, are generative in nature, making them highly effective for tasks like text generation, completion, and conversational AI.

One of the most practical and visible applications of LLMs is in the development of chatbots. Modern chatbots go far beyond scripted responses and are capable of engaging in dynamic, context-aware conversations with users. These chatbots leverage pre-trained language models to understand user queries, extract intent, and generate human-like responses. They are used extensively in customer support, virtual assistants, healthcare, and education. For instance, a GPT-based chatbot can answer complex customer inquiries, resolve issues, and even maintain multi-turn dialogue without needing explicit rules. The use of LLMs in chatbots significantly reduces the need for manually labeled training data and enhances scalability across different languages and domains. However, deploying these models responsibly involves addressing challenges like bias, hallucination, and privacy concerns. As LLMs and chatbots continue to evolve, they are transforming the way humans interact with machines, making communication more natural, intelligent, and accessible.

Large Language Models (LLMs): Large Language Models (LLMs) are advanced deep learning models trained on massive text datasets to understand, generate, and manipulate human language. Models like GPT, BERT, and T5 use transformer architectures that allow them to learn complex language patterns, semantic relationships, and context at scale. LLMs are pre-trained on diverse corpora such as books, websites, and social media, and then fine-tuned for specific tasks like summarization, translation, or question answering. Unlike traditional NLP models, LLMs do not require handcrafted rules or task-specific features, making them highly flexible across domains.

Large Language Models (LLMs) are advanced artificial intelligence systems trained on massive text datasets to understand, generate, and manipulate human language. Using transformer-based architectures, such as those in GPT (Generative Pre-trained Transformer) or BERT (Bidirectional Encoder Representations from Transformers), these models can learn the structure, context, and meaning of language in a highly sophisticated way. LLMs are pre-trained on diverse sources books, websites, articles and can then be fine-tuned for specific tasks like summarization, sentiment analysis, translation, or question answering. Their ability to process language with context awareness enables them to handle complex NLP tasks with high accuracy and fluency.

The importance of LLMs in NLP lies in their versatility and performance. They have drastically reduced the need for manual feature engineering or rule-based systems, enabling faster development and deployment of intelligent language applications. LLMs power tools like virtual assistants, search engines, chatbots, grammar checkers, and even code generators. They also support research, education, healthcare, and accessibility by providing advanced language understanding and generation capabilities. As LLMs continue to scale and improve, they are setting new standards in how machines interpret and communicate using human language, making them a central pillar in the evolution of AI-driven communication and automation.

Importance of Large Language Models (LLMs)

1. **Advanced Language Understanding:** Capture context, semantics, and complex relationships in text for better comprehension.
2. **Versatility:** Can be fine-tuned for a wide range of NLP tasks like translation, summarization, sentiment analysis, and more.
3. **Reduced Manual Effort:** Minimize the need for handcrafted rules or feature engineering in NLP applications.
4. **Improved Accuracy:** Achieve state-of-the-art results on many language benchmarks and real-world tasks.
5. **Scalability:** Handle vast datasets and diverse language styles, enabling broad applicability across domains.
6. **Supports Creativity:** Generate coherent, human-like text, aiding content creation, code writing, and storytelling.

7. **Enables Conversational AI:** Powers intelligent systems like chatbots, virtual assistants, and customer support bots.
8. **Accessibility:** Help build tools that improve communication for people with disabilities or language barriers.

Chatbots: Chatbots are AI-powered applications designed to simulate human-like conversations through text or speech. They are used to interact with users in real time, often through websites, mobile apps, or messaging platforms. Traditional chatbots were rule-based, relying on predefined scripts and keyword matching, but modern chatbots utilize machine learning and large language models (LLMs) to understand natural language, infer user intent, and generate context-aware responses. They can handle multi-turn dialogues, adapt to the tone of the conversation, and even personalize interactions based on user data.

The importance of chatbots in today's digital landscape is immense. They enhance user experience by providing instant, 24/7 support and automating routine tasks like answering FAQs, booking appointments, or processing transactions. This reduces operational costs and improves service efficiency for businesses across industries such as retail, healthcare, education, and finance. When integrated with LLMs like GPT, chatbots become significantly more intelligent, capable of holding fluent, coherent, and dynamic conversations. They are also instrumental in expanding accessibility, allowing users to communicate with systems via natural language instead of complex interfaces. As conversational AI continues to advance, chatbots are evolving into essential tools for digital engagement, personalized service delivery, and efficient communication at scale.

Importance of Chatbots

1. **24/7 Customer Support:** Provide instant assistance anytime, improving user satisfaction and engagement.
2. **Cost Efficiency:** Automate repetitive tasks, reducing the need for human agents and operational costs.
3. **Scalable Communication:** Handle large volumes of inquiries simultaneously without delays.
4. **Personalized Interactions:** Use user data and context to tailor responses and recommendations.
5. **Improved User Experience:** Enable natural, conversational interfaces that are easy to use.
6. **Lead Generation & Sales:** Guide users through buying processes, increasing conversion rates.
7. **Multilingual Support:** Help businesses engage customers worldwide by supporting multiple languages.
8. **Integration with LLMs:** Enhanced understanding and response generation for more natural, human-like conversations.

Differences Between Large Language Models and Chatbots: Table 5 shows the differences between Large Language Models and Chatbots.

Table 5.2

S.No.	Feature	Large Language Models (LLMs)	Chatbots
1.	Definition	AI models trained on massive text data to understand and generate human language	AI applications designed to simulate human conversation and interact with users
2.	Primary Function	Language understanding, generation, and processing	Conversational interaction with users
3.	Core Technology	Transformer-based deep learning architectures (e.g., GPT, BERT)	Often powered by LLMs or rule-based systems
4.	Output	Text generation, summarization, translation, classification	Context-aware, multi-turn dialogue responses
5.	Use Cases	Text summarization, question answering, language translation, content generation	Customer support, virtual assistants, booking, FAQs, lead generation
6.	Interaction Type	Usually non-interactive or single-turn; serves as a backend model	Interactive, multi-turn conversations with users
7.	Dependence	Can be standalone or integrated into applications	Typically rely on LLMs or other NLP models to generate responses
8.	Customization	Fine-tuned for various NLP tasks	Customized for specific business goals and conversational flows
9.	Complexity	High computational resources needed for training and inference	Varies; can be simple rule-based or complex AI-driven systems
10.	User Interface	No direct user interface; accessed via APIs or embedded in applications	Direct interface with users via chat windows, voice, or messaging apps
11.	Examples	GPT-4, BERT, T5	Siri, Alexa, customer support bots, website chat widgets

14. Time Series Analysis

Time Series Analysis is a crucial area of data science focused on analyzing data points collected or recorded at successive time intervals. Unlike traditional data, time series data is ordered chronologically, making it essential to consider the temporal context to uncover patterns, trends, and seasonality. This type of analysis is widely used in finance (stock prices), weather forecasting, economics, healthcare, and many other fields where understanding how data evolves over time is key to making predictions and informed decisions. Key components of time series analysis include identifying trends (long-term movement), seasonality (repeating patterns over fixed periods), and noise (random fluctuations). Techniques such as ARIMA (AutoRegressive Integrated Moving Average) and Exponential Smoothing help model and forecast time series data by capturing these components. More recently, deep learning models like Long Short-Term Memory (LSTM) networks have gained popularity for their ability to learn complex temporal dependencies in large datasets.

The importance of time series analysis lies in its ability to provide accurate forecasting and anomaly detection, which supports planning, resource allocation, and risk management across industries. By leveraging historical data and temporal patterns, businesses and researchers can anticipate future events and trends, optimize operations, and make data-driven decisions.

Key Concepts in Time Series Analysis

1. **Time Series Data:** Time series data consists of observations recorded at regular intervals—seconds, minutes, hours, days, months, or years. Examples include stock prices recorded every minute, daily temperature measurements, monthly sales figures, and quarterly GDP.
2. **Stationarity:** A crucial concept in time series analysis is stationarity. A time series is stationary if its statistical properties such as mean, variance, and autocorrelation structure remain constant over time. Many modeling techniques require stationarity to perform well. Non-stationary series, exhibiting trends or changing variance, often need to be transformed (e.g., by differencing) to achieve stationarity before modeling.
3. **Components of Time Series:** Time series data is typically decomposed into four key components:
    - **Trend:** The long-term upward or downward movement in the series.
    - **Seasonality:** Regular, repeating patterns or cycles occurring at fixed intervals, such as yearly, monthly, or weekly.
    - **Cyclicality:** Fluctuations occurring over irregular time periods, often linked to economic or business cycles.
    - **Noise (Residual):** Random variation or irregular fluctuations that cannot be explained by the other components.

Challenges in Time Series Analysis: Despite its power, time series analysis faces several challenges:

1. **Non-stationarity:** Many real-world series are non-stationary with evolving dynamics, requiring careful preprocessing.
2. **Missing Data and Noise:** Time series data may have gaps or measurement errors, complicating modeling.
3. **Seasonality Changes:** Seasonal patterns may evolve or shift over time.
4. **High Dimensionality:** Multivariate time series involving multiple correlated variables increase model complexity.
5. **Interpretability:** Complex models like deep learning provide high accuracy but often lack transparency.
6. **Data Volume:** Long historical records improve model training but increase computational demands.

Addressing these challenges involves a combination of data preprocessing, feature engineering, model selection, and validation techniques.

Evaluation Metrics: Evaluating time series models requires metrics that capture forecasting accuracy, such as:

1. **Mean Absolute Error (MAE):** Average absolute difference between predicted and actual values.
2. **Mean Squared Error (MSE):** Average squared difference, penalizing larger errors.
3. **Root Mean Squared Error (RMSE):** Square root of MSE, interpretable in original units.
4. **Mean Absolute Percentage Error (MAPE):** Percentage error, useful for comparing across scales.
5. **Symmetric Mean Absolute Percentage Error (sMAPE):** Addresses issues with MAPE on zero or near-zero values.

Trends and Seasonality

In time series analysis, understanding trends and seasonality is fundamental for effective modeling and forecasting. A trend represents the long-term progression or direction in the data over time. It reflects systematic increases or decreases in the variable of interest. For example, monthly sales data for a growing company might show an upward trend, indicating consistent growth over years. Identifying trends helps analysts understand whether the underlying process is improving, declining, or stable, and aids in making strategic decisions.

Seasonality refers to repeating patterns or cycles in the data that occur at fixed intervals, such as daily, weekly, monthly, or yearly. For instance, retail sales often spike during holiday seasons every year, or electricity consumption may peak during summer due to air conditioning use. Seasonal patterns arise from regular influences like weather, holidays, or social behaviors. Recognizing seasonality is crucial for accurate forecasting because ignoring these cycles can lead to misleading predictions.

Decomposing a time series into its components trend, seasonality, and residual (noise) allows better modeling by isolating different influences. Techniques such as moving averages or seasonal decomposition of time series (STL) are commonly used to visualize and separate these components. After decomposition, models can focus on capturing the trend and seasonality explicitly, improving the interpretability and accuracy of forecasts.

Understanding trends and seasonality also supports anomaly detection by distinguishing between normal seasonal fluctuations and unexpected deviations. Businesses use this insight for inventory management, budgeting, staffing, and marketing strategies, ensuring resources are aligned with predictable demand cycles. Overall, effectively identifying and modeling trends and seasonality enables more informed, data-driven decision-making across industries.

Trends in Time Series: A trend in time series refers to the long-term movement or direction in the data, showing a consistent increase or decrease over an extended period. It represents the underlying pattern that persists beyond short-term fluctuations or random noise. For example, a company's sales revenue may show a steady upward trend over several years due to business growth, or average global temperatures may exhibit a rising trend because of climate change.

Identifying trends is crucial because it reveals the general trajectory of the data, helping analysts and decision-makers understand whether values are improving, declining, or stable. Trends can be linear, where the change happens at a constant rate, or nonlinear, involving accelerating or decelerating growth.

Detecting trends allows for more accurate forecasting, as models can incorporate these long-term movements to predict future values effectively. It also aids in strategic planning, enabling businesses or policymakers to make informed decisions based on expected growth or decline. Furthermore, understanding trends helps differentiate between normal data behavior and anomalies, supporting better anomaly detection.

Common methods to identify trends include visual inspection through line plots, statistical tests for stationarity, and decomposition techniques that separate trend from seasonality and noise. Modeling trends explicitly is a key step in many forecasting methods, such as ARIMA and exponential smoothing, ensuring predictions align with the underlying data dynamics.

Importance of Trends

1. **Indicates Long-Term Changes:** Helps identify whether the data is generally increasing, decreasing, or stable over time.
2. **Supports Strategic Planning:** Businesses can forecast future growth or decline and plan investments, production, or marketing accordingly.
3. **Improves Forecast Accuracy:** Modeling trends correctly enhances the precision of predictions by capturing underlying shifts.
4. **Guides Model Selection:** Knowledge of trends helps choose or design appropriate forecasting models, such as incorporating differencing in ARIMA or using trend components in exponential smoothing.
5. **Helps Detect Structural Changes:** Identifying changes in trend patterns can indicate important shifts in the market or environment.
6. **Assists in Anomaly Detection:** Differentiates between normal upward/ downward movement and unusual data spikes or drops.
7. **Informs Policy Making:** For economic or environmental data, trend analysis supports long-term policy decisions.

Seasonality: Seasonality in time series refers to regular, repeating patterns or fluctuations that occur at fixed intervals due to seasonal factors. These intervals could be daily, weekly, monthly, quarterly, or yearly, depending on the nature of the data. Seasonality captures the cyclical behavior driven by external influences such as weather changes, holidays, cultural events, or business cycles. For example, retail sales often spike during the holiday season every year, or electricity consumption may increase during summer months due to higher air conditioning use.

Recognizing and modeling seasonality is critical for accurate time series analysis and forecasting. Seasonal patterns, if ignored, can lead to misleading conclusions and poor predictions. Seasonality is often separated from trend and noise components through decomposition methods, allowing analysts to understand each influence clearly.

Importance of Seasonality

1. **Improves Forecast Accuracy:** Incorporating seasonal patterns results in more reliable predictions by accounting for predictable cyclical changes.
2. **Optimizes Resource Allocation:** Helps businesses plan inventory, staffing, and marketing campaigns around high-demand periods.
3. **Supports Demand Planning:** Enables industries like retail, energy, and tourism to prepare for seasonal fluctuations effectively.
4. **Enhances Anomaly Detection:** Helps distinguish normal seasonal variations from unusual or unexpected data behavior.
5. **Informs Strategy Development:** Seasonal insights guide timing of promotions, product launches, and operational adjustments.
6. **Aids Model Selection:** Knowledge of seasonality helps choose appropriate models like SARIMA or Holt-Winters exponential smoothing.

ARIMA and Exponential Smoothing

ARIMA (Auto Regressive Integrated Moving Average) and Exponential Smoothing are two classical and widely used statistical techniques for time series forecasting, each with distinct methodologies and applications.

ARIMA is a versatile model that combines three components: autoregression (AR), differencing (I for integrated), and moving average (MA). The autoregressive part captures relationships between an observation and its previous values; differencing helps make a non-stationary series stationary by removing trends; and the moving average component models the relationship between observations and past forecast errors. ARIMA models are denoted as ARIMA(p,d,q), where p is the order of AR, d is the degree of differencing, and q is the order of MA. It is powerful for data with trends and autocorrelation but without strong seasonal patterns. Seasonal ARIMA (SARIMA) extends ARIMA to handle seasonality by adding seasonal terms.

Exponential Smoothing methods forecast future values by applying exponentially decreasing weights to past observations, giving more importance to recent data. Simple Exponential Smoothing works well for series without trends or seasonality. Holt's linear trend method extends it to capture trends, while Holt-Winters exponential smoothing models both trend and seasonality. These methods are intuitive, computationally efficient, and adaptive to changing data patterns.

Both ARIMA and Exponential Smoothing have been extensively used due to their interpretability and solid theoretical foundations. While ARIMA offers flexibility for modeling complex autocorrelations, Exponential Smoothing methods excel in simplicity and are often preferred for their ease of implementation in business forecasting. Combining these models with modern machine learning approaches often leads to improved forecasting performance.

LSTMs for Time Series Forecasting

Long Short-Term Memory (LSTM) networks are a specialized type of recurrent neural network (RNN) designed to model sequential data, making them highly effective for time series forecasting. Unlike traditional RNNs, which suffer from the vanishing gradient problem limiting their ability to learn long-term dependencies, LSTMs incorporate memory cells and gating mechanisms that regulate the flow of information. This allows LSTMs to remember important patterns over long periods and ignore irrelevant data, capturing complex temporal dynamics in time series.

LSTMs are especially useful for forecasting time series with nonlinear patterns, seasonality, trends, and multiple interacting variables. They learn directly from raw sequential data without requiring strict assumptions about stationarity or linearity, unlike classical models such as ARIMA. This makes them well-suited for real-world datasets where relationships evolve over time and exhibit noise or irregularities.

In practice, LSTMs take sequences of past observations as input and predict future values, often in a multi-step forecasting setup. They can be stacked in layers or combined with convolutional neural networks (CNNs) for feature extraction, creating powerful hybrid models. LSTMs have been successfully applied in finance (stock price prediction), energy demand forecasting, weather prediction, and anomaly detection.

Despite their advantages, LSTMs require large amounts of data and computational resources to train effectively. They can also be more difficult to interpret compared to classical models. Nonetheless, with advancements in hardware and software frameworks, LSTMs are increasingly popular in time series forecasting for their flexibility and superior performance in capturing complex temporal patterns.

15. Reinforcement Learning

Reinforcement Learning (RL) is a branch of machine learning where an agent learns to make decisions by interacting with an environment to maximize cumulative rewards. Unlike supervised learning, where models learn from labeled data, RL relies on trial and error, using feedback from actions taken to improve future decisions. The agent observes the current state of the environment, takes an action, and receives a reward or penalty based on the outcome. Over time, it learns policies that map states to optimal actions to achieve the best long-term results.

RL is inspired by behavioral psychology and has applications in robotics, gaming, autonomous driving, and resource management. Key concepts include the environment, agent, states, actions, rewards, and policy (the strategy the agent follows).

The agent's goal is to find a policy that maximizes the expected cumulative reward, often discounted over time to prioritize immediate gains.

Techniques like Q-learning use value functions to estimate the utility of actions in particular states, while policy gradient methods optimize the policy directly. Reinforcement learning excels in complex, dynamic scenarios where explicit programming is difficult, enabling agents to adapt and improve through experience. Its ability to solve sequential decision-making problems makes RL a powerful tool in artificial intelligence research and real-world applications.

Basics of Reinforcement Learning

Reinforcement Learning (RL) is a type of machine learning where an agent learns to make decisions by interacting with an environment to maximize cumulative rewards. Unlike supervised learning, RL doesn't rely on labeled data but instead learns through trial and error, receiving feedback in the form of rewards or penalties. The agent observes the current state, takes an action, and transitions to a new state while receiving a reward, gradually improving its strategy, or policy, over time. Key components include states, actions, rewards, a policy function, and value functions that estimate future rewards. RL is widely used in areas such as robotics, game playing, and autonomous systems, where sequential decision-making is crucial. Algorithms like Q-learning, Deep Q-Networks (DQN), and Proximal Policy Optimization (PPO) have achieved remarkable success, enabling machines to outperform humans in complex tasks. RL combines ideas from computer science, neuroscience, and control theory to enable intelligent, adaptive behavior in uncertain environments.

Key Components of Reinforcement Learning: The key components of reinforcement learning are as:

1. **Agent:** The entity that learns and makes decisions.
2. **Environment:** The world or system with which the agent interacts.

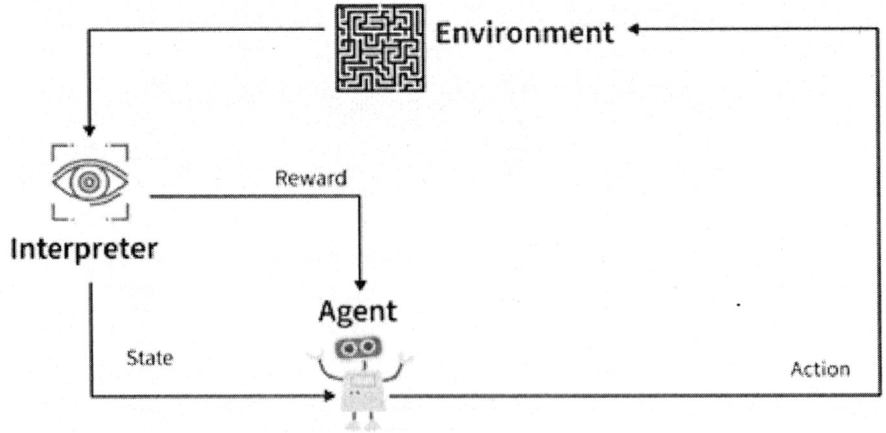

Fig. 5.2

3. **State:** The current situation or condition of the environment.
4. **Action:** The possible moves or choices the agent can take within the environment.
5. **Reward:** Feedback from the environment indicating the success or failure of an action.

How Reinforcement Learning Works?

The RL process involves an agent performing actions in an environment, receiving rewards or penalties based on those actions, and adjusting its behavior accordingly. This loop helps the agent improve its decision-making over time to maximize the cumulative reward. Here's a breakdown of RL components:

1. **Policy:** A strategy that the agent uses to determine the next action based on the current state.
2. **Reward Function:** A function that provides feedback on the actions taken, guiding the agent towards its goal.
3. **Value Function:** Estimates the future cumulative rewards the agent will receive from a given state.
4. **Model of the Environment:** A representation of the environment that predicts future states and rewards, aiding in planning.

Types of Reinforcements in RL

1. **Positive Reinforcement:** Positive Reinforcement is defined as when an event, occurs due to a particular behavior, increases the strength and the frequency of the behavior. In other words, it has a positive effect on behavior.

   Advantages: Maximizes performance, helps sustain change over time.

   Disadvantages: Overuse can lead to excess states that may reduce effectiveness.

2. **Negative Reinforcement:** Negative Reinforcement is defined as strengthening of behavior because a negative condition is stopped or avoided.

   Advantages: Increases behavior frequency, ensures a minimum performance standard.

   Disadvantages: It may only encourage just enough action to avoid penalties.

Application of Reinforcement Learning

1. **Robotics:** RL is used to automate tasks in structured environments such as manufacturing, where robots learn to optimize movements and improve efficiency.
2. **Game Playing:** Advanced RL algorithms have been used to develop

strategies for complex games like chess, Go, and video games, outperforming human players in many instances.

3. **Industrial Control:** RL helps in real-time adjustments and optimization of industrial operations, such as refining processes in the oil and gas industry.
4. **Personalized Training Systems:** RL enables the customization of instructional content based on an individual's learning patterns, improving engagement and effectiveness.

Advantages of Reinforcement Learning

1. **Solving Complex Problems:** RL is capable of solving highly complex problems that cannot be addressed by conventional techniques.
2. **Error Correction:** The model continuously learns from its environment and can correct errors that occur during the training process.
3. **Direct Interaction with the Environment:** RL agents learn from real-time interactions with their environment, allowing adaptive learning.
4. **Handling Non-Deterministic Environments:** RL is effective in environments where outcomes are uncertain or change over time, making it highly useful for real-world applications.

Disadvantages of Reinforcement Learning

1. **Not Suitable for Simple Problems**: RL is often an overkill for straightforward tasks where simpler algorithms would be more efficient.
2. **High Computational Requirements**: Training RL models requires a significant amount of data and computational power, making it resource-intensive.
3. **Dependency on Reward Function**: The effectiveness of RL depends heavily on the design of the reward function. Poorly designed rewards can lead to suboptimal or undesired behaviors.
4. **Difficulty in Debugging and Interpretation**: Understanding why an RL agent makes certain decisions can be challenging, making debugging and troubleshooting complex

Q-Learning and Policy Gradients

Q-Learning is a value-based, model-free reinforcement learning algorithm that aims to learn the optimal action-value function ***Q(s,a)***, which estimates the expected future rewards for taking action ***a*** in states. The agent updates its Q-values using the Bellman equation, gradually improving its knowledge of the environment through experience. A policy is indirectly derived from these values, typically by choosing the action with the highest Q-value (greedy policy). Q-Learning is off-policy, meaning it learns the optimal policy regardless of the agent's current behavior. It is particularly effective in discrete environments but can struggle with high-dimensional or continuous action spaces when used with function approximators like neural networks.

Policy Gradient methods, on the other hand, directly learn the policy π **(a/s)** by optimizing it to maximize the expected cumulative reward. These methods use gradient ascent to update the policy parameters in the direction that increases the probability of taking actions that lead to higher rewards. Unlike Q-Learning, Policy Gradient approaches are well-suited for problems with continuous or large action spaces and can learn stochastic policies, allowing for more flexible decision-making. However, they often suffer from high variance in gradient estimates and slower convergence, though techniques like Actor-Critic and PPO help mitigate these issues.

Q-Learning: Q-learning is a reinforcement learning algorithm where an agent learns to make decisions by interacting with an environment and receiving rewards for its actions. It focuses on learning an optimal action-selection policy by estimating the "quality" (Q-value) of taking a specific action in a given state. Key Components of Q-learning

1. **Q-Values or Action-Values:** Q-values represent the expected rewards for taking an action in a specific state. These values are updated over time using the Temporal Difference (TD) update rule.
2. **Rewards and Episodes:** The agent moves through different states by taking actions and receiving rewards. The process continues until the agent reaches a terminal state which ends the episode.
3. **Temporal Difference or TD-Update:** The agent updates Q-values using the formula:

   Where,

   S is the current state.

   A is the action taken by the agent.

   S′ is the next state the agent moves to.

   A′ is the best next action in state S′.

   R is the reward received for taking action A in state S.

   γ **(Gamma)** is the discount factor which balances immediate rewards with future rewards.

   α **(Alpha)** is the learning rate determining how much new information affects the old Q-values.
4. ***e*-greedy Policy (Exploration vs. Exploitation):** The *e*-greedy policy helps the agent decide which action to take based on the current Q-value estimates:

- **Exploitation:** The agent picks the action with the highest Q-value with probability 1–*e*. This means the agent uses its current knowledge to maximize rewards.
- **Exploration:** With probability *ee*, the agent picks a random action, exploring

new possibilities to learn if there are better ways to get rewards. This allows the agent to discover new strategies and improve its decision-making over time.

How does Q-Learning Works?

Q-learning models follow an iterative process where different components work together to train the agent. Steps-by-steps working of Q-learning is as:

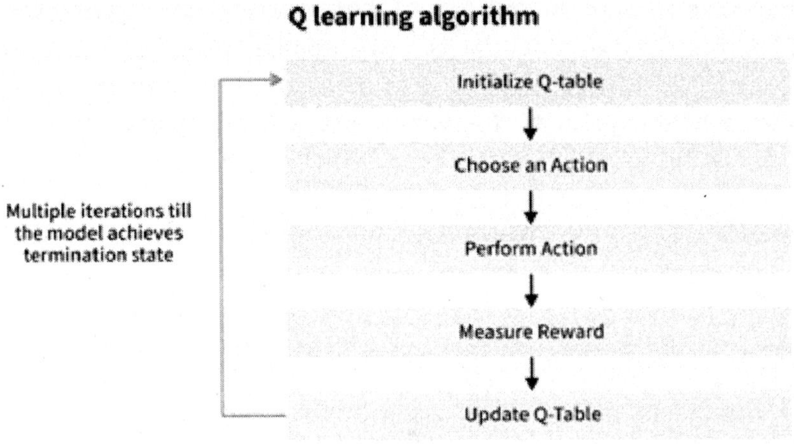

Fig. 5.3

1. **Start at a State (S):** The environment provides the agent with a starting state which describes the current situation or condition.
2. **Agent Selects an Action (A):** Based on the current state and the agent chooses an action using its policy. This decision is guided by a Q-table which estimates the potential rewards for different state-action pairs. The agent typically uses an å-greedy strategy:
   - It sometimes explores new actions (random choice).
   - It mostly exploits known good actions (based on current Q-values).
3. **Action is Executed and Environment Responds:** The agent performs the selected action. The environment then provides:
   - A new state (S2) the result of the action.
   - Reward (R) feedback on the action's effectiveness.
4. **Learning Algorithm Updates the Q-Table:** The agent updates the Q-table using the new experience:
   - It adjusts the value for the state-action pair based on the received reward and the new state.
   - This helps the agent better estimate which actions are more beneficial over time.

5. **Policy is Refined and the Cycle Repeats:** With updated Q-values the agent:
   - Improves its policy to make better future decisions.
   - Continues this loop observing states, taking actions, receiving rewards and updating Q-values across many episodes.

Methods for Determining Q-values: The methods of Q-values are as:

1. **Temporal Difference (TD):** Temporal Difference is calculated by comparing the current state and action values with the previous ones. It provides a way to learn directly from experience, without needing a model of the environment.
2. **Bellman's Equation:** Bellman's Equation is a recursive formula used to calculate the value of a given state and determine the optimal action. It is fundamental in the context of Q-learning and is expressed as:

   $$Q(s,a) = R(s,a) + \gamma \max_a Q(s',a)$$

   Where:

   Q(s, a) is the Q-value for a given state-action pair.

   R(s, a) is the immediate reward for taking action a in state s.

   γ is the discount factor, representing the importance of future rewards.

   $\max_a$ Q(s',a) is the maximum Q-value for the next state s' and all possible actions.

Policy Gradients: Policy gradients are a class of reinforcement learning algorithms that optimize a parameterized policy (a function that maps states to actions) directly by following the gradient of the expected return with respect to the policy's parameters. Essentially, they adjust the policy to favor actions that lead to higher rewards, iteratively improving the agent's decision-making process. Policy Gradient methods in Reinforcement Learning (RL) to directly optimize the policy, unlike value-based methods that estimate the value of states. These methods are particularly useful in environments with continuous action spaces or complex tasks where value-based approaches struggle. Given a policy ð parameterized by è, the goal is to optimize the objective:

$$J(\theta) = \mathbb{E}\left[\sum_t R_t\right]$$

Where R_t is the reward at time t and the expectation is taken over states and actions under the policy $\pi\theta$.

Working of Policy Gradient Methods: The core idea behind policy gradient methods is to compute the gradient of the objective function J(θ) with respect to the policy parameters θ. The general algorithm involves the following steps:

1. **Rollout**: The agent interacts with the environment following the current policy, collecting states, actions and rewards.
2. **Compute the Return**: The return Gt is the cumulative reward obtained from

time step t onwards. This is often computed as the discounted sum of rewards.

3. **Compute the Gradient**: The gradient of the objective function with respect to the policy parameters is computed using the collected data.
4. **Update the Policy**: The policy parameters are updated using gradient ascent to improve the expected return.

Policy gradient helps improve decisions by checking how each action affects the total reward. Using the likelihood ratio method, we adjust the policy to make better choices over time.

Types of Policy Gradient Methods: The different types of policy gradient methods are as:

1. **REINFORCE Algorithm:** REINFORCE is a simple Monte Carlo method that directly estimates the policy gradient using complete episodes from the environment. It updates the policy parameters based on the log probability of actions taken, weighted by the return (cumulative reward) from those actions. While simple it can suffer from high variance in the gradient estimates.
2. **Actor-Critic Methods:** Actor-Critic methods use two parts: the actor which decides what action to take and the critic which evaluates how good that action was. The critic provides feedback to the actor help to improve its decisions. This setup makes learning more stable and reduces the randomness in the updates.
3. **Proximal Policy Optimization (PPO):** Proximal Policy Optimization (PPO) is a method that carefully updates the decision-making rules. It avoids making big changes at once which helps keep training steady. This balance makes PPO reliable and popular for tough problems.

Applications of Policy Gradient Methods: Policy gradient methods have shown remarkable performance in various real-world applications, including:

1. **Robotics:** Help robots learn tasks like picking up objects, walking and moving around obstacles by learning from experience.
2. **Autonomous Vehicles:** Policy gradient algorithms are used to optimize the driving policies for self-driving cars.
3. **Game AI:** Enable systems to develop smart strategies by learning through trial and error in games like Go, Chess and various video games.
4. **Natural Language Processing:** In tasks like machine translation and dialogue generation, policy gradient methods help to optimize policies for generating human-like responses.

Differences Between Q-Learning and Policy Gradients: The differences between Q-Learning and policy gradients are listed in table 5.3.

Table 5.3

S.No.	Features	Q-Learning	Policy Gradients
1.	Type	Value-based	Policy-based
2.	Learning Target	Action-value function Q(s,a)Q(s, a)	Policy (\pi(a
3.	Policy	Derived (greedy or ε-greedy from Q-values)	Learned directly
4.	Policy Type	Deterministic or ε-greedy	Stochastic
5.	Update Mechanism	Temporal Difference (TD) learning	Gradient ascent on expected return
6.	Action Space	Best for discrete action spaces	Handles both discrete and continuous spaces
7.	Exploration Strategy	ε-greedy or similar	Inherent via stochastic policies
8.	Stability with NN	Can be unstable without careful tuning (e.g., DQN)	More stable in high-dimensional problems
9.	Variance	Lower variance in updates	Higher variance (requires techniques like baseline)
10.	Convergence Speed	Generally, faster in simple environments	Slower due to high variance
11-	Off-policy or On-policy	Off-policy	Typically, on-policy (some variants are off-policy)
12.	Use Cases	Tabular environments, simple games	Robotics, continuous control, complex decision-making

Applications in Robotics and Game AI

AI in robotics and game AI are both areas experiencing significant growth and innovation. In robotics, AI enables autonomous navigation, predictive maintenance, surgical assistance, and human-robot collaboration. In game AI, it enhances the behavior of non-player characters (NPCs), creates dynamic environments, and generates new gaming experiences.

Role of Robotics in Artificial Intelligence

Artificial Intelligence has played a very major role not only in increasing the comforts of humans but also by increasing industrial productivity, which includes quantitative as well as qualitative production and cost-efficiency. An artificial intelligence robot can significantly enhance these benefits by integrating advanced algorithms and machine learning capabilities.

Robotics and artificial intelligence (AI) are closely related fields, and when combined, they give rise to a discipline known as robotic artificial intelligence or simply "robotics in artificial intelligence."

1. Robotics in AI involves integrating AI technologies into robotic systems to enhance their capabilities and enable them to perform more complex tasks.
2. AI in robotics allows robots to learn from experience, adapt to new situations, and make decisions based on data from sensors. This can involve machine

learning, computer vision, natural language processing, and other AI techniques.

3. Robots can use machine learning algorithms to analyze data, recognize patterns, and improve their performance over time. This is particularly useful for tasks where the environment is dynamic or unpredictable.
4. AI-powered vision systems enable robots to interpret and understand visual information from the surroundings. This is crucial for tasks like object recognition, navigation, and manipulation.

How AI is used in Robotics?

AI plays a crucial role in modern robotics, bringing intelligence and adaptability to these fascinating machines. An Artificial Intelligence Robot is a perfect example of how AI enhances the capabilities of robots, enabling them to perform a wide range of tasks with increased autonomy and adaptability. There are several ways in which an Artificial Intelligence Robot utilizes AI in robotics:

1. **Object Recognition**: AI-powered computer vision allows robots to recognize and identify objects in their environment. Computer vision helps robots understand their surroundings, create maps, and navigate through complex environments. This is essential for autonomous vehicles, drones, and robots operating in unstructured spaces.
2. **Visual serving:** AI allows robots to track and precisely manipulate objects based on visual feedback, crucial for tasks like welding, painting, or assembling delicate components.

Applications in Robotics and Game AI: Applications in Robotics and Game AI refer to how artificial intelligence (AI) techniques are integrated into robotics and games to enhance autonomy, decision-making, and realism.

Applications in Robotics:

1. **Industrial Automation:** Industrial automation involves using robots and control systems to perform manufacturing tasks such as assembly, welding, and packaging. These robots enhance precision, speed, and efficiency while reducing human error and labor costs. Collaborative robots (cobots) further enable safe interaction between humans and machines on modern factory floors.
   - Robots are extensively used in manufacturing industries for repetitive tasks.
   - Common tasks: welding, painting, assembly, material handling, and packaging.
   - Benefits: Increased precision, speed, efficiency, and reduction in human error.
   - Use of Collaborative Robots (Cobots) allows safe human-robot interaction on the factory floor.

2. **Healthcare and Medical Robotics:** Healthcare and medical robotics assist in surgery, rehabilitation, and patient care. Surgical robots enable precise, minimally invasive procedures, while rehabilitation robots support physical therapy. Telepresence robots allow remote consultations, and companion robots aid elderly care. These technologies enhance treatment accuracy, patient recovery, and access to medical services.
   - Surgical Robots (e.g., Da Vinci System) assist in minimally invasive surgeries with high precision.
   - Rehabilitation Robots help in physical therapy and motor function recovery.
   - Telepresence Robots allow doctors to interact with patients remotely.
   - Companion Robots support elderly care and improve mental well-being.
3. **Service and Hospitality Robots:** Service and hospitality robots are used in hotels, restaurants, and retail to assist with tasks like check-ins, food delivery, cleaning, and customer guidance. They improve efficiency, reduce wait times, and enhance customer experience. These robots operate autonomously or alongside staff, streamlining operations and offering consistent, high-quality service.
   - Robots are used in hotels, restaurants, and retail for customer interaction and service.
   - Applications include automated check-in, food delivery, room cleaning, and guiding customers.
   - Enhance customer experience while reducing reliance on human staff.
4. **Domestic Robotics:** Domestic robotics involves robots designed to assist with household tasks such as vacuuming, lawn mowing, window cleaning, and home security. Devices like robotic vacuum cleaners (e.g., Roomba) automate routine chores, saving time and effort. Integrated with smart home systems, they enhance convenience, safety, and energy efficiency in everyday living.
   - Household robots perform daily chores like vacuuming (e.g., Roomba), lawn mowing, and window cleaning.
   - Smart home integration allows robots to assist with security and environmental control.
5. **Autonomous Vehicles:** Autonomous vehicles use robotics, sensors, and AI to navigate and operate without human input. Equipped with LiDAR, cameras, and GPS, they detect surroundings, make real-time decisions, and ensure safe driving. Applications include self-driving cars, trucks, and public transport, revolutionizing logistics, mobility, and reducing traffic accidents and human error.
   - Self-driving cars and trucks use robotic systems for navigation, perception, and decision-making.

- Utilize sensors (LiDAR, radar, cameras) and AI algorithms for safe travel.
- Applications include ride-sharing, logistics, and public transportation.

6. **Drones and Aerial Robotics:** Drones and aerial robotics are unmanned flying devices used in agriculture, surveillance, delivery, photography, and disaster response. Equipped with cameras, sensors, and GPS, they collect data, monitor environments, and perform tasks in hard-to-reach areas. Their speed, flexibility, and efficiency make them valuable tools across many industries.
   - Unmanned Aerial Vehicles (UAVs) used in agriculture, surveillance, delivery, photography, and disaster response.
   - Agricultural drones monitor crop health and spray fertilizers with precision.
   - Delivery drones are being tested for last-mile logistics (e.g., Amazon Prime Air).
7. **Search and Rescue Operations:** Search and rescue robots assist in locating and saving people during disasters like earthquakes, fires, or floods. Equipped with cameras, sensors, and mobility tools, they access dangerous or collapsed areas unsafe for humans. These robots provide real-time data, enhancing rescue efforts and increasing the chances of saving lives.
   - Robots operate in disaster zones, collapsed buildings, or hazardous areas.
   - Equipped with cameras and sensors to locate survivors or assess damage.
   - Used in firefighting, earthquake rescue, and flood relief operations.
8. **Exploration Robots:** Exploration robots are designed for remote environments like space and deep oceans. Space rovers explore planets, gathering scientific data, while underwater robots investigate the ocean depths. These robots operate in extreme conditions humans cannot easily access, enabling valuable research and discoveries in astronomy, marine biology, and geology.
   - Space Robots (e.g., NASA's Mars rovers) collect data from planets and celestial bodies.
   - Underwater Robots explore oceans and shipwrecks, where human access is limited.
   - Help in collecting scientific data in extreme environments.
9. **Agricultural Robotics:** Agricultural robotics automates farming tasks such as planting, weeding, irrigation, and harvesting. Using AI and sensors, these robots monitor crop health and optimize resource use, increasing efficiency and yield. They reduce labor costs and support sustainable farming practices by precisely targeting inputs like water and fertilizers.
   - Robots automate tasks like planting, weeding, irrigation, and harvesting.
   - Use AI and computer vision for crop monitoring and precision farming.
   - Reduces labor costs and increases food production efficiency.

10. **Military and Defense:** Military and defense robots perform tasks like surveillance, reconnaissance, bomb disposal, and combat support. Unmanned ground and aerial vehicles reduce risks to soldiers by operating in dangerous environments. These robots enhance mission efficiency, provide real-time intelligence, and assist in training and simulations, improving overall defense capabilities.
    - Robots used for surveillance, reconnaissance, and bomb disposal.
    - Unmanned ground and aerial vehicles assist in reducing soldier risk.
    - Robotic systems are also used for training and simulations.
11. **Education and Research:** Education and research robots are used to teach STEM concepts and advance robotics technology. Educational kits like LEGO Mindstorms engage students in programming and engineering. Research robots help test AI, machine learning, and human-robot interaction, driving innovation and preparing the next generation of scientists and engineers.
    - Robots are used as teaching aids in schools and universities.
    - Educational kits (like LEGO Mindstorms) promote STEM learning.
    - Research robots test algorithms in AI, machine learning, and human-robot interaction.

Applications in Game AI: Game AI focuses on creating intelligent, responsive, and believable behaviors in virtual characters:

1. **Non-Player Character (NPC) Behavior**: AI governs NPC actions, enabling dynamic and realistic responses to player interactions. Techniques like behavior trees and finite state machines create engaging and unpredictable opponents or allies, enhancing gameplay depth and immersion.
    - AI controls NPCs to create realistic, dynamic behaviors.
    - Techniques like finite state machines, behavior trees, and utility systems enable characters to react appropriately to player actions.
    - Enhances immersion and gameplay challenge.
2. **Pathfinding and Navigation**: AI algorithms such as A* help characters move efficiently through complex game environments by calculating optimal paths. Navigation meshes guide NPCs around obstacles, ensuring smooth, believable movement essential for strategy and adventure games.
    - AI algorithms (e.g., A*, Dijkstra) guide characters to navigate complex game environments.
    - Navigation meshes and waypoint systems help NPCs move naturally around obstacles.
    - Crucial in strategy, RPG, and open-world games for believable movement.

3. **Procedural Content Generation (PCG)**: AI dynamically creates game elements like levels, maps, quests, and items, ensuring unique experiences in each playthrough. This boosts replayability and reduces developer workload, seen in games like *Minecraft* and *No Man's Sky*.
   - AI generates game content such as levels, maps, quests, and items.
   - Ensures variety and replicability by creating unique experiences.
   - Used in games like Minecraft, No Man's Sky, and Rogue Legacy
4. **Adaptive Difficulty and Dynamic Balancing**: AI adjusts game challenges in real time based on player skill and performance. This maintains player engagement by preventing frustration or boredom, creating a tailored and enjoyable experience.
   - AI monitors player performance and adjusts difficulty to maintain engagement.
   - Prevents player frustration or boredom by scaling challenges.
   - Example: Left 4 Dead uses AI Director to control enemy spawn rates and intensity.
5. **Player Modeling and Personalization**: AI analyzes player behavior and preferences to customize gameplay, storylines, and matchmaking. This personalization increases player satisfaction, retention, and immersion by offering experiences suited to individual styles.
   - AI analyzes player behavior to customize game experience.
   - Can tailor storylines, suggest strategies, or match players in multiplayer games.
   - Enhances player retention and satisfaction.
6. **Game Testing and Quality Assurance**: AI bots simulate player actions to identify bugs, glitches, and balance issues during development. This automated testing accelerates quality assurance, ensuring smoother gameplay and fewer post-release problems.
   - AI bots simulate player actions to test game mechanics and find bugs.
   - Speeds up the testing process and uncovers issues hard to detect manually.
   - Improves game stability and balance before release.
7. **Natural Language Processing (NLP) and Dialogue Systems**: AI enables NPCs to understand and respond to player text or voice input, creating interactive and meaningful conversations. This enriches storytelling and player engagement in RPGs and interactive fiction.
   - AI enables NPCs to understand and respond to player text or voice input.
   - Creates immersive interactions and complex storylines.

- Used in RPGs and interactive storytelling games.

8. **Strategic and Tactical AI**: AI controls opponents in strategy games, planning moves and adapting tactics. It challenges players by simulating intelligent behavior, as seen in chess engines or real-time strategy (RTS) games.
   - AI opponents plan and execute strategies in real-time or turn-based games.
   - Examples include chess engines, RTS game AIs, and fighting game bots.
   - Provides challenging opponents that require skill and adaptation.
9. **Simulation of Realistic Environments**: AI manages environmental factors like weather, day-night cycles, and ecosystems that react to player actions, creating immersive and dynamic game worlds.
   - AI controls environmental elements like weather, day-night cycles, and ecosystems.
   - Creates dynamic, believable worlds that react to player actions.
   - Enhances immersion and narrative depth.
10. **Emotion and Behavior Simulation**: AI models NPC emotions and psychological states, enabling realistic reactions and deeper player connections. This adds narrative complexity and empathy within story-driven games.
    - AI models emotions or psychological states for NPCs to display realistic reactions.
    - Increases player empathy and engagement.
    - Used in narrative-driven games for deeper storytelling.
11. **Multiplayer Matchmaking and Anti-Cheat Systems**: AI matches players by skill level for fair competition and detects cheating behaviors. This maintains game integrity and enhances the multiplayer experience.
    - AI analyzes player skill levels for fair matchmaking.
    - Detects cheating or abnormal behavior to maintain game integrity.
    - Enhances multiplayer experience and fairness.
12. **Training and Coaching AI**: AI provides personalized tutorials, hints, and feedback to help players improve skills. Adaptive coaching adjusts based on player progress, fostering learning and mastery.
    - AI tutors help players improve skills by offering hints, tutorials, or feedback.
    - Adaptive coaching based on player performance encourages learning.
    - Useful in competitive and educational games.
13. **Virtual Reality (VR) and Augmented Reality (AR) AI**: AI enhances VR/AR by controlling responsive virtual characters and environments that adapt to user interactions, increasing immersion and realism in these interactive experiences.

- AI enhances immersion by controlling virtual characters and adapting scenarios in real-time.
- Improves responsiveness and realism in VR/AR environments.
- Enables natural interaction between players and digital worlds.

14. **AI-Driven Storytelling**: AI dynamically alters narratives based on player decisions, enabling branching storylines and personalized plots. This increases replicability and gives players meaningful control over the story.
    - AI dynamically alters narrative paths based on player choices.
    - Supports branching storylines and personalized narratives.
    - Increases replicability and player agency.

SUMMARY OF ADVANCED TOPICS IN DATA SCIENCE

As the field of data science continues to evolve, several advanced topics have become central to pushing the boundaries of what is possible with data-driven insights. This summary explores three such critical areas: Natural Language Processing (NLP), Time Series Analysis, and Reinforcement Learning. Each of these domains offers unique techniques and applications that empower machines to understand language, predict temporal patterns, and make intelligent decisions over time.

13. Natural Language Processing (NLP)

Natural Language Processing (NLP) is a specialized field within artificial intelligence that focuses on enabling computers to understand, interpret, and generate human language. It bridges the gap between human communication and computer understanding by combining computational linguistics with machine learning and deep learning techniques. Key processes in NLP include text preprocessing steps such as tokenization, stemming, and lemmatization, which prepare raw text data for analysis. NLP tasks range from simple functions like language detection and keyword extraction to more complex applications such as sentiment analysis, topic modeling, machine translation, and text summarization. Modern advancements in NLP are driven by large language models (LLMs) like BERT and GPT, which use deep neural networks to comprehend context and semantics. NLP is widely applied in real-world systems, including voice assistants, chatbots, customer support automation, and language-based search engines. It plays a crucial role in making human-computer interaction more natural and efficient.

- **Text Preprocessing:** Effective NLP begins with preprocessing, where raw text is cleaned and structured for analysis. Text preprocessing is the initial step in Natural Language Processing that prepares raw text for analysis. It includes tasks like tokenization, lowercasing, removing punctuation, stop words removal, stemming, and lemmatization. These techniques clean and standardize text, improving the performance of machine learning models by reducing noise and complexity. Key steps include:

- **Tokenization**: This process breaks down text into individual units, such as words or phrases (tokens). Tokenization is essential for most NLP tasks, as it simplifies text for further processing.
- **Stemming**: Stemming reduces words to their root forms. For example, "running" becomes "run." It uses heuristic rules and may result in non-dictionary forms, but it's computationally efficient.
- **Lemmatization**: Unlike stemming, lemmatization reduces words to their base or dictionary form (lemma) using vocabulary and morphological analysis. For example, "better" becomes "good." Though slower, it preserves more meaning.

Together, these techniques standardize text, reduce dimensionality, and improve model performance.

- **Sentiment Analysis and Topic Modeling:** These are popular NLP tasks that extract insights from large volumes of text. Sentiment analysis and topic modeling are key NLP techniques. Sentiment analysis identifies the emotional tone of text, classifying it as positive, negative, or neutral. Topic modeling, often using methods like LDA, uncovers hidden themes within large text corpora. Both are widely used in marketing, social media, and customer feedback analysis.
  - **Sentiment Analysis** aims to determine the emotional tone behind words. It categorizes text as positive, negative, or neutral, often using supervised learning algorithms. Applications include social media monitoring, product reviews, and customer service automation.
  - **Topic Modeling**, an unsupervised learning technique, identifies abstract topics within a collection of documents. Latent Dirichlet Allocation (LDA) is a common method used for this purpose. It uncovers themes in large text datasets, useful in research, journalism, and marketing.
- **Large Language Models and Chatbots:** Large Language Models (LLMs), such as GPT, BERT, and their successors, have transformed NLP by leveraging deep learning and transformer architectures. They are trained on massive datasets and are capable of:
  - Understanding context and nuance
  - Generating coherent and contextually relevant text
  - Performing translation, summarization, and question answering

  Chatbots powered by LLMs can engage in dynamic, human-like conversations. They are used in customer service, education, and personal assistants. Modern chatbots often combine retrieval-based and generative models to balance factual accuracy and natural dialogue.

14. Time Series Analysis

Time series analysis focuses on data points collected or recorded at specific time intervals. This form of analysis is crucial in finance, economics, weather forecasting, and operations. Time Series Analysis involves studying data points collected or recorded at specific time intervals to identify patterns, trends, and seasonal variations. It is widely used in fields like finance, economics, weather forecasting, and operations management. Key components of time series include trend (long-term movement), seasonality (repeating short-term cycle), and noise (random variation). Common methods include ARIMA (AutoRegressive Integrated Moving Average), which models temporal dependencies, and exponential smoothing, which gives more weight to recent observations. More advanced models like LSTMs (Long Short-Term Memory networks) can capture complex temporal patterns. Time series analysis aids in forecasting future values and detecting anomalies.

- **Trends and Seasonality:** Trends and seasonality are fundamental components of time series analysis. A trend represents the long-term direction in the data, showing whether values are increasing, decreasing, or remaining stable over time. Seasonality refers to recurring patterns or fluctuations that occur at regular intervals, such as daily, monthly, or yearly cycles. For example, retail sales may spike every December due to holidays, indicating a seasonal pattern. Identifying these components helps analysts better understand data behavior and improve forecasting accuracy. Decomposing a time series into trend, seasonal, and residual components allows for more effective modeling and insight into underlying processes driving the data. A fundamental step in time series analysis is decomposing data into its components:
  - **Trend**: The long-term movement in a time series. It could be upward, downward, or stationary.
  - **Seasonality**: Regular patterns that repeat at specific intervals (e.g., monthly sales peaks due to holidays).
  - **Cyclic and Irregular Components**: These reflect longer-term economic cycles or random noise.
- **ARIMA and Exponential Smoothing:** ARIMA (AutoRegressive Integrated Moving Average) and Exponential Smoothing are widely used methods for time series forecasting. ARIMA models the relationship between past values and past forecast errors using three components: autoregression (AR), differencing (I), and moving average (MA). It's effective for stationary data or can be adapted for non-stationary data through differencing. Exponential Smoothing assigns exponentially decreasing weights to older observations. Variants include Simple, Holt's Linear, and Holt-Winters (for seasonality). It's intuitive and performs well for short-term forecasts. Both methods are useful for identifying trends and patterns, with ARIMA preferred for complex data and smoothing for simplicity and interpretability. Two classical models dominate traditional time series forecasting:

ARIMA (AutoRegressive Integrated Moving Average): ARIMA models are effective for univariate forecasting and require careful tuning of parameters (p, d, q). Combines three aspects:

- AR (autoregression): Predicts future values using past values.
- I (integration): Makes the data stationary by differencing.
- MA (moving average): Models the error of the prediction as a linear combination of past errors.

Exponential Smoothing assigns exponentially decreasing weights to past observations. Types include:

- Simple Exponential Smoothing (for data with no trend or seasonality)
- Holt's Linear Trend Model (for trending data)
- Holt-Winters Method (for seasonal data)

These models are easy to interpret and implement, making them useful in business forecasting.

- **LSTMs for Time Series Forecasting:** With the rise of deep learning, Long Short-Term Memory (LSTM) networks have become a popular choice for time series tasks. LSTMs, a type of Recurrent Neural Network (RNN), are designed to remember long-term dependencies. LSTMs outperform traditional models in complex, real-world scenarios like stock prediction or energy demand forecasting. However, they require significant computational resources and careful tuning. Advantages include:
  - Handling non-linear patterns
  - Learning from multivariate inputs
  - Robustness to noisy data

15. Reinforcement Learning (RL)

Reinforcement Learning is a machine learning paradigm where agents learn optimal actions through interaction with an environment. It differs from supervised learning in that it uses rewards and punishments rather than labeled data. Reinforcement Learning (RL) is a machine learning paradigm where an agent learns to make decisions by interacting with an environment. The agent receives rewards or penalties based on its actions and aims to maximize cumulative rewards over time. RL involves key concepts like states, actions, rewards, and policies. Algorithms such as Q-learning and policy gradients help agents learn optimal strategies. Unlike supervised learning, RL does not rely on labeled data but learns through trial and error. It's widely used in robotics, game AI, recommendation systems, and autonomous vehicles, where adaptive decision-making in dynamic environments is essential.

- **Basics of Reinforcement Learning:** Reinforcement Learning involves an agent learning to make decisions by interacting with an environment. The agent observes states, takes actions, and receives rewards or penalties. Its goal is to learn a policy that maximizes cumulative rewards through trial and error, improving performance over time without labeled data. The core elements of RL include:

- **Agent**: The decision-maker
- **Environment**: Where the agent operates
- **State**: A snapshot of the environment
- **Action**: What the agent can do
- **Reward**: Feedback received after taking an action

The goal is to learn a policy (a strategy mapping states to actions) that maximizes cumulative rewards over time. RL problems are often formulated using Markov Decision Processes (MDPs), where the next state depends only on the current state and action.

- **Q-Learning and Policy Gradients:** Q-Learning is a value-based, model-free algorithm that estimates the expected utility of taking a given action in a particular state. The Q-table is updated using the Bellman Equation. Deep Q-Networks (DQNs) extend this approach using neural networks, enabling it to handle large or continuous state spaces.

  Policy Gradient Methods: These directly optimize the policy using gradients. Rather than learning value functions, they learn the probability distribution over actions. REINFORCE and Actor-Critic models are prominent examples. Policy gradients are better suited for environments with high-dimensional or continuous action spaces.

- **Applications in Robotics and Game AI:** Reinforcement Learning has made major strides in practical applications:
  - **Robotics**: RL enables robots to learn locomotion, grasping, and manipulation tasks through trial and error, often in simulated environments before transferring to the real world.
  - **Game AI**: One of RL's most famous milestones was DeepMind's AlphaGo defeating world champions in Go. In gaming, RL agents learn strategies that outperform human experts in complex games such as StarCraft, Dota 2, and more.

  Additionally, RL is being explored in areas like recommendation systems, autonomous vehicles, and adaptive control systems.

Chapter 6

Big Data and Data Engineering

Big Data and Data Engineering are critical fields that handle the collection, processing, and management of massive and complex datasets that traditional methods cannot efficiently address. Big Data refers to extremely large volumes of data generated from diverse sources like social media, sensors, transactions, and devices. Its key characteristics include high volume, velocity, variety, and veracity, often summarized as the "4 Vs." Managing big data requires scalable storage and computing solutions.

Data Engineering focuses on designing, building, and maintaining the infrastructure and pipelines that enable efficient data collection, storage, transformation, and retrieval. This includes working with distributed systems such as Hadoop and Spark, as well as cloud platforms for scalable processing. Data engineers develop ETL (Extract, Transform, Load) workflows to clean and prepare data for analysis.

Together, big data and data engineering support data-driven decision-making by ensuring data is reliable, accessible, and in a usable format. They enable organizations to harness insights from vast datasets, powering machine learning models, business intelligence, and real-time analytics. The combination of advanced storage technologies, processing frameworks, and pipeline automation is fundamental to modern data ecosystems.

Big Data

Big Data in Data Science refers to the massive, diverse, and fast-growing datasets that data scientists analyze to extract valuable insights. Unlike traditional datasets, big data is characterized by the "4 Vs": Volume (large scale), Velocity (high speed of data generation), Variety (different data types like text, images, and videos), and Veracity (uncertainty or quality of data). Big data enables more comprehensive and accurate models by providing richer information and patterns. It requires specialized tools and frameworks such as Hadoop, Spark, and cloud platforms to store, process, and analyze data efficiently. Big data analytics powers applications like predictive modeling, recommendation systems, fraud detection, and customer segmentation. By leveraging big data, data scientists can uncover deeper insights, drive innovation, and support better decision-making across industries. Big data services enable a more comprehensive understanding of trends and patterns, by integrating diverse data sets to form a complete picture. This fusion not only facilitates retrospective analysis but also enhances predictive capabilities, allowing for more accurate forecasts and strategic decision-making. Additionally, when combined with AI, big data transcends traditional analytics, empowering organizations to unlock innovative solutions and drive transformational outcomes.

More complete answers mean more confidence in the data which means a completely different approach to tackling problems.

1. **Better insights:** When organizations have more data, they're able to derive better insights. In some cases, the broader range confirms gut instincts against a more diverse set of circumstances. In other cases, a larger pool of data uncovers previously hidden connections and expands potentially missed perspectives. All of this allows organizations to have a more comprehensive understanding into the how and why of things, particularly when automation allows for faster, easier processing of big data.
2. **Decision-making:** With better insights, organizations can make data-driven decisions with more reliable projections and predictions. When big data combines with automation and analytics, that opens an entire range of possibilities, including more up-to-date market trends, social media analysis, and patterns that inform risk management.
3. **Personalized customer experiences:** Big data allows organizations to build customer profiles through a combination of customer sales data, industry demographic data, and related data such as social media activity and marketing campaign engagement. Before automation and analytics, this type of personalization was impossible due to its sheer scope; with big data, this level of granularity improves engagement and enhances the customer experience.
4. **Improved operational efficiency:** Every department generates data, even when teams don't really think about it. That means that every department can benefit from data on an operational level for tasks such as detecting process anomalies, identifying patterns for maintenance and resource use, and highlighting hidden drivers of human error. Whether technical problems or staff performance issues, big data produces insights about how an organization operates—and how it can improve.

Source of Big Data:

1. **Social media:** Today's world a good percent of the total world population is engaged with social media like Facebook, WhatsApp, Twitter, YouTube, Instagram, etc. Each activity on such media like uploading a photo, or video, sending a message, making comment, putting like, etc create data.
2. **A sensor placed in various places:** Sensor placed in various places of the city that gathers data on temperature, humidity, etc. A camera placed beside the

road gather information about traffic condition and creates data. Security cameras placed in sensitive areas like airports, railway stations, and shopping malls create a lot of data.

3. **Customer Satisfaction Feedback:** Customer feedback on the product or service of the various company on their website creates data. For Example, retail commercial sites like Amazon, Walmart, Flipkart, and Myntra gather customer feedback on the quality of their product and delivery time. Telecom companies, and other service provider organizations seek customer experience with their service. These create a lot of data.

Big Data Application: The applications of Big Data are as:

1. **IoT Appliance:** Electronic devices that are connected to the internet create data for their smart functionality, examples are a smart TV, smart washing machine, smart coffee machine, smart AC, etc. It is machine-generated data that are created by sensors kept in various devices. For Example, a Smart printing machine is connected to the internet. A number of such printing machines connected to a network can transfer data within each other. So, if anyone loads a file copy in one printing machine, the system stores that file content, and another printing machine kept in another building or another floor can print out that file hard copy. Such data transfer between various printing machines generates data.
2. **E-commerce:** In e-commerce transactions, business transactions, banking, and the stock market, lots of records stored are considered one of the sources of big data. Payments through credit cards, debit cards, or other electronic ways, all are kept recorded as data.
3. **Global Positioning System (GPS):** GPS in the vehicle helps in monitoring the movement of the vehicle to shorten the path to a destination to cut fuel, and time consumption. This system creates huge data on vehicle position and movement.
4. **Transactional Data:** Transactional data, as the name implies, is information obtained through online and offline transactions at various points of sale. The data contains important information about transactions, such as the date and time of the transaction, the location where it took place, the items bought, their prices, the methods of payment, the discounts or coupons that were applied, and other pertinent quantitative data. These are some of the sources of transactional data: orders for payment, Invoices, E-receipts and recordkeeping etc.
5. **Machine Data:** Automatically generated machine data is produced in reaction to an event or according to a set timetable. This indicates that all of the data was compiled from a variety of sources, including satellites, desktop computers, mobile phones, industrial machines, smart sensors, SIEM logs, medical and wearable devices, road cameras, IoT devices, and more. Businesses

can monitor consumer behaviour thanks to these sources. Data derived from automated sources expands exponentially in tandem with the market's shifting external environment. These sensors are used to capture this kind of information: In a broader sense, machine data includes data that is generated by servers, user applications, websites, cloud programmes, and other sources.

Five "Vs" of Big Data?

Traditionally, we've recognized big data by three characteristics: variety, volume, and velocity, also known as the "three Vs." However, two additional Vs have emerged over the past few years: value and veracity. Those additions make sense because today, data has become capital. Think of some of the world's biggest tech companies. Many of the products they offer are based on their data, which they're constantly analyzing to produce more efficiency and develop new initiatives. Success depends on all five Vs.

1. **Volume:** The amount of data matters. With big data, you'll have to process high volumes of low-density, unstructured data. This can be data of unknown value, such as X (formerly Twitter) data feeds, clickstreams on a web page or a mobile app, or sensor-enabled equipment. For some organizations, this might be tens of terabytes of data. For others, it may be hundreds of petabytes.
2. **Velocity:** Velocity is the fast rate at which data is received and (perhaps) acted on. Normally, the highest velocity of data streams directly into memory versus being written to disk. Some internet-enabled smart products operate in real time or near real time and will require real-time evaluation and action.
3. **Variety:** Variety refers to the many types of data that are available. Traditional data types were structured and fit neatly in a relational database. With the rise of big data, data comes in new unstructured data types. Unstructured and semi structured data types, such as text, audio, and video, require additional preprocessing to derive meaning and support metadata.
4. **Veracity:** How truthful is your data and how much can you rely on it? The idea of veracity in data is tied to other functional concepts, such as data quality and data integrity. Ultimately, these all overlap and steward the organization to a data repository that delivers high-quality, accurate, and reliable data to power insights and decisions.
5. **Value:** Data has intrinsic value in business. But it's of no use until that value is discovered. Because big data assembles both breadth and depth of insights, somewhere within all of that information lies insights that can benefit your organization. This value can be internal, such as operational processes that might be optimized, or external, such as customer profile suggestions that can maximize engagement.

Evolution of Big Data: Past, Present, and Future: Although the concept of big data is relatively new, the need to manage large data sets dates back to the 1960s and '70s, with the first data centres and the development of the relational database.

Past: Around 2005, people began to realize just how much data users generated through Facebook, YouTube, and other online services. Apache Hadoop, an open-source framework created specifically to store and analyze big data sets, was developed that same year. NoSQL also began to gain popularity during this time.

Present: The development of open-source frameworks, such as Apache Hadoop and more recently, Apache Spark, was essential for the growth of big data because they make big data easier to work with and cheaper to store. In the years since then, the volume of big data has skyrocketed. Users are still generating huge amounts of data but it's not just humans who are doing it. With the advent of the Internet of Things (IoT), more objects and devices are connected to the internet, gathering data on customer usage patterns and product performance. The emergence of machine learning has produced still more data.

Future: While big data has come far, its value is only growing as generative AI and cloud computing use expand in enterprises. The cloud offers truly elastic scalability, where developers can simply spin up ad hoc clusters to test a subset of data. And graph databases are becoming increasingly important as well, with their ability to display massive amounts of data in a way that makes analytics fast and comprehensive.

Big Data Use Cases: Big data can help you optimize a range of business activities, including customer experience and analytics. Here are just a few.

1. **Retail and Ecommerce:** Companies such as Netflix and Procter & Gamble use big data to anticipate customer demand. They build predictive models for new products and services by classifying key attributes of past and current products or services and modeling the relationship between those attributes and the commercial success of the offerings. In addition, P&G uses data and analytics from focus groups, social media, test markets, and early store rollouts to plan, produce, and launch new products.
2. **Healthcare:** The healthcare industry can combine numerous data sources internally, such as electronic health records, patient wearable devices, and staffing data, and externally, including insurance records and disease studies, to optimize both provider and patient experiences. Internally, staffing schedules, supply chains, and facility management can be optimized with insights provided by operations teams. For patients, their immediate and long-term care can change with data driving everything such as personalized recommendations and predictive scans.
3. **Financial Services:** When it comes to security, it's not just a few rogue attackers—you're up against entire expert teams. Security landscapes and compliance requirements are constantly evolving. Big data helps you identify patterns in data that indicate fraud and aggregate large volumes of information to make regulatory reporting much faster.
4. **Manufacturing:** Factors that can predict mechanical failures may be deeply buried in structured data—think the year, make, and model of equipment—

as well as in unstructured data that covers millions of log entries, sensor data, error messages, and engine temperature readings. By analyzing these indications of potential issues before problems happen, organizations can deploy maintenance more cost effectively and maximize parts and equipment uptime.

5. **Government and Public Services:** Government offices can potentially collect data from many different sources, such as DMV records, traffic data, police/firefighter data, public school records, and more. This can drive efficiencies in many different ways, such as detecting driver trends for optimized intersection management and better resource allocation in schools. Governments can also post data publicly, allowing for improved transparency to bolster public trust.

Big Data Best Practices: To help you on your big data journey, we've put together some key best practices for you to keep in mind. Here are our guidelines for building a successful big data foundation.

1. **Align big data with specific business goals:** More extensive data sets enable you to make new discoveries. To that end, it is important to base new investments in skills, organization, or infrastructure with a strong business-driven context to guarantee ongoing project investments and funding. To determine if you are on the right track, ask how big data supports and enables your top business and IT priorities. Examples include understanding how to filter web logs to understand ecommerce behavior, deriving sentiment from social media and customer support interactions, and understanding statistical correlation methods and their relevance for customer, product, manufacturing, and engineering data.
2. **Ease skills shortages with standards and governance:** One of the biggest obstacles to benefiting from your investment in big data is not having enough staff with the necessary skills to analyze your data. You can mitigate this risk by ensuring that big data technologies, considerations, and decisions are added to your IT governance program. Standardizing your approach will allow you to manage costs and leverage resources. Organizations implementing big data solutions and strategies should assess their skill requirements early and often and should proactively identify any potential skill gaps. These can be addressed by training/cross-training existing resources, hiring new resources, and leveraging consulting firms.
3. **Optimize knowledge transfer with a center of excellence:** Use a center of excellence approach to share knowledge, control oversight, and manage project communications. Whether big data is a new or expanding investment, the soft and hard costs can be shared across the enterprise. Leveraging this approach can help increase big data capabilities and overall information architecture maturity in a more structured and systematic way.
4. **The top payoff is aligning unstructured with structured data:** It is certainly valuable to analyze big data on its own. But you can bring even greater business

insights by connecting and integrating low-density big data with the structured data you are already using today. Whether you are capturing customer, product, equipment, or environmental big data, the goal is to add more relevant data points to your core master and analytical summaries, leading to better conclusions. For example, there is a difference in distinguishing all customer sentiment from that of only your best customers. Which is why many see big data as an integral extension of their existing business intelligence capabilities, data warehousing platform, and information architecture.

Keep in mind that the big data analytical processes and models can be both human- and machine-based. Big data analytical capabilities include statistics, spatial analysis, semantics, interactive discovery, and visualization. Using analytical models, you can correlate different types and sources of data to make associations and meaningful discoveries.

5. **Plan your discovery lab for performance:** Discovering meaning in your data is not always straightforward. Sometimes we don't even know what we're looking for. That's expected. Management and IT needs to support this lack of direction or lack of clear requirement.

   At the same time, it's important for analysts and data scientists to work closely with the business to understand key business knowledge gaps and requirements. To accommodate the interactive exploration of data and the experimentation of statistical algorithms, you need high performance work areas. Be sure that sandbox environments have the support they need and are properly governed.

6. **Align with the cloud operating model:** Big data processes and users require access to a broad array of resources for both iterative experimentation and running production jobs. A big data solution includes all data realms including transactions, master data, reference data, and summarized data. Analytical sandboxes should be created on demand. Resource management is critical to ensure control of the entire data flow including pre- and post-processing, integration, in-database summarization, and analytical modeling. A well-planned private and public cloud provisioning and security strategy plays an integral role in supporting these changing requirements.

16. Big Data Technologies

Big data technologies encompass the tools, techniques, and systems used to manage, process, and analyze massive datasets that exceed the capabilities of traditional data processing software. These technologies are crucial for extracting valuable insights and making informed decisions from complex, large-scale information. Big Data technologies are tools and frameworks designed to store, process, analyze, and manage massive volumes of structured, semi-structured, and unstructured data. These technologies support scalability, fault tolerance, and high-speed processing. They are broadly categorized as follows:

1. **Data Storage and Management:** Data storage and management in Big Data involve systems that can handle vast amounts of structured and unstructured data reliably and efficiently. Hadoop Distributed File System (HDFS) is a core technology that stores data across multiple machines in a fault-tolerant way, enabling high-throughput access. NoSQL databases like Apache HBase, Cassandra, and MongoDB are designed to scale horizontally, providing real-time access to large datasets. Cloud-based storage solutions such as Amazon S3, Google Cloud Storage, and Azure Blob Storage offer scalable, secure, and cost-effective data storage with global accessibility. These platforms support redundancy, versioning, and integration with analytics tools. Effective data management also involves metadata handling, data lifecycle policies, backup strategies, and access controls. Together, these tools form the backbone of any big data system, allowing organizations to store, retrieve, and manage petabytes of data across geographically distributed environments for analytics, compliance, and business intelligence purposes.
   - **Hadoop Distributed File System (HDFS):** A scalable, fault-tolerant file system for storing large datasets across multiple machines.
   - **Apache HBase:** A NoSQL database that runs on top of HDFS, used for real-time read/write access to big data.
   - **Amazon S3, Google Cloud Storage, Azure Blob Storage:** Cloud-based storage systems for massive and flexible data handling.
2. **Data Processing Frameworks:** Data processing frameworks are essential for analyzing large volumes of data quickly and efficiently. Apache Hadoop's MapReduce provides a programming model for processing data in parallel across clusters. It splits tasks into smaller units that are processed simultaneously, then aggregated. However, Hadoop is mainly suited for batch processing. Apache Spark, a more advanced framework, offers in-memory processing, making it significantly faster for iterative algorithms and real-time analytics. It supports multiple languages (Scala, Python, Java) and libraries for machine learning (MLlib), graph processing (GraphX), and SQL queries (Spark SQL). Apache Flink and Apache Storm are designed for real-time stream processing, handling event-driven data with low latency. These frameworks can integrate with HDFS, Kafka, and cloud services, allowing seamless data flow from storage to computation. They are highly scalable, fault-tolerant, and optimized for distributed computing, making them ideal for complex data science tasks such as predictive modeling, anomaly detection, and log analysis.
   - **Apache Hadoop (MapReduce):** Batch processing engine that splits large datasets and processes them in parallel.
   - **Apache Spark:** In-memory data processing engine known for speed and ease of use, suitable for batch and real-time processing.

- **Apache Flink & Storm:** Real-time stream processing frameworks.

3. **Data Ingestion Tools:** Data ingestion tools move raw data from various sources such as databases, sensors, logs, and applications into storage or processing systems in real or batch time. Apache Kafka is a high-throughput, distributed messaging system used for building real-time data pipelines. It enables decoupling of data producers and consumers, ensuring reliable and scalable data transmission. Apache NiFi is a user-friendly, flow-based tool that supports automated data ingestion, transformation, and routing with a visual interface. It excels in tracking data lineage, prioritizing security and compliance. Apache Sqoop is another tool, mainly used for importing/exporting large volumes of data between relational databases (like MySQL or Oracle) and Hadoop. Flume is optimized for log data collection and aggregation. Effective ingestion tools support high data velocity, transformation during ingestion, and fault tolerance. These tools form the first critical step in the big data pipeline, ensuring that data reaches storage or analysis systems in a timely, consistent, and usable format.
   - **Apache Kafka:** Distributed messaging system for high-throughput real-time data streaming.
   - **Apache NiFi:** Automates data flow between systems, supports data ingestion, routing, and transformation.
4. **Data Querying and Analysis:** Data querying and analysis tools allow users to explore and gain insights from big data using familiar query languages and interfaces. Apache Hive provides a SQL-like interface (HiveQL) on top of Hadoop, enabling analysts to run queries without deep programming knowledge. It translates queries into MapReduce or Spark jobs for execution. Impala, developed by Cloudera, is optimized for low-latency SQL queries on Hadoop, offering faster performance compared to Hive. Presto, now Trino, is another high-performance, distributed SQL engine that allows querying data across multiple sources like HDFS, S3, MySQL, and Kafka simultaneously. These tools enable data scientists and analysts to perform complex joins, aggregations, and filtering on massive datasets efficiently. They integrate well with visualization platforms like Tableau and Power BI. By enabling interactive exploration of data and supporting business intelligence workflows, these technologies help translate raw data into actionable insights, enabling informed decision-making in real-time and batch-processing environments.
   - **Apache Hive & Impala:** SQL-like query engines for big data stored in Hadoop.
   - **Presto:** Distributed SQL query engine for querying large datasets from multiple sources.
5. **Data Orchestration and Workflow Management:** Data orchestration and workflow management tools are crucial for automating, scheduling, and

managing complex data pipelines across systems. Apache Airflow is a widely used tool that allows users to define workflows as Directed Acyclic Graphs (DAGs) using Python. It provides scheduling, logging, monitoring, and retry mechanisms, making it ideal for managing multi-step processes like ETL jobs, machine learning pipelines, and report generation. Apache Oozie is a workflow scheduler for Hadoop, capable of managing MapReduce, Hive, and Pig jobs. It is XML-based and tightly integrated with the Hadoop ecosystem. These tools ensure that data tasks are executed in the correct order, with dependencies and failure recovery mechanisms. They support triggers based on time or external events and provide audit trails for data lineage and debugging. Effective orchestration enhances reliability, scalability, and repeatability in data workflows, which is critical for enterprise-level big data operations where timing, accuracy, and automation are essential.

- **Apache Airflow:** Manages complex data pipelines through DAGs (Directed Acyclic Graphs).
- **Oozie:** Workflow scheduler system for Hadoop jobs.

6. **Big Data Ecosystem Support Tools:** Big Data ecosystem support tools help manage and coordinate the infrastructure that powers data storage, processing, and analytics. Apache ZooKeeper is a centralized service for maintaining configuration information, naming, and synchronization across distributed systems. It ensures coordination and consistency among nodes in big data clusters, which is essential for fault tolerance and resource sharing. YARN (Yet Another Resource Negotiator), a core component of Hadoop, acts as a cluster resource manager. It allocates system resources to various applications running on a Hadoop cluster, enabling multi-tenancy and scalability. Ambari is another tool used for provisioning, monitoring, and managing Hadoop clusters through a web-based interface. Kubernetes, while not Hadoop-specific, is increasingly used for containerized deployment and orchestration of big data services. These support tools ensure efficient operation, monitoring, scalability, and resilience of the big data ecosystem. They are the backbone that keeps distributed systems functioning smoothly, even as workloads and data volumes grow.

   - **Zookeeper:** Coordinates distributed applications and manages configuration.
   - **YARN (Yet Another Resource Negotiator):** Manages cluster resources in the Hadoop ecosystem.

Big data technologies enable organizations to store and analyze petabytes of data efficiently, forming the backbone of data science, machine learning, and real-time analytics applications.

Hadoop and MapReduce

Hadoop and MapReduce are closely related but distinct concepts in big data processing. Hadoop is a framework for distributed storage and processing of large datasets, while MapReduce is a programming model and software framework within Hadoop for parallel data processing. MapReduce utilizes the distributed storage capabilities of Hadoop (HDFS) to process data in parallel across multiple nodes.

Hadoop: Hadoop software is a framework that permits the distributed processing of huge data sets across clusters of computers using simple programming models. In simple terms, Hadoop is a framework for processing 'Big Data. Hadoop was created by Doug Cutting. It was also created by Mike Cafarella. It is designed to scale from single servers to thousands of machines, each having local computation and storage. Hadoop is an open-source software. The core of Apache Hadoop consists of a storage part, known as the Hadoop Distributed File System (HDFS), and a processing part, which may be a MapReduce the programming model. Hadoop splits files into large blocks and distributes them across nodes in a cluster. It then transfers packaged code into nodes to process the info in parallel.

1. **Distributed Storage:** Hadoop's core component, the Hadoop Distributed File System (HDFS), allows for storing massive datasets across a cluster of computers.
2. **Scalability and Fault Tolerance:** Hadoop is designed to handle large volumes of data and is fault-tolerant, meaning it can continue operating even if some nodes fail.
3. **Open-Source Framework:** Hadoop is an open-source framework, widely used for big data processing and analytics.

Mapreduce: MapReduce is a programming model that is used for processing and generating large data sets on clusters of computers. It was introduced by Google. MapReduce is a concept or a method for large-scale parallelization. It is inspired by functional programming map() and reduce() functions.

1. **Parallel Processing:** MapReduce divides data processing tasks into smaller, parallelizable subtasks that can be executed on different nodes.
2. **Two-Phase Processing:** It consists of two main phases: the Map phase, where data is processed and transformed, and the Reduce phase, where the results from the Map phase are combined to produce the final output.
3. **Programming Model:** It provides a programming model that simplifies the development of parallel data processing applications.
4. **Core Component:** MapReduce is one of the core components of the Hadoop ecosystem, playing a vital role in processing structured and unstructured data.

MapReduce program is executed in three stages they are:

1. **Mapping: The** Mapper's job is to process input data. Each node applies the map function to the local data.
2. **Shuffle:** Here nodes are redistributed where data is based on the output keys. (output keys are produced by map function).

3. **Reduce:** Nodes are now processed into each group of output data, per key, in parallel.

Difference Between Hadoop and MapReduce: The differences between Hadoop and MapReduce is listed in table 6.1.

Table 6.1

S.No.	Aspect	Hadoop	MapReduce
1.	Definition	A framework for distributed storage and processing of large datasets	A programming model used for processing data within Hadoop
2.	Functionality	Provides storage (via HDFS) and resource management (via YARN)	Provides data processing using map and reduce functions
3.	Component Type	Complete ecosystem/framework	A processing paradigm or module within the Hadoop ecosystem
4.	Main Components	HDFS, YARN, MapReduce, and tools like Hive, Pig	Map function (splits and processes data), Reduce function (aggregates)
5.	Purpose	To manage and process big data using distributed computing	To execute batch processing tasks in a parallel and distributed manner
6.	Execution	Manages resources and job scheduling across nodes	Executes specific tasks written in MapReduce format
7.	Flexibility	Highly flexible with support for multiple processing engines (e.g., Spark)	Limited to the map and reduce paradigm
8.	Speed	Slower if using only MapReduce	Generally slower compared to modern engines like Spark
9.	Use Case	Broad platform for big data storage and processing	Batch processing of large-scale data

Apache Spark and Distributed Computing

Apache Spark is a powerful open-source distributed computing framework designed for fast and scalable data processing. Unlike traditional MapReduce, Spark performs in-memory computation, significantly speeding up tasks like iterative algorithms and real-time analytics. It supports multiple programming languages, including Python (PySpark), Scala, Java, and R.

Spark provides a unified engine for batch processing, stream processing (via Spark Streaming), machine learning (via MLlib), graph processing (via GraphX), and SQL querying (via Spark SQL). Its Resilient Distributed Dataset (RDD) abstraction ensures fault tolerance and efficient data distribution across clusters. Distributed computing in Spark involves breaking down large tasks into smaller ones, distributing them across multiple nodes in a cluster, and combining the results. This parallelism enables Spark to handle petabytes of data efficiently. It integrates well with Hadoop (using HDFS), cloud storage, and data lakes, making it a go-to solution for modern big data analytics and data science workloads.

Apache Spark: Apache Spark is an open-source, distributed processing system designed for large-scale data analytics and machine learning. It provides a unified engine for handling various workloads, including batch processing, interactive queries, streaming, and machine learning. Spark excels in performance due to its ability to process data in-memory and optimize query execution.

Spark Components: There are several components of Spark ecosystem, some of them are getting developed. Few respective contributions are being made every now and then. Initially, Spark ecosystem empowers following 6 components which are mentioned below:

1. **Apache Spark core:** Spark core is the kernel of Apache Spark and is the foundation of parallel and distributed processing. Spark core is accountable for all the fundamental I/O functionalities. Also, includes monitoring of jobs over cluster, scheduling jobs on the cluster. Self-recovery of fault, task dispatching, networking and efficient memory management also included.

   Due to In-memory computation capability, it provides high speed. In Spark core, we use a special data structure RDD. RDD refers to Resilient Distributed Datasets. While we need to share or reuse data in computing systems like Hadoop MapReduce. That requires data to be stored in intermediate stores. Thus, that slowdowns the speed of computation. Hence, RDD overcomes this limitation by introducing fault tolerant "In-Memory" computation.

Fig. 6.1

2. **Apache Spark SQL:** Spark SQL is one of the Spark Ecosystem components. If the data is too voluminous, we use Spark SQL to perform structured data analysis. Using this component we get more information on data structure and computations. This information helps in performing extra optimization. We can also compute an output on the engine. There is no need for languages to express the computation. Also, allows running Hive queries on existing Hadoop deployment.

   Spark SQL makes the process of extracting and merging various datasets easier. So that we can use the datasets for machine learning. We can access structured as well as semi-structured data in it. Also, acts as a distributed SQL query engine.

3. **Apache Spark Streaming:** This is one of the lightweight components of Spark Ecosystem. It allows developers to perform batch processing and data streaming with ease. To process data in real time, it uses a continuous stream of input data. The great advantage is fast scheduling capacity. Also, helps to perform streaming analytics by ingesting data in mini-batches. On this mini batches of data, we allow transformation process.

4. **Apache Spark Mllib:** MLlib is one of the most important components of Spark Ecosystem. It is a scalable machine learning library, which provides both High-quality algorithms as well as blazing Speed. This library supports all APIs like Java, Scala, and Python as part of Spark applications. Due to this feature, we can include it in our complete workflows. It has quickly emerged as a critical piece in mining Big Data system. MLlib is very simple to use and scalable. It is compatible with various programming languages. This can be easily integrated with other tools also. The deployment and development of scalable pipelines are becoming easier through MLlib.

5. **Apache Spark GrahphX:** It is **a** graph computation engine built on top of Spark. GraphX enables users to build, transform and reason about data at scale. It is available with a library of common algorithms already. For cross-world manipulations, GraphX is an API.

   On top of Apache Spark, this easily solves this problem. Through Graphx Clustering, classification pathfinding is also possible. Also, Graph and GraphX parallel execution are possible through it. Spark has its own Graph Computation Engine for graphs and graphical computations.

6. **Apache Spark R:** R is a language that enhances developer productivity for statistical analysis. To handle processing in the single machine, we can use R language along with Spark through SparkR. Apache Spark R is a boon for users to enable R with the power of Spark. Basically, it is the key component of language R. For data processing, Data Frames are the basic data structure.

7. **Scalability to many cores and machines:** This can run on terabytes of data and clusters with thousands of machines at same time. Also, operations that execute on DataFrames, get distributed across the cluster.

Key Features and Capabilities:

1. **Unified Engine:** Spark offers a single platform for diverse data processing needs, including batch processing, real-time stream processing, machine learning, and graph processing.

2. **In-Memory Processing:** Spark can cache data in memory, significantly speeding up iterative algorithms and interactive queries compared to traditional disk-based systems like MapReduce.

3. **Distributed Processing:** Spark distributes data and computations across a cluster of computers, enabling it to handle massive datasets.
4. **Fault Tolerance:** Spark ensures data reliability by tracking the lineage of data transformations, allowing it to reconstruct lost data in case of failures.
5. **Programming Languages:** Spark provides APIs for Java, Scala, Python, and R, making it accessible to a wide range of developers.
6. **Built-in Libraries:** Spark includes libraries for SQL (Spark SQL), streaming (Spark Streaming), machine learning (MLlib), and graph processing (GraphX), facilitating diverse data analysis tasks.

Distributed Computing: Distributed computing is the process of using multiple computers, or nodes, connected over a network to solve a complex problem or task as if they were a single system. Instead of relying on a single powerful machine, the task is divided into smaller parts, and these parts are processed concurrently on different computers, which then collaborate to deliver the final result. This approach offers several benefits, including increased processing power, scalability, and improved fault tolerance. Key Concepts:

1. **Multiple Computers/Nodes:** Distributed systems utilize a network of individual computers or servers, each with its own processing capabilities and potentially its own data storage.
2. **Network Connection:** These computers are connected through a network, allowing them to communicate and exchange information.
3. **Task Decomposition:** Complex problems are broken down into smaller, independent tasks that can be executed in parallel by different nodes.
4. **Coordination and Collaboration:** The nodes in a distributed system work together, coordinating their efforts to complete the overall task.

Examples of Distributed Systems:

1. **Cloud Computing:** Large-scale cloud platforms like AWS, Azure, and Google Cloud utilize distributed computing to provide services to millions of users.
2. **Big Data Processing:** Systems like Hadoop and Spark are used to process massive datasets by distributing the workload across multiple machines.
3. **Content Delivery Networks (CDNs):** CDNs use distributed servers to store and deliver content to users based on their geographic location, improving performance and reducing latency.
4. **High-Performance Computing (HPC):** Supercomputers often employ distributed computing to tackle complex scientific simulations and calculations.

NoSQL Databases

NoSQL databases, also known as non-relational or "not only SQL" databases, are a departure from traditional relational databases. They are designed to handle a wide variety of data formats, including unstructured and semi-structured data, and are known for their flexibility and scalability. Unlike relational databases that use tables with rows and columns, NoSQL databases employ various data models like document, key-value, wide-column, and graph.

Types of NoSQL Databases

NoSQL databases are generally classified into four main categories based on how they store and retrieve data.

1. **Document databases:** Document databases store data as documents, usually in JSON, BSON, or XML format. Each document is a self-contained unit that includes both the data and its structure (schema). These databases are ideal for handling semi-structured data and allow for flexible, dynamic schemas meaning each document in a collection can have different fields. This flexibility makes them popular for web, mobile, and content-driven applications. They support complex queries, indexing, and aggregation operations. Common use cases include content management systems, user profiles, e-commerce catalogs, and real-time analytics. Document databases scale horizontally and are built for high availability and performance.

   Examples: MongoDB, CouchDB, Amazon DocumentDB

2. **Key-value stores:** Key-value stores are the simplest type of NoSQL database. They store data as a key (unique identifier) and a value (the actual data). This model provides extremely fast data access, making it ideal for scenarios like caching, session management, user preference storage, and real-time data retrieval. These databases typically lack complex querying capabilities, but excel at speed and scalability. They are highly efficient for operations that

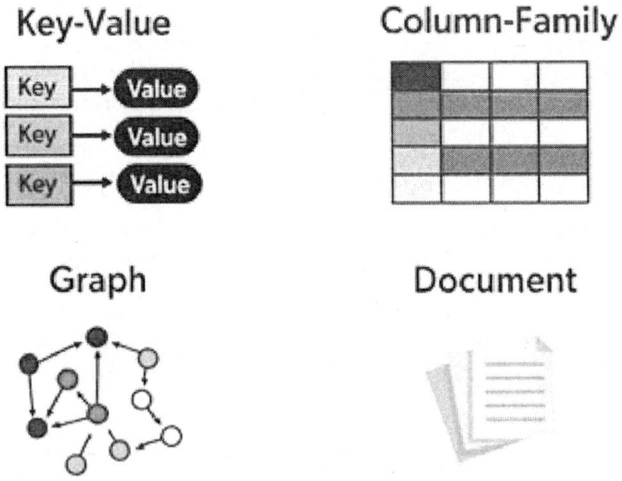

Fig. 6.2

require lookups by key, such as retrieving a shopping cart or user profile quickly.

Examples: Redis, Amazon DynamoDB, Riak

3. **Column-Family Stores:** Column-family stores organize data into rows and columns, but unlike relational databases, columns are grouped into families and stored together. Each row doesn't have to contain the same columns, allowing for more flexible and efficient storage of sparse data. This model is well-suited for analytics, time-series data, and large-scale data warehouses. These databases can handle massive amounts of data across distributed nodes and are optimized for fast reads and writes across columns, rather than rows. Popular in use cases like telemetry, logs, and real-time analytics, column-family stores are designed for high throughput and horizontal scaling.

   Examples: Apache Cassandra, HBase, ScyllaDB

4. **Graph Databases:** Graph databases use nodes, edges, and properties to represent and store data. Nodes represent entities (e.g., people, products), edges represent relationships (e.g., friend, bought), and properties store data about both. This structure allows for fast and complex querying of relationships, which would be slow and inefficient in traditional relational databases. They are ideal for scenarios where relationships between data points are central, such as social networks, recommendation engines, fraud detection, and network topology mapping. Graph queries use pattern matching, making it easy to traverse complex relationships. Graph databases are schema-flexible and can handle changes in the structure of relationships over time without impacting performance.

   Examples: Neo4j, Amazon Neptune, ArangoDB

17. Data Pipelines and Automation

Data pipelines and automation refer to the streamlined, automated processes used to collect, process, transform, and move data from various sources to destinations such as data warehouses, databases, or analytics tools. A data pipeline typically involves a series of steps including data ingestion, cleansing, transformation, and loading (ETL/ELT), often scheduled or triggered to run continuously or at intervals. Automation ensures these steps happen reliably without manual intervention, improving efficiency, consistency, and scalability. Pipelines are crucial in modern data engineering, supporting real-time analytics, machine learning workflows, and business intelligence reporting by ensuring data is fresh, accurate, and accessible. Tools like Apache Airflow, AWS Data Pipeline, and Azure Data Factory are widely used for orchestration, allowing teams to monitor, schedule, and manage complex workflows. Automation also includes error handling, retries, and logging, making pipelines robust and production-ready. As businesses increasingly rely on data for decision-making, automated pipelines reduce latency, minimize human error, and enable faster insights. They are essential in environments dealing with large volumes of data from diverse sources such as web logs, APIs, IoT devices, or databases. In essence, data pipelines and automation form the backbone of modern data infrastructure, enabling continuous data flow and intelligent data-driven operations.

Data Pipelines: A data pipeline is a series of automated steps that move and process data from one or more sources to a destination, where it can be analyzed and used. It's essentially a structured series of operations that enable the flow and transformation of data, turning raw data into valuable insights. Data Pipeline deals with information that is flowing from one end to another. In simple words, we can say collecting the data from various resources than processing it as per requirement and transferring it to the destination by following some sequential activities. It is a set of manner that first extracts data from various resources and transforms it to a destination means it processes it as well as moves it from one system to another system.

Types of Data Pipelines: The different types of data pipeline are as:

1. **Batch Data Pipelines**: Batch data pipelines are designed to process large volumes of data in discrete chunks at scheduled intervals such as hourly, daily, or weekly. They are ideal when real-time processing is not required, and when dealing with historical data, logs, or periodic reports. The process involves extracting data from one or more sources, transforming it (e.g., cleansing, aggregating), and then loading it into a destination like a data warehouse or lake commonly known as ETL (Extract, Transform, Load) or ELT. Batch pipelines are efficient for operations like end-of-day sales reports, monthly billing data, or analytics dashboards that don't require up-to-the-second accuracy. They are relatively simple to implement and cost-effective, especially for predictable workloads. Popular tools include Apache Spark, AWS Glue, and Talend. However, batch pipelines may introduce latency, as data is only updated after each scheduled run, which can limit use in time-sensitive applications. Despite that, their reliability, scalability, and ease of orchestration make them suitable for many enterprise and analytical use cases where data freshness is less critical than data completeness and consistency.

Fig. 6.3

2. **Real-Time Data Pipelines**: Real-time data pipelines process and transmit data immediately as it's generated, enabling near-instant insights and actions. They

are essential for applications that require low latency and continuous data flow, such as fraud detection systems, recommendation engines, live dashboards, and IoT monitoring. These pipelines ingest data from streaming sources like Apache Kafka, Amazon Kinesis, or Google Pub/Sub, process it using tools such as Apache Flink or Apache Spark Streaming, and deliver it to destinations such as real-time databases or alerting systems. Real-time pipelines often include windowing functions, event-time handling, and out-of-order event correction to ensure accuracy in time-sensitive processing. Unlike batch pipelines, they are designed to operate continuously, handling high-throughput data with milliseconds to seconds of latency. While more complex to develop and maintain, real-time pipelines enable dynamic decision-making and improve user experiences through personalized, adaptive systems. They often complement batch pipelines by covering use cases where immediate feedback or response is critical. Real-time pipelines also need to be highly resilient and fault-tolerant to prevent data loss and ensure reliable delivery, making monitoring, scalability, and message durability essential design considerations.

3. **Cloud-Native Data Pipelines**: Cloud-native data pipelines are built to run seamlessly in cloud environments, leveraging the scalability, flexibility, and managed services offered by cloud providers. These pipelines use cloud-based tools and services such as AWS Glue, Azure Data Factory, Google Dataflow, and Snowflake to automate data movement, transformation, and orchestration. Being cloud-native means the pipeline architecture takes advantage of the cloud's elasticity resources can scale up or down based on demand without manual intervention. These pipelines are designed to be highly available, cost-efficient, and resilient, often supporting both batch and streaming workloads. They also offer integrated monitoring, security, and compliance features, making them ideal for enterprise-grade operations. Cloud-native pipelines reduce the need for managing infrastructure, thus enabling teams to focus on data logic and business goals. They can easily connect with other cloud-native systems like cloud storage, databases, AI/ML services, and BI tools, creating a fully integrated data ecosystem. As organizations increasingly migrate to the cloud, cloud-native data pipelines offer a future-proof, maintainable solution for handling large-scale data flows across hybrid or multi-cloud environments, promoting agility, automation, and innovation in data operations.

4. **Open-Source Data Pipelines**: Open-source data pipelines are built using community-driven, freely available tools and frameworks that offer flexibility, transparency, and customization for building end-to-end data workflows. These pipelines are popular among data engineers who want full control over data processing logic, infrastructure, and integration without vendor lock-in. Tools like Apache Airflow (workflow orchestration), Apache Kafka (real-time messaging), Apache Spark (batch/stream processing), and dbt (data transformation) are widely used in open-source ecosystems. They allow teams

to create robust pipelines tailored to specific needs, from ingestion to transformation to storage. Open-source pipelines are often modular and composable, making it easier to integrate various tools and scale systems horizontally. While they offer cost advantages and community support, they do require technical expertise to deploy, configure, and maintain, especially in production environments. Open-source pipelines are ideal for organizations that prioritize customization, transparency, and portability. They can be run on-premises or in the cloud, and offer flexibility to avoid proprietary ecosystems. Additionally, many open-source tools now integrate well with modern cloud and container environments (e.g., Kubernetes), making them a powerful choice for hybrid and complex data infrastructure. However, they also require investments in monitoring, security, and governance to ensure long-term reliability and compliance.

Data Pipeline Architecture: Fig.6.4 shows the representation of data pipeline architecture.

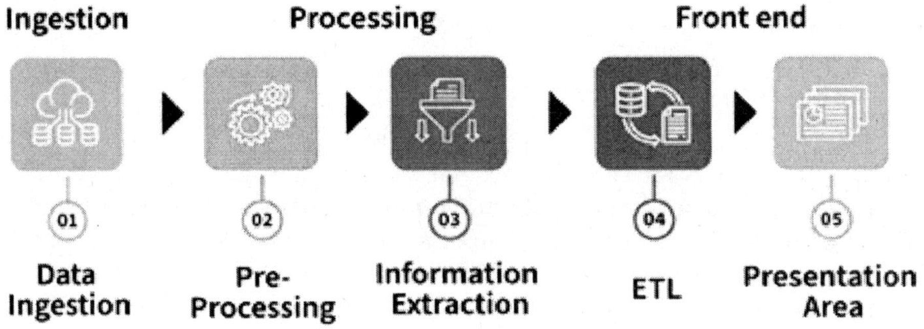

Fig. 6.4

1. **Ingestion Layer**: The ingestion layer is the entry point of the data pipeline, responsible for collecting raw data from various sources and feeding it into the system. Data can come from structured databases, APIs, logs, files, social media, or IoT devices. This layer supports both batch and real-time (streaming) ingestion depending on the pipeline's design. Tools like Apache Kafka, AWS Kinesis, Apache NiFi, or Flume are commonly used to handle ingestion efficiently and reliably. The ingestion layer ensures that data is collected in its original form, while handling challenges like data loss, latency, duplication, and schema changes. It's crucial that this layer is resilient, scalable, and fault-tolerant to ensure data flows continuously and accurately. It often includes checkpoints or buffering to deal with spikes in data volume. In essence, the ingestion layer serves as the foundation of the pipeline, setting the stage for downstream processing and transformation by collecting and moving data reliably from source systems to the next stage in the pipeline.
2. **Processing Layer:** The processing layer transforms raw, ingested data into meaningful, structured, and usable formats. It includes tasks such as data

cleansing, validation, transformation, enrichment, deduplication, aggregation, and filtering. This layer is crucial for making the data analytics-ready. Depending on the use case, processing can be done in batch mode (e.g., Apache Spark, AWS Glue) or real-time streaming (e.g., Apache Flink, Spark Streaming, Kafka Streams). In this layer, business logic is applied to convert raw input into standardized output that fits organizational goals—like turning log data into user activity reports or combining multiple datasets into a unified format. The processing layer also handles schema evolution, data formatting, and, often, data quality checks to ensure that only valid data moves forward. This is where much of the complexity of a pipeline lives, and good design here ensures high performance, data accuracy, and scalability. It acts as the "brain" of the pipeline, making raw data meaningful for analytics, machine learning, or decision-making systems downstream.

3. **Storage Layer:** The storage layer is responsible for storing data after it has been ingested and processed. It serves as the long-term repository where both raw and transformed data reside, enabling easy access for analysis, querying, and reporting. Depending on the pipeline architecture, this can include data lakes (e.g., Amazon S3, Azure Data Lake), data warehouses (e.g., Snowflake, BigQuery, Redshift), NoSQL stores (e.g., Cassandra, MongoDB), or relational databases (e.g., PostgreSQL, MySQL). A well-designed storage layer balances performance, scalability, cost, and accessibility. It supports different data formats such as JSON, Parquet, Avro, or CSV and is often optimized for querying and indexing. It also incorporates data partitioning, compression, and cataloging to manage large datasets efficiently. Data in this layer may be organized in raw, curated, and trusted zones to support different user needs. Security and compliance (e.g., encryption, role-based access) are critical here, especially in regulated industries. Ultimately, the storage layer acts as the "memory" of the pipeline storing all historical and real-time data that fuels downstream analytics, dashboards, and decision-making tools.

4. **Monitoring Layer:** The monitoring layer ensures the data pipeline is running reliably, accurately, and efficiently. It tracks the health, performance, and behavior of pipeline components in real time. This includes monitoring for failures, delays, data loss, throughput, latency, and resource usage. Tools like Prometheus, Grafana, Datadog, AWS CloudWatch, and Apache Airflow's built-in monitoring are commonly used to visualize metrics, send alerts, and automate remediation. In data pipelines, monitoring isn't limited to just infrastructure—it also includes data quality monitoring, such as schema drift, missing values, duplicates, and anomalies. Alerting systems are set up to notify teams if something goes wrong, such as an ingestion job failing or a data delay that could impact reporting. The monitoring layer plays a critical role in achieving data reliability, observability, and operational excellence. It ensures compliance with SLAs (Service-Level Agreements) and helps engineering teams debug issues quickly to avoid business disruption. A strong monitoring

layer turns a pipeline from a passive system into an active, self-aware infrastructure that can respond to issues in real time.

5. **Consumption Layer:** The consumption layer is the final stage of the data pipeline where end users and applications access the processed data for analysis, reporting, or decision-making. This includes BI tools (like Tableau, Power BI, Looker), data science notebooks (e.g., Jupyter, Databricks), dashboards, or machine learning platforms that pull data from the storage layer to generate insights or predictions. The data must be accurate, timely, and formatted according to the consumer's needs. This layer supports ad hoc querying, scheduled reporting, and real-time alerting, depending on the organization's requirements. It often includes access control and auditing to manage permissions and track usage. In modern architectures, the consumption layer may also expose APIs, data marts, or semantic layers to allow multiple teams or services to consume data in a self-service manner. The goal is to democratize access to high-quality data so business units, analysts, and data scientists can act on it effectively. A well-designed consumption layer ensures that data is not just stored but is actively used to drive decisions, innovation, and value across the organization.

ETL (Extract, Transform, Load)

ETL (Extract, Transform, Load) process plays an important role in data warehousing by ensuring seamless integration and preparation of data for analysis. This method involves extracting data from multiple sources, transforming it into a uniform format, and loading it into a centralized data warehouse or data lake. ETL is essential for businesses to consolidate vast amounts of data, enhancing decision-making processes and enabling accurate business insights. In today's digital ecosystem, where data comes from various sources and formats, the ETL process ensures that

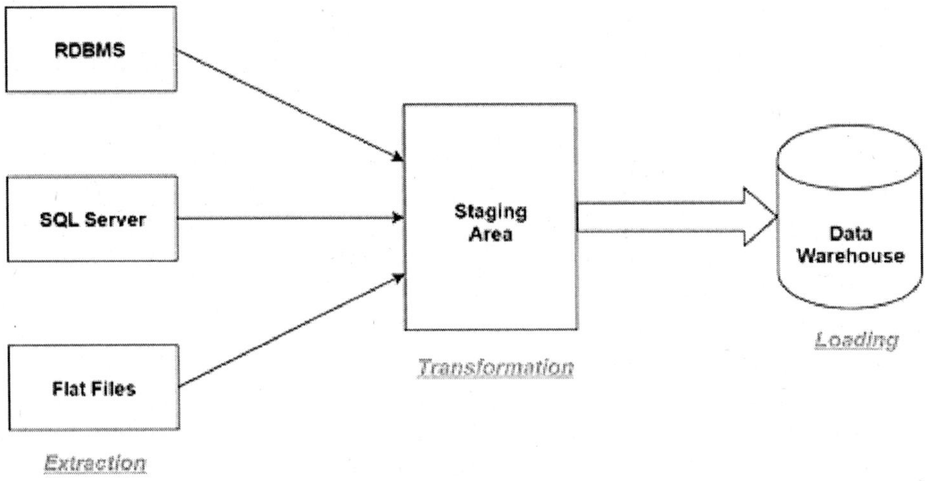

Fig. 6.5

organizations can efficiently clean, standardize, and organize this data for advanced analytics. It provides a structured foundation for data analytics, improving the quality, security, and accessibility of enterprise data.

ETL Process: The ETL process, which stands for Extract, Transform, and Load, is a critical methodology used to prepare data for storage, analysis, and reporting in a data warehouse. It involves three distinct stages that help to streamline raw data from multiple sources into a clean, structured, and usable form.

A detailed breakdown of each phase:

1. **Extraction:** The Extract phase is the first step in the ETL process, where raw data is collected from various data sources. These sources can be diverse, ranging from structured sources like databases (SQL, NoSQL), to semi-structured data like JSON, XML, or unstructured data such as emails or flat files. The main goal of extraction is to gather data without altering its format, enabling it to be further processed in the next stage. Types of data sources can include:
   - **Structured:** SQL databases, ERPs, CRMs
   - **Semi-structured:** JSON, XML
   - **Unstructured:** Emails, web pages, flat files
2. **Transformation:** The Transform phase is where the magic happens. Data extracted in the previous phase is often raw and inconsistent. During transformation, the data is cleaned, aggregated, and formatted according to business rules. This is a crucial step because it ensures that the data meets the quality standards required for accurate analysis. Common transformations include:
   - **Data Filtering:** Removing irrelevant or incorrect data.
   - **Data Sorting:** Organizing data into a required order for easier analysis.
   - **Data Aggregating:** Summarizing data to provide meaningful insights (e.g., averaging sales data).

   The transformation stage can also involve more complex operations such as currency conversions, text normalization, or applying domain-specific rules to ensure the data aligns with organizational needs.
3. **Loading:** Once data has been cleaned and transformed, it is ready for the final step: Loading. This phase involves transferring the transformed data into a data warehouse, data lake, or another target system for storage. Depending on the use case, there are two types of loading methods:
   - **Full Load:** All data is loaded into the target system, often used during the initial population of the warehouse.
   - **Incremental Load:** Only new or updated data is loaded, making this method more efficient for ongoing data updates.

Importance of ETL

- **Data Integration:** ETL combines data from various sources, including structured and unstructured formats, ensuring seamless integration for a unified view.
- **Data Quality:** By transforming raw data, ETL cleanses and standardizes it, improving data accuracy and consistency for more reliable insights.
- **Essential for Data Warehousing:** ETL prepares data for storage in data warehouses, making it accessible for analysis and reporting by aligning it with the target system's requirements.
- **Enhanced Decision-Making:** ETL helps businesses derive actionable insights, enabling better forecasting, resource allocation, and strategic planning.
- **Operational Efficiency:** Automating the data pipeline through ETL speeds up data processing, allowing organizations to make real-time decisions based on the most current data.

Challenges in ETL Process

The ETL process, while essential for data integration, comes with its own set of challenges that can hinder efficiency and accuracy. These challenges, if not addressed properly, can impact the overall performance and reliability of data systems.

- **Data Quality Issues:** Inconsistent, incomplete, or duplicate data from multiple sources can impact transformation and loading, leading to inaccurate insights.
- **Performance Bottlenecks:** Large datasets can slow down or cause ETL processes to fail, particularly during complex transformations like cleansing and aggregation.
- **Scalability Issues:** Legacy ETL systems may struggle to scale with growing data volumes, diverse sources, and more complex transformations.

Solutions to Overcome ETL Challenges:

- **Data Quality Management:** Use data validation and cleansing tools, along with automated checks, to ensure accurate and relevant data during the ETL process.
- **Optimization Techniques:** Overcome performance bottlenecks by parallelizing tasks, using batch processing, and leveraging cloud solutions for better processing power and storage.
- **Scalable ETL Systems:** Modern cloud-based ETL tools (e.g., Google BigQuery, Amazon Redshift) offer scalability, automation, and efficient handling of growing data volumes.

ETL Tools and Technologies

ETL (Extract, Transform, Load) tools play a vital role in automating the process of data integration, making it easier for businesses to manage and analyze large datasets. These tools simplify the movement, transformation, and storage of data from multiple sources to a centralized location like a data warehouse, ensuring high-quality, actionable insights.

Some of the widely used ETL tools include:

- **Apache Nifi:** Open-source tool for real-time data flow management and automation across systems.
- **Talend:** Open-source ETL tool supporting batch and real-time data processing for large-scale integration.
- **Microsoft SSIS:** Commercial ETL tool integrated with SQL Server, known for performance and scalability in data integration.
- **Hevo:** Modern data pipeline platform automating ETL and real-time data replication for cloud data warehouses.
- **Oracle Warehouse Builder:** Commercial ETL tool for managing large-scale data warehouses with transformation, cleansing, and integration features.

Workflow Automation with Apache Airflow

Apache Airflow is a powerful open-source platform used to programmatically author, schedule, and monitor workflows. It excels at automating complex data pipelines and other tasks by representing workflows as Directed Acyclic Graphs (DAGs) of tasks. This allows for precise scheduling, dependency management, and efficient execution of tasks, making it a valuable tool for data engineering and other automation needs. A more detailed look at how Airflow is used for workflow automation:

1. **Defining Workflows with DAGs:** In Apache Airflow, workflows are defined as DAGs (Directed Acyclic Graphs) using Python code. A DAG is a collection of tasks that are executed in a specified order without any cycles, meaning no task can depend on itself either directly or indirectly. This ensures a clear, repeatable execution path. Each task in a DAG is defined using Operators, such as PythonOperator, BashOperator, or EmailOperator, which encapsulate the logic of the task.

   DAGs are defined in .py files placed inside the Airflow DAGs directory. Each DAG includes metadata like dag_id, start_date, schedule_interval, and a set of tasks with defined dependencies using task1 >> task2 or task2.set_upstream(task1). This structure allows for version-controlled, readable, and easily modifiable workflows. Airflow dynamically parses these DAGs to construct execution plans. Airflow also supports templating with Jinja, making DAGs dynamic and parameterized. This lets developers reuse workflows across multiple environments or datasets. Clear visualizations of DAGs are available in the Web UI, helping teams understand dependencies and data flow. Overall, DAGs are the foundation of Airflow's automation and orchestration capabilities.

- Airflow represents workflows as DAGs, which are essentially Python code that defines the tasks and their dependencies.
- Each task in a DAG represents a unit of work, and the edges between tasks define the order in which they should be executed.
- This approach allows for dynamic and scalable workflows, making it suitable for various automation scenarios.

2. **Scheduling and Execution:** Scheduling in Apache Airflow determines when a DAG should be run. It is configured using the schedule_interval parameter in the DAG definition. This can be a cron expression (e.g., "0 0 * * *" for daily at midnight), a timedelta object (e.g., timedelta(days=1)), or predefined presets like @hourly, @daily, @weekly. Airflow also uses the start_date to determine the first execution and automatically manages the following schedules based on this interval. An important concept in scheduling is the execution date, which represents the logical time the DAG is run for, not the actual time it runs. For example, a DAG scheduled for "@daily" with a start_date of 2025-07-10 will run at 2025-07-11 00:00 but is labeled with the execution date 2025-07-10. Airflow supports backfilling, which means running DAG instances for previous intervals that were missed or not yet run. It also provides options like catchup=False to skip old runs if backfilling isn't desired. The scheduler daemon constantly parses DAGs and triggers task instances when they're due, handling dependency resolution and queueing them for execution via the executor backend.

   Execution in Airflow involves running each task in a DAG at the right time and in the right order. Once the scheduler determines a DAG run should occur, it creates a DAG Run and sets up Task Instances for each task. These tasks are then sent to the executor, which is responsible for running them, either locally, on Celery workers, Kubernetes pods, or other supported environments. Each task follows its dependency rules, so tasks only start once all upstream dependencies have succeeded (unless configured otherwise). Airflow handles retry, timeouts, and failure handling automatically. You can configure each task with parameters like retries, retry_delay, and execution_timeout. Task logs, states (e.g., success, failed, skipped), and metadata are stored in the Airflow metadata database and accessible via the Web UI or CLI. Developers can view logs, rerun failed tasks, or mark tasks as successful for manual intervention. During execution, tasks can communicate using XComs (cross-communications) to pass small pieces of data. Larger data transfers should be handled externally (e.g., via databases or cloud storage). Airflow's pluggable architecture also allows for custom operators and sensors to fit specific execution needs.

   - Airflow provides a web-based UI for visualizing and monitoring workflows.

- It allows users to schedule tasks based on various triggers, such as cron expressions or events.
- The scheduler ensures that tasks are executed in the correct order and at the specified time, while the executor handles the actual execution of tasks.

Flexibility and Scalability: Airflow can handle complex workflows with numerous tasks and dependencies, scaling to meet the demands of large-scale data processing.

1. **Automation:** It automates the execution of tasks, reducing manual effort and potential errors.
2. **Monitoring and Logging:** Airflow provides comprehensive monitoring and logging capabilities, allowing users to track the progress of workflows, identify issues, and troubleshoot problems.
3. **Integration:** Airflow can integrate with various systems and platforms, making it a versatile tool for automating a wide range of tasks.

Common Use Cases:

1. **Data Pipelines:** Airflow is widely used for automating data extraction, transformation, and loading (ETL) processes.
2. **Machine Learning Pipelines:** It can be used to automate the training, deployment, and monitoring of machine learning models.
3. **Business Process Automation:** Airflow can automate various business processes, such as report generation, data analysis, and more.

In essence, Apache Airflow provides a robust and flexible platform for automating workflows, improving efficiency, and reducing manual effort in various domains.

DataOps and MLOps

DataOps and MLOps are both inspired by DevOps principles, but they focus on different aspects of the data and AI lifecycle. DataOps streamlines data management and analytics, ensuring high-quality, reliable data pipelines, while MLOps focuses on the machine learning model lifecycle, from development to deployment and monitoring. Essentially, DataOps ensures the right data, and MLOps ensures the right decisions.

DataOps: DataOps (Data Operations) is a collaborative, agile, and process-oriented methodology focused on improving the quality, speed, and reliability of data analytics and data pipeline workflows. It applies principles from DevOps, Agile development, and Lean manufacturing to the field of data engineering and analytics.

The central goal of DataOps is to streamline the flow of data from source systems to end-users (data analysts, data scientists, business intelligence tools) in a way that ensures data is accurate, timely, and trustworthy. Unlike traditional data management practices that are often siloed, slow, and manual, DataOps promotes automation, continuous integration, continuous delivery (CI/CD), and monitoring across the data lifecycle. The components of DataOps are as:

1. **Automated Data Pipelines**: DataOps encourages the use of orchestration tools (like Apache Airflow, Prefect, or Dagster) to automate ETL/ELT processes. These pipelines can be tested, version-controlled, and deployed just like software code.
2. **Data Testing & Validation**: Frameworks like Great Expectations or dbt tests help enforce data quality rules and catch anomalies early in the pipeline. This is critical to ensuring that downstream consumers trust the data they use.
3. **Collaboration and Version Control**: DataOps brings Git-based workflows to data engineering. Data transformations, schema changes, and even dashboards can be versioned and collaboratively developed, improving reproducibility and reducing human error.
4. **Monitoring and Observability**: Just like DevOps monitors applications, DataOps uses tools to monitor the health, freshness, lineage, and quality of data. Tools like Monte Carlo and Datafold help with data observability, catching issues like schema changes or pipeline failures before they affect users.
5. **CI/CD for Data**: Teams can deploy changes to data pipelines in a structured, tested, and automated way using CI/CD tools (e.g., GitHub Actions, Jenkins), ensuring quicker iterations without compromising reliability.

Benefits of DataOps

1. Faster delivery of data products (dashboards, reports, models)
2. Improved data quality and trust across the organization
3. Reduced manual errors and increased team productivity
4. Enhanced collaboration between data engineers, analysts, and operations

In essence, DataOps is about treating data pipelines as software engineering products. By doing so, organizations ensure that data is not only available but also reliable, traceable, and scalable for downstream use cases like analytics, business intelligence, and machine learning.

MLOps: MLOps (Machine Learning Operations) is the practice of automating, standardizing, and managing the lifecycle of machine learning models from development and training to deployment, monitoring, and retraining. It brings DevOps principles to the unique challenges of machine learning, helping teams operationalize AI and scale ML across organizations.

Where traditional software development ends with code deployment, machine learning requires ongoing maintenance due to data drift, model decay, and evolving business needs. MLOps bridges the gap between data science and IT, ensuring that ML systems are production-ready, reproducible, and continuously improving. Key Components are as:

1. **Model Development & Experimentation**: Tools like MLflow, Weights & Biases, or TensorBoard allow data scientists to track experiments, model versions, hyperparameters, and metrics — ensuring reproducibility and collaboration.
2. **Versioning and Packaging**: Just like software, models and their dependencies (data, code, libraries) need to be versioned. Tools like DVC (Data Version Control) and Docker help create portable, reproducible model packages.
3. **Automated Training Pipelines**: Using workflow orchestration tools (like Airflow, Kubeflow Pipelines, or Metaflow), MLOps teams automate data ingestion, feature engineering, model training, evaluation, and validation.
4. **Model Deployment**: MLOps supports multiple deployment strategies (batch, real-time, A/B testing, shadow deployment). Platforms like SageMaker, Vertex AI, or KServe manage scalable, low-latency model serving.
5. **Monitoring and Retraining**: After deployment, models are continuously monitored for performance degradation, drift in data distributions, or bias. Alerts can trigger automated retraining workflows when thresholds are breached.
6. **Governance and Compliance**: MLOps ensures traceability of every model — what data it was trained on, what code was used, who approved it helping organizations meet regulatory and ethical standards.

Benefits of MLOps

1. Faster deployment of ML models into production
2. Improved reproducibility and collaboration in model development
3. Robust monitoring for performance, drift, and anomalies
4. Reduced operational burden on data science and engineering teams
5. Better alignment with business and regulatory goals

Differences Between DataOps and MLOps: The differences between DataOps and MLOps are listed in table 6.2.

18. Cloud Computing for Data Science

Cloud computing for data science enables scalable, flexible, and cost-effective access to computing resources, making it easier to collect, process, analyze, and model large volumes of data. Instead of relying on limited local infrastructure, data scientists can use cloud platforms like AWS, Google Cloud, and Azure to run complex analytics, machine learning, and deep learning workloads on demand. These platforms offer a wide range of services such as cloud storage (S3, Blob Storage), virtual machines (EC2, Compute Engine), big data tools (BigQuery, Databricks), and AI/ML services (SageMaker, Vertex AI) that support end-to-end data science workflows. Cloud environments also enable collaboration through shared notebooks, real-time access to data, and integration with version control systems like Git. Elastic computing allows

Table 6.2

S.No.	Aspect	DataOps	MLOps
1.	Primary Focus	Managing and automating data pipelines and workflows	Managing the lifecycle of machine learning models
2.	Main Objective	Deliver clean, reliable, and timely data	Deploy, monitor, and maintain ML models in production
3.	Key Users	Data engineers, data analysts, BI teams	Data scientists, ML engineers, DevOps
4.	Core Activities	ETL/ELT, data quality, validation, transformation	Model training, deployment, monitoring, retraining
5.	Pipeline Type	Data pipelines	ML pipelines (training, serving, monitoring)
6.	Versioning Focus	Data and data transformation code	Models, datasets, code, experiments
7.	Tools & Frameworks	Airflow, dbt, Great Expectations, Monte Carlo	MLflow, Kubeflow, SageMaker, DVC, TFX
8.	Monitoring Focus	Data freshness, data quality, pipeline health	Model accuracy, drift detection, prediction performance
9.	Automation	Automated data ingestion, testing, and deployment	Automated model training, deployment, and retraining
10.	CI/CD Usage	For deploying data pipelines and transformations	For deploying and updating machine learning models
11.	Governance	Data lineage, schema validation, compliance	Model lineage, audit trails, ethical compliance
12.	Business Value	Ensures trusted data for analytics and decision-making	Enables scalable, production-ready AI/ML systems
13.	Challenges Addressed	Data quality issues, broken pipelines, slow delivery	Model drift, reproducibility, deployment complexity

users to scale resources up or down based on workload demands, ensuring performance without overpaying. Additionally, managed services reduce infrastructure overhead, allowing teams to focus on data and model development. With features like auto-scaling, built-in security, and easy deployment, cloud computing is now essential for modern data science, especially for projects involving big data, AI, and cross-functional collaboration.

Why is Cloud Computing Important in Data Science?

Let's imagine for a second that there was no Cloud Computing for Data Science. Then companies would have to locally store data in servers and every time a Data Scientist needed to perform data analysis or extract some information from the data, they would need to transfer the data to their system from the central servers and then perform the analysis. Can you imagine the complications in this?! This is not just a little bit of data as data analysis by companies uses a huge volume of data.

Moreover, it is very expensive to create servers for the data and while big companies can manage this easily, it is very different for the smaller companies. These smaller companies cannot use servers as they require space to keep them. These servers require constant maintenance and upkeep and also require backups in case anything goes wrong. Having servers also require immense planning and it may also happen that companies may obtain more or fewer servers than they need according to their data requirements. And this is where cloud computing comes in! Companies can use the cloud to host their data and they don't need to worry about servers anymore as this is the headache of the cloud provider now! The companies can access server architecture in the cloud according to their needs and even save money by only paying as much as the data they are using on the cloud.

Cloud computing has democratized data in a manner that is unique in these times. Now, smaller companies can perform data analytics and compete with larger multinationals in the market without worrying about the insane costs associated with Data Science. In fact, Data Science with Cloud Computing has become so popular now that it has given birth to Data as a Service (DaaS).

Cloud Computing Platforms for Data Science

1. **Amazon Web Services:** Amazon Web Services is a cloud computing platform that is a subsidiary of Amazon. It was launched in 2006 and is currently one of the most popular cloud computing platforms for data science. AWS provides various products for data analytics which include Amazon QuickSight (business analytics service), Amazon RedShift (data warehousing), AWS Data Pipeline, AWS Data Exchange, and Amazon Kinesis (real-time data analysis), Amazon EMR (Big data processing), etc. Amazon Web Services also provides products for databases which include the Amazon Aurora (relational database) and Amazon DynamoDB (NoSQL database). Some of the more popular companies that use AWS include Netflix, NASA, etc.
2. **Google Cloud:** The Google Cloud Platform is a cloud computing platform that is provided by Google. It provides the same infrastructure for companies that Google itself uses in its internal products such as Google Search, YouTube, Gmail, etc. Google Cloud provides various products for data analytics which include BigQuery (Data warehouse), Dataflow (Streaming analytics), Dataproc (Running Apache Hadoop, Apache Spark clusters), Looker (Business Intelligence Analytics), Google Data Studio (Visualization Dashboards, Data Reporting), Dataprep (Data Preparation), etc.
3. **Microsoft Azure:** Microsoft Azure is a cloud computing platform created by Microsoft. It was initially released in 2010 and is a popular cloud computing platform for data science and data analytics. Some of the Microsoft Azure products for data analytics are Azure Synapse Analytics (Data Analytics), Azure Stream Analytics (Streaming analytics), Azure Databricks (Apache Spark analytics), Azure Data Lake Storage (Data Lake), Data Factory (Hybrid data integration), etc. Microsoft Azure also has support for databases including Azure Cosmos DB (NoSQL database), Azure SQL Database (SQL database), etc.

Use Case: Predictive Customer Churn Model Using AWS: A telecommunications company wants to predict customer churn to proactively retain users. They use cloud computing via AWS to build, train, and deploy a machine learning model for this purpose.

1. **Data Storage**: Customer data (e.g., usage history, billing info) is uploaded to Amazon S3, a scalable cloud storage service.
2. **Data Processing**: Using AWS Glue (a serverless ETL service), the data team cleans and transforms the data into a structured format suitable for machine learning.
3. **Exploratory Data Analysis**: Data scientists use Amazon SageMaker Studio (a cloud-based Jupyter environment) to explore the data, visualize trends, and engineer features.
4. **Model Training**: A logistic regression model is trained on the prepared dataset using SageMaker's built-in algorithms, running on GPU-enabled EC2 instances for speed.
5. **Model Deployment**: The trained model is deployed as an API endpoint via SageMaker, enabling real-time predictions of customer churn from web or mobile apps.
6. **Monitoring & Retraining**: SageMaker Model Monitor tracks prediction accuracy over time. If performance drops, the pipeline automatically triggers model retraining.

Deploying Models on AWS, GCP, and Azure

Deploying machine learning models on cloud platforms like AWS, Google Cloud Platform (GCP), and Microsoft Azure offers robust, scalable infrastructure for putting AI solutions into production. Each provider offers tools tailored for different skill levels from beginner-friendly autoML options to advanced containerized model deployment. On AWS, Amazon SageMaker allows users to train, deploy, and monitor models seamlessly. With a few clicks or lines of code, users can deploy models as scalable REST APIs with built-in logging, versioning, and A/B testing. SageMaker supports real-time, batch, and asynchronous inference and even allows for model deployment on edge devices using SageMaker Edge Manager.

On GCP, Vertex AI serves as the unified platform for end-to-end ML workflows. It supports custom model training with TensorFlow, scikit-learn, or PyTorch, and integrates with Google Kubernetes Engine (GKE) for large-scale deployment. Vertex AI also offers AutoML and pre-trained APIs for those who prefer not to build models from scratch. Azure provides Azure Machine Learning, a cloud-based environment for training and deploying models with automated ML, drag-and-drop tools, and full Python SDK support. Azure also offers managed endpoints for real-time and batch scoring, with easy integration into enterprise applications using Power BI or Logic Apps. All three platforms offer seamless CI/CD integration, monitoring tools, and governance support, making them enterprise-ready. Importance of Deploying Models on AWS, GCP, and Azure are as:

1. **Scalable Infrastructure**: Easily handle increasing loads and serve models to millions of users with automatic scaling.
2. **Fast and Reliable Deployment**: Quickly move from development to production using managed services like SageMaker (AWS), Vertex AI (GCP), and Azure ML.
3. **Built-in Model Monitoring**: Track model performance, detect drift, and set alerts using integrated monitoring and logging tools.
4. **Support for Real-Time and Batch Inference**: Deploy models for both real-time API serving and scheduled batch processing with high availability.
5. **AutoML and Custom Model Support**: Use both low-code AutoML features and full-code environments for advanced ML workflows.
6. **Secure and Compliant**: Take advantage of enterprise-grade security, authentication, and compliance standards built into cloud platforms.
7. **Integrated MLOps Tools**: Access CI/CD pipelines, version control, model registries, and deployment automation for streamlined ML operations.
8. **Cost-Efficiency Through Managed Services**: Avoid the complexity and cost of managing your own infrastructure with serverless and pay-as-you-go options.
9. **Cross-Service Integration**: Easily integrate with cloud storage, databases, data pipelines, and business intelligence tools within the same ecosystem.
10. **Global Availability and Redundancy**: Deploy models across multiple regions and zones to ensure low latency and high availability for global users.

Serverless Data Science Applications

Serverless computing in data science refers to building and running applications or models without provisioning or managing servers. This architecture is ideal for tasks like event-driven data pipelines, lightweight machine learning inference, and dynamic data processing. Cloud platforms offer serverless tools like AWS Lambda, Google Cloud Functions, and Azure Functions, which allow small bits of code to be executed in response to events like file uploads, HTTP requests, or time-based triggers. For instance, a data scientist could build a serverless pipeline that triggers a function to preprocess data every time a new CSV is uploaded to a storage bucket, run a model inference, and store the results in a database—all without managing any server infrastructure.

Serverless applications are highly scalable and cost-effective, as they only consume resources during execution. Combined with other cloud services like S3, BigQuery, or Azure Blob Storage, serverless functions create powerful, event-driven workflows. For ML use cases, lightweight models can be hosted on serverless endpoints, or trigger model scoring functions that respond in milliseconds. Additionally, serverless frameworks like AWS Step Functions, Google Cloud Workflows, or Azure Durable Functions can orchestrate multi-step data science workflows, including ETL, inference, and logging. This makes serverless architecture a strong fit for dynamic, low-latency, and cost-sensitive data science applications. Importance of Serverless Data Science Applications are as:

1. **No Server Management Required**: Developers and data scientists can focus on code and analysis without worrying about provisioning or maintaining infrastructure.
2. **Scales Automatically**: Serverless platforms automatically handle scaling based on demand ideal for unpredictable workloads.
3. **Cost-Efficient**: Pay only for what you use no charges for idle compute, which reduces costs significantly for intermittent tasks.
4. **Faster Development and Deployment**: Serverless functions are lightweight and modular, allowing rapid iteration and deployment of data science features.
5. **Ideal for Event-Driven Workflows**: Easily trigger functions with events like file uploads, API calls, or schedule-based automation (e.g., daily model scoring).
6. **Improves Productivity**: Eliminates the need for managing servers or container orchestration, allowing teams to focus on data, models, and results.
7. **Simplifies Maintenance**: Infrastructure updates, patching, and availability are handled by the cloud provider, reducing operational overhead.
8. **Supports Microservices Architecture**: Encourages modular, loosely coupled components, which improves reusability and maintainability of code.
9. **Enables Real-Time Processing**: Great for real-time inference, streaming analytics, or instant alerts triggered by data changes.
10. **Integrates Easily with Other Cloud Services**: Seamlessly connects to cloud storage, databases, machine learning services, and APIs for full pipeline automation.

Scaling and Cost Optimization

Scaling data science workloads in the cloud means dynamically adjusting computing resources to meet demand without over-provisioning. Modern cloud platforms offer vertical (bigger machines) and horizontal (more machines) scaling options. Tools like auto-scaling groups (EC2, GKE, AKS) and managed services like BigQuery or SageMaker handle large-scale processing and model training efficiently. For big data or deep learning tasks, users can spin up clusters of GPU-enabled instances or distribute processing using Spark or Ray. The ability to scale infrastructure on-demand allows data teams to accelerate training, handle large data volumes, and deploy models to millions of users without bottlenecks.

Cost optimization is crucial, especially with large-scale or long-running data workloads. Cloud providers offer multiple strategies: use of spot instances (temporary, cheap compute), auto-shutdown of idle resources, and serverless services which charge per execution. Tools like AWS Cost Explorer, Google Cost Management, and Azure Cost Analysis help track and forecast expenses. For model training, preemptible VMs (GCP), spot instances (AWS), and low-priority VMs (Azure) can cut compute costs significantly. Teams can also optimize storage costs by using lifecycle rules (e.g., moving infrequently accessed data to cheaper tiers like S3 Glacier or Azure Archive). Efficient resource allocation, automation, and monitoring are key to balancing performance and budget. Importance of Scaling and Cost Optimization are as:

1. **Ensures Performance and Availability**: Automatically scales resources to handle growing or fluctuating workloads without service disruption.
2. **Supports Big Data and ML Workloads**: Enables efficient processing of large datasets and complex model training using scalable infrastructure.
3. **Enhances Flexibility and Agility**: Allows data science teams to experiment, deploy, and iterate faster without infrastructure limitations.
4. **Reduces Infrastructure Management Overhead**: Auto-scaling removes the need for manual provisioning and monitoring of resources.
5. **Prevents Overprovisioning and Resource Waste**: Optimizes usage by allocating exactly the resources needed no more, no less.
6. **Minimizes Cloud Costs**: Uses strategies like spot instances, auto-shutdown, and storage tiering to avoid unnecessary expenses.
7. **Improves Budget Predictability**: Helps forecast and control spending by monitoring usage and setting alerts.
8. **Maximizes Return on Investment (ROI)**: Aligns resource spending with actual business value and outcomes.
9. **Supports Sustainable Growth**: Scales efficiently as data and user demand grow, without incurring linear cost increases.
10. **Enables Long-Term Operational Efficiency**: Creates a balance between high performance and cost control for sustainable cloud operations.

SUMMARY OF BIG DATA AND DATA ENGINEERING

In the era of digital transformation, the volume, velocity, and variety of data have reached unprecedented levels. This phenomenon, known as Big Data, has driven the evolution of technologies and practices that help organizations store, process, and extract insights efficiently. At the core of this evolution lies data engineering, which focuses on building systems and workflows that support the movement, transformation, and integration of data for analytics and machine learning.

16. Big Data Technologies

Big Data technologies enable the storage, processing, and analysis of massive and complex datasets that traditional systems cannot handle efficiently. Tools like Hadoop introduced a distributed storage and processing model using HDFS and MapReduce, allowing data to be managed across multiple nodes. However, newer frameworks like Apache Spark have improved performance by enabling in-memory computation, real-time analytics, and machine learning capabilities. In parallel, NoSQL databases such as MongoDB, Cassandra, and HBase have emerged to handle unstructured and semi-structured data with flexible schemas and horizontal scalability. These technologies collectively support applications involving real-time streaming, big data analytics, recommendation systems, and large-scale AI training. Their ability to manage high-volume, high-velocity, and high-variety data makes them essential in industries such as finance, healthcare, retail, and telecommunications, where quick insights and large-scale data processing are crucial for competitiveness and innovation.

- **Hadoop and MapReduce:** Hadoop was one of the pioneering technologies in the big data revolution. It introduced a framework for storing and processing vast amounts of data across distributed clusters using commodity hardware. The Hadoop Distributed File System (HDFS) allows large datasets to be stored across multiple machines, while MapReduce is a programming model that enables parallel processing of these datasets. In MapReduce, data is processed in two steps: the "Map" step performs filtering and sorting, and the "Reduce" step aggregates results. While Hadoop provided an initial solution for handling big data, it has largely been supplemented by faster and more versatile frameworks like Spark.
- **Apache Spark and Distributed Computing:** Apache Spark is a fast, in-memory distributed computing engine that significantly improves upon MapReduce. It enables real-time data processing, machine learning, and streaming analytics across clusters. Spark supports multiple languages (Python, Scala, Java, and R), and its libraries like Spark SQL, MLlib, and GraphX make it suitable for advanced analytics. Unlike MapReduce, Spark retains data in memory, drastically reducing the time needed for iterative computations. It also integrates well with Hadoop ecosystems and other data storage systems, making it a versatile tool for modern big data applications.
- **NoSQL Databases:** Traditional relational databases struggle with the scalability and flexibility demands of big data. NoSQL databases were developed to address these challenges. These databases including MongoDB, Cassandra, Redis, and HBase allow for the storage and retrieval of unstructured, semi-structured, and large-scale structured data. They are schema-less, horizontally scalable, and support a variety of data models (document, key-value, column-family, and graph). This makes NoSQL an excellent choice for real-time analytics, large-scale web apps, and IoT data streams.

17. Data Pipelines and Automation

Data pipelines and automation are crucial for efficiently moving, processing, and preparing data for analysis and machine learning. The ETL (Extract, Transform, Load) process extracts data from various sources, transforms it into a clean, usable format, and loads it into storage systems. Tools like Apache Airflow automate and orchestrate these complex workflows using Directed Acyclic Graphs (DAGs), managing dependencies and scheduling tasks reliably. Additionally, methodologies like DataOps and MLOps bring software engineering best practices to data and model pipelines, improving collaboration, quality, and continuous delivery. Together, these enable scalable, repeatable, and reliable data-driven workflows essential for modern analytics and AI projects.

- **ETL (Extract, Transform, Load):** A foundational concept in data engineering, ETL refers to the process of extracting data from various sources, transforming it into a usable format, and loading it into a target system such as a data warehouse. ETL pipelines ensure data consistency, cleanliness, and readiness for analysis or machine learning. Modern tools like Apache NiFi, Talend, and dbt allow for automation and orchestration of ETL workflows. The "T" (Transform) phase often includes normalization, enrichment, and validation tasks, which are critical for ensuring high-quality datasets.
- **'Workflow Automation with Apache Airflow:** Manual orchestration of data workflows is inefficient and error-prone. Apache Airflow solves this by allowing users to define workflows as DAGs (Directed Acyclic Graphs) using Python code. Each task in a DAG represents a step in the pipeline, and Airflow handles dependencies, scheduling, retries, and monitoring. It integrates with major cloud services, databases, and APIs, making it a powerful tool for managing complex workflows in both ETL and machine learning projects. Its modular and extensible design allows for scaling across distributed environments and maintaining reliability in production systems.
- **DataOps and MLOps:** DataOps and MLOps extend DevOps principles to data and machine learning workflows. DataOps focuses on improving the quality, reliability, and delivery speed of data pipelines through version control, testing, CI/CD, and monitoring. Tools like Great Expectations and Datafold are used for data validation and observability. MLOps, on the other hand, addresses the unique challenges of deploying and managing ML models in production. It includes experiment tracking, model packaging, deployment automation, and monitoring model performance and drift. Platforms like MLflow, Kubeflow, and SageMaker help streamline the ML lifecycle. Together, DataOps and MLOps ensure that data and models are trustworthy, reproducible, and scalable.

18. Cloud Computing for Data Science

Cloud computing for data science provides scalable, flexible, and cost-effective infrastructure to store, process, and analyze vast amounts of data. It eliminates the need for heavy upfront investment in hardware by offering on-demand access to powerful compute resources, storage, and managed services through platforms like

AWS, Google Cloud Platform (GCP), and Microsoft Azure. These platforms support end-to-end data science workflows from data ingestion and cleaning to model training, deployment, and monitoring. Cloud services also enable collaboration through shared environments and integrated tools such as Jupyter notebooks, AutoML, and serverless functions. Moreover, cloud computing facilitates scaling to handle large datasets and compute-intensive models while providing cost optimization options like spot instances and automated resource management. This combination accelerates innovation, reduces operational overhead, and democratizes access to advanced analytics and machine learning capabilities for organizations of all sizes.

- **Deploying Models on AWS, GCP, and Azure:** Cloud platforms provide the infrastructure and tools needed to deploy machine learning models at scale. On AWS, Amazon SageMaker allows you to train, deploy, and monitor ML models with built-in versioning and scalability. Google Cloud Platform (GCP) offers Vertex AI, a unified environment for managing the ML lifecycle, from AutoML to custom training and deployment. Microsoft Azure provides Azure Machine Learning, which supports drag-and-drop interfaces, Jupyter notebooks, and automated deployment endpoints. All platforms support real-time and batch inference, offer model registries, and integrate with CI/CD pipelines. Deploying models on these platforms allows for secure, scalable, and highly available machine learning services.
- **Serverless Data Science Applications:** Serverless computing abstracts infrastructure management, allowing data scientists to focus purely on code and logic. Functions like AWS Lambda, Google Cloud Functions, and Azure Functions execute small pieces of code in response to events such as file uploads, API calls, or time-based schedules. This makes serverless ideal for lightweight data transformations, on-demand model inference, and dynamic pipelines. Serverless applications are highly cost-effective, as you only pay for execution time, and they automatically scale to meet demand. Additionally, they integrate easily with other services (e.g., cloud storage, messaging queues, APIs), enabling the creation of fully automated, event-driven data science workflows without managing servers.
- **Scaling and Cost Optimization:** Cloud computing offers unmatched scalability, allowing teams to process terabytes of data or train large models on GPUs with ease. However, scaling must be matched with effective **cost optimization** to avoid overspending. Platforms provide tools like auto-scaling, spot/preemptible instances, and resource scheduling to manage usage efficiently. Storage costs can be controlled by using lifecycle rules to archive unused data to cheaper tiers (e.g., S3 Glacier or Azure Archive). Cost monitoring tools like AWS Cost Explorer, Google Cloud Billing, and Azure Cost Management help track resource usage, set budgets, and analyze trends. Efficient scaling ensures performance under load, while optimization strategies ensure long-term financial sustainability.

Big Data and Data Engineering are at the heart of modern data-driven decision-making. With technologies like Hadoop, Spark, and NoSQL, organizations can handle massive datasets efficiently. Data pipelines and automation tools, especially Apache Airflow and modern ETL practices, enable the reliable flow of data from source to insight. Incorporating DataOps and MLOps ensures that both data and models are managed with rigor and repeatability. Meanwhile, cloud computing has revolutionized the way models are deployed, scaled, and maintained. Serverless architectures offer new levels of efficiency, while smart scaling and cost management ensure these powerful capabilities remain sustainable. Altogether, these tools and practices form the backbone of scalable, efficient, and intelligent data systems in today's digital world.

Chapter 7

Real-World Applications and Ethics

Real World Applications and Ethics in data science and AI span transformative use cases across industries alongside profound ethical responsibilities. AI-driven systems are used in healthcare to predict patient outcomes, personalize treatment, and detect diseases from medical imagery; in finance, algorithms help automate credit scoring, fraud detection, and algorithmic trading; and in public policy, predictive policing tools attempt to forecast areas of concern. These applications can bring enormous benefits but carry serious risks when models rely on biased data or opaque logic. High profile failures have shown the perils: Amazon's scrapped hiring algorithm reinforced gender bias; COMPAS risk scores misclassified Black defendants at twice the rate of white defendants; Cambridge Analytica harvested Facebook data without consent to target voters spotlighting privacy and transparency failures (Medium). Algorithmic bias persists in facial recognition systems that inaccurately classify individuals with darker skin tones, deepfake technologies that erode trust, and credit systems that penalize protected groups. To address this, proponents advocate for ethical frameworks such as a "Hippocratic oath" for data scientists, ethical matrices for algorithm evaluation, third-party audits, inclusive datasets, and rigorous human oversight (wired.com). Ethical data science also requires transparent consent mechanisms, robust security controls, fairness assessments, and continuous monitoring after deployment. As technology accelerates, anchoring innovation in ethical stewardship is essential to empower trust, mitigate harm, and ensure that advanced systems align with human values and social equity.

Real-world Applications: Data science has become a transformative force across various industries, enabling organizations to leverage data for improved decision-making, efficiency, and innovation. Below are some notable real-world applications of data science. Data science has numerous real-world applications across various industries. It's used to analyze data, build predictive models, and extract insights to improve decision-making, optimize processes, and enhance customer experiences.

1. **Healthcare: Disease Diagnosis and Personalized Medicine:** Data science is revolutionizing healthcare by enhancing disease diagnosis and enabling personalized treatment plans. Machine learning algorithms analyze medical images, such as X-rays and MRIs, to detect conditions like cancer and eye

diseases with remarkable accuracy. For instance, Google's DeepMind developed an AI system capable of diagnosing over 50 eye diseases, achieving accuracy comparable to leading ophthalmologists. Additionally, predictive models assess patient data to develop personalized treatment plans, improving patient outcomes.

2. **Finance: Fraud Detection and Risk Management:** Financial institutions employ data science techniques to detect fraudulent activities and manage risks effectively. Machine learning models analyze transaction data in real-time to identify anomalies and prevent fraud. JPMorgan Chase, for example, utilizes a combination of supervised learning models and unsupervised clustering techniques to process millions of transactions daily, significantly reducing financial losses.

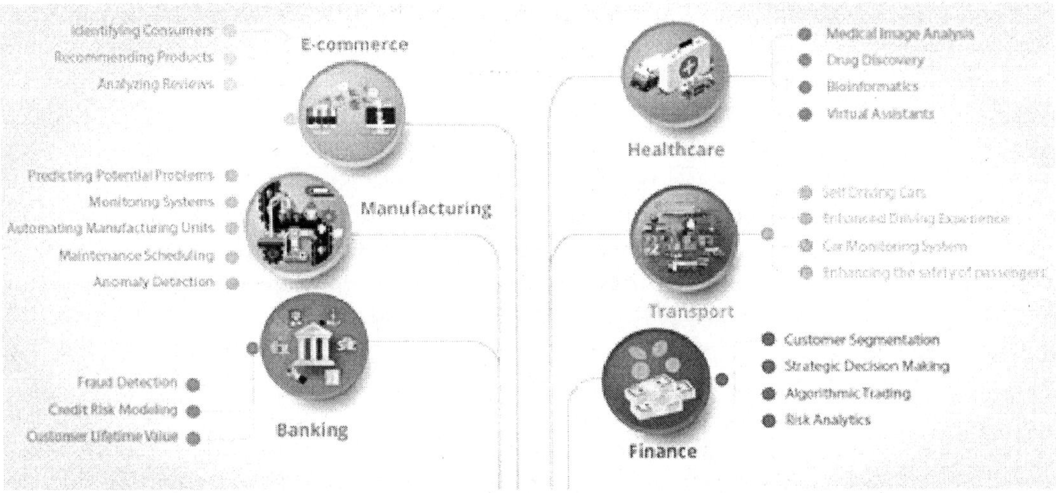

Fig. 7.1

3. **Retail: Customer Segmentation and Inventory Optimization:** Retailers leverage data science to understand customer behavior and optimize inventory management. By analyzing purchasing patterns and demographics, businesses can segment customers and tailor marketing strategies accordingly. Walmart, for instance, uses machine learning to forecast demand for 500 million item-store combinations weekly, optimizing inventory and reducing waste.

4. **Transportation: Route Optimization and Autonomous Vehicles:** Data science enhances transportation by optimizing routes and enabling autonomous vehicles. Ride-sharing platforms like Uber analyze historical traffic data and demand patterns to suggest optimal routes, reducing wait times and fuel consumption. Tesla's Autopilot system employs machine learning algorithms to process sensor data, enabling semi-autonomous driving capabilities and continuous improvement through software updates.

5. **Agriculture: Precision Farming and Crop Monitoring:** In agriculture, data science facilitates precision farming by analyzing data from sensors, drones, and satellite imagery. Farmers can monitor soil conditions, weather patterns, and crop health to make informed decisions on irrigation, fertilization, and pest control. This data-driven approach increases crop yields, conserves resources, and promotes sustainable agricultural practices.
6. **Entertainment: Content Recommendation Systems:** Streaming platforms like Netflix and Spotify utilize data science to analyze user preferences and recommend personalized content. By examining viewing history, search patterns, and user ratings, these platforms suggest movies, shows, and music tailored to individual tastes. This personalization enhances user experience and engagement, driving platform growth and user retention.
7. **Manufacturing: Predictive Maintenance and Quality Control:** In the manufacturing sector, data science enables predictive maintenance and quality control. Sensors embedded in machinery collect data on performance metrics, which are analyzed to predict potential failures and schedule maintenance proactively. This approach reduces downtime, extends equipment lifespan, and ensures consistent product quality.
8. **Education: Personalized Learning and Student Performance Analysis:** Educational institutions employ data science to personalize learning experiences and analyze student performance. By examining data on student interactions, assessments, and engagement, educators can identify learning gaps and tailor instructional strategies to individual needs. This data-driven approach improves learning outcomes and supports student success.
9. **Energy: Smart Grid Management and Consumption Forecasting:** Data science enhances energy management through smart grid technologies and consumption forecasting. By analyzing data from smart meters and sensors, utilities can monitor energy usage patterns, detect inefficiencies, and optimize energy distribution. This leads to cost savings, reduced energy waste, and more sustainable energy consumption practices.
10. **Environmental Conservation: Wildlife Monitoring and Habitat Preservation:** Data science aids in environmental conservation efforts by analyzing data from sensors, satellites, and drones to monitor wildlife populations and habitats. Machine learning models process this data to detect changes in ecosystems, identify threats, and inform conservation strategies. These efforts contribute to biodiversity preservation and sustainable environmental practices.

Ethics: Ethics in data science is a critical aspect that guides professionals in responsibly handling data throughout its lifecycle from collection and analysis to interpretation and dissemination. As data-driven technologies increasingly influence various sectors, ethical considerations ensure that these practices uphold societal values and protect individual rights. Key Ethical Practices in Data Science are as:

1. **Bias Detection and Mitigation:** Regularly audit datasets and algorithms to identify and address biases that could lead to discriminatory outcomes. For instance, a study revealed that an AI system used in healthcare disproportionately flagged white patients over Black patients, despite the latter group comprising a larger portion of the actual high-risk population.
2. **Transparency and Accountability:** Maintain clear documentation of data sources, methodologies, and decision-making processes. This transparency allows stakeholders to understand and trust the outcomes of data analyses.

Fig. 7.2

3. **Privacy and Data Protection:** Implement measures such as data anonymization, encryption, and access controls to safeguard personal information. Adhering to privacy laws like GDPR and CCPA is crucial in protecting individuals' data rights.
4. **Informed Consent:** Ensure that individuals are fully aware of how their data will be used and have the option to consent. This practice is fundamental in maintaining ethical standards in data collection and usage.
5. **Human Oversight:** Incorporate human judgment in automated decision-making processes, especially in sensitive areas like healthcare and criminal justice, to prevent errors and ensure ethical outcomes.

19. Data Science in Business and Industry

Data science has become a cornerstone of modern business and industry, revolutionizing operations, decision-making, and customer engagement across various sectors. By leveraging vast amounts of data, organizations can derive actionable insights that drive efficiency and innovation. For instance, predictive analytics enables companies to forecast market trends, optimize supply chains, and personalize customer experiences. Retail giants like Amazon and Walmart utilize data science to manage inventory, predict demand, and enhance customer satisfaction. In finance, institutions employ machine learning algorithms to detect fraudulent activities and assess credit risks in real-time, ensuring security and compliance. Healthcare providers analyze patient data to improve treatment outcomes and streamline operations. Manufacturers adopt smart technologies to monitor production processes, reduce downtime, and maintain quality standards. Moreover, data science facilitates strategic planning by identifying growth opportunities, optimizing pricing strategies, and enhancing product development. However, the integration of data science also presents challenges, including data privacy concerns, the need for skilled professionals, and the requirement for robust infrastructure. Despite these hurdles, the strategic application of data science is essential for businesses aiming to maintain a competitive edge and achieve sustainable growth in today's data-driven world. Data science is applied in different business contexts:

1. **Improved Decision-making:** Data science provides businesses with the tools to analyze data and make informed decisions based on evidence rather than intuition. By identifying trends and patterns, businesses can optimize resource allocation, improve efficiency, and develop more effective strategies.

   For example, in retail, data science can help optimize inventory management, personalize product recommendations, and predict customer demand.

2. **Enhanced Customer Experience:** Data science helps businesses understand customer behavior, preferences, and needs, enabling them to personalize products and services. By analyzing customer data, businesses can identify areas for improvement in customer service, personalize marketing campaigns, and improve customer satisfaction. For instance, in e-commerce, data science can be used to personalize product recommendations, optimize website design for better user experience, and improve customer support through chatbots.

3. **Increased Efficiency and Productivity:** Data science can automate repetitive tasks, optimize processes, and improve resource allocation, leading to increased efficiency and productivity. For example, in logistics, data science can optimize delivery routes, reduce transportation costs, and improve delivery times.

4. **Fraud Detection and Risk Management:** Data science algorithms can analyze vast amounts of data to identify fraudulent transactions, detect anomalies, and manage financial risks. In finance, data science is used to detect fraudulent transactions, manage credit risk, and personalize financial advice. For instance, PayPal uses data science algorithms to evaluate transaction risks in real-time, preventing fraud attempts.

5. **Predictive Analytics:** Data science enables businesses to build predictive models to forecast future outcomes and trends, including customer behavior, market demand, and sales performance. This allows businesses to anticipate future challenges and opportunities, enabling them to make proactive decisions and optimize their operations.

Key Applications of Data Science in Business and Industry

1. **Supply Chain Optimization**: Companies like Amazon and XPO Logistics utilize data science to forecast demand, optimize inventory, and streamline logistics. This approach enhances efficiency and reduces costs.
2. **Customer Personalization**: Platforms such as Netflix and Spotify employ machine learning algorithms to analyze user behavior, enabling personalized recommendations that improve user experience and retention.
3. **Financial Risk Management**: JPMorgan Chase leverages data science to assess credit risk by analyzing a wide range of data points, leading to more accurate loan approvals and reduced default rates.
4. **Manufacturing Efficiency**: General Electric uses data analytics to monitor jet engine performance, identifying inefficiencies and reducing defects, thereby enhancing product quality.
5. **Human Resources and Corporate Social Responsibility (CSR)**: Advanced HR platforms and AI analytics assist companies in collecting and interpreting social data, such as workforce diversity and pay gaps, to support CSR initiatives and ensure compliance with ESG criteria.

Jobs and Career in Data Science: Some of the key data science job roles:

1. **Data Scientist:** Analyzing large datasets, developing machine learning models, interpreting results, and providing insights to inform business decisions.

   Skills: Proficiency in programming languages like Python or R, expertise in statistics and machine learning algorithms, data visualization skills, and domain knowledge in the relevant industry.
2. **Data Analyst:** Collecting, cleaning, and analyzing data to identify trends, patterns, and insights. Often involves creating reports and dashboards to communicate findings to stakeholders.

   Skills: Strong proficiency in SQL for data querying, experience with data visualization tools like Tableau or Power BI, basic statistical knowledge, and familiarity with Excel or Google Sheets.
3. **Machine Learning Engineer:** Building and deploying machine learning models at scale, optimizing model performance, and integrating them into production systems.

   Skills: Proficiency in programming languages like Python or Java, experience with machine learning frameworks like TensorFlow or PyTorch, knowledge of cloud platforms like AWS or Azure, and software engineering skills for developing scalable solutions.
4. **Data Engineer:** Designing and building data pipelines to collect, transform, and store large volumes of data. Ensuring data quality, reliability, and scalability.

Skills: Expertise in database systems like SQL and NoSQL, proficiency in programming languages like Python or Java, experience with big data technologies like Hadoop or Spark, and knowledge of data warehousing concepts.

5. **Business Intelligence (BI) Analyst:** Gathering requirements from business stakeholders, designing and developing BI reports and dashboards, and providing data-driven insights to support strategic decision-making.

   Skills: Proficiency in BI tools like Tableau, Power BI, or Looker, strong SQL skills for data querying, understanding of data visualization principles, and ability to translate business needs into technical solutions.

6. **Data Architect:** Designing the overall structure of data systems, including databases, data lakes, and data warehouses. Defining data models, schemas, and data governance policies.

   Skills: Deep understanding of database technologies and architectures, experience with data modeling tools like ERWin or Visio, knowledge of data integration techniques, and familiarity with data security and compliance regulations.

Data-Driven Decision Making

Data-driven decision-making (DDDM) is a strategic approach where organizations utilize data analytics to inform and guide business decisions, moving beyond intuition or personal experience. This methodology involves systematically collecting relevant data, analyzing it to uncover insights, and applying these findings to optimize operations, marketing, product development, and customer engagement. For instance, predictive analytics enables companies to forecast market trends, optimize supply chains, and personalize customer experiences. Retail giants like Amazon and Walmart utilize data science to manage inventory, predict demand, and enhance customer satisfaction. In finance, institutions employ machine learning algorithms to detect fraudulent activities and assess credit risks in real-time, ensuring security and compliance. Healthcare providers analyze patient data to improve treatment outcomes and streamline operations. Manufacturers adopt smart technologies to monitor production processes, reduce downtime, and maintain quality standards. Moreover, data science facilitates strategic planning by identifying growth opportunities, optimizing pricing strategies, and enhancing product development. However, the integration of data science also presents challenges, including data privacy concerns, the need for skilled professionals, and the requirement for robust infrastructure. Despite these hurdles, the strategic application of data science is essential for businesses aiming to maintain a competitive edge and achieve sustainable growth in today's data-driven world.

Fundamentals of Making Decisions based on Data: As organizations increasingly adopt data-driven decision-making (DDDM) approaches, several key principles have emerged for putting this into practice effectively:

1. **Evidence-Based Insights:** At its core, DDDM is about basing decisions on verifiable data points and statistical analysis rather than gut feelings or intuition. The data provides concrete evidence to support more rational, analytical decision-making.
2. **Ongoing Analysis:** DDDM is not a one-time initiative - it requires building capabilities for continuous data gathering, modeling, and analysis. To adjust strategies in response to changing market conditions, consumer behaviors, or internal metrics, companies need to foster a data-driven culture across the organization.
3. **Data Quality Assurance:** No analytics model can provide reliable guidance if the underlying data is incomplete, inaccurate, or skewed. Investing in data governance, cleaning, and management is essential to ensure the insights derived are valid.
4. **Alignment with Business Objectives:** Data analysis should be focused on serving the company's overarching vision and goals. Leaders must define key business questions and use data modeling to derive answers that lead to better strategic decisions.
5. **Collaborative Decision-Making:** DDDM brings together decision-makers from across departments to interpret data and align on actions. This fosters enterprise-wide engagement vs top-down mandated analysis. Diverse viewpoints enrich the insights gleaned.

In today's hypercompetitive and fast-changing business landscape, data is a crucial asset. Organizations that commit to continuous, collaborative, and strategically-focused DDDM are best poised to leverage data for sustained success.

Importance of Making Decisions Based on Data: In today's highly competitive and disruptive business landscape, relying on data to drive decisions has become a strategic imperative across industries. Organizations that embrace data-driven decision making (DDDM) stand to gain several key advantages:

1. **Improved Decision Accuracy:** Basing decisions on quantitative analysis minimizes cognitive biases, gut feelings, or intuition that can lead to poor outcomes. Data provides empirical evidence to inform strategic choices.
2. **Competitive Edge:** Leading companies use data to identify market opportunities, optimize operations, boost efficiency, and respond quickly to trends ahead of rivals. DDDM provides a competitive differentiator.
3. **Customer Centricity:** Analyzing customer behavior, feedback, and market research enables more tailored products, services and enhanced customer experiences. Data reveals what customers truly want and value.
4. **Operational Efficiency:** Analyzing operational metrics helps identify issues, bottlenecks, and improvement opportunities to streamline workflows, reduce costs, and allocate resources optimally.

5. **Risk Management:** By modeling different scenarios, organizations can forecast risks and make contingency plans. This allows more prudent decision making amidst uncertainty.

Fraud Detection and Risk Management

Fraud detection and risk management are critical components in safeguarding businesses and financial institutions from losses caused by deceitful activities. Fraud detection involves identifying suspicious behavior or transactions that deviate from normal patterns, often using advanced analytics, machine learning models, and rule-based systems. These systems analyze large volumes of data in real-time, flagging anomalies that could indicate fraudulent activities such as credit card fraud, identity theft, or insurance scams. The goal is to detect fraud early and accurately to prevent financial damage and maintain trust. Risk management complements fraud detection by assessing, controlling, and mitigating potential threats across an organization. It involves identifying risks, evaluating their impact, and implementing policies or controls to minimize exposure. Effective risk management combines quantitative models with expert judgment to prioritize risks and allocate resources efficiently. In financial services, risk management ensures compliance with regulations, manages credit and market risks, and supports decision-making to maintain operational stability. Together, fraud detection and risk management create a proactive defense mechanism that protects assets, enhances customer confidence, and sustains long-term business viability.

Fraud Detection: Fraud detection is the process of identifying and preventing unauthorized or deceitful activities that cause financial loss or damage to organizations and individuals. It is especially critical in industries like banking, insurance, e-commerce, and telecommunications, where large volumes of transactions occur daily. Fraud can take many forms, including credit card fraud, identity theft, insurance scams, and cyber fraud. Modern fraud detection relies heavily on data analytics and machine learning techniques. By analyzing historical transaction data, behavior patterns, and user profiles, algorithms can detect anomalies that may indicate fraudulent activity. For example, sudden changes in spending patterns or transactions from unusual locations can trigger alerts. Machine learning models are trained to recognize both known fraud patterns and adapt to new, emerging threats, improving detection accuracy over time.

Real-time monitoring is often used to prevent fraud before it happens, minimizing financial loss and protecting customers. Additionally, fraud detection systems incorporate rules-based engines, risk scoring, and cross-channel data analysis to enhance effectiveness. Challenges include balancing false positives (flagging legitimate transactions as fraud) with missing actual fraud cases. Overall, fraud detection is a vital defense mechanism that helps organizations maintain security, reduce financial risks, and preserve customer trust in an increasingly digital world.

Types of Fraud Detection: The different types of Fraud Detection are as:

1. **Payment Fraud:** Detecting fraudulent credit card transactions, unauthorized account access, and other payment-related scams.
2. **Insurance Fraud:** Identifying false claims, exaggerated injuries, or other deceptive practices in insurance applications or claims.
3. **Financial Fraud:** Detecting money laundering, insider trading, and other illegal financial activities.
4. **Identity Theft:** Identifying fraudulent attempts to impersonate individuals for financial gain or other malicious purposes.
5. **Cybercrime:** Detecting and preventing various forms of cyberattacks, including phishing, malware, and ransomware.

Benefits of Data Science in Fraud Detection:

1. **Reduced Financial Losses:** Early detection of fraud helps prevent financial losses for businesses and individuals.
2. **Improved Efficiency:** Automated fraud detection systems can handle a large volume of transactions and identify anomalies much faster than manual methods.
3. **Enhanced Accuracy:** Machine learning algorithms can identify subtle patterns and anomalies that humans might miss, leading to more accurate detection.
4. **Proactive Prevention:** Data science enables organizations to not only detect fraud but also predict and prevent future fraudulent activities.
5. **Adaptability:** Machine learning models can be continuously updated and retrained to adapt to evolving fraud techniques.

Recommender Systems

Recommender systems are algorithms designed to predict and suggest items that users might find interesting, improving personalization and user experience. Widely used in e-commerce, streaming services, and social media, these systems help users navigate large catalog of products, movies, music, or content by offering tailored recommendations based on their preferences and behavior. There are several types of recommender systems, including collaborative filtering, which leverages similarities between users or items; content-based filtering, which uses item features to suggest similar content; and hybrid approaches combining both methods for enhanced accuracy. These systems analyze historical data, such as purchase history, ratings, clicks, and search patterns, to identify trends and preferences. By effectively predicting user preferences, recommender systems increase engagement, sales, and customer satisfaction. They also help businesses retain users by providing a more relevant and enjoyable experience. Challenges include dealing with sparse data, avoiding popularity bias, and protecting user privacy. Overall, recommender systems play a pivotal role in personalizing digital experiences and driving growth across various industries.

There are three main types of recommender systems:

1. **Collaborative Filtering:** This approach relies on user-item interactions (such as ratings, clicks, or purchases) to identify patterns. There are two subtypes:
   - **User-based collaborative filtering**, which recommends items that similar users liked.
   - **Item-based collaborative filtering**, which recommends items similar to those a user previously liked.

   Collaborative filtering is effective but can struggle with the "cold start" problem difficulty recommending for new users or items due to lack of data.
2. **Content-Based Filtering:** This method recommends items based on the attributes of items and the user's past preferences. For example, if a user has watched many action movies, the system will suggest similar movies based on genre, director, or keywords. This approach works well for new users with sufficient profile data, but it may lack diversity, repeatedly suggesting similar items.
3. **Hybrid Systems:** These combine collaborative and content-based approaches to improve recommendation accuracy and overcome individual limitations. For instance, Netflix uses a hybrid model to suggest TV shows and movies, blending user preferences with item features and viewing history.

Application of Recommender Systems

1. **E-Commerce:** Recommender systems are heavily used in online retail platforms (e.g., Amazon, Flipkart) to suggest products based on user behavior, past purchases, and preferences. These systems:
   - Improve product discovery.
   - Increase cross-selling (e.g., "Customers who bought this also bought...").
   - Personalize shopping experiences.
   - Boost sales and customer retention.
2. **Entertainment and Media:** Streaming services like Netflix, Spotify, and YouTube rely on recommender systems to suggest content based on viewing/ listening history.
   - Help users discover new music, movies, or shows.
   - Increase watch/listen time.
   - Tailor homepages and playlists to individual tastes.
3. **Social-media:** Platforms like Facebook, Instagram, and TikTok use recommendation algorithms to:
   - Suggest friends or connections.
   - Prioritize content in feeds.
   - Recommend groups, events, or pages to follow.
   - Keep users engaged longer by showing content they're likely to interact with.

4. **Online Education:** Educational platforms like Coursera, Khan Academy, and Udemy use recommender systems to:
   - Suggest relevant courses based on user progress and interests.
   - Personalize learning paths.
   - Recommend readings, quizzes, and peer interactions.
5. **News and Publishing:** News apps and sites (e.g., Google News, Flipboard) use recommendations to:
   - Show personalized news feeds.
   - Suggest articles based on reading habits and trends.
   - Improve engagement through targeted content delivery.
6. **Healthcare:** In healthcare, recommender systems are emerging to:
   - Suggest treatment options based on patient history.
   - Recommend health and wellness programs.
   - Guide doctors with diagnostic decision support.
7. **Job Portals and Recruitment:** Sites like LinkedIn and Indeed use recommender systems to:
   - Recommend jobs based on user profiles and activity.
   - Match candidates to job postings.
   - Suggest skills or certifications to improve employability.
8. **Travel and Tourism:** Travel platforms (e.g., TripAdvisor, Airbnb, Booking.com) use recommendation engines to:
   - Suggest destinations, hotels, and activities.
   - Personalize travel packages.
   - Recommend based on user preferences, location, and reviews.
9. **Online Dating:** Apps like Tinder and Bumble use recommender systems to:
   - Match users based on preferences, activity, and compatibility algorithms.
   - Improve match quality and user satisfaction.
10. **Finance and Banking:** Financial institutions use recommender systems to:
    - Suggest financial products like credit cards or loans.
    - Recommend budgeting or investment advice.
    - Detect anomalies and support fraud prevention.

20. Ethics and Bias in Data Science

Ethics and bias in data science are critical concerns that shape the fairness, accuracy, and social impact of data-driven decisions. As data science increasingly influences areas such as healthcare, finance, criminal justice, and hiring, the ethical implications of algorithms and models cannot be ignored. Bias can enter at multiple stages data collection, model design, or interpretation leading to outcomes that reinforce existing inequalities or unfairly discriminate against certain groups.

For example, biased training data can cause algorithms to make discriminatory predictions, such as lower credit scores for minority groups or flawed facial recognition systems. Transparency, accountability, and fairness must guide the development and deployment of data science tools. Ethical data scientists strive to understand the societal context of their work, actively seek to identify and mitigate bias, and ensure that data is used responsibly.

Ethical practices include anonymizing data to protect privacy, obtaining informed consent, auditing models for bias, and involving diverse perspectives in the development process. Regulatory frameworks like GDPR and AI ethics guidelines help enforce these principles. Ultimately, ethical data science is about building trust—ensuring that models serve all communities equitably and contribute positively to society, rather than reinforcing historical injustices or creating new harms.

Key Aspects of Ethics and Bias in Data Science:

1. **Data Bias:** Bias in data can arise from various sources, including flawed data collection methods, skewed datasets, or biased algorithms. For example, if a facial recognition system is trained primarily on images of one race, it may perform poorly on individuals of other races.
2. **Algorithmic Bias:** Algorithms can reflect and amplify existing societal biases, leading to unfair or discriminatory outcomes. For instance, an algorithm used for loan applications might unfairly deny loans to individuals from certain demographics if the training data reflects past lending biases.
3. **Ethical Considerations:** Data scientists need to consider ethical implications at every stage, from data collection to model deployment. This includes respecting privacy, ensuring transparency, and promoting fairness.
4. **Mitigation Strategies:** Several strategies can help mitigate bias and promote ethical data practices, such as using diverse and representative datasets, employing fairness metrics, and continuously auditing models for bias.

Consequences of Ethical Lapses and Bias:

1. **Disparate Impact:** Biased systems can have a disparate impact on certain groups, leading to unfair or discriminatory outcomes.
2. **Erosion of Trust:** Ethical lapses can erode public trust in data-driven technologies and organizations.
3. **Legal and Reputational Risks:** Unethical data practices can lead to legal challenges and reputational damage.

Fairness and Transparency in AI

Fairness and transparency are foundational principles in the responsible development and deployment of artificial intelligence (AI). Fairness in AI ensures that algorithms make unbiased decisions and treat all individuals and groups equitably, regardless of race, gender, age, or socioeconomic status. Without fairness, AI systems can perpetuate or even amplify existing social inequalities, as seen in biased hiring tools, facial recognition systems, or predictive policing models. Transparency refers to the ability to understand how an AI system works, including how decisions are made and what data influences those decisions. It is essential for building trust and accountability. Transparent AI allows stakeholders developers, regulators, and users to scrutinize models, identify potential biases, and correct harmful behaviors.

Achieving fairness and transparency involves careful data selection, algorithmic auditing, and the use of explainable AI (XAI) techniques that make model decisions interpretable. It also requires open communication about the limitations and risks of AI systems. Legal and ethical frameworks, such as the EU AI Act and responsible AI guidelines, are helping to standardize these practices. Together, fairness and transparency ensure AI technologies are used ethically and justly, minimizing harm and promoting positive outcomes for all members of society.

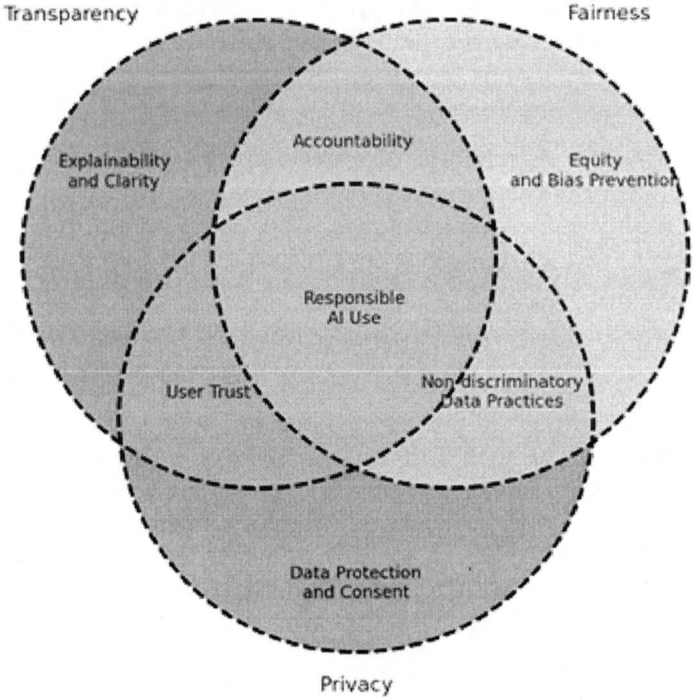

Fig. 7.3

Fairness in AI: Fairness in AI refers to the development and deployment of systems that make decisions without unjust bias or discrimination. Biases can manifest in various forms, such as racial, gender, age-related, or socioeconomic, often leading to unequal treatment or outcomes for certain groups. In algorithmic decision-making, fairness means ensuring that outcomes are equitable, inclusive, and free from systemic bias.

However, fairness is not a one-size-fits-all concept. It can be defined in multiple, sometimes conflicting, ways. For instance:

1. Demographic parity ensures equal outcomes across groups (e.g., equal loan approval rates for men and women).
2. Equal opportunity focuses on fairness among those who qualify (e.g., equal approval rates among applicants with similar creditworthiness).
3. Individual fairness emphasizes that similar individuals should receive similar outcomes.

These definitions highlight the complexity of operationalizing fairness, as meeting one criterion may violate another.

Transparency in AI: Transparency in AI involves making systems understandable and open to scrutiny. It includes both technical transparencies how the system works and procedural transparency how it was developed, tested, and deployed. Transparency also involves explainability, the ability of AI systems to provide clear and comprehensible reasons for their decisions. In black-box models such as deep neural networks, achieving explainability can be particularly difficult. Yet, without transparency, it is nearly impossible to assess whether an AI system is fair, accountable, or safe.

Why Transparency Matters: Transparency fosters trust among users, developers, regulators, and affected communities. It allows:

1. **Auditing and Accountability**: Clear documentation and explanations make it easier to identify and fix problems in AI behavior.
2. **User Trust and Adoption**: People are more likely to use and accept AI tools when they understand how decisions are made.
3. **Regulatory Compliance**: Transparency is often a legal requirement, especially under regulations like the EU's General Data Protection Regulation (GDPR), which grants users the right to explanations for automated decisions.

Moreover, transparency can help detect unintended consequences early, such as discriminatory outcomes or harmful feedback loops, allowing for timely intervention.

Challenges to Fairness and Transparency: Despite their importance, achieving fairness and transparency in AI comes with numerous challenges:

1. **Complexity of AI Models**: Advanced models, especially deep learning architectures, are often opaque and difficult to interpret.
2. **Trade-offs Between Fairness and Accuracy**: Efforts to make models fairer

may reduce their predictive performance, raising debates about acceptable compromises.

3. **Conflicting Fairness Definitions**: Implementing one fairness standard may result in perceived unfairness under another, making universal agreement difficult.
4. **Data Limitations**: High-quality, unbiased, and representative data is essential but often hard to obtain.
5. **Proprietary Systems and Secrecy**: Commercial interests may limit how much companies are willing to disclose about their models or data sources.

These challenges highlight the need for interdisciplinary collaboration among data scientists, ethicists, sociologists, and legal experts.

Best Practices for Promoting Fairness and Transparency: To address these challenges, organizations can adopt the following practices:

1. **Bias Audits and Fairness Metrics**: Regularly test models for disparate impact across different demographic groups. Use fairness metrics tailored to the use case.
2. **Diverse and Inclusive Teams**: Build development teams with diverse backgrounds to spot blind spots and incorporate broader perspectives.
3. **Explainable AI (XAI)**: Use techniques like LIME (Local Interpretable Model-Agnostic Explanations) or SHAP (SHapley Additive exPlanations) to improve interpretability.
4. **Transparent Documentation**: Maintain clear documentation through tools like model cards and datasheets for datasets, detailing the purpose, performance, and limitations of AI systems.
5. **Public Engagement and User Feedback**: Involve stakeholders, including the public, in discussions about AI deployment, especially when it affects rights or opportunities.
6. **Ethical Review Boards and Governance**: Establish internal review processes to evaluate the ethical and social impacts of AI systems.
7. **Open Source and Research Collaboration**: Sharing models and methodologies with the broader research community can improve accountability and encourage innovation.

Fairness and transparency are not just technical features they are ethical imperatives that determine the legitimacy and impact of AI systems. As AI continues to shape decisions that affect lives, jobs, and rights, we must prioritize inclusive, explainable, and equitable practices. Achieving these goals requires a combination of technological innovation, ethical awareness, diverse collaboration, and regulatory oversight. Only by embedding fairness and transparency into the core of AI design and governance can we ensure that these systems serve the public good and foster trust in a future increasingly driven by intelligent machines.

Differences Between Fairness and transparency: Table 7.1 shows the differences between Fairness in AI and Transparency in AI.

Table 7.1

S.No.	Aspect	Fairness in AI	Transparency in AI
1.	Definition	Ensuring AI decisions are unbiased and equitable across all individuals and groups	Making AI systems and their decision-making processes understandable and open
2.	Primary Goal	Prevent discrimination and promote equity	Foster trust, accountability, and interpretability
3.	Focus Area	Outcomes and impacts of AI decisions	Internal logic, processes, and reasoning of AI models
4.	Key Questions	Is the AI treating different groups fairly?	How does the AI system arrive at its decisions?
5.	Common Techniques	Bias detection, fairness metrics (e.g., demographic parity, equal opportunity)	Explainable AI (XAI), model documentation, interpretability tools (e.g., SHAP)
6.	Challenges	Defining fairness (multiple definitions), data imbalance, conflicting goals	Complexity of models, proprietary systems, lack of explainability in deep learning
7.	Impact	Affects social justice, equality, and legal compliance	Affects user trust, accountability, and regulatory understanding
8.	Measurement	Quantified using fairness metrics across different demographic groups	Assessed by level of interpretability and accessibility of system information
9.	Examples of Concern	Hiring bias, loan approval discrimination, unequal healthcare diagnosis	Black-box models, lack of explanation for credit score changes
10.	Relation to Users	Ensures equitable treatment of users	Helps users understand and question AI decisions

Bias in Machine Learning Models

Machine Learning (ML) is revolutionizing industries by automating decision-making processes and improving efficiency across areas like healthcare, finance, marketing, criminal justice, and education. However, as ML models become more widely used, concerns about bias and fairness have become increasingly significant. Bias in machine learning models can lead to unequal, discriminatory, or unjust outcomes, particularly when models are used in high-stakes domains such as hiring, policing, or healthcare. Understanding the nature of bias in ML, its causes, consequences, and how to mitigate it is essential for building ethical and trustworthy AI systems.

Types of Bias in Machine Learning Models: The different types of bias are crucial for identifying and mitigating them effectively:

1. **Data Bias:** Data bias occurs when the training data does not accurately reflect the real-world distribution or population. This can happen if certain groups are overrepresented or underrepresented in the data.

   Example: An ML model trained on English-language news articles from Western countries may fail to generalize well to users from non-Western regions.

2. **Sampling Bias:** Sampling bias is a type of data bias where the sample used to train the model is not representative of the target population.

Example: A health prediction model trained primarily on data from urban hospitals may not perform well in rural healthcare settings.

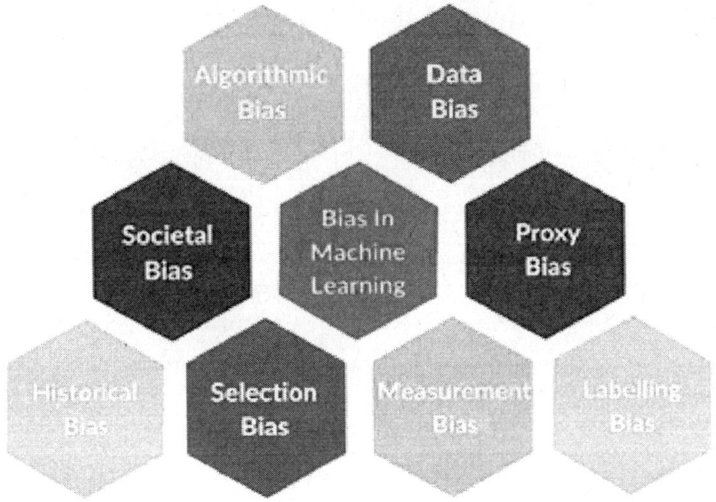

Fig. 7.4

3. **Label Bias:** Label bias occurs when the labels or outcomes in the dataset are themselves biased. This often happens when labels reflect subjective human judgments or historical inequities.

   Example: In crime prediction systems, if historical arrest data reflects biased policing, models trained on this data may unfairly target minority communities.

4. **Measurement Bias:** Measurement bias arises when the variables or features used in the model are poor proxies for what they're meant to represent, or are measured inconsistently across groups.

   Example: Using income as a proxy for creditworthiness may inadvertently disadvantage individuals from historically marginalized communities.

5. **Algorithmic Bias:** Algorithmic bias is introduced through choices made in model design, such as selecting certain features, optimization objectives, or decision thresholds.

   Example: A model that maximizes overall accuracy might unintentionally perform worse for smaller demographic groups, if their data is underrepresented.

6. **Historical Bias:** Historical bias stems from real-world inequalities that are embedded in data, regardless of how clean or representative the data may appear.

   Example: A resume screening tool trained on past hiring data might inherit gender biases if the company historically hired fewer women.

7. **Representation Bias:** Representation bias occurs when a model fails to capture the full diversity of a population, often due to imbalanced training data.

   Example: A facial recognition system that performs well on lighter-skinned individuals but poorly on darker-skinned individuals due to imbalanced training images.

8. **Confirmation Bias:** Confirmation bias happens when developers or researchers selectively interpret or use data in a way that supports their pre-existing beliefs.

   Example: Only highlighting performance metrics that show strong results while ignoring evidence of poor subgroup performance.

Data Privacy and Compliance (GDPR, CCPA)

Data privacy and compliance ensure organizations handle personal data lawfully, transparently, and securely. The General Data Protection Regulation (GDPR) governs data processing of EU residents, requiring lawful bases for processing, clear consent, and rights such as access, erasure, and data portability. GDPR mandates data breach notifications within 72 hours and imposes significant fines for violations. The California Consumer Privacy Act (CCPA) provides California residents with rights to know, delete, and opt out of the sale of their personal data, along with protections against discrimination for exercising those rights. Businesses must offer clear privacy notices and maintain robust data protection practices. Non-compliance can lead to legal action and reputational damage. To stay compliant, organizations should implement data audits, consent management systems, employee training, and secure data handling procedures. Both laws reflect a growing global emphasis on individual control over personal information and corporate accountability.

General Data Protection Regulation (GDPR): The General Data Protection Regulation (GDPR) is a comprehensive data privacy law implemented by the European Union in May 2018. It applies to all organizations that process the personal data of EU residents, regardless of where the organization is based. GDPR is designed to give individuals greater control over their personal data and to standardize data privacy laws across Europe.

Key principles include lawful processing, transparency, data minimization, and accountability. It grants individuals rights such as access to their data, the right to rectification, erasure (right to be forgotten), data portability, and the right to object to processing. Organizations must obtain clear and informed consent, ensure data security, and report data breaches within 72 hours. Non-compliance can lead to heavy fines up to €20 million or 4% of annual global revenue, whichever is higher. GDPR has influenced global privacy standards and emphasizes protecting individuals in an increasingly data-driven world.

Principles of GDPR: GDPR establishes six core principles that govern all personal data processing:

1. **Lawfulness, Fairness, and Transparency**: Data must be processed lawfully,

fairly, and in a transparent manner. Organizations must inform data subjects about how their data will be used.

2. **Purpose Limitation**: Personal data must be collected for specified, explicit, and legitimate purposes and not processed in a manner incompatible with those purposes.
3. **Data Minimization**: Only personal data necessary for the intended purpose should be collected and processed.
4. **Accuracy**: Personal data must be accurate and kept up to date. Inaccurate data must be corrected or deleted without delay.
5. **Storage Limitation**: Personal data must not be kept longer than necessary for the purposes it was collected.
6. **Integrity and Confidentiality (Security):** Data must be processed securely, protected against unauthorized or unlawful processing, accidental loss, destruction, or damage.

Data Subject Rights: GDPR significantly enhances the rights of individuals regarding their personal data:

1. **Right to Access:** Individuals can request confirmation whether their data is processed, access to their data, and supplementary information.
2. **Right to Rectification:** The right to have inaccurate or incomplete data corrected.
3. **Right to Erasure ("Right to be Forgotten"):** The right to request deletion of personal data when it is no longer necessary, consent is withdrawn, or data was unlawfully processed.
4. **Right to Restrict Processing:** Data subjects can limit how their data is processed under certain conditions.
5. **Right to Data Portability:** Allows individuals to receive their data in a structured, commonly used format and transfer it to another controller.
6. **Right to Object:** The right to object to data processing for direct marketing, research, or legitimate interests.
7. **Rights Related to Automated Decision-Making and Profiling:** Individuals have the right not to be subject to decisions based solely on automated processing, including profiling, that produces legal effects or similarly significant impacts.

California Consumer Privacy Act (CCPA): The California Consumer Privacy Act (CCPA) is a landmark privacy law enacted to protect the personal data of California residents. It went into effect on January 1, 2020, making California the first U.S. state to implement comprehensive data privacy rights. Inspired in part by the European Union's General Data Protection Regulation (GDPR), the CCPA represents a major shift in how companies handle and disclose consumer data in the United States.

CCPA provides consumers with greater control over their personal information by granting specific rights and imposing obligations on businesses that collect and process this data. It also reflects growing public concern about how companies use personal data for advertising, tracking, and monetization.

Consumer Rights Under the CCPA: The CCPA grants California consumers several key rights:

1. **Right to Know:** Consumers have the right to request information about the categories and specific **pieces** of personal data a business has collected about them in the past 12 months, including:
   - Sources of the information,
   - Business purposes for collecting or selling the data,
   - Categories of third parties the data is shared with.
2. **Right to Delete:** Consumers can request that a business delete their personal information, with some exceptions (e.g., when data is needed to complete a transaction or comply with a legal obligation).
3. **Right to Opt Out:** Consumers have the right to opt out of the sale of their personal information. Businesses must provide a clear and conspicuous "Do Not Sell My Personal Information" link on their websites.
4. **Right to Non-Discrimination:** Businesses may not discriminate against consumers for exercising their CCPA rights. This includes refusing service, charging different prices, or providing a different level of service although financial incentives for data sharing are permitted if they are disclosed and consented to.

Differences Between GDPR and CCPA: The differences between GDPR and CCPA is listed in table 7.2.

21. Building a Career in Data Science

Building a career in data science involves a combination of strong technical skills, analytical thinking, and domain knowledge. It typically begins with a solid foundation in mathematics, statistics, and programming especially in languages like Python or R. Aspiring data scientists should also gain proficiency in data wrangling, machine learning, data visualization, and tools such as SQL, Pandas, Scikit-learn, and Tableau. Earning a degree in computer science, statistics, or a related field is helpful, though many professionals transition from other disciplines through bootcamps, online courses, or certifications. Practical experience is crucial, so building a portfolio with real-world projects, participating in competitions like Kaggle, and contributing to open-source projects can demonstrate capabilities to employers. Data scientists must also possess soft skills such as problem-solving, communication, and the ability to translate complex insights into actionable business strategies. Networking, attending industry conferences, and staying updated with trends and tools also play key roles in advancing a data science career. Core Skills and Tools are as:

Table 7.2

S.No.	Aspect	GDPR (General Data Protection Regulation)	CCPA (California Consumer Privacy Act)
1.	Jurisdiction	Data controllers and processors	California, USA; applies to businesses handling data of California residents
2.	Effective Date	Any information relating to an identifiable person	January 1, 2020 (updated by CPRA in 2023)
3.	Scope	Special categories defined (e.g., health, religion, biometric data)	For-profit businesses meeting specific thresholds
4.	Applies to	Access, rectification, erasure, portability, restriction, objection, etc.	Businesses meeting revenue/data thresholds
5.	Personal Data Definition	Mostly **opt-in**, especially for consent	Broad, includes household and device information
6.	Sensitive Data	Yes, comprehensive (with exceptions)	Introduced under CPRA (e.g., SSN, geolocation, race, health)
7.	Consumer Rights	Yes	Access, deletion, opt-out of sale, non-discrimination, correction (via CPRA)
8.	Opt-In/Opt-Out	Yes, including to profiling and direct marketing	**Opt-out** of data sale/sharing
9.	Right to Erasure	Regulated and subject to restrictions	Yes, but more limited
10.	Right to Data Portability	National data protection authorities in each EU country	Yes
11.	Right to Object	Up to €20 million or 4% of global annual turnover (whichever is higher)	No direct right to object (opt-out of sale only)
12.	Automated Decision-Making	No general right (only in some EU countries); mostly regulator-driven enforcement	Not specifically addressed under CCPA
13.	Enforcement Body	Required for many types of data processing	California Privacy Protection Agency (CPPA)
14.	Penalties for Violations	Within 72 hours to regulator	Up to $7,500 per intentional violation; $2,500 for unintentional
15.	Private Right of Action	Consent required under age 16 (can be lowered to 13 by member states)	Yes, for data breaches due to lack of security
16.	Consent Requirements	Explicitly required	Required only for minors; otherwise opt-out model for sale
17.	Data Breach Notification	High – model for many other global privacy laws	No specific time, but required for qualifying breaches
18.	Children's Data	European Union (EU) and European Economic Area (EEA); extraterritorial effect	Opt-in required for sale of data of minors under 16 (13 with parental consent)
19.	Purpose Limitation & Minimization	May 25, 2018	Introduced under CPRA
20.	Global Influence	All organizations processing personal data of EU residents	Growing – influences U.S. state laws like Colorado, Virginia, etc.

1. **Programming:** The ability to write code is fundamental. Two of the most commonly used programming languages in data science are:
   - **Python**: Widely used due to its simplicity and rich ecosystem (NumPy, Pandas, Scikit-learn, TensorFlow).
   - **R**: Strong in statistical analysis and data visualization.

   Additional knowledge of SQL (Structured Query Language) is crucial for working with databases.
2. **Statistics and Mathematics:** Understanding concepts such as probability, distributions, hypothesis testing, and linear algebra is vital for building reliable models and interpreting data correctly.
3. **Machine Learning:** Machine learning is at the heart of modern data science. Key concepts include:
   - Supervised and unsupervised learning
   - Regression and classification
   - Clustering and dimensionality reduction
   - Neural networks and deep learning

   Familiarity with tools like Scikit-learn, Keras, PyTorch, and XGBoost is often required.
4. **Data Wrangling and Cleaning:** Much of a data scientist's time is spent preparing data. This involves handling missing values, removing duplicates, correcting errors, and normalizing data to make it usable.
5. **Data Visualization:** Data must be communicated effectively. Tools like Matplotlib, Seaborn, Tableau, and **Power BI** help create charts and dashboards that translate complex data into clear insights.
6. **Big Data Tools (Optional but Valuable):** For working with large-scale data, tools like Apache Spark, Hadoop, and Google BigQuery are useful. Understanding cloud platforms such as AWS, Azure, or Google Cloud Platform adds value.

Essential Skills and Certifications

To build a successful career in data science, mastering a diverse range of technical and analytical skills is crucial. At the core, programming proficiency is essential Python is the most widely used language in data science due to its simplicity and vast library support (NumPy, Pandas, Scikit-learn, TensorFlow). R is another powerful language, especially in statistical modeling and data visualization. SQL is fundamental for querying relational databases, while experience with big data tools like Apache Spark or Hadoop can be an advantage for handling large-scale datasets. Apart from programming, strong statistical and mathematical knowledge is critical. Data scientists must understand probability, hypothesis testing, linear regression, classification, and clustering. Knowledge of machine learning algorithms and how to apply them in real-world scenarios is equally important. Being able to clean, preprocess, and visualize data effectively is vital to ensure accurate model outcomes and communicate results clearly.

Alongside technical capabilities, soft skills are equally important. The ability to communicate insights to non-technical stakeholders, work in cross-functional teams, and solve ambiguous problems creatively sets successful data scientists apart. For those looking to formalize their skills or stand out in a competitive job market, various certifications and courses can add credibility. Recognized programs include the IBM Data Science Professional Certificate, Google Data Analytics Certificate, and Coursera's Data Science Specialization by Johns Hopkins University. Additionally, Microsoft Certified: Azure Data Scientist Associate, and AWS Certified Machine Learning Specialty validate cloud and machine learning expertise. Though not mandatory, these certifications can help beginners enter the field and professionals demonstrate up-to-date knowledge, especially when transitioning from non-technical backgrounds.

Importance of Essential Skills and Certifications (Continuous Points):

1. **Forms the foundation of technical problem-solving**: Core skills in programming, statistics, and machine learning are essential to tackle data-driven challenges.
2. **Enables hands-on data manipulation and analysis**: Tools like Python, R, and SQL are critical for working with large and complex datasets.
3. **Equips you to build predictive models and AI solutions**: Knowledge of machine learning helps create solutions that drive business decisions.
4. **Ensures efficient data cleaning and preprocessing**: A must-have skill to prepare raw data for accurate analysis and modeling.
5. **Improves communication of insights**: Visualization tools like Tableau or Matplotlib help present data findings clearly to non-technical audiences.
6. **Enhances employability and job-readiness**: Candidates with strong technical skills are more likely to be hired and succeed in competitive roles.
7. **Provides confidence in technical interviews**: A solid skillset makes it easier to handle coding tests, case studies, and whiteboard problems.
8. **Supports career transitions from non-technical backgrounds**: Certifications act as proof of knowledge for career changers entering the data science field.
9. **Demonstrates commitment to the field**: Pursuing certifications shows motivation, discipline, and genuine interest in continuous learning.
10. **Validates your expertise to employers**: Industry-recognized certifications like Google, IBM, or Microsoft add credibility to your profile.
11. **Fills knowledge gaps**: Structured courses help you learn in a logical order, reducing confusion and building confidence.

12. **Keeps your skills current**: Certifications are often updated to reflect the latest tools and technologies in data science.
13. **Boosts chances of promotion or role change**: Certified professionals are more likely to be considered for internal advancement or specialized positions.
14. **Builds a competitive edge in a saturated job market**: When many candidates have similar degrees, certifications help you stand out.
15. **Increases salary potential**: Professionals with in-demand certifications and advanced skills often earn higher salaries than their uncertified peers.

Creating a Data Science Portfolio

A strong data science portfolio is one of the most powerful tools for landing a job or internship in the field. Unlike traditional resumes that list qualifications, a portfolio demonstrates your ability to apply skills to real-world problems. It gives employers insight into how you think, your coding style, and your problem-solving approach. Portfolios typically include a mix of projects that cover different stages of the data science pipeline—data collection, cleaning, exploration, modeling, and visualization. Beginner projects may involve analyzing publicly available datasets (e.g., from Kaggle or UCI Machine Learning Repository) such as predicting housing prices, classifying images, or customer segmentation. As you progress, you should showcase end-to-end projects involving data scraping, preprocessing, building models, and presenting results via dashboards or interactive apps (e.g., using Streamlit or Flask).

Hosting your portfolio online is crucial. GitHub is the standard platform for publishing code and notebooks. Creating a personal website or blog (e.g., using GitHub Pages, WordPress, or Medium) to explain your projects, challenges faced, and outcomes adds an extra layer of professionalism and clarity. Write-ups should be easy to follow and aimed at both technical and non-technical audiences. You can also include Jupyter notebooks, data visualizations, and links to deployed models. Showcasing your ability to interpret results and provide actionable insights is just as important as technical accuracy. Finally, contributing to open-source projects, participating in data science competitions (like Kaggle), and engaging in GitHub discussions helps build a reputation in the data community and improves your visibility to potential employers.

Importance of a Data Science Portfolio:

1. **Demonstrates Practical Skills**: Shows your ability to apply data science concepts to real-world problems beyond theoretical knowledge.
2. **Replaces the Need for Experience**: Ideal for beginners or career switchers to prove their capabilities when they lack formal job experience.
3. **Showcases the Full Workflow**: Allows you to present end-to-end projects, including data collection, cleaning, analysis, modeling, and visualization.
4. **Highlights Problem-Solving Ability**: Reflects how you approach challenges, select models, interpret results, and draw actionable insights.

5. **Improves Visibility to Recruiters**: A strong, public portfolio (on GitHub, personal website, or LinkedIn) increases your chances of being noticed by hiring managers.
6. **Reveals Communication Skills:** Explaining projects clearly in write-ups or blogs demonstrates your ability to convey complex ideas to non-technical audiences.
7. **Builds Confidence and Identity**: Curating your work over time helps you track your growth and develop a professional identity as a data scientist.
8. **Encourages Continuous Learning**: Maintaining a portfolio motivates you to keep learning and experimenting with new tools, techniques, and datasets.
9. **Facilitates Technical Discussions in Interviews**: Serves as a conversation starter in interviews, allowing you to walk through your thought process and coding approach.
10. **Validates Your Passion for the Field**: A well-maintained portfolio signals genuine interest and long-term commitment to data science.

Job Roles and Salary Expectations

The field of data science offers a variety of job roles, each focusing on different aspects of data management, analysis, and modeling. Common entry-level roles include Data Analyst, who primarily interprets and visualizes data to support decision-making, and Junior Data Scientist, who may assist in building and testing predictive models. As you gain experience, roles such as Data Scientist, Machine Learning Engineer, and Data Engineer become accessible. Data Scientists build advanced statistical models and machine learning algorithms, while Machine Learning Engineers focus on scaling and deploying those models in production environments. Data Engineers, on the other hand, manage data pipelines and architecture, ensuring data is clean, accessible, and reliable. Specialized roles like NLP Engineers, Computer Vision Specialists, and AI Researchers are also emerging in companies focusing on deep learning and advanced AI applications.

Salaries in data science are highly competitive and depend on experience, location, industry, and skill set. In the United States, entry-level data scientists typically earn between $75,000 and $95,000 annually. Mid-level professionals with 3–5 years of experience can expect $100,000 to $130,000, while senior data scientists and machine learning engineers often make upwards of $150,000 per year, especially in tech hubs like San Francisco, Seattle, or New York. In countries like the UK, Canada, Germany, and India, the salaries are slightly lower but still well above the average for tech roles. Moreover, companies in finance, healthcare, and tech generally pay higher than education or non-profit sectors. Certifications, advanced degrees, and niche skills like cloud computing or deep learning can significantly boost earning potential. As organizations become increasingly data-driven, the demand for skilled professionals continues to rise, making data science one of the most future-proof and rewarding career paths today.

Importance of Job Roles and Salary Expectations:

1. **Helps Identify the Right Role Based on Skills and Interests:** Clarifies what each data science role entails so you can pursue one that fits your background and career goals.
2. **Guides Targeted Learning and Certification Paths**: Knowing what a Data Analyst vs. a Machine Learning Engineer needs allows you to focus on relevant tools and techniques.
3. **Supports Career Progression Planning**: Understanding the hierarchy (junior → senior → lead → principal) helps you set achievable milestones.
4. **Clarifies Expectations for Each Position**: Prevents confusion by outlining specific tasks, such as model deployment in ML Engineering vs. visualization in BI roles.
5. **Boosts Confidence in Job Interviews**: Knowing your role prepares you to answer technical and scenario-based questions confidently.
6. **Improves Resume and Portfolio Targeting**: Allows you to highlight role-specific skills and achievements, increasing chances of being shortlisted.
7. **Reveals the Financial Value of Each Role**: Helps you assess the return on investment for time and money spent on learning or certifications.
8. **Enables Strategic Job Searching**: Knowing high-demand, high-paying roles lets you focus on industries and companies that value your expertise.
9. **Promotes Better Salary Negotiation**: With benchmark data, you can negotiate offers based on market standards and your experience level.
10. **Shows Which Skills Are High-Earning**: Helps prioritize learning in areas like cloud computing, NLP, or deep learning, which offer better pay.
11. **Encourages Geographic and Industry Flexibility**: Understanding salary variation across locations and sectors can influence relocation or industry switch decisions.
12. **Supports Freelancing or Consulting Decisions**: For independent professionals, role clarity and salary benchmarks help price services competitively.
13. **Assists in Budgeting and Financial Planning**: Salary expectations help you make informed decisions about lifestyle, savings, and career-related investments.
14. **Helps Set Realistic Entry-Level Expectations**: Prevents disappointment by aligning first-job expectations with market norms.
15. **Motivates Long-Term Skill Development**: Awareness of how salaries grow with expertise and experience inspires ongoing learning and specialization.

SUMMARY OF REAL-WORLD APPLICATIONS AND ETHICS

Data science plays a transformative role in modern industries by enabling smarter, faster, and more accurate decision-making. In business, data-driven decision-making has become a core strategy, helping companies optimize operations, reduce costs, and improve customer experiences. For example, banks and fintech firms use data science for fraud detection and risk management, employing machine learning models to flag suspicious transactions in real time. E-commerce platforms and streaming services rely heavily on recommender systems that analyze user behavior to personalize product or content suggestions, boosting engagement and revenue.

However, with great power comes great responsibility. As data science becomes deeply embedded in society, ethical concerns are increasingly critical. One major issue is bias in machine learning models, which can result from imbalanced training data and lead to unfair or discriminatory outcomes. Ensuring fairness and transparency in AI is crucial, especially in sensitive areas like hiring, lending, or criminal justice. The push for explainable AI aims to make model decisions more understandable and accountable. Additionally, data privacy and compliance with regulations like the General Data Protection Regulation (GDPR) and California Consumer Privacy Act (CCPA) are essential. These laws protect individual rights and ensure that organizations handle personal data responsibly, with clear consent and transparency.

19. Data Science in Business and Industry

Data science has become a critical asset in modern business and industry, enabling smarter, faster, and more informed decision-making. By analyzing large volumes of structured and unstructured data, companies gain valuable insights that drive strategic planning, operational efficiency, and customer engagement. Data-driven decision making allows organizations to move beyond intuition, using analytics to guide actions in marketing, finance, logistics, and more. In fraud detection and risk management, machine learning models identify suspicious patterns in real time, reducing financial losses and enhancing security, particularly in banking and insurance sectors. Another major application is recommender systems, which personalize user experiences by suggesting relevant products or content based on past behavior. These systems are widely used by platforms like Amazon and Netflix to boost user engagement and sales. Overall, data science transforms raw data into actionable intelligence, giving businesses a competitive edge in an increasingly digital and data-centric world.

- **Data-Driven Decision Making:** Data science empowers organizations to base decisions on analytics and factual insights rather than intuition. Businesses use data to forecast trends, measure performance, and make strategic choices in areas like marketing, operations, and finance.
- **Fraud Detection and Risk Management:** Machine learning algorithms detect anomalies in financial transactions, helping institutions identify and prevent fraud. Predictive models assess risks more accurately, enhancing decision-making in banking, insurance, and cybersecurity.

- **Recommender Systems:** Recommender systems personalize user experiences by analyzing past behavior to suggest relevant products or content. Used by platforms like Amazon, Netflix, and Spotify, these systems increase engagement and revenue.

20. Ethics and Bias in Data Science

Ethics and bias in data science are critical concerns as AI and machine learning increasingly influence real-world decisions. Bias in models can arise from unbalanced or flawed data, leading to unfair or discriminatory outcomes, particularly in areas like hiring, lending, and law enforcement. Ensuring fairness and transparency is essential, with growing emphasis on explainable AI to make decisions understandable and accountable. Additionally, data privacy regulations like GDPR and CCPA mandate responsible data handling, emphasizing user consent and transparency. Ethical data science practices are crucial for building trust, promoting equity, and ensuring that technology serves all users fairly.

- **Fairness and Transparency in AI:** AI systems must be explainable and equitable. Fairness ensures that models don't discriminate against individuals or groups, and transparency builds trust by making model decisions understandable.
- **Bias in Machine Learning Models:** Bias often arises from skewed or incomplete training data, leading to unfair predictions. It's crucial to detect and mitigate bias to avoid reinforcing social inequalities through AI.
- **Data Privacy and Compliance (GDPR, CCPA):** Laws like the GDPR and CCPA protect personal data rights, requiring organizations to obtain consent, ensure transparency, and offer users control over their information. Compliance is critical to maintaining ethical standards and trust.

21. Building a Career in Data Science

A career in data science is both dynamic and rewarding, offering opportunities across industries such as finance, healthcare, technology, and e-commerce. To succeed, aspiring data scientists must develop core skills in programming (Python, R), statistics, machine learning, and data visualization. Earning certifications from recognized platforms like Coursera, IBM, or Google helps validate expertise and strengthens job applications. Building a portfolio of real-world projects hosted on GitHub or personal websites demonstrates practical ability and problem-solving skills. Understanding various job roles (e.g., Data Analyst, Data Scientist, ML Engineer) helps align skills with career goals. Salaries are highly competitive, with potential for growth based on experience and specialization. In this rapidly evolving field, continuous learning and adapting to new tools and technologies are essential. With the right mix of technical skills, real-world experience, and strategic planning, a career in data science can be both impactful and future-proof.

- **Essential Skills and Certifications:** Key skills include Python/R programming, statistics, SQL, and machine learning. Certifications (e.g., from IBM, Google,

Microsoft) validate expertise and help candidates stand out, especially those transitioning from other fields.

- **Creating a Data Science Portfolio:** A strong portfolio showcases practical project work across data cleaning, modeling, and visualization. Hosting projects on GitHub or personal websites allows recruiters to evaluate a candidate's real-world capabilities.
- **Job Roles and Salary Expectations:** Data science offers diverse roles like Data Analyst, Data Scientist, ML Engineer, and Data Engineer. Salaries are competitive, with higher earnings linked to specialization, experience, and industry.

Appendices

GLOSSARY OF DATA SCIENCE TERMS

This glossary covers essential terms that span the data science lifecycle, from data collection and cleaning, through modeling and evaluation, to deployment and automation. Understanding these concepts is vital for practitioners and stakeholders in data-driven projects, ensuring effective communication and execution of data science initiatives.

1. **Algorithm:** A step-by-step procedure or formula for solving a problem. In data science, algorithms are used to perform tasks such as classification, regression, clustering, or recommendation by learning patterns from data.
2. **Artificial Intelligence (AI):** A broad field of computer science focused on creating systems capable of performing tasks that normally require human intelligence, such as reasoning, perception, language understanding, and decision-making.
3. **Big Data:** Datasets whose size, complexity, and variety exceed the ability of traditional data processing systems to manage and analyze them efficiently. Big data often involves the "3 Vs": volume, velocity, and variety.
4. **Bias:** Systematic error introduced in the data collection, model training, or evaluation processes that cause the model to make inaccurate or unfair predictions. Bias can lead to unethical outcomes and reduced model effectiveness.
5. **Classification:** A supervised machine learning task where the goal is to assign input data points into one of several predefined categories or classes.
6. **Clustering:** An unsupervised learning technique that groups similar data points into clusters based on features or patterns without pre-labeled outcomes.
7. **Confusion Matrix:** A table used to evaluate the performance of a classification model by showing the true positives, true negatives, false positives, and false negatives.
8. **Data Cleaning:** The process of detecting, correcting, or removing errors,

inconsistencies, and inaccuracies from datasets to improve data quality and reliability.

9. **Data Engineer:** A professional responsible for designing, building, and maintaining data pipelines and infrastructure that enable data collection, storage, and accessibility for analytics and modeling.
10. **Data Lake:** A centralized repository that stores vast amounts of raw data in its native format until needed for analysis or processing.
11. **Data Mining:** The process of discovering meaningful patterns, correlations, and insights from large datasets using statistical, machine learning, and database systems.
12. **Data Pipeline:** A series of automated processes that move data from sources to destinations, often including steps for extraction, transformation, validation, and loading into data warehouses or data lakes.
13. **Data Science:** An interdisciplinary field that combines statistics, computer science, domain expertise, and machine learning to extract insights and knowledge from data.
14. **Data Visualization:** The graphical representation of data through charts, graphs, and dashboards to help communicate insights and trends clearly and effectively.
15. **Dataset:** A structured collection of data points, often organized in rows and columns, used for training or evaluating machine learning models or conducting analyses.
16. **Decision Tree:** A supervised learning algorithm that splits data based on feature values to create a tree-like model of decisions, useful for classification and regression.
17. **Deep Learning:** A subset of machine learning involving neural networks with many layers (deep neural networks) that can model complex patterns in data, especially in images, speech, and text.
18. **Dimensionality Reduction:** Techniques like PCA (Principal Component Analysis) or t-SNE used to reduce the number of features in a dataset while preserving its meaningful structure, often to improve model performance or visualization.
19. **ETL (Extract, Transform, Load):** A data integration process that extracts data from source systems, transforms it into a clean, consistent format, and loads it into a destination database or data warehouse.
20. **Exploratory Data Analysis (EDA):** An initial approach to analyzing datasets using summary statistics and visualization to discover patterns, anomalies, and test hypotheses.
21. **Feature Engineering:** The process of creating, selecting, and transforming

variables (features) from raw data to improve the performance of machine learning models.

22. **Feature Selection:** Techniques used to identify the most important features in a dataset to reduce dimensionality and enhance model accuracy and interpretability.
23. **Gradient Boosting:** An ensemble learning method that builds models sequentially by correcting errors from previous models, widely used for structured data prediction tasks.
24. **Hyperparameter:** Parameters that control the behavior of machine learning algorithms (e.g., learning rate, number of trees) and are set before training begins, usually tuned via techniques like grid search or random search.
25. **K-Means Clustering:** A popular unsupervised algorithm that partitions data into K clusters by minimizing the variance within each cluster.
26. **Label:** The target variable or outcome in supervised learning tasks, representing the ground truth used to train models.
27. **Linear Regression:** A statistical method used to model the relationship between a dependent variable and one or more independent variables by fitting a linear equation.
28. **Machine Learning (ML):** A subset of AI focused on developing algorithms that enable computers to learn patterns from data and make decisions or predictions without explicit programming.
29. **Model Deployment:** The process of integrating a trained machine learning model into a production environment where it can make predictions on new data.
30. **Model Evaluation:** Assessing a model's performance using metrics such as accuracy, precision, recall, F1-score for classification, or RMSE, MAE for regression.
31. **Natural Language Processing (NLP):** A branch of AI that enables computers to understand, interpret, and generate human language text or speech.
32. **Neural Network:** A computational model inspired by the human brain's structure, consisting of layers of interconnected nodes (neurons) capable of learning complex patterns.
33. **NoSQL Databases:** Non-relational databases designed to handle large volumes of unstructured or semi-structured data, offering high scalability and flexibility (e.g., MongoDB, Cassandra).
34. **Overfitting:** A modeling error where a machine learning model learns noise and details from the training data, resulting in poor generalization to unseen data.

35. **Pandas:** A widely used Python library providing data structures and functions for data manipulation and analysis, especially for tabular data.
36. **Precision and Recall:** Metrics used to evaluate classification models: precision measures the accuracy of positive predictions, while recall measures the ability to find all positive instances.
37. **Python:** A versatile, high-level programming language favored in data science for its readability, rich libraries, and community support.
38. **Random Forest:** An ensemble learning method using multiple decision trees to improve predictive accuracy and control overfitting.
39. **Reinforcement Learning (RL)**: An area of ML where an agent learns optimal actions by interacting with an environment to maximize cumulative rewards.
40. **Regression:** A type of supervised learning task focused on predicting continuous numerical values.
41. **SQL (Structured Query Language):** A standard language for managing and querying relational databases.
42. **Supervised Learning:** Machine learning where models are trained on labeled datasets to predict outcomes for new data.
43. **TensorFlow:** An open-source deep learning framework developed by Google for building and deploying machine learning models.
44. **Time Series Analysis:** Techniques for analyzing data points collected or recorded at specific time intervals to identify trends, seasonal patterns, or forecasting.
45. **Training Set:** The subset of data used to train machine learning models
46. **Transfer Learning:** A technique where a pre-trained model is adapted to a new but related problem, reducing training time and data requirements.
47. **Unsupervised Learning:** Learning patterns from data without labeled outcomes, such as clustering and dimensionality reduction.
48. **Validation Set:** Data used to tune model hyperparameters and prevent overfitting during training.
49. **Variance:** A measure of how much a model's predictions change with different training data; high variance indicates overfitting.
50. **Workflow Automation:** Automating repetitive data tasks and machine learning pipelines using tools like Apache Airflow to increase efficiency and reliability.
51. **Apache Airflow:** An open-source platform for programmatically authoring, scheduling, and monitoring workflows, widely used for data pipeline orchestration.

52. **Apache Hadoop:** A distributed storage and processing framework designed for big data applications, using HDFS and MapReduce for batch processing.
53. **Apache Spark:** A fast, in-memory distributed computing system for big data processing, enabling real-time analytics and machine learning.
54. **Cloud Computing:** Delivery of computing services servers, storage, databases, networking, software over the internet ("the cloud") on a pay-as-you-go basis.
55. **DataOps:** A set of practices combining Agile, DevOps, and statistical process control to improve the quality, speed, and reliability of data analytics.
56. **ETL Automation:** Using tools and platforms to automate the extract, transform, and load process to improve pipeline efficiency and reduce errors.
57. **MLOps:** A discipline combining machine learning and DevOps practices to automate and monitor all steps of ML lifecycle from data preparation to deployment and monitoring.
58. **NoSQL:** Databases designed for flexible schema and scalability to handle big data with unstructured or semi-structured formats.
59. **Serverless Computing:** Cloud computing model where the cloud provider dynamically manages resource allocation, allowing developers to run code without managing servers.
60. **Spot Instances:** Discounted cloud compute instances that can be interrupted and reclaimed by the provider, used for cost-efficient scalable computing.

RECOMMENDED BOOKS

1. ***Python for Data Analysis* by Wes McKinney**

   Written by the creator of Pandas, this book is a go to resource for data cleaning, manipulation, and analysis using Python libraries like Pandas, NumPy, and Jupyter notebooks. Ideal for hands on learning.

2. ***Data Science for Business* by Tom Fawcett & Foster Provost**

   Explains how data science frameworks and methods apply directly to business decisions, bridging analytic thinking with practical strategy. Perfect for decision-makers and technical professionals alike.

3. ***Data Science for Dummies* by Lillian Pierson**

   A beginner friendly guide introducing core concepts like data wrangling, machine learning, and analytics using Python or R. It's structured and accessible for non-technical audiences.

4. ***Naked Statistics* by Charles Wheelan**

   Simplifies statistical fundamentals with engaging storytelling and real-world examples, making probability and regression clear even for novices.

5. ***Data Science and Predictive Analytics* by Ivo Dinov**

Focused on biomedical and health data using R, this comprehensive guide walks you through techniques, statistical modeling, and real-world case studies. Updated in 2023.

RECOMMENDED COURSES

1. **Top Beginner-Friendly Programs**
   - **IBM Data Science Professional Certificate (Coursera × IBM)**

     A robust 9-course program covering Python, SQL, data visualization, machine learning, and a capstone project. Highly rated and suited for beginners, with real-world tools like JupyterLab and IBM Watson.
   - **Applied Data Science with Python Specialization (University of Michigan, Coursera)**

     A 5-month specialization focused on Python-based data wrangling, visualization, and ML using Pandas, scikit-learn, NLTK, and more. Great for hands-on learners with basic Python familiarity.
   - **Data Science and Machine Learning Program by Scaler (InterviewBit)**

     An industrial-grade curriculum designed with inputs from top tech companies. It includes real-world projects and mentorship, covering topics from OOP to reinforcement learning.
2. **Programs with Academic Rigor**
   - **UC San Diego Data Science MicroMasters (edX)**

     A comprehensive, credit-bearing program covering statistics, machine learning, data visualization, and big data analytics. Suitable for learners aiming for academic depth.
   - **MITx: Statistics and Data Science MicroMasters (edX)**

     A year-long program teaching foundational statistics and probability along with machine learning applications. Ideal for those pursuing serious technical mastery.
   - **Udacity Data Scientist Nanodegree**

     A project-driven course with content developed alongside industry partners like IBM and Amazon. Covers data wrangling, visualization, modeling, and capstone projects.

RECOMMENDATIONS BASED ON YOUR GOALS

1. **If you're new to the field:** Start with *Data Science for Dummies* and the IBM Data Science Professional Certificate for guided introduction and project-based learning.
2. **For Python-powered analytics & modeling:** *Python for Data Analysis* plus Applied Data Science with Python Specialization offer excellent hands-on experience.

3. **For deep academic or technical rigor:** Consider the MITx or UCSD MicroMasters programs for a solid statistics and ML foundation.
4. **For career acceleration and mentoring:** The Scaler Data Science program and Udacity Nanodegree provide structured projects, real-time feedback, and industry relevance.
5. **To build portfolio fast on a budget:** Udemy bootcamps like *Complete Data Science Bootcamp* or *Python for Data Science and ML Bootcamp* deliver practical skills affordably.

HANDS-ON PROJECTS FOR DATA SCIENCE PRACTICE

Project 1: End-to-End Customer Churn Prediction

Objective:

Build a predictive model to identify customers likely to *churn* (leave a service), enabling businesses (e.g. telecom, retail, SaaS) to take preventive actions.

Problem Framing and Data Understanding: This stage focuses on clearly identifying a real-world business issue and translating it into a data-driven problem. It begins with stakeholders: What is the context? What outcome or goal such as increasing sales, reducing churn, or optimizing logistics is being pursued? One effective approach is the Current State–Future State (CS-FS) framework, where you document the current situation, desired target, and the gap the analysis should close. Clear framing ensures alignment across stakeholders and provides measurable objectives guiding the analytics process.

Once the problem is framed, the next step is understanding the data you have. This phase involves four steps: collecting initial data, describing it, exploring its patterns, and verifying. You document data sources, types (e.g., numeric, categorical), and volume, and create a data dictionary describing each field. Exploratory Data Analysis (EDA) using histograms, scatter plots, and summary stats helps uncover trends, outliers, and missing values. Verifying data quality involves identifying inconsistencies, duplicates, or gaps to determine if the data is sufficient or if additional sourcing or cleaning is needed. Well-documented data understanding builds trust, prevents rework, and sets the stage for effective modeling.

Data Preparation and Feature Engineering (Approx. 180 words)

Clean and prep the data by:

1. Converting TotalCharges to numeric, filling missing values.
2. Encoding categorical variables: one-hot encoding or label encoding. Or use CatBoost directly for categories.
3. Normalizing/standardizing numerical features to ensure good model performance.
4. Generating new features like contract tenure, service count, or engagement metrics (e.g., 'SeniorCitizen', internet usage, payment method).

5. Splitting the data into training and test sets (e.g., 80/20 split, with stratification to preserve the churn ratio).
6. Use Scikit-learn's pipeline for preprocessing + modeling, ensuring consistent transformations and tidy code structure.

Model Selection, Training & Tuning: Start with baseline models:

1. Logistic Regression
2. Decision Tree or Random Forest
3. Gradient Boosting (XGBoost/LightGBM)
4. Powerful gradient-based model: CatBoost (handles categorical features) .

Use pipelines built with Scikit-learn:

```
from sklearn.pipeline import Pipeline
from sklearn.preprocessing import StandardScaler, OneHotEncoder
from sklearn.compose import ColumnTransformer
preprocessor = ColumnTransformer([
 ('num', StandardScaler(), numeric_cols),
 ('cat', OneHotEncoder(drop='first'), categorical_cols)
])
pipeline = Pipeline([
 ('pre', preprocessor),
 ('clf', RandomForestClassifier(random_state=42))
])
```

Train models and evaluate on the validation set using metrics like accuracy, precision, recall, F1-score, and ROC-AUC . For example, Random Forest gives ~78% accuracy. CatBoost often outperforms with fewer encoding efforts Medium.

Apply hyperparameter tuning: grid search or randomized search on parameters like tree depth, number of estimators, learning rate, and class weights. Optimize based on ROC-AUC or F1 on the validation set to balance precision and recall.

Model Evaluation & Interpretation: After training, assess performance using:

1. Confusion matrix to evaluate classification errors (false positives vs. negatives).
2. ROC curve and AUC to understand ranking ability.
3. Precision-recall curve or F1-score if false negatives are costly.

This evaluation phase reveals whether the model aligns with business logic. For example, contracts and monthly charges often influence churn significantly.

Deployment and Monitoring: Pack your model and pipeline using joblib or pickle. Optionally create an API with:

1. FastAPI or Flask to deploy the model endpoint, as in real-world SaaS applications.
2. Optionally wrap in Docker for portability.

For front-end interaction: Create a simple UI using Streamlit, allowing users to input customer features and get churn predictions.

Automate deployment:

1. Write CI/CD scripts (e.g., GitHub Actions) to retrain on new data, update the model, and redeploy.
2. Add monitoring for data drift (distribution changes) and model performance decay. Alert business teams if churn predictions shift significantly over time.

Hands-On Summary: This project guides you through an end-to-end pipeline: data extraction, EDA, preprocessing, modeling, tuning, deployment, and monitoring. It touches on core data science areas: classification, feature engineering, hyperparameter optimization, model explainability, and deployment.

You'll gain familiarity with tools like pandas, Scikit-learn, CatBoost, FastAPI, Streamlit, Docker, and CI/CD frameworks skills crucial for full-stack data science roles. The project meshes theory with practice, and makes a strong addition to your portfolio with real-world relevance.

Project 2: Real-Time Sentiment Analysis (Twitter/YouTube)

Objective

Build a real-time system to analyze public sentiment on social media (e.g. Twitter or YouTube comments), visualized through live dashboards. Ideal for brand analytics or event tracking.

Use Case & Data Acquisition: Real-time sentiment analysis is valuable across marketing, politics, or media brands track public opinion during campaigns or event launches. You'll build a system that streams comments or tweets, processes sentiment, and visualizes trends live. Use APIs like Twitter's or YouTube's. For example, a Reddit-shared project ingests YouTube comments via Kafka, processes with Spark, and streams to Streamlit . Similarly, Twitter sentiment monitoring helps detect real-time mood shifts around specific events. This project merges big data, NLP, and dashboards into a full pipeline.

1. **Data Ingestion & Streaming:** Use Kafka for streaming ingestion to ensure scalable, resilient pipelines:
2. **Producer**: Fetch messages from API (Twitter using Tweepy or YouTube).
3. **Kafka cluster**: Orchestrate topics and brokers to buffer message streams.
4. **Consumer**: Spark Structured Streaming or Python script reads messages.

Kafka enables horizontal scaling and decoupled producers/consumers Reddit.

Data Processing & NLP: In the consumer:

1. Preprocess the text: lowercase, remove noise, strip punctuation, handle emojis, normalize repetitions ("loooove") Wried.
2. Use lexicon-based methods (e.g., VADER) for quick sentiment, or transformer-based models like DistilBERT for deeper understanding arXiv.
3. With Spark, apply NLP in a distributed fashion across partitions for scalability.

Enrich results with timestamp and metadata. Use window aggregations in Spark to compute sentiment trends over time for instance, 1-minute sliding windows computing positive/negative counts.

Storage and Visualization: Store results in a time-series database (InfluxDB or PostgreSQL). This supports analytics dashboards. Visualize live analytics through:

1. Streamlit dashboard (bar charts, line plots) to monitor sentiment trends and recent messages.
2. Alternatively, integrate with Power BI or Grafana via connectors.

Enable filtering by keyword, sentiment, or time range. Show latest negative message to catch potential issues early.

Scaling, Deployment & Automation: Use Docker to containerize:

1. Kafka components
2. Spark stream processor
3. Dashboard app

Orchestrate using Docker Compose or Kubernetes for horizontal scaling (e.g., multiple Kafka brokers and Spark executors).

Use cloud platforms (AWS/GCP/Azure) to deploy:

1. Kafka cluster via managed services
2. Spark via EMR, Dataproc, or HDInsight
3. Streamlit app on cloud VMs or serverless services

Add automation:

1. CI/CD pipeline to rebuild Docker images, push to registry, and deploy updated services when code changes.
2. Alerting system using Slack or email when sentiment across key keywords turns overly negative.

Insight Extraction & Real-World Impact

Interpret live data:

1. Track sentiment changes during events (e.g. product launches, speeches).
2. Use anomaly detection to catch viral negative sentiment spikes.

Use cases include:

1. Brand reputation monitoring
2. Early detection of social media crises
3. Engagement scoring (political campaigns, media premieres)

Key Learnings

This project blends streaming architecture, NLP (lexicon + transformers), time-series aggregation, and real-time visualization. You'll work across Kafka, Spark, Docker, and dashboard frameworks a full-stack data engineering + data science build. Skills gained: streaming design, distributed NLP, containerization, real-time analytics, and operational dashboards all critical for modern data roles.

Final Summary: These two projects deliver deep exposure to core data science capabilities:

1. **Churn Prediction** marries classification, feature engineering, model deployment, and MLOps.
2. **Real-Time Sentiment Analysis** integrates streaming, NLP, time-series analytics, and cloud scaling.

Together, they cover data wrangling, modeling, deployment, automation, and real-time intelligence making them excellent portfolio additions and skill accelerators for aspiring data scientists and engineers.

About the Authors

Dr. Pooja Mittal, currently working as Associate Professor, Department of Computer Science & Applications, Maharshi Dayanand University (NAAC A+ State University), Haryana. She has approx. 23 years of total teaching experience. She did her Ph.D in Computer Science from Maharshi Dayanand University (NAAC A+ State University), Haryana under supervision of Prof. Nasib Singh Gill in 2017. She is SLET (Haryana) and TOEFL qualified. She did her MCA from IGNOU, B.Sc (Computer Science) from Kurukshetra University. Before joining the teaching domain, she had worked as Corporate Trainer with Tata Infotech Ltd. Convened various important committees like AICTE, Women Cell, Anti Ragging Squad and many more at University level. She has more than 65 research papers to her credits published in renowned SCI, SCIE, ESCI, SCOPUS and Web of Science indexed journals. More than 50 papers presented in different International and National Conferences/Seminars/Webinars at different platforms. Also acting as reviewer in different reputed journals. She has authored chapters with renowned publishers and seven patents (published) to her credentials. She has guided four research scholars and currently guiding 02 research scholars working in Data Analytics, Smart Technology (IoT) and Machine Learning/ Deep Learning areas.

Dr. Ramesh Kait is a distinguished academician and dedicated researcher, currently serving as an Assistant Professor in the Department of Computer Science and Applications at Kurukshetra University, Kurukshetra. Since joining the department in 2002, he has played a pivotal role in shaping the academic landscape through his unwavering commitment to teaching, research, and innovation.

With a profound passion for knowledge dissemination and scholarly inquiry, Dr. Kait has successfully guided numerous research scholars, fostering a culture of critical thinking and academic excellence. His prolific contributions to the field are reflected in the publication of over one hundred research papers in esteemed international journals. In addition, he has actively participated in more than fifty national and international conferences and seminars, sharing his insights and engaging with scholars worldwide.

An accomplished author, Dr. Kait has also contributed to academia through the publication of 8 books, earning recognition for his depth of knowledge and scholarly rigor. His enduring dedication continues to inspire students and researchers alike, marking him as a respected figure in the academic community.